LONDON'S
COUNTRY HOUSES

Twickenham, Orleans House, interior of the Octagon, designed by Gibbs in 1720. This summer house or banqueting house was given exuberant plasterwork by the immigrant craftsmen Artari & Bagutti.

English Country Houses Series

LONDON'S COUNTRY HOUSES

Caroline Knight

Phillimore

2009, reprinted 2010

Published by
PHILLIMORE & CO. LTD
Andover, Hampshire
www.phillimore.co.uk
www.thehistorypress.co.uk

ISBN 978-1-86077-646-5

Printed and bound in Malta.
Manufacturing managed by Jellyfish Print Solutions Ltd.

CONTENTS

PART THREE   MINOR HOUSES

LIST OF ILLUSTRATIONS

ILLUSTRATION ACKNOWLEDGEMENTS

Unacknowledged illustrations are either photographs taken by the author or taken from material belonging to her. The author is grateful to Julia Brown, George Carter, Richard Gapper, Ann Gore, Fred Hauptfuhrer and Sir Henry Warner for permission to use material in their possession, and also to the following institutions:

Bridgeman Art Library
Buckinghamshire County Museum Collections
Conway Library, The Courtauld Institute of Art, London
Country Life Picture Library
Croydon Local Studies
Edifice
The Georgian Group, Pardoe Collection
Guildhall Library
© Historic Royal Palaces
Howarth-Loomes Collection/National Monument Record
A.F. Kersting
Knight, Frank
London Borough of Barking & Dagenham Archives
London Borough of Hackney Archives
London Borough of Haringey, Bruce Castle
London Borough of Waltham Forest, Vestry House Museum
National Monument Record
© The National Trust Photo Library
Royal Borough of Kensington & Chelsea Collection
Palace of Westminster Collection
Phillimore & Co. Ltd.
RIBA Library, Drawings & Archives Collections
The Royal Collection © 2007, Her Majesty Queen Elizabeth II
The Trustees of Sir John Soane's Museum
John D. Wood & Co.
Victoria & Albert Museum, Drawings Collection

ABBREVIATIONS

BL	British Library
Cherry & Pevsner, *London 2*	*London 2: South*, 1983
Cherry & Pevsner, *London 3*	*London 3: North West*, 1991
Cherry & Pevsner, *London 4*	*London 4: North*, 1998
Cherry, O'Brien & Pevsner, *London 5*	*London 5: East*, 2005
EH	English Heritage
GLC	Greater London Council
LB of …	London Borough of …
LCC	London County Council
LMA	London Metropolitan Archives
Lysons, *Environs*	Daniel Lysons, *The Environs of London*, 1792–6
NA	National Archives (formerly Public Record Office)
NAL	National Art Library, Victoria & Albert Museum
NAS	National Archives of Scotland
NMR	National Monument Record, English Heritage
NRO	Norfolk Record Office
Pevsner	Nikolaus Pevsner, *The Buildings of England* series
QVJ	Queen Victoria's Journal
RBK & C	Royal Borough of Kensington & Chelsea
RCHM	Royal Commission on Historical Monuments
RIBA	Royal Institute of British Architects, British Architectural Library, Drawings & Archives Collection
SPAB	Society for the Protection of Ancient Buildings
SRO	Scottish Record Office
Survey	*Survey of London*
V & A	Victoria & Albert Museum
VCH	*Victoria County History*
WRO	Wiltshire Record Office

PREFACE AND ACKNOWLEDGEMENTS

This book cannot pretend to cover the country houses round London exhaustively. They were built so densely, were replaced so frequently, and have disappeared in such large numbers that their history is very different from that of most country houses. These suburban houses have not been looked at as a separate type until now, although many of them have been carefully researched. In this book I have tried to bring together as many important examples as it was possible to cover, including a few – but only a few – of the houses which have disappeared. I hope that this is enough to allow these near-London houses and the social life that went with them to be better understood.

Not as many suburban houses have been taken over by heritage organisations as have large country houses with important contents, although English Heritage and the National Trust do each own several of them. Most of these are open to the public, but it is hard to visit many of the others. Most are institutions or offices, and are therefore in everyday use. This is good in itself – an unused house is a wasted building – but it does not encourage public interest or understanding. Those which are empty are often also under threat, and I was unable to gain access to two of these. Most of the institutions or their tenants were extremely helpful in allowing me access to the buildings in their charge, as were the owners of often very private houses. I would like to thank all those who made my visits useful and often enjoyable.

I am also grateful to the friends and colleagues who were supportive over the long gestation of this book. John Newman first encouraged me to research this neglected subject and Nicholas Cooper pressed me into writing this book. My fellow students at the Courtauld, Tabitha Barber, Claire Gapper, Karen Hearn, Paula Henderson and Cathal Moore have all helped me at various stages. I would also like to mention the late Annabel Ricketts with whom I visited several of these houses, and enjoyed her pungent comments. The following were also very helpful: Malcolm Airs, Susie Barson, Michael Bidnell, Susan Bracken, Neil Burton, George Carter, Rosalys Coope, Joe Friedman, Terry Friedman, Ann Gore and the late Alan Gore, John Harris, Richard Hewlings, Sally Jeffery, Richard Sachs, Pat Smith, Pete Smith and Geoffrey Tyack. I am most grateful to the estate of the late A.F. Kersting for making his photographs available to me, to Julia Brown for her constant advice over illustrations, and to Miles Thistlethwaite, without whose encouragement this book might not have been finished.

PART ONE

INTRODUCTION

First impressions of London and its environs suggest that country houses are unlikely to survive in large numbers, but closer inspection reveals that many are still standing. Some of these are of outstanding importance while many others are of interest. Some are now surrounded by high-rise housing, some by industrial premises; others have small areas of park or garden, and a few still have extensive, almost rural surroundings; most are still intensively used. This book is the first to address the history of these houses, concentrating on those that still exist, while giving some indication of the major lost ones as well.

How are these houses comparable to the country houses which still exist in the wider landscape? The proximity of London meant that each parish might have several houses of some distinction, unlike the situation in the country. As Defoe writes, these were not 'the ancient residences of ancestors, the capital messuages of estates … but these are all houses of retreat, gentlemen's meer [sic] summer-houses, or citizen's country-houses, whither they retire from the hurry of business … to draw their breath in a clean air and to divert themselves and their families in hot weather.'[1] Those with business in London might be bankers and merchants; others came for the legal and parliamentary terms: members of Parliament, bishops, and lawyers. Many came for the London season, bringing their wives and families with them. These families either owned a London house or rented one when required. Some also owned large country estates with substantial houses, others were gentry with smaller properties in the country; in both cases these would be their family seats, and the country house would act as the administrative centre of the estate. The suburban houses would be able to accommodate many people: households would be large, guests might stay for long visits, entertaining neighbours would be a requirement, the estate might be run from the house itself. A house close to London with only a few acres would be simpler to run and the owners would not have the social obligations which went with landowning in the country. They could please themselves to a far greater extent – this was one of the attractions of the suburban life.

There were disadvantages to living in London: it was densely inhabited, noisy, busy and polluted. By the late 17th century the smoke from burning coal meant that a pall of smoke hung over it, although with the prevailing west wind the air was somewhat cleaner in the West End. It was also unhealthy, due to overcrowding, poor water and drainage, and it was swept by infections, particularly in the summer. So a house close to London was a pleasant place to escape to, with clean air and water and a kitchen garden to provide fresh fruit and vegetables. These houses were close enough to travel to and from the city with ease. They were usually not permanent residences, but houses which were used by families from time to time, especially during the summer. The head of the family had more reason to be in

London than his dependants, so wives and children tended to spend longer in them than him. Many children were born in them, as good doctors in London were within easy reach. I describe these as suburban houses, to distinguish them from country houses at a greater distance from London.

Definitions

The area covered by this book extends from London to the M25, which sliced through the country round London in the late 20th century. It makes an arbitrary but practical boundary for the purposes of this book. It is sad to leave out important houses such as Copt Hall, Essex, or Combe Bank, Kent, when their grounds lie on both sides of the road, but it seemed logical to exclude them when the houses themselves are outside the motorway. So this book does not have the county boundaries of the other guides in this series. Anyway, the expansion of London over the last century or so and the consequent changes in local government mean that county boundaries have changed more here than elsewhere. Middlesex, the only county to be wholly within the area I am dealing with, was rich, fertile and well-populated; many of the houses in this book were once in that county, which is now reduced to no more than a postal address and a county cricket team. To the north lies Hertfordshire, and a small area of that county falls within the M25. Essex began on the eastern bank of the River Lea. As Morant wrote, Essex was one of the best situated counties for 'its nearness to the capital, conveniency of water carriage and good roads in general.'[2] Roman roads meant that much of it was within easy reach of the City and it had many distinguished suburban houses. South of the Thames, part of Surrey could easily be reached by water, although roads were generally bad further from London. Kent too could be reached either by water or by the Roman road leading to Canterbury. To the west, a small part of Buckinghamshire also falls within the M25. So this book will cover parts of those five counties, and will therefore overlap slightly with other volumes. In these outlying areas there was not the same pressure on land as there was closer to London, houses were not used as retreats in quite the same way and some, such as Chevening or Denham were the centre of modest estates within easy reach of London.

The peculiar nature of these houses near London goes back to late medieval days, although very few from that period survive. With the great changes in land ownership triggered by the Reformation many more were built through the Tudor and Stuart periods. During the 18th century greater prosperity meant that many more people were able to afford a suburban house and they tended to be built further from the centre of London as it expanded. By the late 19th century London had spread over so large an area that any building that can be termed a country house had to be much more distant from the city, so I am excluding any house begun after 1900, and being selective in my choice of 19th-century houses. There are simply too many to include them all. I am confining myself to country houses, free-standing in their own grounds, and am therefore excluding houses in village settings, such as the large houses along Chiswick Mall, on Richmond Green or in the centre of Petersham or Hampstead. Nor am I making any stylistic definition: types of houses varied enormously, and the word 'villa' can only occasionally be usefully applied.

The houses are listed by parish, using the parish name in use when the house was built. So The Grove, with an address today in Sarratt, is listed under Watford since it was in that parish when built. I have made two exceptions to this: the village of Highgate, a place with a strong sense of identity in spite of being split down the middle between the parishes of Hampstead and Hornsey until the early 19th century, and Mill Hill, another hilltop settlement which developed differently from the parish of Hendon of which it was a part. In keeping with the other volumes in the series the houses are divided into major and minor; this is not always a clear distinction in practice, and readers will have to accept my arbitrary choices.

Many more houses have been demolished in the London area than in most counties. Since recording all these would make this book unwieldy, I am discussing the reasons for their disappearance in a separate chapter, and including short entries on only a handful of the most architecturally significant. Where part of an important house still exists, such as Holland House in Kensington or Orleans House in Twickenham, I am treating it as a surviving house.

Landscape

The Thames, winding from west to east, dominates the area, not least because it also provided the most reliable method of transport until improvements in road transport in the 18th century. So it was an important factor in the location of houses. There were no bridges west of London Bridge until Kingston-upon-Thames, so the bridge-building programme of the 18th century was crucial in opening up travel round London. Ferries were plentiful, but getting coaches across the river was a slow and cumbersome process. Bridges were built at Putney in 1729, Westminster in 1750, Hampton in 1753 and Richmond in 1774.

The Thames valley has a gentle climate, good for gardens, which were an important feature of most of these houses. It is pleasant, unspectacular country with a good water supply. The soil is mainly clay, though light and gravelly in some areas. The clay is good for brick-making, so London was encircled by brick-fields providing the materials for the ever-expanding city. Beside the Thames the land is fairly flat, but to the north a ridge of high ground stretches from Harrow in the west to Havering in the east; the hill-top villages of Hampstead and Highgate, about 400 feet above sea level, have fine views towards the city. To the south the chalky high ground of Blackheath, Charlton and Eltham leads to the hills of Kent; and to the south-west the hill-top village of Wimbledon opens the way to the Surrey hills. Most of the area was agricultural land, much of it used for market gardening to feed the capital. It had originally been wooded, and some ancient forest survives even today in Highgate Wood and Queen's Wood in north London and in Epping and Hainault Forests to the east. There were also areas of common land, much of it being enclosed from the 16th century onwards. As London expanded inexorably there was public pressure to save at least some of it as open space. After the foundation of the Commons Preservation Society in 1865 there were successful campaigns which resulted in saving Blackheath, Wimbledon Common and Hampstead Heath from further development.

Building Materials

There is no good building stone in the area. The only easily available stone is Kentish rag-stone which could be transported along the Thames. It was widely used for churches in both the medieval and Victorian periods, but was not often used for houses as it is rough and cannot be cut into large blocks. Flint, widely used in medieval churches and vernacular buildings in the South-East, was hardly used for large houses in the London area. Hall Place, Bexley, built partly of flint in the 16th century, is therefore exceptional. Most medieval

1 Bexley, Hall Place. Knapped flint and chalk in a chequerboard pattern are unusual materials for the entrance front of this mid-16th-century house.

houses in East Anglia and the South-East were timber framed, and a few timber-framed buildings still exist, such as Lauderdale House in Highgate and Valence House in Dagenham; both are modest in scale, even if once slightly larger than they are today. The plentiful clay meant that from the 15th century brick was replacing timber-framing as the main building material for houses. Early examples are the surviving fragment of late 15th-century Esher Place and the courtyard of Fulham Palace. The bricks are small and fairly uneven in outline

2 Highgate, Lauderdale House, east side. This timber-framed house was built *c*.1580. The jettied first floor was given a pediment in the 18th century and a pebbledash finish in the 20th. The terrace overlooks the formal gardens.

3 Esher Place, Wayneflete's Tower. This was the *c.*1460 gatehouse of Bishop Wayneflete's palace with the original diaper brickwork. It was embellished by William Kent in the 1730s for the Hon. Henry Pelham, who was later prime minister.

so the mortar is a noticeable feature, and both houses have diaper decoration in vitrified bricks. By the early 17th century brickwork has become a decorative feature in its own right: houses such as Cromwell House, Highgate and Kew Palace have moulded bricks making decorative door and window surrounds, cornices and quoins. In the late 17th and early 18th centuries cut and rubbed brickwork of the finest quality is common in the London area, as at Ranger's House in Blackheath or Roehampton House.

Stone was barely used until the 18th century, and was usually brought by sea from the South-West. It was used only for the largest and most expensive houses, such as Wricklemarsh, built of Portland stone *c.*1725. The much smaller Stone House, Lewisham was unusual enough for its material to provide its name, and even more unusually was built of rough Kentish ragstone. But a brick house faced in stucco could be lined out to resemble stone, while being built more quickly and cheaply. Marble Hill, Twickenham, completed in 1729, is a good example of this treatment, which continued through the 18th and into the 19th centuries. By the later 18th century bricks were made of grey or yellow clays, closer to stonework in colour, as we can see at Plaistow Lodge or Pitzhanger Manor. Over the same period roofing

4   Kew Palace, entrance front. This merchant's house was built of brick in 1631. Recently research has shown that it was originally limewashed, and this has now been reinstated.

5   Bexley, Red House, showing the garden front and the well with its conical roof. Designed by Philip Webb for William and Jane Morris in 1859. The high roofs were tiled instead of slated, as was usual by this date.

6   Harrow Weald, Grim's Dyke. The entrance front of the 1870 Norman Shaw house is tile-hung and half-timbered below tiled roofs. The pre-Roman Grim's Ditch was incorrectly filled with water as if it were a moat.

materials changed, and the red of locally made clay tiles is replaced by slates, brought first by sea or canal and later by rail. These cooler colours make an enormous difference to the appearance of houses, both in London and outside. Later in the 19th century the Arts and Crafts movement, consciously echoing earlier styles, brought back the warm red brick and tiles of two hundred years earlier as we can see at Red House, Bexley, where again the material was unusual enough to suggest the name of the house.

House Plans

Experiments in planning were being made throughout the period, especially in these suburban houses. Where successful, they often became standard throughout England. In late medieval times there was little distinction in plan between town and country houses; a large town house would be built round one or more courtyards, as would a country house. Suburban houses are similar: Fulham Palace is a rambling multi-courtyard house of the late 15th century, while the contemporary but more modest Wickham Court has a very small central courtyard, making it a more innovative outward-looking design. Osterley and Syon are large single courtyard houses of the 16th century, but with the gradual reduction in the size of households this scale of house was both extravagant and inconvenient and there were important experiments with more compact plans even during the 16th century. It appears that suburban houses were leading the way, and key examples are the H-plan of Sutton House, Hackney or the half H-plan of Wimbledon House, both consisting of a central range with two projecting wings. By the early 17th century the H-plan has replaced the courtyard house, and Charlton House near Greenwich is an especially fine example. Traditionally the hall was the main room of the house, entered by a screens passage which separated the service rooms from the living quarters, but its importance was declining. The hall was beginning to lose its function as a communal space for a large household and was becoming simply an impressive entrance hall; and these suburban houses had less formal household structures than large country houses, with greater privacy for their owners. A small group of houses built in the first half of the 17th century shows experiments with this. At Charlton House, Eagle House in Wimbledon and Holland House in Kensington the hall was in the centre of the house running from front to back. This does not disrupt the symmetry of the façade, and also means that the centre block is two rooms deep, both important innovations. Danvers House in Chelsea (demolished) was another example of a through hall within an almost square plan, but here the main stairs seem to have risen through the hall, allowing four corner apartments on each floor. These houses with through halls are the

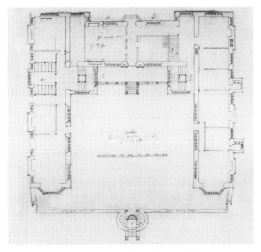

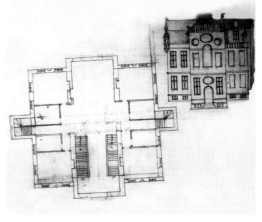

7 Wimbledon House, plan of ground floor by John Thorpe, *c*.1600, showing half H-plan with chapel and reception rooms on the left and service rooms on the right.

8 Danvers House, Chelsea, plan of ground floor by John Thorpe *c*.1622, showing the through hall with main staircase, and projecting stair turrets each side. The inset elevation shows the transition from Jacobean to Jonesian style.

beginnings of the double-pile house, which first appears in the London area. These houses are square or rectangular blocks two rooms deep. They are cheaper to build, easier to keep warm, and give better access from room to room. They can be quite small, with four rooms per floor, or can be extended to a much larger size. John Thorpe's drawings show many variants on this type, some long rectangular houses such as Dorchester House, Highgate (demolished) or smaller ones with four rooms to a floor, such as Mr Taylor's house at Potter's Bar.[3] These houses were built of brick; some had shaped gables, others had decoration in moulded brickwork round the doors, windows and cornice. Many of these, such as Danvers

House in Chelsea, have gone, but others such as Forty Hall in Enfield remain, although somewhat altered externally. It is such a practical and convenient type that it continues into the 18th century: Eagle House in Mitcham and Rainham Hall are good examples. It is these two compact plans, the H-plan and the double-pile, which go on to influence the design of country houses in the post-Restoration period, showing how designs could be tried out in the London area before being adopted in other parts of England.

Until the later 17th century it is rarely possible to attribute the design of a house to a particular architect. Designs were put together by surveyors or by master craftsmen, such as bricklayers or carpenters, with or without the assistance of the patron. Visits to outstanding recent houses might be made, prints and illustrated books studied, then drawings and perhaps a model prepared. But increasingly the architect took over the design of the house, and sometimes supervised the building process as well. Leading architects from the mid-17th century designed compact houses near London as well as major royal palaces. John Webb designed Gunnersbury, Wren may have designed Ranelagh House in Chelsea, Hugh May designed Eltham Lodge and Morton Hall in Chiswick; all except Eltham Lodge have been demolished. By the early 18th century houses in the suburbs and the country were getting larger and more imposing: Thomas Archer's Roehampton House or Thornhill's Moor Park, Rickmansworth were substantial houses with central blocks flanked by wings. Even if these two houses are Baroque in style, this type of house – a central block with outlying pavilions – became the standard design for the Palladian house from the 1720s. Marble Hill, Twickenham, by Roger Morris, is a fine example, although it has lost its flanking wings; Wrotham Park, Barnet is an interesting mid-18th-century variation on this type.

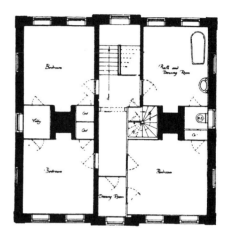

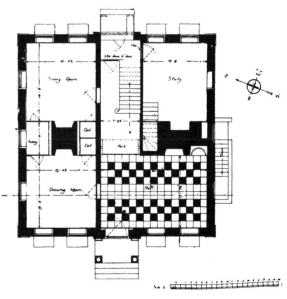

9 Rainham Hall, Essex, ground and first-floor plans. This house of 1720 shows the four-rooms-to-a-floor plan. The deep chimneybreasts allow for closets or access from room to room.

A return to a more compact plan came with the neo-classicism of the later 18th century, partly due to the demand for medium-sized houses within easy reach of London for the increasingly prosperous middle classes. The owners refer to their houses as their country house, or their house in Chelsea or wherever; they do not talk about their 'villa.' But some ingeniously planned compact houses are villa types. Sir Robert Taylor was among the most innovative and interesting of these architects, with his clients drawn mainly from City families. His cleverly planned houses with elegant cantilevered staircases and varied room shapes, such as Asgill House, Richmond, and Danson Park, Bexley, have variety within a comparatively small space and a series of interconnecting reception rooms with refined detailing. Stone House, Lewisham, is an extreme example of a tightly-planned villa on a very small scale, designed by an architect for himself. By the end of the 18th century there is a taste for a more picturesque style with a looser grouping of the different parts of a house and symmetry loses its hold. John Soane's own house at Pitzhanger has a central block but two completely different wings, one from an earlier house, the other designed by Soane. John Nash's Sundridge Park in Kent is a triangular house sited to take advantage of its beautiful setting, while William Atkinson's Twyford Abbey has an asymmetrical plan with a loose grouping of service buildings, responding to the historic house originally on the site. By the later 19th century there is usually more distinction between the servants' rooms and those of the family. Richard Norman Shaw's Grim's Dyke, Harrow Weald has an exterior with many projections and changes in level which in fact reflects a carefully composed sequence of reception rooms and service rooms; its organic nature allowed a vast music room to be added later without disrupting the overall plan. Philip Webb's Red House for William Morris was one of the first houses to explore a more domestic scale and to integrate service areas with the rest of the house in a manner that has become usual today. It is a compact L-shaped house, with one wing for the family and another for the servants, but both sharing views into the gardens. By the 20th century there was a return to classicism. Trent Park was radically altered by Sir Philip Sassoon, who transformed an asymmetrical 19th-century house into a symmetrical neo-Georgian one, while Stephen Courtauld added L-shaped wings in a pastiche of Wren's style to the medieval hall at Eltham Palace.

Gardens and Grounds

The gardens of these houses were of unusual importance to their owners, and the relationship between house and garden was much closer than in contemporary country houses. Since London was an expanding city, unhealthy and polluted, escape from a town house meant an opportunity to relax in a more natural environment, to grow your own produce, to let your children run about. The areas closest to London were always more suburban than rural: villages such as Chelsea, Hackney or Islington might have fields and trees, but were much visited by Londoners who could go there for an afternoon or evening, as Samuel Pepys described in his diaries. With transport slow and expensive it was important to keep London supplied with food, and market gardening was an important industry in Middlesex and other neighbouring counties. One of the advantages of owning a house and a few acres of land near the city was the provision of home-produced milk, butter, fruit and vegetables. These could be delivered to the London house if the family was there, or consumed in the suburban one. In addition, riding and carriage horses needed grazing in summer and hay in winter, so some grassland was needed too. The print of Balms in Hackney shows the early 17th-century house surrounded by formal gardens, orchards and kitchen gardens, with horses and cattle in the adjoining fields; yet this house was only a mile from the City. The records of many houses show that additional grazing was rented as required; hay was harvested and sent regularly to their London houses. This demand for land must also have

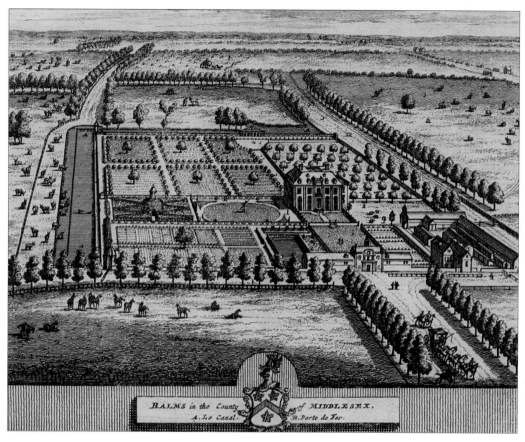

10   Hackney, Balms, 1707 print. The bird's-eye view shows the formal gardens, orchards and outbuildings. Cattle and horses are grazing in the fields.

been a boost to the local economy. Ideally a suburban house would have 15-30 acres, but land in the more fashionable villages was in demand and this might not be possible. When Sir Stephen Fox bought a house in Chiswick in 1663 it had only two acres. The much larger house next door, bought by the 1st Earl of Burlington in 1682, had only 15 acres until the 3rd Earl was able to buy the adjoining property and considerably extend his gardens and grounds. Riverside plots in a desirable village such as Twickenham were hard to come by; the trustees of the Countess of Suffolk were able gradually to buy up several different landholdings for her, so that when building began her new house at Marble Hill had about 25 acres. When Horace Walpole wanted to buy a suburban property in Twickenham, the only available land was a four-acre plot almost in the adjoining parish of Teddington, a much less fashionable village. In other areas it was possible to own large amounts of land, especially for families who had been there over several generations. Important early houses such as Syon and Osterley still stand today in large gardens as well as having parks, farmland and extensive, almost rural views.

Further from London it was possible to own enough land to form a true estate, even if on a small scale: both Dawley in Harlington and Wimbledon House had deer parks large enough for hunting, and James I was invited to hunt at the latter in 1616. But these large landholdings were tempting to developers, and both these parks were built over after the houses were demolished. Others only just inside the M25, such as Chevening in Kent or Wrotham in Hertfordshire, have large landholdings and still have farmland as well as grounds around the house. Switzer described these large grounds in his book, noting that he was discussing gardens 'six or seven miles out of town, whither the fatigues of court and senate often force the illustrious patriots of their country to retreat, and breathe the sweet and fragrant air of gardens [with] woods, coppices and groves.'[4] Cassiobury has gone, but the bird's-eye view of 1714 shows this type of landscape. The house has walled gardens with formal parterres on two sides, and on another a *patte d'oie* leads through woodland and wilderness to round ponds. In the distance are stables, a dovecot and farm buildings, with a walled kitchen garden beyond. This is landscaping on a massive scale.[5]

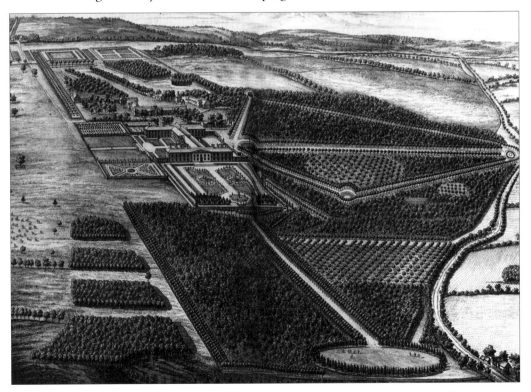

11   Cassiobury Park, Watford, bird's-eye view from *Britannia Illustrata*, 1714. This large late 17th-century house has formal gardens and extensive outbuildings.

With the improvements in agriculture during the 18th century owners might become enthusiastic agriculturalists even near London. At Woburn Park near Weybridge the owner, Philip Southcote, *c.*1750 laid out a *ferme ornée* on his 135 acres. Part of this was gardens, but the rest was fields for his cows and sheep, with carefully placed clumps of trees and the hedges embellished with flowers. A winding walk took visitors past flowers and shrubs as they walked round the farm. There were seats scattered about, a Gothic poultry house, and an octagonal temple designed by Lord Burlington. At nearby Painshill Charles Hamilton did something similar, making a landscape with carefully contrived views but also planting a vineyard on a south-facing slope; he even included a small tile-making factory disguised as a lakeside ruin. In Hampstead the 2nd Earl of Mansfield commissioned new service and farm buildings at Kenwood from George Saunders in 1793. These included a dairy (now rather neglected), while just across Hampstead Heath Lord Southampton laid out a *ferme ornée* at Fitzroy Farm. A visitor described the friendly rivalry between the men's wives 'both admirable dairy women, and so jealous of each other's fame that they ... have once or twice been very near a serious falling-out on the dispute: which of them could make the greatest quantity of butter from such a number of cows.'[6] The fashion continued well into the 19th century, with the late 18th-century dairy at Syon being rebuilt by Decimus Burton c.1847 and fitted with marble-topped tables and a Minton tile floor, and the 17th-century dairy at Ham House being refitted with cow's leg supports to its marble shelves. At Laleham J. B. Papworth, an

architect who specialised in the design of small houses and *cottages ornées*, designed a dairy. He knew his clientèle, writing 'When the fashionable amusements of the town are relinquished for those of the country, there are few so interesting to the female mind as the dairy.'[7] Keeping cows was common practice in most of these households and remained so; cows were kept at Mount Clare in Roehampton until the Second World War. There was even a commercial dairy herd at Twyford Abbey, just next to a busy stretch of the North Circular Road, until 1975 – probably the last commercial dairy herd so close to central London by that date.

To offset the limitations of the flat land round London, the Thames offered its own attractions. Picnics, boating and fishing by and on the Thames were popular amusements in the summer. Syon still has an elegant fishing lodge on the Thames, designed by Robert Mylne, and David Garrick kept two boats at his house

12   Petersham, Ham House. Interior of the dairy, built 1672 and refurbished in the early 19th century with ivy-leaf tiles and cow's legs supporting the marble shelves.

in Hampton. The gardens beside the Thames were embellished with garden buildings, such as the Octagon added to Orleans House by Secretary Johnston or the elaborate domed octagonal summer-house used by Lady Walpole at her house in Chelsea. One of the few survivors of these is David Garrick's Shakespeare Temple adorning the riverbank at Hampton, painted by Zoffany with its owners beside it. Even away from the Thames, waterside amusements were possible. A print shows elegantly dressed visitors fishing in the canal at the Duke of Argyll's house at Whitton, at Canons a gondola was kept on the lake, at Osterley they had a Chinese sampan. Humphry Repton designed a delicious boathouse-cum-cottage for the lake at Highams and the young William Morris boated, swam and fished in the moat at Water House in Walthamstow. Perhaps surprisingly, moated houses

13   Hampton. David Garrick and his wife pose with their dogs outside the Shakespeare Temple which they built in the grounds of their riverside house. By Johann Zoffany, *c.*1762.

do exist in Greater London: Fulham Palace has a tiny fragment of the enormous moat it once had, Twyford Abbey used to be moated, Valence in Dagenham still has its moat, and at Whitton a moat was constructed in the 18th century.

The grounds of most houses have shrunk or disappeared but some do still have gardens, even if altered. A few have become golf clubs with golf courses laid out in the grounds. Moor Park is a good example, where celebrated gardens were made in the early 17th century by Lucy, Countess of Harrington which were much altered later, as was the house. Today the house still has a landscape setting, although there is hardly a trace of the former gardens and the golf course comes close to the house. If the house is in public ownership it is very hard to preserve the historic character of its gardens. Fulham Palace is unusual in still having its walled kitchen gardens intact, even if very overgrown. Chiswick House and Gunnersbury have both kept areas of their formal 18th-century gardens, alongside changes made in the later 18th century and adjustments made since then for public access. Public use means that open areas with grass and paths are basic requirements; playing fields are needed, areas for children to play, cafés, and sometimes car parks. Increasingly safety, ease of access and low maintenance are important considerations for over-stretched council budgets. So where historic gardens have survived, they are all the more precious.

16

But most gardens have gone, and we have only descriptions, prints and drawings to tell us about them. Some of the earliest detailed information we have on gardens comes from Robert Smythson's plans, drawn in 1609 when he was visiting London and looking at some key buildings and their surroundings. His plan of Wimbledon House and its gardens shows the elaborate terraced approach, and the loggia on the east side of the house leading to the privy garden. These loggias were an effective way of integrating house and garden, an important aspect of these suburban houses. Behind the house are the productive areas, a kitchen garden, extensive orchards and a vineyard. Smythson also recorded Ham House in Petersham, recently built by Sir Thomas Vavasour. He uses the same method of recording the house and grounds as at Wimbledon, with an outline plan of the house, although he is clearly at least as interested in its setting. He shows the various compartments: the walled forecourt, the stable court beside it, and behind the house an early example of a formal garden laid out on the axis of the house. The National Trust took over the house in 1947 and has restored part of the garden, basing their design on later 17th-century evidence. Danvers House in Chelsea of 1622-3 has gone, but Aubrey describes the highly original garden with its oval bowling green surrounded by 'a kind of wildernesse of lilacs, syringas, sweet briar, holly, juniper etc … and apple and pear trees.' Here Sir John Danvers arranged an innovative mixture of mythological and naturalistic sculptures: mythological figures in the main walks, but a gardener and his wife in the 'boscage' and shepherds and shepherdesses to represent 'rustic beauty … and innocent simplicity.'[8]

14 Fulham Palace. The large walled kitchen gardens would once have produced enough fruit and vegetables for the Bishop of London's large household, but are semi-derelict today.

Among post-Restoration gardens John Evelyn's at Sayes Court in Deptford was one of the most celebrated. Deptford was so close to London that Evelyn had no London house, using the Thames to travel easily to either the City or Whitehall while enjoying suburban peace at home. The large Tudor house had been leased by his royalist father-in-law, Sir Richard Browne, from the Crown, so it had been confiscated and sold after the execution of Charles I in 1649. Evelyn managed to buy it back in 1652 after returning from his extensive travels in Europe, which had given him the opportunity to study Italian and French garden design. This influenced both his own gardens and his advice to other owners. He was laying

15 Tottenham. Bruce Castle, painted by Wolridge in 1686. The house has a walled forecourt where a boy is rolling the lawn. The enclosed garden on the right has pots of flowers and a fountain, and the service court is on the left.

out his 10-acre garden from *c*.1652; it was intensively cultivated, and with his fields beyond it provided him with a place to research his books on trees and gardens.[9] He also advised others on the design and planting of gardens, such as his friend Sir Stephen Fox who was laying out the grounds of Morton Hall in Chiswick. But even in his lifetime the shipyards at Deptford and its population were expanding, and after he inherited his elder brother's property at Wotton in Surrey he moved there in 1694. The proximity of the shipyards made Sayes Court the perfect place for William III to rent for Peter the Great. He was a most unsatisfactory tenant during his three months there in 1698, while he was studying ship-building in Deptford. The house became a victim of its position close to the industrial premises along the Thames. It was demolished in the 18th century and a workhouse built on the site.

Botanical experiments were made in these gardens. Plants were brought in to London docks from sea voyages, to be snapped up by plant collectors and nurserymen. The climate was milder round London than in many parts of the country, so it was easier to establish them; and there was a concentration of people interested in the subject. Garden owners and their head gardeners could compare their plants and techniques with neighbours, foreign visitors could see a number of gardens in a small area, and papers on botany were given at the Royal Society. London and Wise were the major late-17th-century garden designers, working for William and Mary at Kensington Palace and Hampton Court, and later for Sir Richard Child at Wanstead. They also provided plants for their clients from their extensive nurseries in Brompton. Queen Mary was particularly interested in the new plants which were being brought back from east and west by merchant and naval ships, which were carefully nurtured as 'exoticks' in her hot houses. A contemporary of the queen who was equally serious in her pursuit of botanical knowledge was Mary Capel, married to the 1st Duke of Beaufort. She collected botanical books and employed an artist to paint some of her choicest plants; these watercolours are still at Badminton, as well as various plant lists. In 1681 they bought the house in Chelsea which had once belonged to Sir Thomas More, the most important and historic house in the area. It had 15 acres of grounds and a view of the Thames, and in this sheltered spot she developed a fine garden. There was a well-stocked flower garden as well as fruit and nut trees, currants, gooseberries and a wide range of vegetables. When her husband died in 1700 she had to give up her gardens at Badminton; as usual the widow kept the suburban house, and she died aged 85 in Chelsea in 1714.[10]

Another important garden was made by the Hon. Henry Compton, Bishop of London from 1675 until his death in 1713. The bishop's suburban house was Fulham Palace and the post also gave him responsibility for the Anglican Church in the American colonies. Although he never crossed the Atlantic he asked his chaplains there to send him back rare plants and trees which he planted at Fulham, building up a remarkable collection and sharing

16   Esher, Claremont. Anonymous painting *c*.1740 showing Bridgeman's amphitheatre and the lake, after changes made by William Kent.

19

it with other botanists.[11] As a friend and adviser to Queen Mary since her childhood he shared many of her interests, and planted exotics as well as trees. Wisely realising that future bishops might not share his botanical interests he bequeathed specimens of many of his choicest plants to the Physic Garden in Oxford to ensure their survival. Other gardens depended on grass, trees and water for effect; they were more the product of landscape gardening than of botanical knowledge. Chiswick House, where a major restoration project is now under way on the gardens, is a good example of the early 18th-century formal style of Charles Bridgeman overlaid by the innovative, looser designs of William Kent. At Claremont Kent was also employed to soften an existing Bridgeman design, and although the Duke of Newcastle's house there has gone the gardens are owned by the National Trust and are much visited. Claremont's grassy amphitheatre overlooking the pond with a central obelisk probably inspired a smaller version of the same at Chiswick. Most of these houses could be visited and they were used constantly for entertaining so visitors could quickly pick up ideas on plants and garden design.

In these large gardens water could be harnessed to good effect, although the flatness of much of the Thames Valley made spectacular effects difficult. William Kent designed the cascade at Chiswick, inspired by Italian examples which he had seen; the lack of natural water pressure was a problem, and the cascade probably works better since its restoration in the 1990s than ever before. The rough-hewn rockwork used for cascades was also popular for grottoes. One of the most famous was below the riverside house in Twickenham designed by James Gibbs in 1719 for Alexander Pope (demolished). A double flight of steps framed the entrance to the grotto, which was also a passage through his basement and under the road behind his house to connect the front garden with that at the back. It was a succession of spaces, the walls of rock or covered in shells, with water from a spring rippling through and reflected in mirrors on the ceiling. William Kent, who may have played a part in designing the garden behind the house with its winding walks and temple, sketched the owner seated in his vaulted grotto and writing away in a shaft of light. Joseph Lane of Tisbury, the most famous designer of grottoes in the mid-18th century, designed the grotto on the island at Painshill near Cobham, decorating it with tufa and quartz to reflect the light. The rest of the gardens were laid out by the owner, Charles Hamilton, with a sure hand. Thomas Wright, another leading designer of grottoes and garden buildings, planned the garden lay-out and the grotto at Hampton Court House.

Major architects and designers were employed to lay out the grounds and garden buildings of these houses round London. Charles Bridgeman designed the early gardens at Chiswick House and Claremont, William Kent then came in to alter both; he also altered the grounds and garden buildings at Esher Place and probably helped Pope with his gardens in Twickenham. Lancelot 'Capability' Brown, the foremost landscape designer of his age, worked at Claremont, Kew Gardens and Syon. Gibbs designed the Octagon Room at Orleans House and the 'Greenhouse' at Whitton Place; Robert Adam designed the tea house at Moor Park and the semi-circular garden house at Osterley; and Chambers added several garden buildings to his own grounds at Whitton. Humphry Repton worked on many of these suburban houses, and, as he describes in his *Memoir*, enhanced existing landscapes with judicious planting and areas of flower garden.[12] In the early part of his career he was in partnership with John Nash, and they worked together at Sundridge, Repton choosing a new site for the house on higher ground so that the main rooms faced south over a valley

17 Heston, Osterley Park, the Garden House. This was designed by Robert Adam in 1780, both to protect tender plants and to provide an elegant place to take tea. It has a set of Windsor chairs inside, the usual type for indoor/outdoor use.

and wooded slopes. But the partnership ended acrimoniously, and Repton then worked independently. At Castle Hill, Ealing (demolished) he laid out new grounds in the 1790s for a house remodelled by James Wyatt, and although Repton's 'Red Book' has not survived, he described the place as 'a perfect little *bijou*'. He also worked at Highams, where he linked the views into the gardens to the distant prospect of Epping Forest.

The shift to the more formal garden which affected country houses in the early 19th century is also seen in suburban ones. The Italian Garden at Chiswick House reflects this more formal style. It was laid out for the 6th Duke of Devonshire in 1813, with a symmetrical arrangement of flower beds designed by Lewis Kennedy in front of a domed conservatory

18 Chiswick House. The conservatory designed by Samuel Ware in the Italian Garden, which was laid out by Lewis Kennedy in 1813.

by Samuel Ware. The use of cast iron for slender supports allowed these conservatories to be glass-roofed, so much more effective than the earlier orangeries where the light could enter only from large south-facing windows. They could also be heated by a system of stoves on the back wall and hot pipes. The Chiswick conservatory was largely rebuilt in the 1930s, at Syon the Great Conservatory is unaltered. This was added by the 3rd Duke of Northumberland in 1827, designed by Charles Fowler. Like that at Chiswick it overlooks a newly laid out formal garden, but is much more magnificent with its high dome and enclosing wings. On a smaller scale, Smirke designed a top-lit orangery at Gunnersbury for Lionel Rothschild in 1835, whose gardens had many hothouses for exotic fruit and flowers. The gardens at Chevening were formalised after 1816 when the 4th Earl Stanhope inherited, with a maze laid out west of the house and parterres reinstated below the south front. Later gardens relied for their effects on dense planting, so Sir Philip Sassoon at Trent Park had an exquisite flower garden close to his house as well as hothouses supplying exotic plants for indoors.

19   Isleworth, Syon House. The Great Conservatory was designed by Charles Fowler and built 1827-30. The glazed roofs and dome allowed the plants much more light than in earlier orangeries.

A Note on Sources

Suburban houses changed hands far more often than country estates, and therefore their history is often complex and scattered through many sets of family papers. Biographical information on the owners and their reasons for wanting a suburban house need to be addressed. The revised edition of the *Dictionary of National Biography* is invaluable, as well as Cokayne's *Complete Peerage* and Beaven's *Aldermen of London*. The papers held at the London

Metropolitan Archives and the National Archives are also precious resources. In terms of building records there is considerable evidence for lost and surviving houses, both published and unpublished. Royal properties are recorded in the Office of Works papers and in the Royal Archives, and properties such as Bushy House and Henrietta Maria's Wimbledon House were carefully recorded in the Commonwealth Inventories of 1649. The Hearth Tax returns of the late 17th century tell us about the comparative size of houses, a useful source when later changes have obscured evidence of the early history of a house. Local libraries often hold collections of visual and other material, in the form of maps, prints, old photographs and press cuttings. Sale documents are a particularly rich source from the late 19th century onwards and tell us about the lay-out of houses, room sizes, service buildings and land-holdings; when illustrated with photographs, plans or estate maps they are even more useful.[13]

The environs of London were easily accessible to visitors, so foreigners wrote descriptions of the houses and gardens they saw, such as Thomas Platter's *Travels in England* of 1599 or Prince Pückler-Muskau's letters in the 1820s.[14] Guide books and histories, such as Stow's *Survey of London* of 1598 or John Norden's *Speculum Britanniae* of 1593 proudly describe the fertile land dotted with houses.[15] Daniel Lysons in his *Environs of London* traces the history of the more ancient of these properties parish by parish, while local historians of the 19th and 20th centuries record in detail houses that have sometimes disappeared.[16] The *Survey of London* volumes, inspired by C. R. Ashbee's campaign to save The Old Palace, Bromley-by-Bow, are still being published, and the series includes monographs on buildings of particular interest. The *Victoria County History* is another ongoing series which publishes invaluable historical research. Both series started over a century ago and therefore include records of houses which existed then but have now gone. The *Buildings of England* volumes were originally arranged by Nikolaus Pevsner as county volumes, but the recently revised and expanded volumes on outer London are particularly useful in bringing the story up to date.

Visual evidence is plentiful too. Many of the plans and drawings by John Thorpe, that precious source for evidence of early houses, are of houses round London and provide intriguing designs and plans for medium-sized and large houses. The lavishly illustrated books of the early 18th century, such as Kip and Knyff's *Britannia Illustrata* or Colen Campbell's *Vitruvius Britannicus*, with their plans, elevations and bird's-eye views are also rich sources. Architects such as James Gibbs, William Chambers and Robert and James Adam produced books with engravings of their buildings. Publishers commissioned prints recording the homes of famous men such as Alexander Pope or Horace Walpole, both of Twickenham. By the early 19th century books such as Britten's *The Beauties of England & Wales* or Neale's *Views of Seats* combine text with topographical views, thereby recording the rural setting of these houses which was in many cases soon to disappear. It is striking how many houses shown in Watts' *Seats* of 1787 are round London, showing both their importance and their high profile.[17]

Maps are another vital source, and are increasingly produced from the early 17th century onwards. The elegant mid-18th-century maps by John Rocque, some with vignettes of houses and gardens, some with the names of owners, are packed with information; they are particularly useful in showing gardens just before the fashion for opening them up in the 'Capability' Brown style arrived. From the mid-19th century Ordnance Survey maps are both detailed and accurate, and looked at in sequence show the encroaching development as London expanded. Estate maps and maps of parishes are also useful records. Country

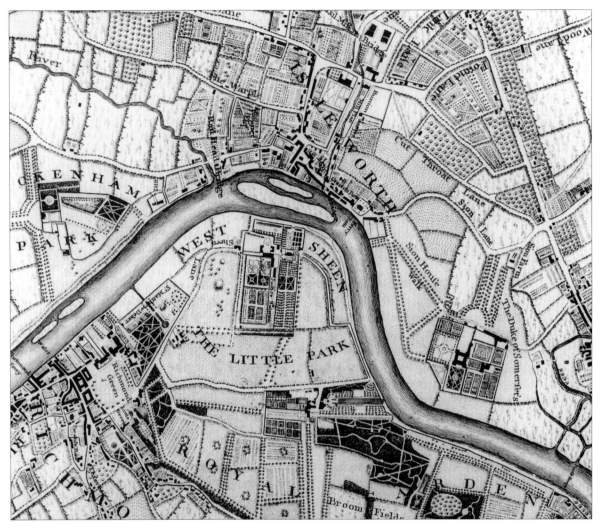

20   John Rocque, detail from his *Exact Survey of … London and the Country ten miles round* published in 1745. This shows the formal gardens round Syon House and the royal gardens at Kew across the Thames.

house views are another valuable source, and some artists include so much detail that their topographical views are especially useful, especially when their depictions can be checked against other evidence. The oil paintings of Jan Siberechts, Canaletto and Samuel Scott and the watercolours of Paul Sandby all provide fairly reliable information. By the 19th century picturesque old houses such as Eltham Palace or Wimbledon Rectory were being drawn and painted. Houses which were about to be demolished were also recorded, such as in the group of watercolours by G.W. Toussaint of Balms in Hackney, painted in 1852, just before its demolition. Amateur artists, often women, also painted charming views, such as Elizabeth Gulston's watercolours of Chelsea houses or the interiors of Aubrey House by Mrs Goldsmid. And throughout the 20th century *Country Life* articles record a selection of these houses, combining the history of the building and its owners with superb photographs.

Chapter I

MANNERS AND MONEY: THE SOCIAL CONTEXT

The social background of the owners of these suburban houses is different to that of country landowners, and is much more varied; some had a City background, others were courtiers with no involvement in business. Outside London and its environs the owner of a large estate held a special role in his area. He might be a Member of Parliament; he would usually control the local living, with the right to appoint the vicar to his local church; and he would administer the law as a Justice of the Peace. A major landowner, such as the Duke of Northumberland in Northumberland or the Duke of Devonshire in Derbyshire, might be Lord Lieutenant of the county and would be at the apex of provincial society. But in and around London the situation was different: the royal family were the leaders of society, and most of the royal houses were not far from London. As far as the aristocracy was concerned, the major landowners might be ministers in the government or sit in the House of Lords, with their wives or children in royal service. They needed to be in attendance in London or wherever the king or queen might be, and their suburban retreats therefore were within easy reach of the favourite royal houses. As these changed over the centuries, so the fashionable places to live changed too.

The Court and the Church

When not in central London, the Tudors mainly used the palaces of Greenwich, Eltham and Richmond, to which Henry VIII added Hampton Court and Nonsuch. All these had deer parks where hunting could be arranged, as did Oatlands in Surrey. James I gave the latter to his wife, Anne of Denmark; and Charles I completed the Queen's House at Greenwich for Henrietta Maria, as well as buying Wimbledon House for her (demolished). Some royal palaces survived the Civil War and Commonwealth unscathed, but others suffered considerable damage and were never in royal use again, such as Nonsuch and Eltham. After the Restoration Charles II made major alterations to Windsor Castle, just outside the area covered in this book, and William and Mary rebuilt Hampton Court, as well as buying and enlarging what we now call Kensington Palace. These three places continued in royal use under George I and George II, but Kew and Richmond also became favoured retreats, and various fairly modest houses there continued to be used by George III and his family. So there was a gradual move from the large old palaces east of London to palaces and houses west of the capital from the 16th and 17th centuries, and by the 18th century it is the riverside villages west of London which are the natural haunts of courtiers and politicians. Places such as Kew, Richmond and Twickenham became very fashionable, and houses there were in great demand. And since these villages remained comparatively unspoilt by industrial development, a surprisingly large number of houses have survived. By the late 18th century turnpike roads and the building of bridges meant that travel by coach was faster and easier than ever. So by the 19th century the monarch could be further from London and still keep in touch with the government. Visits to the seaside became part of the summer season: the future George IV built the Brighton Pavilion, while Queen Victoria and Prince Albert built Osborne on the Isle of Wight for family holidays. With the arrival of the railways they were able to travel to Scotland and visit their estate at Balmoral every summer. This meant that courtiers had to be in attendance far from London, another factor in the decline in popularity of suburban houses.

Until the Reformation the Church was the other major landowner, but following the Dissolution of the monasteries from 1536 monastic land became Crown property, although some ecclesiastical land remained in church hands. Some was given away to courtiers, some was sold. For instance the Brigettine nunnery of Syon was dissolved, and was converted by Protector Somerset into his private house. Canonbury, the summer retreat of the Abbot of St Bartholomew the Great in Smithfield, became a private house and like many others changed hands frequently over the next few years as speculators bought and sold it. Some properties were already leased and simply changed owners: Belsize House (demolished), a large courtyard house south of Hampstead which had belonged to the Abbot of Westminster, passed to the Dean and Chapter of Westminster Abbey and was leased by the Waad family for several generations. Wimbledon Rectory had been leased to various courtiers from c.1500, who had to pay for modest lodgings elsewhere for the Rector. From 1550 it was rented by William Cecil, later Lord Burghley, who paid his rent to the Dean and Chapter of Worcester. Other properties belonged to particular dioceses: archbishops and bishops were more often in London than not, attending the House of Lords or the court. The Archbishop of Canterbury stayed at Croydon Palace when travelling to London, while the Bishop of Winchester used Esher Place; the former remained church property post-Reformation, the latter did not. The house with greatest continuity of ecclesiastical ownership is Fulham Palace, one of the seats of the Bishops of London from at least 704 and used until 1973 by the Bishops of London; it is still owned by the Church Commissioners today.

Another upheaval in property ownership was caused by the Civil War and the execution of Charles I in 1649. After his death all royal property was inventoried, and most was put up for sale; these inventories provide fascinating information about the houses, ancillary buildings and contents of the royal palaces and houses. New owners were supporters of the new regime: Wimbledon House was sold to Captain Adam Baynes, who sold it on to the Parliamentarian Major-General Lambert. In 1660 it was restored to Henrietta Maria, who no longer wanted it and it was soon resold. Nonsuch with its parks was also sold, being divided between General Lambert and Colonel Pride; it too was restored to Henrietta Maria at the Restoration. Eltham Palace was bought by Nathaniel Rich and returned to the Crown in 1660. Lodges or rangers' houses in the royal hunting parks also became available, and Bushy House in Bushy Park was taken over by James Challenor, brother of the regicide Thomas. (He lost it in 1660 when it was given to General Monck as a reward for his role in restoring Charles II to the throne.) Bishoprics were abolished, and in 1646 a law was passed allowing the sale of some church properties. Croydon Palace, seat of the Archbishops of Canterbury, was given by Parliament to Sir William Brereton who desecrated the chapel. Fulham Palace was sold to Colonel Harvey in 1647; both reverted to the Church in 1660. Many royalists lost their houses; some were so crippled by fines that they sold up. Others had their properties taken on spurious legal grounds, such as the Countess of Home, who was forced to give up Lauderdale House to the Parliamentarian John Ireton. The Waad family had rented Belsize House for generations, but as royalist tenants were forced to surrender the lease, and were unable to reclaim it after the Restoration. The 2nd Duke of Buckingham was forced out of Beaufort House in Chelsea in 1649, and Bulstrode Whitelocke, a Parliamentarian, lived there till the Restoration. A few impressive new houses were built by influential men in Cromwell's circle, such as Sir John Maynard, who employed Webb to design Gunnersbury House; but on the whole this was not a propitious time for investing in new building.

The City

The City was, as it is today, the centre of financial and commercial life, and for many families was the source of great wealth. For them, a suburban house might be the only country house, although they might have investments in land scattered across more distant counties. Their pattern of use was therefore different: they would not have the option of going to a distant country house, perhaps for the summer or for Christmas; they would use their suburban house instead. And often they retired there. The landowning class was rich in assets but often poor in cash and sometimes died deeply in debt, while many City families could afford to build themselves fashionable new houses out of their accumulated capital. They were less dependent on the royal family and were likely to be members of City livery companies, to serve as Justices of the Peace and as Aldermen, and eventually perhaps to become Lord Mayor. They expected to live in comfort, near enough to the City for the men to travel easily between their town and country houses. In the 16th and early 17th centuries this might mean close to the City. Sir John Spencer bought Canonbury House in Islington and improved it in the late 16th century. Slightly later Sir George Whitmore, Lord Mayor in 1631-2, bought Balms in Hackney (demolished); both these houses were barely a mile from the City. The increasing industrialisation of the Thames to the east of the City meant that the most desirable houses were away from the poverty and pollution along the Thames and the River Lea. A few men took advantage of the business possibilities, such as Captain Harle of Rainham Hall in Essex, who in 1729 built himself a house close to his wharves and industrial premises, but most people preferred to escape to more countrified settings. Sir Edmund Wright, Lord Mayor in 1640-1, built Swakeleys at Ickenham, even today on the western fringes of London. Fine houses were built in the 18th century in the Bexley and Bromley areas of Kent, such as Plaistow Lodge for the Thellusson banking family, and Danson for the Boyds. North of the Thames Essex villages such as Walthamstow and Wanstead had distinguished houses built by City families. The Goldsmid brothers, highly respected City financiers, both had suburban houses, Benjamin building himself Elm Grove in Roehampton and Abraham buying Morden Hall in Blackheath (demolished). John Julius Angerstein, who played a large part in developing the insurance industry and Lloyds in particular, built himself Woodlands in Greenwich. Others moved to the west of London, such as the Child banking dynasty of Osterley, or the banker Sir Charles Asgill who built Asgill House at Richmond, and in the 19th century Nathan Mayer Rothschild bought the large estate at Gunnersbury where he built himself a new house on the site of the earlier house by Webb.

The international trading companies also brought great wealth to some. Robert Bell, a founder of the East India Company, built Eagle House in Wimbledon in 1613 and Josiah

Child bought Wanstead in 1674. In the early 18th century South Sea Company profits enabled Sir John Fellowes to buy Carshalton House, Edward Gibbon to build Lime Grove, Putney (demolished) and Benjamin Styles to rebuild Moor Park, Rickmansworth. Later in the 18th century George Clive's profits from the East India Company financed the building of Mount Clare, Roehampton. Clive of India came back to England fabulously rich and bought the substantial estate at Claremont in Surrey, where he proceeded to demolish the old house and build anew. Sugar was also a highly profitable commodity in the mid-18th century, and John Boyd partly financed the building of Danson from the profits of his West Indian sugar plantations.

The army and navy could also provide huge bonuses. Prize money financed the building of Wrotham Park by Admiral Byng, although he did not live long enough to enjoy it; and Admiral Sir George Pocock of Orleans House, Twickenham, was awarded £123,000 for taking Havana in 1762. But the most lucrative post of all was Paymaster-General. Sir Stephen Fox founded the fortunes of his family and rebuilt Morton Hall in Chiswick through the profits of that post, to which he was appointed in 1661; the Earl of Ranelagh held the same post from 1685 and built Ranelagh House beside the Royal Hospital, Chelsea; both these house have been demolished. Richer still was James Brydges, later Duke of Chandos, who was Paymaster-General when the Duke of Marlborough was commander of British troops in the War of the Spanish Succession: his house at Canons in Edgware (demolished) was one of the most magnificent in the London area. Slightly later Sir Lawrence Dundas, another army contractor who became immensely rich during the 1745 rebellion and the Seven Years' War, was able to buy Moor Park, Rickmansworth as well as a town house in Arlington Street and land in England, Scotland and Ireland.

Businesses were also being established in the West End of London, so men such as the successful cabinet maker John Gumley with his shop in the Strand had a house in Isleworth. William Hallett senior, also a well-known cabinet maker, bought Canons and built himself a much more modest house there than that of the Duke of Chandos. Brewing was another profitable business, and the brewer Peter Hamond built Belmont on the summit of Mill Hill. Henry Thrale lived close to his brewery in Southwark but under pressure from his wife Hester they spent the summers in a substantial house in Streatham (demolished) with extensive grounds, where Dr Johnson became a frequent visitor. By the 19th and early 20th centuries fortunes were being made from new industries, and the owners were buying some of the largest houses in the London area even if their businesses were elsewhere. Thomas Willan, who rebuilt Twyford Abbey in 1807, was an entrepreneur with business interests in many fields, from dairies to stage coaches. Railway magnates were making fortunes, such as Sir John Kelk who bought Bentley Priory in 1863, the same year that Alfred Bean, another railway magnate, bought Danson. In the 20th century Lord Leverhulme of Lever Bros bought Moor Park, Lord Waring of the furniture firm Waring & Gillow bought Foot's Cray in Kent, Arthur du Cros of the Dunlop Rubber Company bought Canons, and Stephen Courtauld, whose wealth came from his family's textile manufacturing business, leased Eltham Palace and built a new house on that historic site.

Professionals and Women

Artists and architects did not usually own country estates; they lived in London to be near their clients, and if successful were able to afford a house near London to escape to. Sir

Godfrey Kneller was a hugely successful portrait painter and in 1709 built himself the grandiose Kneller Hall near Twickenham, set in formal gardens. Others are too modest to feature in this book, such as William Hogarth's small house at Chiswick, Johann Zoffany's at Strand-on-the-Green, and Turner's house near Twickenham, two of these three overlooking the Thames. Thomas Hudson also had a riverside house in Twickenham, while Joshua Reynolds commissioned Sir William Chambers to design him a house on Richmond Hill. Chambers had his own house nearby. Around 1780 he bought part of the Duke of Argyll's property at Whitton and made alterations to his house there. Sir John Vanbrugh bought an estate near Esher, later called Claremont, and built himself a house there (demolished); he later built himself a house in Greenwich. John Soane bought and partially rebuilt Pitzhanger Manor in Ealing, and Samuel Ware bought Hendon Hall. In the 19th century William Morris asked his friend Philip Webb to design Red House, Bexley, and the artist Frederick Goodall commissioned Grim's Dyke in Harrow Weald.

Married women could not hold property in their own name until the Married Women's Property Act of 1882; but as widows they could be property owners and they often inherited the suburban house. In the case of City and business families who might not have a distant country estate, the London house and business would probably be inherited by the eldest son, while the widow would be left the house near London. In the case of major landowners the country estate might be entailed on the eldest son, and the London house would also be left to the new head of the family. It was customary for a widow to be left one-third of her husband's assets, so a valuable but not too large house near London and some capital would enable her to live comfortably and keep in touch with friends and family. In the absence of a son, a daughter might be left a suburban property. Elizabeth Murray, Countess of Dysart in her own right, inherited Ham House in Petersham from her father, so already owned it when she married her second husband, the future Duke of Lauderdale. She played an important part in enlarging and furnishing it in highly fashionable taste between 1672-5 and she remained there as a widow. So these houses, usually the second home of a well-off family, often became, for at least a few years, the only house of a single and perhaps older woman. At her death, or if she remarried, the house might be sold – another factor contributing to the constant changes of ownership of these houses.

Some women built their own houses, though this was unusual. Boston Manor in Brentford was built by a young widow, Lady Reade c.1622-3, and c.1725 Henrietta Howard, the separated wife of the Earl of Suffolk, built Marble Hill, Twickenham, as a perfect Palladian villa for her occasional use. Sarah, Duchess of Marlborough, an immensely rich widow with strong ideas of what she wanted, built herself a house at Wimbledon in 1732-3 (demolished), only settling on Roger Morris as her architect after dismissing two others. Miss Elizabeth Chauncy, daughter of a well-off East India Company director, built herself an elegant house overlooking the Thames in Fulham c.1763; it has convincingly been attributed to Robert Taylor.[1] A single woman might have a suburban property for other reasons: Lady Mary Coke, the separated wife of Viscount Coke, agreed to live outside central London as one of the conditions of her financial settlement. Once widowed she had her own London house but she continued to rent a suburban house, first Aubrey House in Kensington, then Morton Hall in Chiswick till her death in 1811.

There were many foreigners in London, although unless naturalised British they were unable to own property in England. But there was always a large number of properties available to rent for the long or short term. Theodore de Mayerne, a French immigrant who was physician to James I and Charles I, arranged for trustees to buy Lindsey House in Chelsea on his behalf. Fernandez Mendez, physician to Queen Catherine of Braganza and like her Portuguese, built Eagle House in Mitcham, an elegant small house of 1705. Samuel Fortrey, a French immigrant, c.1630 built himself Kew Palace (also known as The Dutch House) on the Thames, while the Huguenot David Papillon developed property in Roehampton at about the same time. There were also Dutch immigrants in the 18th century who had successful businesses, such as Theodore Janssen of Wimbledon and Joshua Vanneck who had a house in Putney; both houses have disappeared. These two men were naturalised British, so were able to own property. Jewish immigrants also bought houses in the environs of London, the first being Alvarez da Costa from Portugal, who bought Cromwell House in Highgate in 1675. Benjamin and Abraham Goldsmid, brothers of Dutch extraction and remarkably successful business men, owned respectively Elm Grove, Roehampton and Morden Hall, Blackheath. And later John Julius Angerstein, a Russian Jew, built himself Woodlands in Greenwich, Nathan Mayer Rothschild bought Gunnersbury and built himself a new house there, while Sir Edward Sassoon rented Trent Park in Southgate, a house which his son later altered after buying the freehold.

21   Petersham, Ham House. The Queen's Antechamber was furnished c.1675 and still has its original textile hangings, grained panelling and japanned furniture.

Access and Display

These suburban houses were much loved by their owners, providing as they did an escape from the pressures of London without having to spend too long on uncomfortable travel. More so than in remote country houses entertaining was easy, with friends and relations having their own houses nearby.[2] It was often in these London and suburban houses that the best pictures and furnishings were placed, so they could be admired by the constant visitors. One of the few suburban houses to keep its original contents into the 20th century is Ham House, where the sumptuous furnishings have hardly been altered since the mid-18th century; the Queen's Antechamber has its original textile hangings and a unique set of 'japanned' chairs. Another example is Osterley, with equally finely furnished state rooms. The country house might be empty much of the year, the rooms shuttered and sheeted; and when entertaining took place, it was mainly local gentry. Family portraits might be hung there, but the newer pieces were much more likely to be in or near the capital.

22　Heston, Osterley Park, the Tapestry Room. Robert Adam ordered the set of Gobelin tapestries for the anteroom to the state bedchamber in 1772.

23 Ickenham, Swakeleys. The *c.*1700 paintings on the staircase are possibly by Lanscroon.

24 Canonbury House, Islington. Detail of the woodwork in the Oak Room, dated 1599.

These houses were conveniently close to London, so it was easier to attract top craftsmen who might be reluctant to spend months in the more remote corners of England. We do not know the name of the craftsman who carved the stylish Renaissance decoration in the Oak Room at Canonbury, but it is fine workmanship. The same house has fine plasterwork ceilings, as do other houses round London, from late Elizabethan examples such as this to the exuberant Baroque decoration in the hall at Moor Park or the Octagon of Orleans House. Many major artists, such as Verrio, Laguerre and Thornhill painted walls and ceilings in Baroque houses, and although many have gone they can still be seen in many places, from Arnos Grove in Southgate to Swakeleys in Ickenham. Some houses had superb art collections: Gregory Page at Wricklemarsh had a splendid collection of Dutch, Flemish and Italian paintings, as did the 1st Duke of Chandos at Canons. The Earl of Bessborough had fine paintings and classical sculpture in his Roehampton house, and Syon still has a large collection of antique and 18th-century sculpture. On a smaller scale, Angerstein had part of his great art collection in Woodlands, and John Soane had paintings including Hogarth's *Rake's Progress* as well as classical sculptures and casts in his house at Pitzhanger. Wrotham still has some of the fine paintings collected by the Byngs, and the Duke of Northumberland's pictures at Syon still give us a glimpse of how these houses would have looked with Old Master paintings hung in a series of sumptuous rooms (although some of these came from Northumberland House). It was only when these houses declined in the late 19th century, which the London houses did slightly later, that in most cases their contents were sent to the country house, giving a completely misleading impression of the richness of country house interiors. An exception was Trent Park where Sir Philip Sassoon filled his house in the 20th century with 18th-century conversation pieces and fine walnut furniture, both of good enough quality to form the nucleus of exhibitions arranged by him.[3]

With the ever-increasing improvements in road travel it became easier to reach these houses. John Evelyn describes leaving the St James's Square house of the Earl of Essex early one morning and arriving at his Hertfordshire house, Cassiobury, at 10 a.m. Lord Perceval, who rented Charlton House in the 1730s, describes going there from London for the day to pick up some papers, and another time goes with his wife for dinner (then an afternoon rather than an evening meal); these are brief winter visits, when London was a more enticing place to be.[4] Horace Walpole describes going up to London from Twickenham for dinner and back again, and Lady Mary Coke regularly went for dinner on Sunday with her sister at Sudbrook in Petersham when she lived at Aubrey House in Kensington. John Julius Angerstein could stay in summer at his house in Greenwich, be at his office in the City by 11 and be home again for dinner at 6.[5] There were risks – coming back in the dark with drunken coachmen led to some accidents, and highwaymen were another.[6] The desolate expanse of Hounslow Heath was notorious for highwaymen, and Lord Ossulstone was attacked *en route* to visit his friends at Dawley in Harlington. In spite of this women were particularly enthusiastic about visiting these suburban houses. Henrietta Pye in her *Short Account of Houses round Twickenham* published in 1760 noted that women rarely travel abroad so these little trips from London, especially taking in the houses along the Thames, were for many women the equivalent of the male Grand Tour. The houses were easily seen: in Twickenham alone Marble Hill, Pope's Villa and Orleans House faced the river, and the road passed very close to Strawberry Hill. The number of visitors to Walpole's Strawberry Hill was such that from 1774 he had printed tickets, and later he had to print rules of behaviour and ban children. Even so he often retreated to his cottage across the road in order to get on with his reading and writing. Sophie von la Roche, that observant traveller, visited Osterley in 1786 through a friend, who had 'sent us a ticket admitting five people.' She saw the gardens and all the state rooms but also went upstairs where she was shown Mrs Child's apartments. She nosed around the room and found 'my *Sternheim* in English translation

25 Twickenham, with Orleans House seen from the Thames. Visitors could see many of the houses from a boat. Print after Heckell, 1749.

26 Twickenham, Strawberry Hill. A late 18th-century view shows how close the house was to the road from Twickenham to Hampton. Horace Walpole put up the obelisk on the crossroads.

among Mrs Child's books, and on the fly-leaf I wrote down something of the joy and pleasure I had experienced at Osterley Park – in English too, as well as I was able.' What did Mrs Child make of this, I wonder?[7]

By the 19th century, house-visiting was becoming not just an upper-class pastime but a commercial venture. Hassell's *Picturesque Rides*, published in 1817, was clearly addressed to tourists, telling them how to reach various places round London and giving information on opening arrangements. For instance he warned visitors to Wanstead that they would only be allowed inside the house on Saturdays.[8] Washington Irving rented a room in Canonbury House in the early 19th century so he could write. He was horrified to find that on Sundays 'the late quiet road beneath my window was alive with the tread of feet and the clack of tongues; and, to complete my misery, I found that my quiet retreat was absolutely a "show house" the tower and its contents being shown to strangers at sixpence a head. There was a perpetual streaming upstairs of citizens and their families to look at the country from the top of the tower, and to take a peep at the city through the telescope to try if they could discern their own chimneys.'[9]

From 1900 onwards cars began to replace horses, though it was hard to beat the smartness of a well-matched pair of carriage horses. The last house to have new and impressive stables built was Roehampton House, just before the First World War. Stables began to be replaced by or to co-exist with garages, and cottages for chauffeurs were of a higher standard than grooms' quarters; they were paid more and expected better housing. As London grew some suburban houses were used as London houses as it expanded. Sir Hugh Lane used Lindsey House, his Thames-side house in Chelsea as his London house from 1909 until his death. Stephen Courtauld had no London house from 1936-44, using his new house at

Eltham Palace instead. The improved roads of the 1960s meant that the 10th and 11th Dukes of Northumberland used Syon House when in London, rather than having a house or flat in the centre, although the huge increase in traffic makes this less practical today. Many houses switched to institutional use in the 20th century. Many are now schools, such as Claremont, Plaistow Lodge, Wickham Court, Hare Hall, Canons, Belmont, Highams and Gumley House. In each case, large extensions have been required as the schools have expanded. Some are used as colleges of further education, such as Grove House, Mount Clare and Parkstead, all in Roehampton. Others have become clubs, which means that their landscaped setting is at least partially preserved. Moor Park, Rickmansworth, Sudbrook in Petersham and Eltham Lodge are all golf clubs, and proud of their distinguished buildings. The Hurlingham Club, a late 18th-century riverside house in Fulham, still keeps its air of seclusion. Some are hotels, such as Addington Palace, Hendon Hall and Grim's Dyke. A few are monasteries or nunneries, such as Gumley House in Isleworth and Holcombe House on Mill Hill. Others have switched to office use, such as Swakeleys and Sundridge Park, and Bromley Hall has recently been rescued from its previous very poor state and restored as offices.

27   Heston, Osterley Park. The stables, seen from the roof of the house. A large household would need stabling for at least a dozen horses, as well as coach houses and accommodation for grooms and outdoor staff.

Local authorities bought up many of these properties as London expanded, not because they wanted the house, but because of the pressing need for public open space. A map of the outskirts of London with its green spaces is a guide to the existence of a house. Marble Hill in Twickenham, Kenwood in Hampstead, and Gunnersbury were all saved from probable destruction by having their grounds made into parks. But local authorities have problems in funding the maintenance of a historic house and finding a suitable use for it. A few have become museums, such as Gunnersbury, Valence House in Dagenham or the

28 Foot's Cray, Kent, the entrance front with a coach and pair. Photographed by Bedford Lemere in 1900, just before motor cars were introduced.

William Morris Gallery in Water House, Walthamstow (although the latter is now about to be closed down). Others are seriously under-funded. Charlton House and Boston Manor, both exceptionally interesting early 17th-century houses, need greater investment and deserve greater recognition.

Other houses have been taken over by the major heritage organisations, and are therefore well researched and mainly open to the public. English Heritage now owns Marble Hill in Twickenham, Ranger's House in Blackheath, Eltham Palace and Kenwood, and has recently been deeply involved in the restoration of Danson in Bexley and the setting up of a trust to run Chiswick House and its grounds. The National Trust owns two of the finest properties with superb contents, Ham House and Osterley, and the smaller Fenton House in Hampstead. Lindsey House in Chelsea and Rainham Hall in Essex are both owned by the Trust but leased to tenants and rarely open to visitors. Eastbury Manor in Barking was acquired as early as 1918, and Sutton House in Hackney in 1938, so both before the Country Houses Scheme of the post-war years; both are 16th-century houses of great historic interest. The Trust has also recently taken on Red House in Bexley, once William Morris's house. The number of houses owned by these two organisations in the London area shows how important these surviving suburban houses are.

Remarkably, quite a few houses are still in private ownership. Sometimes this is due to continuity of ownership, for instance at Syon, which has belonged to the Percy family since

29 Isleworth, Gumley House. The 18th-century house with its colonnaded forecourt was surrounded by much larger convent buildings after its conversion into a school.

1594, or Wrotham Park, Barnet, which the Byng family has owned since it was built in 1754. Canonbury has not been sold since Sir John Spencer bought it in 1570; part of it has gone, part is split into various different houses but it is still largely in residential use. Wayneflete's Tower, the only remaining part of the old house of Esher Place, is lived in today. It is not surprising that smaller houses, such as Argyll House in Chelsea or Stone House in Lewisham are still in private hands, but remarkable that Denham Place has reverted recently from office use to being a family home. It is being extensively restored at the moment. Aubrey House in Kensington and Asgill House in Richmond have both been immaculately restored.

So what is the future for these suburban houses round London? C. R. Ashbee's idea of drawing up a list of historic buildings in Greater London, inspired by the destruction of the Old Palace at Bromley-by-Bow, led in 1894 to the setting up of a Survey Committee to record historic buildings in London and its environs. It was supported by the LCC and although there was then no statutory protection it meant that campaigns could be mounted quickly and effectively if these buildings came under threat. This work has been taken over by English Heritage, and most of the houses covered in this book are listed Grade 1 or 2. Listing has undoubtedly preserved many buildings from insensitive changes or wholesale demolition, and will probably continue to do so in spite of proposed changes in the planning laws. A few houses are still at risk, and these will be looked at in the following chapter, but on the whole the future of these houses is more hopeful than it has been for many years. The HLF has provided funds for some careful restorations, Friends groups often support buildings in local authority hands, and private owners were, until the recession, keener to take on these often fascinating buildings than they had been for decades.

Chapter II

THE DESTRUCTION OF SUBURBAN HOUSES

London has always been by far the largest city in England, and its population has consistently grown faster than that of other towns. In 1801 its population was under one million, by 1901 it was 4½ million, so it has expanded over more of the surrounding countryside than even the great industrial cities of the Midlands and the North-East. The growth of London and its effect on its surroundings are of course the main reasons why so many houses have disappeared in the London area. This chapter will explore the underlying reasons for the loss of some of these suburban houses.

Planning regulations of the late 16th and early 17th centuries tried to prevent London's growth by banning new building outside the City and Westminster, but these had very little effect against the constant pressure of inward migration from the countryside. First to be absorbed were parishes to the east of London, such as Stepney and Bromley-by-Bow, villages which adjoined the River Lea. This river marked the boundary between Middlesex and Essex, and as a navigable river flowing into the Thames east of London Bridge, it was industrialised early on. During the 17th century docks were developing at its junction with the Thames, and shipping-related industries such as rope works and tar factories were set up. Inevitably the area became polluted, and full of poor labourers. If houses in these places survived they lost their semi-rural surroundings and country views, and rapidly became less desirable as retreats for the rich. Some became schools, some industrial premises, others were subdivided into smaller houses or tenements. The Old Palace at Bromley-by-Bow was all of these before its demolition in 1893, and the campaign to prevent its destruction alerted conservationists to the threat to historic houses in the London area.

Hackney was also too close to the City and lost its appeal as housing spread far beyond the City boundaries. Balms in Hackney is a case in point. A print of 1707 shows it surrounded by formal gardens, orchards and farm buildings, but by the mid-18th century it had become a lunatic asylum; it was demolished in 1851 and the site developed with housing as part of the De Beauvoir estate. Some houses were sold for redevelopment even earlier. Highgate was always a desirable village which led to an early instance of redevelopment. Dorchester House (also called The Blewhouse) was a large house built *c.*1600 by John Warner, a City merchant, on the summit of the hill. The interesting plan is among John Thorpe's drawings, and shows the exceptionally spacious staircase leading to the 'flats' on the roof, which would have had extensive views south over London.[1] It was demolished *c.*1688-90 and six semi-detached houses built on the site of the gardens. These attractive houses are now numbers 1-6 The Grove, and their terraced gardens overlooking Hampstead Heath preserve some of the brickwork from the garden walls of Dorchester House.

Villages to the west of London were also becoming less rural as the West End developed after the Restoration, although they largely remained pleasanter to live in and less industrial than villages in the east. Beaufort House was one of the most famous houses in Chelsea, having been built by Sir Thomas More in the early 16th century. By the late 17th century it was also celebrated for its gardens, cultivated by the Duchess of Beaufort. This historic house was demolished, ironically, by Sir Hans Sloane, antiquarian and founder of the British Museum, and today Beaufort Street commemorates the site. Danvers House, close to Beaufort House, was an innovative house built by Sir John Danvers *c*.1623 and demolished about 1716; it too has given its name to a street on the site. Ranelagh House was also in Chelsea, a fine house possibly by Wren which lost its status as a suburban retreat when it was bought in 1741 by the syndicate who were setting up Ranelagh Gardens. When they were closed down Ranelagh House was sold back to the Royal Hospital who built their Infirmary on the site.[2] Belsize House went downhill when the owners did not wish to use it themselves. It was the most historic property in Hampstead, belonging to the Dean and Chapter of Westminster, and had been partially rebuilt by Daniel O'Neill in 1661.[3] It was inherited by the Earl of Chesterfield, but he sublet it to an entrepreneur who cut down the timber and neglected the house. This was sub-let again and rather dubious pleasure gardens opened in

30 Hampstead, Belsize House, early 18th-century print. This late 15th-century house was partially rebuilt in 1661. It became pleasure gardens in 1720, went downhill and was demolished in 1853.

1720, which were closed down after complaints from the local residents. The Chesterfields successfully applied to the Dean and Chapter in 1733 for permission to demolish it and a few years later it had gone.

Other houses went because they were too expensive to keep up, and outdated in style. Wimbledon House was a fine 1580s house built by Thomas Cecil, later 1st Earl of Exeter, on a hillside site outside the village; its gardens have already been referred to. Sir Theodore Janssen, a Dutch immigrant who had a successful career in the City, bought it in 1717. He wanted the land but not the house, which he demolished and planned to replace with a smaller house on a slightly different site. But the collapse of the South Sea Company in 1721 meant that as a director his assets were frozen and he was heavily fined, so he had to sell some of the land and scale down his plans. It was the widowed Duchess of Marlborough who built a house on that land instead. Another early house which disappeared was Nottingham House, the core of what later became Kensington Palace. It was built by Sir George Coppin c.1610 and bought c.1629 by Sir Heneage Finch, whose grandson was 2nd Earl of Nottingham. He sold it to William and Mary in 1689 as a temporary retreat from Whitehall Palace while alterations were going on at Hampton Court. But they became so fond of it that it was constantly being enlarged, and William III continued to use it after Mary's death and the completion of Hampton Court. Wren added pavilions and wings, but the core remained until 1718.[4] Then dry rot and the ambitious plans of George I to turn it into a small ceremonial palace meant that the old house was destroyed, and today the only remains of that house are a few foundations.[5]

Three of the largest and most impressive houses disappeared within a very short time: Wricklemarsh south of Blackheath, Wanstead in Essex and Canons in north Middlesex. All replaced earlier houses and were rebuilt in the first part of the 18th century by newly rich families; all were built of stone, and were noted for their rich interior decoration and fine furnishings. In each case top architects were employed, John James at Wricklemarsh, Colen Campbell at Wanstead and a bewildering succession of architects at Canons, where Talman, James, Vanbrugh, Gibbs and Thornhill were all consulted to a greater or lesser extent. These houses were eagerly visited by connoisseurs and there are many descriptions of them, though very little visual evidence for the interiors. All three were built on a grand scale by families whose wealth came from trading and the City. They all had more land than was usual for these suburban houses, but even so it was not comparable to the great estates further from London. It was partly this factor – the inability of the land to support the house – which led to their disappearance. The 2nd Duke of Chandos inherited an indebted estate and was unable to continue living at Canons, as his father-in-law's pithy comments demonstrate. 'Cannons [sic] was always too big a house for the family, and indeed for any family that has the biggest estate, but still more strongly where the estate is not great and the encumbrances are very great.'[6] And they were just too big; unlike a medium-sized house, such as Wrotham, which could provide elegant and comfortable space for family life and entertaining, without the requirement for a huge household to maintain it. So Wricklemarsh was demolished in 1787, soon after Page's death, by the son who had inherited it. Canons was sold by the 2nd Duke of Chandos immediately after his father's death and demolished in 1747. Wanstead remained in the same family into the 19th century, but the extravagance of the young heiress and her husband, combined with the terms of her marriage settlement, left them with little choice but to sell the contents in 1822 and to demolish the house the following year, although they retained the land.

31 Wanstead. William Hogarth's *Wanstead Assembly* of 1729 shows the lavish interior decoration and furnishing of Lord Castlemaine's house. He sits at a silver table with tapestry hung walls behind him.

These houses were demolished for scrap and various of their parts and those of other houses were reused elsewhere. The portico of Wanstead may have been removed to Hendon Hall, a chimneypiece went to Chillingham Castle in Northumberland, while an obelisk from the grounds moved down the road to Epping Forest. Stone columns and a pair of Venetian window surrounds were removed from Wricklemarsh to Beckenham Place, and some chimneypieces went to the Admiralty. Many parts of Canons were recycled: the staircase went to Chesterfield House in Mayfair, the wrought iron gates to Hampstead parish church and many of the windows and paintings in the chapel were moved to Great Witley church in Worcestershire. Trent Park in Southgate was altered in 1926 using bricks and stone window surrounds from Devonshire House in Piccadilly. Garden buildings were easily moved: in Roehampton a temple from Parkstead was moved to Mount Clare, and a fine brick niche was taken from the garden of Bradmore House, Hammersmith to the grounds of the Geffrye Museum. Mrs Thrale's house, Streatham Park, had a summer house where Dr Johnson used to sit. This was moved to the gardens of Kenwood to preserve it but it was completely destroyed in an arson attack in 1991.

32 Hendon Hall, detail of entrance front. The portico may have come from Wanstead when it was demolished in 1823.

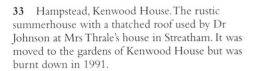

33 Hampstead, Kenwood House. The rustic summerhouse with a thatched roof used by Dr Johnson at Mrs Thrale's house in Streatham. It was moved to the gardens of Kenwood House but was burnt down in 1991.

Occasionally one owner would build up his landholdings until he dominated an area, as happened at Chiswick. Thus in 1728 the 3rd Earl of Burlington bought Sutton Court in order to add its gardens to his own; his descendant demolished the house in 1896. The 6th Duke of Devonshire bought Morton Hall in 1812; he kept the gardens but demolished the house. In 1828 he added Corney House to his property portfolio, a riverside house which had belonged to the Earls of Bedford from 1549 for over a century; the Duke kept its 15 acres and demolished the house. The 7th Duke bought Grove House, a substantial Palladian house set in a park, in 1861. He let the house but kept the land, developing it as Grove Park and thereby ensuring that the old house became less desirable; it too was eventually demolished. So by the early 20th century Chiswick House appeared to be the only major house in the parish, although historically it had been one of several and not the most important.

Of course houses disappeared due to fire. Earl Spencer's house at Wimbledon was burnt down in 1785. It was not rebuilt it till 1801, instead he adapted some service buildings for his occasional use. Foot's Cray in Kent was a fine Palladian house attributed to Isaac Ware, one of the group of English houses closely related to Palladio's Villa Rotonda near Vicenza. The design of the latter, with its centralised plan, four porticoes and domed saloon was adapted for Foot's Cray *c.*1754. The last private owner was Lord Waring who died during the Second World War. In 1946 it was bought by Kent Education Committee and was being adapted as a museum when it was burnt down in 1949, just before its opening. They demolished the remains soon afterwards. Broomfield House in Southgate, owned by the LB of Enfield, is another victim of fire. Standing empty in a public park, it has suffered a succession of arson attacks. It is not wholly destroyed but is a sad shell at present, and has been awaiting funding for restoration for over a decade.

Industrialisation was a major cause of houses going out of domestic use, and sometimes being demolished. Bromley Hall in Bromley-by-Bow was a Tudor hunting lodge near the River Lea, which had declined in status along with its surroundings. After years in industrial use the Northern Approach to the Blackwall Tunnel was built in 1971, so heavy traffic hurtles past day and night just outside its front door. Its excellent recent restoration as offices has saved a house which appeared to have no future. Croydon Palace became a calico printing works after it was sold by the See of Canterbury in 1780, with the great hall used as a drying shed and lengths of material hung from the beams. Its condition deteriorated over the 19th century until it was saved by the Duke of Newcastle who presented it to a religious foundation to become a school. Bradmore House in Hammersmith is another case where industrial use combined with road traffic nearly brought about its destruction. As traffic increased in central Hammersmith it was bought by a bus company which brutally converted it into a garage, part of the house remaining only because of pressure from the LCC. It has recently been restored and now forms an unlikely component in a new development of shops and offices beside the tube station.

34 Bromley-by-Bow, Bromley Hall seen from the south. This recently restored Tudor hunting lodge is now on the approach road to the Blackwall Tunnel.

Gibbs's additions to the earlier 18th-century house at Dawley in Harlington for Henry St John, 1st Viscount Bolingbroke, made it into one of the finest houses on the western fringes of London, and being further from the city it was surrounded by large gardens, a deer park and farmland. But after many changes in ownership the Grand Junction Canal was cut through part of the estate in 1797, rendering light industries such as brick-making and gravel extraction viable. This was followed in 1838 by the Great Western Railway; gradually the whole place descended into industrial use and the last part of the house went in 1951. Gravel extraction also caused the loss of Orleans House in Twickenham in 1926, although the Octagon was not demolished. Sometimes photographs were taken of the demolition process, showing plasterwork, staircases and doorways being ripped out and destroyed. The recycling which was commonplace in the 18th century rarely seems to have been worthwhile in the 20th.

Railways were the death knell of the suburban house, destroying swathes of land close to London, especially to the south of the Thames. Many different companies were competing for this lucrative business, and acquiring land for it was a chaotic and unplanned process. A map of the railways in Surrey shows the jumble of lines which led out of London from Victoria, Charing Cross, Waterloo and Holborn Viaduct.[7] Railway lines cut through estates, such as Twyford Abbey and Dawley; Bentley Priory and Twyford Abbey were made much less attractive and valuable properties by the arrival of the railway close to them, although they were not demolished. Railways were built distressingly close to houses, such as the exquisite Asgill House in Richmond. A railway bridge over the Thames was built so close that the house shakes when a train passes. The park of Arnos Grove had a viaduct built across it for the Piccadilly Line, both bringing commuters and dominating the landscape. Occasionally the landowner did not understand the implications: the Earl of Essex at Cassiobury, having encouraged the construction of the Grand Union Canal within sight of his house, did not try to prevent the railway running parallel to it. As railways developed, this became a source of noise and pollution and it was a contributory factor in the eventual decision to demolish it. In the case of Hare Hall, Romford, the railway company actually bought the whole estate in order to acquire the land they needed. There were more long-term effects than the destruction caused by the laying of the lines and the building of stations: railways also meant that workers could live much further from their place of work, so areas which had been rural, such as Bromley and Bexley in Kent or Southgate and Hadley Wood in Middlesex, became dormitory suburbs in the early 20th century and the pressure to develop accelerated.

Crucially, the railways changed the pattern of entertaining, as landowners could get back to their estates easily and quickly. The weekend in the country became the standard form of hospitality, with hunting, shooting or summer parties taking place on the country estate rather than the suburban one. Places as far afield as Yorkshire or Gloucestershire came within easy reach by rail. For instance, after the death of the 6th Duke of Devonshire in 1858 Chiswick House was hardly used by his successors, who had a London house and who could now easily reach Chatsworth in Derbyshire by rail; Chiswick was let to a succession of tenants, including the Prince of Wales. The new rich expanded their country houses for weekend entertaining, adding more service rooms and increased space for living-in servants as well as many more guest bedrooms. London's suburban houses also had to compete with the lure of the seaside and holidays abroad.

The agricultural slump of the 1870s also affected suburban houses, as those families most dependent on agricultural rents had to retrench by the 1880s. Substantial savings could be made by giving up a suburban house, and several which were put on the market failed to find buyers. They were no longer valuable assets, and were sometimes difficult to sell. Boston Manor in Brentford was put up for sale by the Clitherow family after the First World War, but was withdrawn due to lack of interest; Laleham Abbey remained unsold in 1899, and after being offered for sale again in 1922 remained empty for six years. Other houses were threatened by development, such as Eagle House in Wimbledon. This was bought by the architect T.G. Jackson so that he could preserve it from demolition; he restored it and lived in it himself.

Some houses were requisitioned during the First World War. Hare Hall in Romford became the home of the Artists' Rifles, and men such as Charles Jagger, John Nash and John Lavery were stationed there.[8] Roehampton House became a hospital, and did not return to private use after the war, although Lutyens had only recently enlarged it for a private owner. So by the outbreak of the Second World War not many of these houses remained as private houses for occasional use, and the war did not alter the situation much. Some were requisitioned for use by the services, such as Trent Park in Southgate, requisitioned after the death of its owner in 1939 and used as an interrogation centre. Some suffered severe damage, such as The Round House, Havering-atte-Bower, which was vandalised by troops and barely survived. Bombing was, in principle, far more of a risk to these suburban houses than to houses in the country, but actually destroyed surprisingly few houses round London. Ravenscourt Park in Hammersmith, a modest mid-18th-century house in Council ownership and used as a public library, was hit in 1941 and not rebuilt, although its grounds remain a public park.[9] Brooke House in Hackney was a rambling late 15th-century double-courtyard house which had become a lunatic asylum, but had luckily been evacuated before it was badly damaged by bombs in 1940. After the war it was not restored, instead a *Survey of London* monograph was produced, recording the house in detail before its shell was demolished.[10] Holland House in Kensington was also badly hit and did not continue as a private house, although enough was left for a new use to be found for one wing after the war. It was a well-known house and its ravaged interiors were photographed for local newspapers. Other houses were slightly damaged: Fulham Palace lost some of its outbuildings, the hall of Eltham Palace was

35   Holland House, Kensington, the library after bomb damage in 1940.

damaged, as was one side of Charlton House and Red House, Bexley had blast damage. Some houses went soon after the war, such as Earl Spencer's Wimbledon Park House, an elegant villa by Henry Holland.

From the mid-20th century the pace of destruction has slowed as the historic interest of these houses has been more widely recognised, together with their value in preserving green space in built up areas. Chiswick House lost its late 18th-century wings and its late 17th-century stables but the core of the house as designed by Burlington was preserved. Local people and organisations have been instrumental in saving some of these houses. Recently the campaign to preserve Sutton House in Hackney for community use was enormously effective, and in Hammersmith local opinion was mobilised to prevent the total destruction of Bradmore House by a new transport and office development scheme. It may overlook one of the busiest roundabouts in London, but it is still there. Other houses have an uncertain future; the LB of Waltham Forest has made worrying decisions recently regarding Water House, Walthamstow, which has for many years housed the William Morris Gallery with its fine collection of Arts and Crafts decorative arts. This collection is soon going to be moved out of the house, and may be at least partially in store; the house is at present in good condition, but funds could be slashed when it is no longer a museum. Others are seriously at risk. Broomfield House, Southgate, already referred to, was a museum until devastated by fires in the 1990s. It is still encased in scaffolding ten years on, its painted decoration in store and not available for inspection, and there is little prospect of its restoration at present. Woodlands in Greenwich used to be a library, but is now sitting empty and forlorn with holes

36 Wimbledon Park House, designed by Holland in 1800 for 2nd Earl Spencer, was demolished in 1949.

37 Hammersmith, Bradmore House, on a busy roundabout. It was saved from demolition and was restored as part of a recent development of shops, offices and public transport.

38   Southgate, Broomfield House. This suffered a succession of fires and has been under scaffolding for several years while the council considers its future.

in its roof while a new use is found for it. These three houses are owned by local authorities, while Loughton Hall in Essex, an excellent example of Nesfield's work, has recently been sold by Essex County Council. Now it is empty, boarded up and in a shocking state, with an uncertain future. Twyford Abbey in Ealing is now on English Heritage's register of Buildings at Risk. For many years various developers have been trying to subdivide and alter a Grade 2 listed house and to surround it with other buildings. However its 16-acre grounds are a green space in a densely built up area close to the North Circular Road, providing a haven for plants and wild-life as well as being a historic site which might require further archaeological investigation. A recent planning application has been turned down, although the house is in very poor condition and its future remains uncertain.

PART TWO

ADDINGTON

ADDINGTON PALACE

The little village of Addington is still comparatively rural, although only 13 miles from London and three from Croydon. Near the village church are the lodges to the much-altered house which was for almost a century the country seat of the archbishops of Canterbury, hence its name.

The old house near the church belonged to the Leigh family in the 17th and early 18th centuries. With the death of Sir John Leigh in 1737 a long-drawn battle about its inheritance began, finally won in 1767 by his cousin Anne Spencer. She immediately sold the estate for £38,500 to Alderman Barlow Trecothick (*c*.1718-75), a City merchant involved in the trade with North America, who became Lord Mayor in 1770. It was he who rebuilt the house, much of which remains.[1] He chose a new site away from the village on high chalky ground and appointed Robert Mylne as his architect. The house, then called Addington Park, was

39 Addington Palace. The house designed by Mylne for James Trecothick and built 1773, then called Addington Park.

begun in 1773 and the result was a typical neo-classical villa: a pedimented seven-bay house, the hipped roof with attics; single-storey arcaded wings led to pedimented pavilions each with a Venetian window. Unusually, it was built of stone, a mark of Trecothick's wealth. The entrance front faced N-W over parkland, while the garden front had an extensive view over the Surrey countryside, still partially green and wooded today. The fall in the ground means that the semi-basement is a full storey high on this front, with fine rusticated stonework supporting the ashlar of the upper storeys. Trecothick died in 1775 so did not live to see his house completed, and his nephew, James Ivers, inherited the partially built house. He took his uncle's surname and completed the house in 1779. Its plan is simple: a large entrance hall led to a central top-lit staircase, with three reception rooms beyond overlooking the fine view to the S-E. The house has been vastly extended, but Mylne's delicate plasterwork decoration can still be seen in two of these three rooms.

The history of this house is also linked with that of Croydon Palace, only three miles away. By the late 18th century this ancient building was in poor condition and did not seem a suitable summer residence for the archbishops of Canterbury and their wives. Instead the archbishop 'was accustomed to establish himself for a portion of every year, either by the seaside, or it might be in some watering place, where it was totally impossible he could ever hope to be private.'[2] In 1780 the old palace was sold and in 1808 Archbishop Manners-Sutton (1805-28) bought Addington Park 'just such an unpretending mansion as any country gentleman with £4,000 a year might occupy.'[3] He bought back parts of the estate which had been sold off, but surprisingly failed to make a chapel in his new house.

40 Addington Palace. The house, much enlarged by Norman Shaw, was used as a hospital in the First World War.

William Howley (1828-47) had greater ambitions. As Bishop of London he had already rebuilt parts of Fulham Palace, and he now got to work on Lambeth Palace and Addington, employing Henry Harrison as his architect at the latter in 1828-30. Harrison raised Mylne's arcaded wings to two storeys and added service buildings at each end, so the frontage extended to 223 ft. The entrance was made more Grecian with an Ionic porch with a shallow pediment, which remains; and he made a simple chapel, which was moved to the elegant barrel-vaulted room in Mylne's west pavilion in the later 19th century. Internally his alterations have been largely swept away by the major invasive changes made in 1900.[4]

In 1897 the house was sold by Archbishop Temple, who felt that the archbishop should have a Canterbury residence rather than a country seat near London; a new archbishop's palace was built beside the Cathedral in 1897-8. The buyer of Addington was Frederick Alexander English, a financier and diamond merchant from South Africa. He vastly enlarged the house at a cost of about £70,000, employing Richard Norman Shaw as his architect.[5] By 1900 Shaw was semi-retired, and he took on William Gilmour-Wilson, a young architect from Liverpool, as his partner on this project. Mylne's reception rooms remained, one redecorated by Shaw in Wren style, and the attic storey was replaced by a mansard roof to provide more and better rooms on the second floor. The entrance front was replaced by an overpowering new front, three storeys high and topped by a balustraded parapet; Howley's porch was brought forward and attached to this. Unusually for Shaw, this new range closely matched the smooth ashlar and austere detailing of the Mylne and Harrison house. The staircase was replaced and a billiard room and winter garden made, but the main purpose of this extension was to provide an enormous double-cube hall or saloon (60 by 30 ft) on the entrance front. Like a medieval hall it was given a screens passage leading directly from the entrance to the stairs, and like an early hall it was a double-height room for entertaining; but in style it drew on the early and late 17th century. The walls are panelled in Italian walnut with tapestries above and the Serlian chimneypiece is in alabaster and coloured marbles,

41 Addington Palace. Norman Shaw's saloon, designed in 1900 for F.A. English. The opulent chimneypiece and chandelier are still there.

42 Addington Palace, aerial view. The garden front of Mylne's house can be seen, with the roof of Norman Shaw's addition behind it, and 19th- and 20th-century extensions each side.

while the ceiling has wreaths of foliage like a Restoration ceiling. English bought a vast chandelier in Paris which still hangs in the room. This was converted for electricity, which was supplied from his own 'electricity lighting station' in the grounds. He also had a 'furnace house' for centrally heating parts of the house, and rebuilt the stables, which included a 'motor house' with space for two cars; so modern technology was being introduced.

But this huge expenditure was not enjoyed by him for long: he died childless in 1909, and his widow sold the house soon afterwards. The lavishly illustrated sale brochure of 1911 tells us that the estate was then 1,151 acres, of which 460 was parkland. The grounds included the walled kitchen garden close to Addington church, and a vineyard on the chalky south-facing slope 'which in favourable years produces a wine crop'.[6] The plan of the grounds shows that development was proposed, with the park divided into plots for substantial detached houses, keeping the main house. Instead part of the grounds became the Addington Palace Golf Club and the house itself was requisitioned in the First World War as a hospital. In 1951 Croydon Council bought the house and 140 acres of the grounds; it was in bad state with dry rot, but was restored and leased to the Royal School of Church Music 1954-94. An organ was installed in the saloon, and Dykes-Bower converted English's winter garden in the west wing into a chapel – the third to be made in the house. In 1994 the LB of Croydon offered a 999-year lease on the house, but at a substantial price and with only 3.75 acres. Since then it has been run as a venue for conferences and weddings, and most traces of the 18th-century landscape have been obliterated by the golf course in the grounds.

BARKING

Eastbury Manor House

The River Roding has or had some good houses on the high ground beside it and Eastbury Manor is the southernmost, where the ground falls away to Barking Creek and the Thames. The survival of this mid-16th-century house through many vicissitudes is remarkable and is largely due to public pressure and the National Trust, which has owned it since 1918.

The land had belonged to Barking Abbey before the Reformation and had a farmhouse on a slightly different site. Henry VIII had granted it to Sir William Denham in 1545, at which time he owned 200 acres of arable land and 300 of pasture which with areas of 'furze and heath' made an estate of 810 acres 'overlooking the marshes'.[1] Clement Sysley, a City merchant with property in the nearby village of East Ham, was almost certainly the builder. He bought the land in 1556 and recent dendrochronology dates some of the timbers to that time, so it was probably built over the next few years: a rainwater head was recorded with the date 1573, although it has now gone. Eastbury is a fine example of an early Elizabethan country house of medium size, built of brick in English bond with diaper decoration. It is a

43 Barking, Eastbury Manor House from the south, before 1914. The east range had animals on the ground floor and was derelict above. Several families were living in the west range.

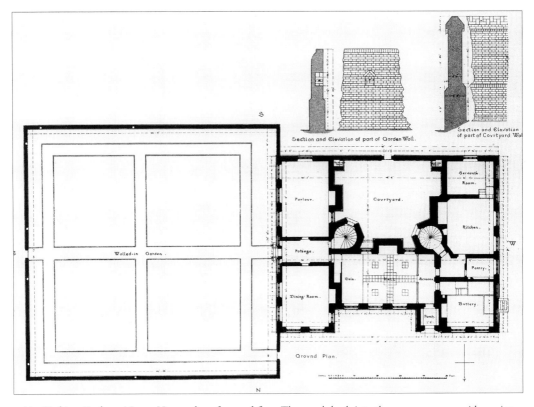

44 Barking, Eastbury Manor House, plan of ground floor. The porch leads into the screens passage with service rooms on the right and the hall leads to parlours on the left. The staircase towers project into the courtyard.

compact house of two main storeys but appears taller due to the many gables, tall octagonal chimneys and the one remaining staircase tower. It would have had even more vertical emphasis when the gables still had their tall finials, which disappeared in the 18th century. No stone was used, although the brick hood-moulds and window surrounds were originally plastered to imitate stone.[2]

The house was approached from the north where the façade is almost symmetrical with three-light mullion and transom windows. The two ranges project slightly in front of the hall and the off-centre porch rises through three storeys. It is a slightly truncated H-plan with the wings projecting more deeply at the south side where they flank a courtyard; this still has its enclosing wall. The porch led into the screens passage (the screen has gone) and the hall also had two windows on the south wall, flanking a large fireplace. The ground floor of the west range had the kitchen and service rooms while the east range had the family parlours. An unusual and attractive feature is the short corridor between the parlours leading into the walled garden on the east side. Two octagonal staircase towers were tucked into the angles of the courtyard, the main one on the east side partially destroyed, the secondary one with a good oak staircase remaining on the west side. On the first floor the great chamber was not, as one might expect, above the single-storey hall but in the east range. This range suffered most in the 18th and 19th centuries and is now shown as a gallery with its partition walls removed. Over the hall is the Painted Room which was originally two rooms with fireplaces on the south wall: their chimneys can be seen from the courtyard. Its name derives from the painted decoration which survives, faintly, on the walls and is dated to *c*.1603. The paintings were recorded in 1834 and show that the plastered walls were divided into panels by chunky Salomonic columns framing sea and landscape views above a painted dado. It was probably commissioned by John Moore, a tenant at that time whose arms were included in the decoration.[3] Family lodgings would have been over the service rooms, and there was a garderobe at the south end of both east and west ranges. The rooms on the top floor were high-ceilinged and with large windows with a gallery on the east side. This would have had spectacular views over the Thames estuary, as would the prospect room at the top of one of the staircase towers.

Sysley died in 1578, leaving to his widow 'my house called Eastbury Hall with all barnes stables dove houses orchards and gardens thereto belonging'.[4] She remarried and her son by her first marriage, a rather hopeless boy called Thomas Sysley, leased Eastbury to his step-brother Augustine Steward in 1592 and later sold it to him, on condition his mother could remain there for life. In the early 17th century it was sold to the Knightley family, and in 1650 was sold again to Thomas Vyner, the founder of the goldsmith and banking firm in the City and a man who managed to be knighted by both Cromwell and Charles II. (His nephew Sir Robert Vyner bought Swakeleys.) It passed to multiple heirs in 1690 and in 1714 was sold but again was soon in joint ownership. As a result the house was let over several generations to tenant farmers.[5] It was impossible for them to maintain a house of this size and deterioration set in. As early as 1724 Defoe described Eastbury as 'a great house,

45   Barking, Eastbury Manor House, after restoration by the National Trust, showing the entrance front with its asymmetrical porch and the west front with service rooms.

ancient and almost fallen down.'[6] The finials on the gables went, the east range descended into stabling and cowsheds, the farmers lived in the kitchen and two other rooms in the west range and had families of labourers living upstairs. By 1813 the main staircase tower had collapsed after being struck by lightning, many of the windows were bricked up and in 1840 some of the chimneypieces were removed to Parsloes, a nearby house since demolished.[7]

Its striking architecture appealed to early 19th-century antiquarians and artists and its site was prominent enough for it to be well-known. Buckler made detailed drawings of it in 1823, 1825 and 1836, and Thomas Hunt in his *Exemplars of Tudor Architecture* based one of his design on Eastbury, saying it had inspired 'the tower surmounted by angular turrets … the high-pitched roof; the chimneys; and the pinnacled gables.'[8] By 1914 the heirs had no interest in the house and decided to sell the land for building. This provoked an outcry, SPAB mounted a campaign, the *Survey of London* produced a monograph on the house and in 1918 the National Trust stepped in to buy it.[9] In 1934 it was leased to Barking Council to be used as a local museum. The architect William Weir carried out work, especially restoring the bricked-up windows and working on the east range, where ground-floor rooms were made out of the stabling and the gallery space was created on the first floor. The museum opened in 1935 but was short-lived as the Second World War intervened and the house suffered some bomb damage in 1941. It was restored in 1964 and was opened for community use and to the public. It has recently had further HLF support for research and restoration, including installing a modern staircase in the ruined S-E tower. This work was carried out by Richard Griffiths Architects and completed in 2004. The walled kitchen gardens have recently been investigated and replanted, and the niches in the original walls of the east garden have been recognised as bee-boles. With its 1½ acres of gardens it provides a much-needed green space in a densely inhabited area of Barking and is a reminder of the past in an area where there are few pre-20th-century buildings.

46 Barking, Eastbury Manor House. 1834 print showing the early 17th-century painted decoration on the first floor.

BARNET

WROTHAM PARK

Rarely does a house near London still belong to the family which built it, but Wrotham is still owned and lived in by the Byng family, descendants of Admiral Byng who built it in 1754. It is also one of the finest mid-18th-century houses in this survey and is Isaac Ware's most important country house, which he illustrates in his *Complete Body of Architecture*.

The Hon. John Byng (1704–57) came from a naval family, and although a younger son he had prize money to help finance his building project. He began buying land in the Barnet area in 1748, when he acquired Pinchbeck House and 150 acres for £6,500, and later added more land.[1] His London house was in Berkeley Square; it was new-built and Isaac Ware arranged the interiors, and was also asked to design his country house, which was to be called Wrotham to reflect the family's Kentish roots.[2] This was to be on a new site with fine views westwards, and remarkably the outlook from the house even today is essentially rural and well-wooded, although it is only 12 miles from central London. Byng

47   Barnet, Wrotham Park. 1781 print of garden front, designed by Isaac Ware for Admiral Byng.

48   Barnet, Wrotham Park, entrance front. The second floor was added and the wings heightened in 1855.

was unmarried, although his mistress Mrs Susannah Hickson lived with him in London and came to Wrotham from time to time. Ware provided him with a house that could be described as a villa – a compact but elegant building nicely adapted to its landscape setting, a type that was to be perfected by Sir Robert Taylor over the next decade.

The five-bay main block has a heavily rusticated semi-basement supporting the *piano nobile*, with a bedroom floor above. The entrance has wide steps leading to an Ionic porch, the pediment above having spirited carving of naval and military trophies flanking a cartouche. On the garden front there is also a Rococo touch in the double staircase which curves down from the portico and connects the saloon with the gardens below. The shape of the pediment – again finely carved – was echoed in the attic room rising above the roofline, although this has been lost in later alterations. Two pyramid-roofed wings connected the main block of the house to domed pavilions with canted bays; the northern pavilion contained the kitchen and service rooms. The whole design has a liveliness which belies Ware's Burlingtonian credentials, and has the Rococo touches with which Ware liked to lighten his buildings. The plan was straightforward: an entrance hall with a screen of columns led to the three main reception rooms on the garden front; the imposing main staircase filled one-third of the entrance front, and a corridor across the main block linked the two pavilions. But Admiral Byng did not live to see his house completed: he was commanding part of the British fleet in the Mediterranean against the French, failed to protect the British troops on Menorca and was arrested and court-martialled on his return to England. The expected royal pardon was not given, and he was executed by firing squad in March 1757. However his portrait by Hudson hangs in pride of place in the dining room, in a magnificent giltwood frame with naval trophies.[3]

Wrotham was inherited by his nephew George Byng who managed to acquire 53 acres of Enfield Chace when that royal hunting park was being partially enclosed; he probably also finished the interiors. His son, also George Byng and MP for Middlesex, inherited in 1789 and made tactful enlargements to the house in 1811. Around this time he was also buying works of art in Paris, at a time when many fine quality objects were available, so the house contains some fine Sèvres porcelain and Boulle furniture. He added an additional storey to both the connecting wings and the domed pavilions, and bow windows replaced the Venetian windows flanking the portico on the garden front. A bow was also added to the side of the south pavilion which contains the dining room, a most beautiful room with one of the few possibly original chimneypieces in the house, and filled today with a fine series of family portraits by Sir Francis Grant. The house as built was of red brick with stone enrichments, but to disguise these changes it was stuccoed, giving it the stone-coloured appearance we see today. He also commissioned Lewis Kennedy to design a flower garden beside the house, sheltered from the N-E by a new stable block. This is a deceptively simple design: an oval courtyard of brick, punctuated by Tuscan columns supporting wooden pediments with deep eaves, the windows set in depressed arches.

49 Barnet, Wrotham Park. The dining room in the south pavilion has a portrait of Admiral Byng in the alcove.

In 1854 George Stevens Byng, Viscount Enfield and later 2nd Earl of Strafford, inherited and soon made further changes, using the London decorators Morant & Boyd. To house his large family William Cubitt & Co. added an attic storey to the main block, diminishing the effect of the pediments but otherwise in keeping with the 18th-century house. Odder was his decision in 1863 to ask S.S. Teulon to add an asymmetrical tower; fortunately this was not built, and Teulon's only addition was the curious oriel window added to the N–W pavilion, although he designed the Kentish ragstone lodge and the little brick village church and nearby cottages in Bentley Heath. In 1883 there was a serious fire, and although most of the contents were saved the house was gutted. Cubitt was called in again, to restore the house to its original appearance; his work was just completed when Strafford died, and his widow promptly removed as much as possible from the house, leaving only the heirlooms. The 3rd Earl, who inherited 1886, used the London decorators Frederick Muntzer to arrange the interiors after his step-mother's depredations. So what we see today is essentially a late 19th-century reconstruction of the 1754 house.

During the 20th century there was the usual pressure to develop the farmland for housing and light industrial use, but the 6th Earl of Strafford resisted, and it is largely due to him that the estate survives today with its park and farmland just inside the M25. He left the house to his daughter Elizabeth, whose son took the name Byng after the death of his grandfather. The family still lives in the house, which is not open to the public, and the elegant and well-proportioned rooms still house a fine collection of pictures and furniture.

BEXLEY

DANSON HOUSE

Danson is one of the success stories of recent years, the house reclaimed from a state of dereliction under local authority control, the fabric restored and the history researched. It is now run by a trust to ensure its future viability, and with its grounds providing parkland in a built-up outer suburb. There is no sign of the busy A2 only a mile away, just beyond the confines of the park. This is one of the best examples of how these houses have come to enhance the lives of local people.

The house faces south over a wide valley with the glimpse of a lake below. The old house was in the valley, the site submerged when it was landscaped *c*.1770. It was probably enlarged and modernised in the 17th century, and in 1695 was sold to John Styleman, a nabob returning from India who lived there till 1723. He then let the house to John Selwyn MP, who enlarged the old house. Styleman died in 1734 leaving it to his widow. The buyer of various lands in Bexley was John Boyd (1718-1800), builder of the house we see today. He was a London merchant, his considerable wealth coming from his East India Company interests and from his West Indies sugar plantations; he was also involved in the slave trade. He lived in the City and ran his business from his office in Austin Friars, but soon moved to

50   Bexley, Danson House. Print by Malton of the house designed by Taylor for Sir John Boyd.

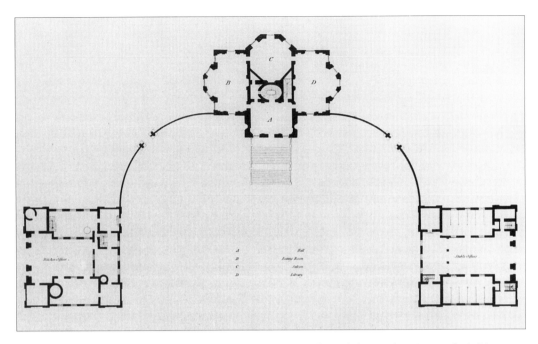

51 Bexley, Danson House. Plan of main floor with its rooms of varied shapes. The wing on the left has the kitchens, that on the right the stables.

Westminster, a mark of social mobility. Now he wanted a country estate as well, but within easy reach of London, a place where he could farm and enjoy country sports and where his wife and young children could spend the summer. In 1753 he leased the old house in the valley and began buying up parcels of land in the parish, eventually having an estate of about 600 acres. In 1759 he bought the freehold of the old house from the Styleman family for £3,500 – so he could build a new house while living in the old until it was ready. The architect Robert Taylor had a wide practice in the City and was commissioned *c.*1761 to build the new house, making it contemporary with Asgill House, Richmond, built for another City client. At the same time the landscape designer Nathaniel Richmond was called in, and his design survives. Did the trio of client, architect and designer choose the new site? The new house was to be on higher ground and building begun in 1762; Boyd's wife, already ill, died in 1763. Building continued, but with his remarriage in 1766 the finishing of the interiors was decided. The result is one of Taylor's most successful villas.

Most of these houses are of brick and stucco, but Boyd was rich enough to build in stone. The house has a rusticated semi-basement with service rooms and a breakfast room; the main rooms are on the ashlar-faced *piano nobile*, with a low-ceilinged bedroom floor above. A neat stone dentil cornice wraps round the whole house below the slate roof, which has a few small servants' rooms within it. The entrance front is pedimented but astylar, the wide flight of stone steps to the front door making a most impressive entrance. Inside, the house is a fine example of Taylor's planning skills. Only the hall is rectangular, opening into an oval staircase hall in the centre of the house. Round it are the three main reception rooms: the dining room with a canted bay to the east matched by the library in the west; and the smaller octagonal saloon facing south. All the rooms are filled with light and have magnificent views over Boyd's newly-acquired estate. The bedroom floor, approached by a toplit cantilevered stone staircase or the small service stair tucked in close to it, had six bedrooms most with closets; the main difference today being the raising of the canted bays at the sides to provide additional closet space; it was decided to leave this during the recent restoration, although it gives the house a less interesting silhouette.

During the completion of the house William Chambers was brought in – perhaps Boyd thought Taylor was too associated with his City origins, and wanted the King's architect to be involved. He embellished the door surround of the entrance, and replaced some of Taylor's chimneypieces; he also designed picture frames for various paintings.[1] But Taylor's detailing is exquisite, and Boyd really had no need to look elsewhere. The door surrounds, the ironwork balustrade to the stairs, the staircase itself and the plasterwork in the saloon are all of superb quality.

Boyd was buying contemporary paintings to decorate his new house, and remarkably some of these are still in situ. Charles Pavillon, a French artist who had come to London but soon moved on to Edinburgh, was asked to paint mythological scenes for the eating room: the overmantel painting is *The Sacrifice to Bacchus*, and tall narrow panels are painted with Ceres paired with Bacchus, Pomona with Vertumnus and Apollo with Euterpe. These are flanked by decorative strips with scrolling vines and flowers; all are oil on canvas. Pavillon helped provide an introduction to Claude-Joseph Vernet who sent over a dramatic landscape with cliffs, a waterfall and a distant view of the sea, an expensive painting to go over the saloon chimneypiece by Chambers.[2] To celebrate his new house and his enhanced status he also commissioned a view by George Barrett of the north front of his new house with the Boyds in the foreground. This large painting now hangs above a door in the saloon in one of Chambers' white and gold frames.

Barrett's painting also shows the additions which were soon made: two pyramid-roofed pavilions were added, the west one with stables, the east with kitchens; these were demolished by Boyd's son. They formed a deep forecourt, screened from south side of the house by curved walls. The original groin-vaulted kitchen was below the dining room – perhaps this remained as a serving room, as there was no corridor linking the new wings to the main block of the house. Chambers also designed a Doric temple and a bridge across the lake in 1770.[3] The lake, formed by damming a small stream, was part of Richmond's early design but was not executed until the new house was ready. There was also a chapel and farm buildings. Boyd was made a baronet in 1775; he took his family to Italy, where he bought the 'Piranesi Vase'.[4] His career and social position seemed assured.

Boyd's business was not going well, especially the sugar trade, which was badly hit by the American War of Independence; there were also the first stirrings of agitation about the slave trade. He continued to buy paintings, acquiring Richard Wilson Italian landscapes, a Rembrandt, a Caracci and a Luca Giordano.[5] But his finances were in poor shape and by the time he died in 1800 the estate was mortgaged to the tune of £40,000. His eldest son, also John, made significant alterations to the house. He demolished the wings and built a fine stable block further from the house, probably reusing stone from the wings.[6] But he could hardly afford these works and some of his father's pictures were offered for sale in 1802, and more in 1805. That year the whole estate was put on the market; he gave up his Grafton Street townhouse and moved to the more middle-class Baker Street. The new owner was another City merchant, John Johnston, who paid £36,000 – less than the mortgage. He did

52   Bexley, Danson House. The stables, shown here before restoration, were rebuilt on a new site in 1800.

little to the estate beyond building a picturesque thatched gamekeeper's cottage and a pair of lodges (all demolished). His widow remained in the house after his death in 1828, while his son employed George Stanley Repton to design him Little Danson, a smaller house in the grounds (demolished). When Mrs Johnston died in 1860 he briefly moved into the main house and soon afterwards put it on the market, but not before his sister Sarah had recorded the house in a series of watercolours, which proved very useful during the restoration of the house.

In 1862 it was bought by Alfred Bean, a successful railway engineer who was involved in the laying-out of railways in the area. He could afford to update the house, installing metal-framed basement windows, gas lighting, better heating and plumbing, but on the whole respecting the neo-classical character of the house. Bean died in 1890 and his widow stayed on till her death thirty years later – thus preserving the house through a time of rapid change in the Bexley area. Some of the land was sold for development in 1922 and the house was offered for sale. But like many others at that time, no-one wanted a country house in an increasingly built-up area and it remained unsold. In 1924 Bexley Urban District Council bought the house and 200 acres for £16,000, driven by the need for public open space rather than by the quality of the historic house.

It is always difficult for a council to maintain a historic house when they have so many conflicting demands for funds, and as usual Danson deteriorated, gradually at first then rapidly. The house opened as a café and local museum but was never adequately maintained; it was requisitioned during the war, and reverted to council use afterwards. Poor quality stonework repairs were carried out, the results of which can still be seen in the discolouration of the stonework; window surrounds were hacked off, and one of the wings almost collapsed.[7] The house was structurally unsound and was closed to the public in 1970, the 1766 organ was removed from the library and the Pavillon paintings from the eating room. From this time on its survival was in doubt. A campaign organised by SAVE resulted in the council off-loading its responsibilities to a private owner who offered to restore the house and stables. Unsupervised by the council, he removed valuable doors, doorcases and chimneypieces. Only after considerable wrangling were they brought back, in return for immunity from prosecution. Finally a course of action was agreed: EH would lease the house and organise a thorough restoration, after which a trust would take over the house and open it to the public. Some income would be provided by the conversion of the stables into a restaurant, serving the visitors to the park even when the house was closed.

In 1995 a £4 million restoration began, using the architects Purcell Miller Tritton. A considerable programme of research was carried out by EH, resulting in a detailed history of the house.[8] In 2003 it was returned to the LB of Bexley which handed it over to the Bexley Heritage Trust, and in 2004 it reopened to the public. This has been a great success, with the Pavillon paintings back in the eating room, the saloon hung with a richly coloured wallpaper and with a copy of Vernet's painting over the fireplace, and the library with its organ and mahogany bookcases back where they stood originally. Its recent history is an example of what can be done by determined action, even after years of neglect.

HALL PLACE

Bexley has a concentration of interesting houses, Danson and Red House being two of the finest, but Hall Place is the oldest, partly Tudor and partly mid-17th-century. Although the A2 is within a mile of the house to the south, it still has its gardens down to the River Cray and open space round about. The current restoration of house and grounds should enhance it further.

The low-lying site is an ancient one: the At-Hall family owned it till 1368, when it passed to the Shelleys; they had permission from the Lord of the Manor, the Archbishop of Canterbury, to rebuild the house in 1469, probably as a timber-framed house. In 1537 William Shelley sold the house and its estate to a City merchant living in Tower Street, Sir John Champneys (or Champneis) who had recently served as Lord Mayor of London. The north front that we see today is largely his rebuilding of Hall Place. The house is a half H-plan built of flint and chalk. In the most prominent areas this is arranged in a chequerboard pattern, but where the walling is more irregular large amounts of monastic stone have been reused, probably from nearby Lesnes Abbey. The house was entered from the south, with a porch (since gone) leading into the screens passage of the double-height hall which had a single bay window at the high end. The hall range was flanked by two irregular cross wings to the north. The east wing contained the kitchen and service rooms, the west wing the parlour and a chapel, with a great chamber on the first floor. The chapel was small, only 10 x 20 ft, but was correctly oriented: its three-light window still faces into the courtyard, although the chapel itself has long gone.[1]

Sir John died in 1556, and his son Sir Justinian Champneis inherited; he had local as well as City interests, and was Sheriff of Kent. He wanted a more symmetrical front to his house, so the existing bay window on the north front was replicated, giving the unusual two-bay front we see today. He also enlarged the east wing and raised the narrower west wing to two storeys

53 Bexley, Hall Place. The entrance front of the mid-16th-century house, built of stone and flint. Taken in 1951, before restoration.

beyond the chapel, making a more symmetrical and impressive approach to the house. The west side facing the gardens has a staircase tower linking the parlour and great chamber, both of which were given bay windows, and a privy tower for the first-floor lodgings.

The Champneis family owned the house until *c.*1640, when it was sold to Robert Austen who made major changes to it. Not many people were enlarging their houses through the troubled years of the Civil War and the Commonwealth, but Austen doubled the size of the house by adding a large courtyard to the south. This is in marked contrast to the earlier part of the house: it is a fine example of mid-17th-century domestic architecture, built of brick and dated variously 1649, 1651 and 1653. Its main feature is the square brick staircase tower behind the hall with irregularly placed mullion and transom and oval windows and topped by a turret; this can be seen on the approach to the house, appearing above the roofline of the hall. The oak staircase round an open well is well-lit, the balustrade with simple chunky balusters and ball finials on the newels. The courtyard behind it was originally arcaded, and traces of this can be seen: it had brick piers and arches with stone keystones and a stone string course. Some of the wide mullion and transom windows are still in place, but on the external walls they have been replaced with sashes. The hipped roof is tiled and has dormer windows to light the attics, and there is a deep bracketed eaves cornice. The interiors of the new ranges are mainly simple service rooms. Austen redecorated the most important room of the house, the great chamber on the first floor of the west wing. He gave it a superb coved plaster ceiling, one of the glories of the house, the central panels with oval and circular wreaths of leaves and flowers, the side panels covered with foliage scrolls and half-figures. It is a fascinating demonstration of the transition from Jacobean to the Restoration style of ceilings which developed from Inigo Jones's interiors.

Robert Austen was made Sheriff of Kent at the Restoration and given a baronetcy, and his descendants held onto Hall Place into the 20th century. But the family finances suffered and few changes were made after this, apart from adding the fine wrought-iron gates to the north forecourt, now the main entrance. Through the marriage of Sir Robert's grandson to Rachel Dashwood it became the property of Sir Francis Dashwood of West Wycombe, later Lord Le Despencer. He had no intention of living in Hall Place, and his successor let it from 1800-70 as a 'school for young gentlemen'.[2] Occasionally a member of the Dashwood family might live there for a while; Maitland Dashwood retired there in 1870 and modernised the house without altering its architectural character. The Dashwoods tried to sell it in 1912, but like many of these houses near London it did not meet its reserve and was withdrawn, in spite of the lure of development land being offered.[3] From 1917 it was let to May, Countess of Limerick (1862-1943) who lived there till her death. She was an Irish beauty who had married the owner of Dromore Castle in Co. Limerick, but was living apart from her husband and no longer wanted to remain in politically unstable Ireland. At Hall Place she entertained lavishly and filled the house with antique furniture; she also made alterations to the house, stripping off plasterwork to expose stonework and beams in a way which would now be considered unsympathetic to its history.[4] Her daughter had married a rich American, James Cox Brady, who bought the house from the Dashwoods in 1926, although his mother-in-law remained there. He died soon afterwards, and his trustees made

54   Bexley, Hall Place. The mid-17th-century addition from the S-W.

55   Bexley, Hall Place. Mid-17th-century plasterwork in the earlier first-floor great chamber. Taken in 1951, before restoration.

an agreement with Bexley Borough Council. The area was becoming increasingly built up and the council wished to preserve the historic house with the grounds for public use: it bought the house and 160 acres for £25,000, with Lady Limerick remaining as tenant for life. After her death in 1943 the contents were sold and the house was used by the U.S. army and after the war was part of Bexley High School for Girls, although the grounds were open as a public park from 1952. It was only in 1968 that the house was restored, without the care and research that would now be considered essential for a Grade 1 listed house; part was opened to the public and the rest used for exhibitions and as the centre for Local Studies. Sadly, local authorities are notoriously bad at maintaining the historic buildings in their care, and by the late 1990s Hall Place was in need of a large amount of money to update it sensitively. So was Danson, the other historic house owned by the LB of Bexley, and it was decided that ownership of the two houses should be transferred to the newly set up Bexley Heritage Trust. The Trust has recently closed Hall Place for the £2 million restoration of the house and its outbuildings, which include a fine 17th-century barn.[5] When it reopens in 2009 the barn and stables to the east of the house will be used for visitor services, freeing up the interiors of the house for displays of historic furniture and objects from the Bexley Museum, as well as some furnishings which were sold after the death of Lady Limerick.[6]

RED HOUSE

Red House is fascinating in many respects: its architecture, its richly coloured furnishings, and the way in which it established a new style, based more on vernacular buildings than on the revival of Gothic forms. It is also the beginning of a new type of house, no longer the summer retreat of a prosperous family, but the dream-home close enough to the capital for its owner to commute to his business and to have his friends down for the weekend. It was a very personal creation by William Morris, even if he only lived there for five years.

When William Morris (1834-96) married Jane Burden in 1859 he had already decided to build a new house to embody some of his ideals: a love of nature and of rural life and a passion for craftsmanship. The land he bought was close to Bexley in Kent in the hamlet of Upton, which had otherwise only a small farming community. Its attractions were its rural tranquillity combined with accessibility from London. He could be driven in a pony trap to the railway station at Abbot Wood, take the train to London and work there during the day. His architect was his great friend Philip Webb, whom he had met while both were working in the office of G. E. Street. It was Webb's first commission, and although some areas of the design are slightly clumsy, it expresses forcibly the ideals of the two young men and was to have an importance in architectural history far beyond its comparatively small scale. So was the friendship between them: they later were co-founders of SPAB, which did (and still does) so much to alert the public to the threat to old buildings and to prevent unsympathetic restoration.[1]

The house is built of red brick, in contrast to the white bricks or stucco which had been so common earlier in the 19th century; and Webb's brickwork is particularly good, laid in English bond and clearly revealing the structure of the house, for instance in the relieving arches over the windows. Red House is approached from the north. Webb's small stable block is still in the N-E corner of the grounds, hidden in the trees; Morris was careful to cut down as few trees as possible during the building. A short drive reveals the house, its severe two-storey entrance front dominated by tall chimneys and a series of steep tiled roofs. The porch has an unusually low arch echoed in the recessed arch with its paired sash windows of the bedroom above. The narrow north window of the ground-floor dining room has triple lancet windows above, suggesting the importance of the drawing room within. The L-shaped plan allowed the Morris and his wife to live mainly in this range, with the extension to the south for their servants. But this does mean that the main rooms used by Morris and his wife were mainly north-facing and dark, while the servants had the light and sunny rooms. The house looks far more inviting from the garden, where the L-plan embraces a well which is given a conical tiled roof, linking it to the varied roofs of the house itself.[2] From this side we can appreciate Webb's insistence that the exterior reflect the lay-out of the house. The tower in the angle with its large windows at different heights clearly contains the staircase and has its own high roof surmounted by a turret with a weathervane and Morris's initials; the service staircase is given a long narrow window running through two storeys. Morris and his wife did not want to relegate the servants to a basement or a gloomy wing, but even so it seems wilful to place the larders facing into the sunny gardens on one side, and have the kitchen facing west into the other garden so it often over-heated; perhaps it was a sign of the inexperience of the two young men.[3]

The interior of the house was to be filled with furniture, textiles and objects designed by Webb and Morris – they could not find the pieces they were after, so the foundation of the

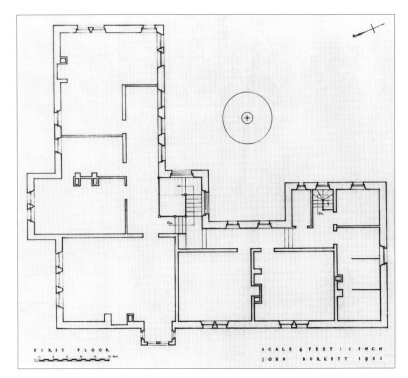

56 Bexley, Red House, plan of first floor. Morris's studio was in the L-shaped room top left, and servants in the small rooms on the right.

immensely influential firm of Morris & Co. was very much a result of the need to furnish Red House. Not much remains in the house today, but the hall is still dominated by the large settle-cum-cupboard by Webb and partly painted by Morris, although the panelling and hangings have gone. On one side of the hall is a passage leading to the garden porch and to a library, while on the other is the dining room, where the massive brick fireplace is inset with old Dutch tiles – an early and influential example of the Arts and Crafts taste for using old blue-and-white tiles in fireplaces. This is a practical place for eating, being close to the kitchen and pantries. Webb designed a red-painted dresser, another example of his multi-purpose pieces of furniture: as well as having storage and display space, a little lantern hangs from the central gable.

The most important rooms are on the first floor, approached up Webb's impressive oak staircase. Balusters are replaced by plain boards, broken only by the pinnacled newels, a reflection of Webb's Gothic training in Street's office. The space extends into the tower above where through its exposed timbers can be seen the original decoration. The outlines of the stylised patterns were pricked into the plasterwork as a guide for the painters. A bare brick arch leads to the two guest bedrooms and on to the dormitory for the maidservants, while the drawing room is over the dining room. This is the most important room in the house, overlooking the west gardens and the Kentish countryside beyond from the oriel window, which is supported externally on carefully corbelled brickwork. It is open to the rafters and is dominated by the tall brick fireplace, its simple lines a foretaste of the simplicity of Arts and Crafts design. This room also houses a strange piece of furniture, originally designed by Morris for his London lodgings. Like Webb's hall dresser, it combined seating with storage space, but for this room Webb added an overhanging canopy to act as a minstrel's gallery, with a ladder built onto one side to give access. From the gallery a simple boarded door with elegant ironwork led into the loft. Not surprisingly this very large piece of furniture has never left this room since it was installed in 1860, although the painted panel by Rossetti is now in Tate Britain. With his fascination with the medieval past Morris commissioned his friend Edward Burne-Jones to paint murals in this room, but of the seven planned only three were executed, and they have not lasted well. The Morris's bedroom was a narrow and poorly-lit room over the hall and porch, now plain and bare, but once enlivened by blue wall-hangings embroidered with daisies by Jane Morris, and by another piece of painted furniture, the Chaucer wardrobe designed by Webb and decorated by Burne-Jones and given them as a wedding present. The most attractive feature of the upper floor is the wide corridor, south-facing, with its *oeuil-de-boeuf* windows overlooking the gardens. These windows have some of the earliest stained glass designed by Morris, which allow the sunlight to flood through. This leads to Morris's study or studio, a well-lit L-shaped room with views over the gardens; again stylised painted decoration has survived on the sloping ceilings. Here he began to work out his ideas for wallpapers and furnishings which led to the foundation of William Morris & Company with its works at Merton Abbey on the River Wandle in south London, inspired

partly by the gardens he created at Red House. Here he countered the austerity of Webb's architecture with luscious planting. The walls were covered with climbing roses, jasmine and honeysuckle, and the flower garden was arranged in medieval style with wattle fences enclosing the beds of roses and lilies. The kitchen garden and orchard provided fruit and vegetables for the household.

The house cost about £3,750 to build and was the fruit of so much thought and inspiration, but it was not to last. Morris had hoped that Edward and Georgina Burne-Jones would join them, and in 1864 Webb proposed adding two more wings to form a courtyard house round the well; but, wisely perhaps, Burne-Jones decided to remain in London. Disappointed, and after a severe illness in 1864 finding the two-hour commute to his business tiring, Morris and his wife decided to move back to London with their two children; they lived in Queen Square and in 1871 rented Kelmscott in Oxfordshire as their country retreat, a nice example of the need to move ever further from London to enjoy country life. He sold Red House in 1865 for only £2,000 so made a considerable

57 Bexley, Red House. Oak staircase designed by Philip Webb, as it was in 1951.

loss on this project. The enormous pieces of furniture designed for Red House were far too large for a London house and were left behind, hence their survival in the rooms for which they were designed.[4]

The house had not then achieved the fame it now enjoys, and it changed hands many times, although usually attracting people responsive to its unusual qualities. From 1889-1903 it belonged to Charles Holme, the founder of *The Studio*; the architect Edward Maufe was brought up there; and in the 1920s Alfred Horsfall, editor of *The Studio* lived there. Most importantly two LCC architects bought it in 1953 for only £3,500, Ted Hollamby and his wife buying out their friends in 1964. They recognised its historic interest at a time when Victorian was a term of abuse and carefully repaired the fabric, which had suffered some bomb damage in the Second World War. He preserved the historic features of the house while researching Morris's life and work, and suitably enough his architect's desk sits today in Morris's studio. After the death of his widow in 2003 the house was sold to the National Trust and is now the subject of a five-year research project. This is particularly timely, as the future of the William Morris collection at Water House, Walthamstow is now so uncertain. As Lawrence Weaver wrote, Red House was 'a fresh starting-point for domestic architecture, of which the importance cannot be exaggerated'.

BLACKHEATH

THE RANGER'S HOUSE

The high ground above Greenwich has fine views and was easily reached from central London, being just off the old Roman road to Canterbury. Greenwich was a populous village by 1700 with royal connections: the palace had been converted into the Royal Naval Hospital and the royal hunting park extended up the hill to the Observatory. Naval bases and all the trades associated with ship-building were concentrated on the Thames from Deptford to Chatham and this area appealed particularly to naval families. Admiral Sir Francis Hosier (1673-1727), as he later became, was born in Deptford and was a captain who had won enough prize money to acquire a Crown lease on a plot of land between Greenwich Park and the common of Blackheath, probably about 1700.

He built a compact double-pile two-storey house of warm red brick set back behind a shallow forecourt. It has a seven-bay entrance front with a slightly recessed centre, a balustraded roof-line and tall brick chimneys. The windows on the outer bays have rubbed red brick surrounds while those in the centre are emphasised by Portland stone dressings: a crisply carved pedimented doorcase with a mask of Neptune and Ionic columns, a stone surround to the arched window above the door and stone panels linking the narrow side windows. There

58   Blackheath, Ranger's House, the entrance front *c*.1700. This was built of red brick, with Chesterfield's 1749 addition on the right and Hulse's later wing on the left in darker brick.

is no known architect and it is the sort of competent design that could have been provided by a London bricklayer. The stone-paved hall leads into the saloon which faces east over Greenwich Park. There were three smaller rooms on this floor, with the fine oak staircase with its twisted balusters on the north side. On the first floor there is a narrow but effective central corridor giving access to the bedrooms; most of the first floor still has its original panelling. The semi-basement had the kitchen and other service rooms and there were further service rooms opposite the stable block to the north. It was a compact, well-planned, medium-sized house. When Hosier died an inventory was made of the contents of the house, which show it to have been richly furnished.[1]

In 1748 the house was inherited by Philip Stanhope, 4th Earl of Chesterfield (1694-1773) who was building Chesterfield House in Mayfair with its superb Rococo interiors at this time. Isaac Ware was his architect, and it is almost certain that he employed him at Ranger's House too (then called Chesterfield House). There was no really large reception room in Hosier's house and by this time a 'great room' was a requirement of fashionable life so he immediately enlarged his Blackheath house by adding a wing on the south side. This is a single-storey extension, differentiated by its larger scale and lighter brickwork. It provided a gallery 75 by 20 ft with bowed ends and a bow in the centre, its ceiling with Palladian plasterwork. The eastern bow actually projected through the park wall, giving views across to the Observatory and towards the Thames.[2] It was a well-lit room, designed for entertaining and for displaying some of Chesterfield's fine collection of paintings. He made the saloon into his dining room, giving it a Palladian cornice and a new chimneypiece and removing the panelling so the plastered walls would provide more space for his pictures; and made a library out of one of Hosier's parlours.

As Chesterfield got older he became very deaf and used Ranger's House not just in the summer but for much of the time, his wife probably spending very little time there with him. When he died it was inherited by a cousin, the 5th Earl, who held a Christie's sale of the contents in 1782.[3] The lease of the house was bought by Richard Hulse, a lawyer. He needed more service rooms so added a wing on the north side, carefully designed to match the gallery wing. He was serious art collector and in the last twenty years of his life bought Dutch, Flemish and Italian pictures, building up a collection not dissimilar to Chesterfields. He was childless and after his death in 1805 the pictures were all sold.[4]

In 1806 Princess Caroline of Brunswick, the separated wife of the Prince of Wales, was made ranger of Greenwich Park by her uncle, George III. At this time the Ranger's House which went with the post was the Queen's House, but it was about to become a school so she rented Montagu House next to the Ranger's House instead.[5] Her mother, the Dowager Duchess of Brunswick, came to London the following year to keep an eye on her wayward daughter and took on the lease of the Ranger's House, then known as Brunswick House. After her death her belongings were sold, and Princess Caroline left Montagu House to go abroad.[6] The lease was taken over by the Crown and it acquired its present name of Ranger's House. From 1815-44 the ranger was Princess Sophia Matilda, a cousin of the Prince Regent. The alterations carried out for her included the construction of a covered passage from the gate to the front door, a practical but intrusive addition.[7] She also had Chesterfield's gallery divided into three inter-connected reception rooms. After her death the house was given by the Crown to various public servants and was also used by Prince Arthur of Connaught, one of Queen Victoria's many children. The last person to use it as a private house was Field-Marshal Lord Wolseley. His wife was a noted collector of early 18th-century English furniture and in 1888 they employed Bodley of Watts & Co. to make some minor alterations, including adding Dutch tiles to some of the fireplaces and redecorating the house.[8]

In 1897 the house was transferred to the Department of Woods & Forests and the 15 acres of parkland which the Duchess of Brunswick had been given as her garden was returned to Greenwich Park. Two years later ownership of the house was transferred to the LCC but no proper plans had been made for its future use or maintenance. The covered porch was removed and the forecourt reinstated, although plans to make a museum in the house did not materialise and from 1902 it was used as a tearoom for visitors to the park (a similar fate to that of Chiswick House). The fabric of the house suffered, even more so during the war when it was requisitioned by the army and the stable block was largely destroyed by a bomb. After the war there was local pressure to do something about it and in 1959-60 restoration was carried out which included opening up Chesterfield's gallery. In 1974 the Suffolk Collection of mainly 17th-century portraits was given to the house and looked superb hanging in the gallery and other rooms. Both Ranger's House and Kenwood House were transferred from the GLC to English Heritage and recently the Suffolk Collection has been moved to Kenwood House, making space to install the newly acquired Wernher Collection at Ranger's House. Within the rooms of Hosier's house a semblance of the rich dark interiors of Sir Julius Wernher's Mayfair house has been recreated, in which this fine collection of Renaissance ivories, bronzes, jewellery and paintings can be seen.[9]

WRICKLEMARSH

Wricklemarsh was one of the group of very grand and expensive houses built in the early 18th century which did not last long. Built *c.*1725, it was John James's most accomplished house; it was demolished in 1787. There had, as usual, been an earlier house on the site which had belonged since 1669 to Sir John Morden (1623-1708). He was a member of the Levant Company and had been a merchant in Aleppo before returning to London. He also belonged to the East India Company and was the founder of Morden College, an almshouse in Blackheath for impoverished merchants. Lady Morden remained in the house after his death and since they were childless it was sold by executors after she died in 1721. The buyer was Sir Gregory Page Bt. (1689-1775) who had just got married. He was a City merchant whose family owned a brewery in Wapping; his father had been a director of the East India Company. Thanks to his father's shares in the South Sea Company having been sold just before the crash he was immensely rich, worth perhaps £600,000 at a time when many people were hit by the collapse in share prices. He already had links with Greenwich, as his father had owned a large house on Maze Hill. They too were to be childless, perhaps a contributory factor in its early disappearance.

John James was well known in City circles, and was also involved in the completion of the Royal Naval Hospital in Greenwich from 1705. As a result he built himself a house on Maze Hill, which still stands. Most of his commissions were for smaller houses, such as Orleans House in Twickenham. Wricklemarsh was different, a most impressive house, built of Portland stone and erected within a year.[1] It was therefore contemporary with Sir Robert

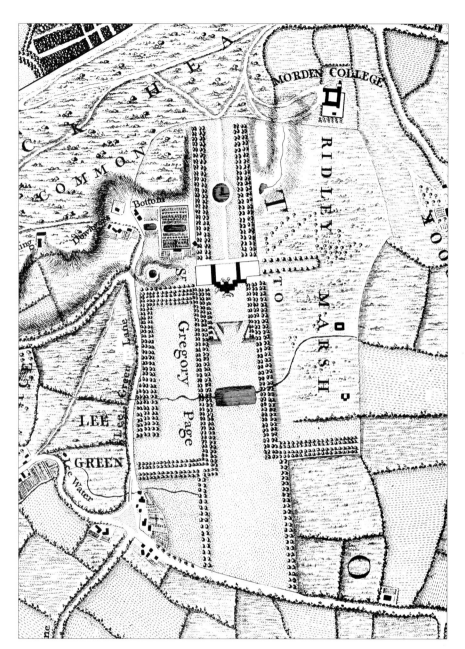

59 Blackheath, Wricklemarsh. Rocque's 1745 map shows Sir Gregory Page's house and Morden College. The grounds are dominated by extensive avenues, with a walled kitchen garden N-W of the house.

Walpole's Houghton Hall, designed by Colen Campbell and James Gibbs. But while that house was a conventional Palladian plan, a central block with pavilions linked by quadrant colonnades, Wricklemarsh was more innovative. There was a deep forecourt, similar to some of Vanbrugh's houses, flanked by lavish stabling (there were stalls for 28 horses) on one side and kitchens, laundries etc on the other, all masked by a Tuscan colonnade. These framed the astylar nine-bay front with horseshoe-shaped steps up to the entrance. Could these possibly have been inspired by the stairs at the Queen's House in Greenwich? The garden

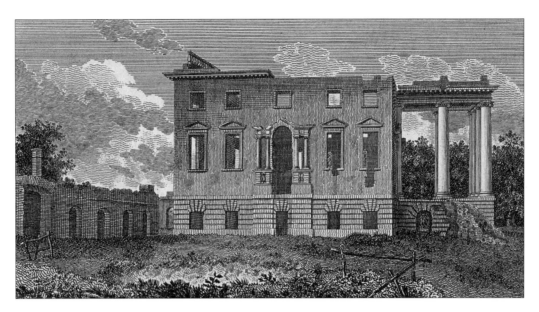

60 Blackheath, Wricklemarsh, print by J. P. Malcolm of 1800 showing the house being demolished. The portico and Venetian windows were removed to Beckenham Place.

front had the same steps leading to a deep unpedimented Ionic portico.[2] It had a *piano nobile* with pedimented windows over a rusticated semi-basement and an attic floor with bedrooms below a hipped roof, partly hidden by a balustrade. In plan Wricklemarsh provided a circuit of rooms, an early example of the type of plan which was developed over the mid-18th century. Hasted, usually more interested in the genealogy of the owners than in the architecture, was impressed, describing it as 'one of the finest seats in England, belonging to a private gentleman, and much admired for its fine situation and excellent air'.[3] The site was impressive. Rocque's map of 1747 shows the north-facing entrance front overlooking the deep forecourt, with a double avenue leading to the edge of Blackheath. There was a walled kitchen garden to the west, while the south front looked down another avenue to a canal. Sir John Clerk of Penicuik visited with William Adam in 1728 and noted that 'the gardens are very natural … and of a new taste consisting only of gravel walks with large squares of green turf, few or no evergreen trees or shrubs'.[4]

The section in *Vitruvius Britannicus* shows the hall with its paired columns. On one side was the dining room with a serving recess, and on the other was the very large library with its screen of paired columns.[5] Could this have been an early example of a library doubling as a living room? A gallery 60 ft long filled all the east side of the house with a Venetian window in the centre, and here Page hung some of his magnificent art collection, which being close to London was well known and much visited. It was a typical choice for its date, with paintings by Rubens, van Dyck, Preti, Luca Giordano and Imperiali; he also had views of Venice and Rome by Canaletto and Panini. In the dressing room were his Dutch cabinet pictures, a particularly fine collection which included several van der Werffs.[6] Sir John Clerk noted the richness of the furniture, and John Soane's set of padouk wood chairs inlaid with mother-of-pearl come from Wricklemarsh. The arms on the back are of Sir Gregory Page and his bride, and they seem to have been made in China for their marriage.

   When Page died in 1775 the house was inherited by his great-nephew Gregory Turner, who added the name Page to his.[7] He did not want the house, letting it while he got an Act of Parliament allowing him to sell it. The picture collection was dispersed gradually through several sales and in 1784 the estate was sold to John Cator. Three years later Christie's held a sale of the fabric of the house, after which it fell into disrepair and was demolished about 1800.[8] Turner painted an evocative watercolour of the unroofed portico and prints were made of the gaunt remains of the house. We know it today only from a few descriptions and from various fittings which were sold in 1787. Cator removed the two Venetian windows from the side walls and the four Ionic columns of the portico and incorporated them clumsily into his house, Beckenham Place. Some chimneypieces also went to Beckenham Place, but were removed by one of the Cators to Woodbastick Hall in Norfolk.[9] Two marble chimneypieces went to the Admiralty and are still there. They are very fine quality, one richly carved with swags of fruit and flowers, the other with comic and tragic masks and festoons of flowers. These are all that remain of this splendid but short-lived house.

BRENTFORD

BOSTON MANOR

Boston Manor is a rare example of a Jacobean house surviving on the outskirts of London; it can be glimpsed among its cedar trees from the M4. The land, once belonging to St Helen's Bishopsgate, is a curious strip, a southward extension of the parish of Hanwell between the parishes of Ealing and Isleworth. It was granted by Elizabeth I to the Earl of Leicester in 1572, who immediately sold it on to Sir Thomas Gresham, the builder of Osterley nearby. When he died, childless, his widow Anne inherited both properties and left them to her son by her first marriage, Sir William Reade, who was probably already living at the old Boston Manor.

Reade died in 1621, leaving Boston Manor (but not Osterley) to his young second wife, born Mary Goldsmith. Women rarely commissioned buildings in the 17th century, but it was she who built the house we see today. She built it immediately: a lead downpipe is dated 1622 and initialled MR, and a plasterwork ceiling is dated 1623. It is a double-pile house of

61 Brentford, Boston Manor, entrance front. The house was built in 1621, with the cornice and window surrounds added in the late 17th century and the porch in the 19th century.

three storeys, built of brick, an interesting if not totally satisfactory example of the compact plan which was becoming popular by this date, especially in the areas round London. There are three gables on the east and west fronts, but the fenestration, none of it original, on the west front is very irregular.

The plan of the house was interesting. The entrance on the east side probably led directly into the screens passage of the hall, although a wall now separates them. So the plasterwork ceiling of the present hall presumably reflects the design of the (lost) ceiling of the rest of the room (now called the dining room). However, it is possible that the present hall is original, and that this was therefore an interesting early example of an entrance hall as a self-contained space.[1]

The principal stairs divided the hall and parlour from the service rooms to the north; although the staircase has been altered, the oak balusters are mainly original, with some later embellishment, and wall paintings below the dado reflected their design; fragments of the painting can still be seen. The original kitchen was probably in the room to the right of the entrance, although it was soon moved out of the main house to separate it further from the living rooms. On the first floor the great chamber is above the hall, with the best bedchamber off it. This can also be approached from the landing via an ante-room. Presumably the family rooms were at the north end of the house, above the service rooms. The upper floor has bedrooms with mainly windowless roof space above. The three attic rooms are at the service end of the house, approached by the secondary staircase; their windows, some with original lead glazing, look inwards onto the valley between the roofs, allowing the gables on the facades to be decorated with small round-headed niches.[2]

It is the quality of the surviving interior details, especially the plasterwork, which makes Boston Manor so interesting. The great chamber has a fine plaster ceiling and a splendid chimneypiece. The overmantel, its design based on Netherlandish prints, has grotesque ornament with a pair of winged horses and a central panel of the *Sacrifice of Isaac*, the whole flanked by caryatids; while the frieze decoration of the chimneypiece itself has a central mask and chunky festoons of fruit in a more classical style. The ceiling, dated 1623 and with Mary Reade's initials, is made up of moulded ribs with flower and leaf decoration surrounding panels of the four seasons and the five senses. The latter are based on late 16th-century engravings by Nicholas de Bruyn.[3] There is another early 1620s plasterwork ceiling and frieze in the state bedchamber.[4]

Later owners of the houses made their mark. Mary Reade remarried, her second husband being Sir Edward Spencer of Wormleighton and Althorp and although the house was meant to be left to some Reade relatives, she bought them out and left it to a member of her own family, John Goldsmith, who inherited it at her death in 1658. When Goldsmith died in 1670 his trustees sold the house and 50 acres of land for £5,336 to James Clitherow, whose descendants owned the house till 1924, thus ensuring its survival through a time when so many other houses on the edge of London were demolished.[5]

James Clitherow I (1618-1682), a younger son of a Lord Mayor of London, was a merchant and investor in voyages to the East Indies, as well as holding money on deposit and speculating in land. He had a house in Cornhill in the City, but it had been destroyed in the Fire of 1666. He was rebuilding it at the time he bought Boston Manor: like many of these City owners, he was well able to afford property purchases and improvements. He rebuilt his Cornhill house as a property investment and let it to an upholsterer. He seems to have lived at Boston Manor for the last 17 years of his life, and was buried in the chapel of ease at New Brentford. He spent £1,439 in improvements at Boston Manor, modernising the fenestration, possibly adding the heavy cornice which wraps round the building, and adding a service wing to the north with the new kitchen.[6]

In 1712 the estate, then belonging to Christopher Clitherow, was 230 acres, of which three acres were gardens, and a further four and a half acres were grounds. The gardens were remodelled in the mid-18th century, and a plan of 1752 shows the walled forecourt and a formal enclosed garden to the south.[7] In 1752 the house had passed to Christopher's grandson, James Clitherow III, and the plan is probably a record of the existing gardens, prior to updating them. One of the proposals was to turn the three fishponds N-W of the house into one ornamental piece of water; another was to remove the old-fashioned axial approach to the east front, and to make a longer drive from slightly further north along the line of the present drive. The painting of 1759 by Arthur Devis of Mr and Mrs James Clitherow

62 Brentford, Boston Manor. The great chamber has a plasterwork ceiling dated 1623, and an overmantel with the Sacrifice of Isaac in the centre.

posing in their garden, with a stretch of water and a view of the house through the trees, is probably an approximate record of their updated grounds.[8] The wallpaper on the stairs, showing Roman ruins, is a fine example of the pictorial papers made in the mid-18th century. Although only part of it survives, on the stairs leading from the first to the second floor, it probably reflects a complete decorative scheme of that time, and happily was not considered worth replacing at the upper levels in the 1847 redecoration.

General John Clitherow (1782-1852) who inherited the house from a cousin in 1847, carried out some sensitive restoration of the interiors in 1847, at a time when the Jacobean style was very fashionable. Accounts record work by the London firm of Hawkesley on the plasterwork ceilings, with that in the great chamber being repaired, painted and partly gilt, a scheme that is still visible today. The staircase was also repaired and grained, and it was at this time that the composition lion heads were added.[9] The rather clumsy but practical porch was probably added at the same time.

At the end of the First World War the house was offered for sale by Colonel John Stracey Clitherow; by this time the family lived mainly on their Yorkshire estate and no longer wanted the house. Its surroundings were becoming built up and such houses were less desirable. It failed to meet the asking price and was withdrawn, although the contents were sold in 1922. In 1924 the house and 20 acres were offered to Brentford Urban District Council for £23,000. As so often in these cases, it was not the house so much as the land which went with it which the council wanted; it would provide public open space, badly needed with the rapid westward expansion of London.

There was some bomb damage in 1944, and after essential post-war repairs the ground floor was used as a school. The house deteriorated badly and in 1960 the firm of Donald Insall & Partners was asked to restore the house and to make some flats in the upper floors; following this, parts of the house were opened to the public in the summer of 1963. At this time part of the park was compulsorily purchased to make an elevated section of the M4. The house and grounds are now administered by the LB of Hounslow, and there is limited public access; its historic interest would justify greater efforts being made to present it to the public.

BROMLEY

SUNDRIDGE PARK

The collaboration between John Nash and Humphry Repton was not always a happy one, but here at Sundridge it produced a striking and unusual house, sited to take advantage of a particularly fine landscape. However it was not the first house on the estate. A courtyard house stood on lower ground (down the drive from the present house) which was replaced during the 18th century by a substantial brick house with stone detailing.[1] In 1792 it was bought by Edward George Lind, who summoned Humphry Repton to help him with ideas for laying out the grounds and James Wyatt to produce ideas for rebuilding the house. Repton produced a 'Red Book' but nothing came of these plans and in 1796 Lind sold the house to Claude Scott, a merchant and MP who later became Sir Claude Scott Bt. He dropped Wyatt but continued to consult Repton who was in partnership at this time with Nash, and the new house and grounds are the result.

63   Bromley, Sundridge Park. View of the south front of the house in its picturesque landscape, drawn by Repton.

The estate lies N–W of Bromley and consists of one valley running east–west with minor valleys leading into it. The hills are well-wooded even today, with grassland below. Repton proposed rebuilding the house higher up the hill to the N–W, giving it views into the valleys while keeping it sheltered from the north by the woods. Did Repton also have a say in the design of the house? When he first met Nash in 1790, he wrote that 'we were charmed with each other at the very first interview. Two such congenial minds were never brought together since the days of David and Jonathan … We jointly designed and built houses.'[2] But in 1796, when they were working on several joint projects, they fell out. It is difficult to know where the division of responsibility lay, but it is generally assumed that the landscape and the siting of the house were the work of Repton, with the architecture by Nash.

The house is approached by a long drive through parkland, past the site of the old house. The stables were rebuilt as a semi-circle behind and above the house, and with the central clock tower make a picturesque composition seen from the drive. Repton 'suggested the idea of cutting down a small hill, so as to form an ample area on which to place the house: this has been executed in a masterly manner and now has the appearance of being the natural shape.'[3] The creamy stucco of the house stands out against the background of a wooded hillside. It is a complex and unusual shape designed to take advantage of the variety of prospects. The dominant feature is a deep bow with a ring of columns and topped by a dome which sits at the apex of a triangle, with two porticoes set further back. All of them have Nash's slightly coarse and over-scaled Corinthian capitals above stuccoed columns; only the steps to the gardens are of Portland stone. Nash and Repton were pioneers in the linking of house and gardens, and here the main reception rooms are on the ground floor with easy access to the gardens. The portico on the west leads into the oval entrance hall, with the service rooms at the back of the house facing into the hillside, and the main rooms overlooking the view. The most dramatic is the circular saloon; this has neo-classical plasterwork which was probably

64 Bromley, Sundridge Park, east front, designed by Nash. The projecting block on the right was added by Claude Scott's son.

added *c*.1870. This room leads through to the drawing room and dining room beyond, the latter with direct access to the gardens through its long windows in the east-facing portico. The core of this deep house is the top-lit cantilevered central staircase, where a single flight leads up between two *scagliola* columns to the niched half-landing where it divides into two; another pair of columns is placed on the landing. The balustrade is of ironwork with a strong French influence, and the dome has neo-classical plasterwork, again possibly added in the 1870s. The space has a sense of drama as one passes from the dark ground-floor corridor to the brilliantly lit staircase itself. A secondary top-lit staircase, steep but elegant with fine brass balusters, leads from near the entrance to family rooms above. The main bedrooms and dressing rooms face south and east over the views. It is an ingenious plan which only makes sense when considered in conjunction with the landscape, as Repton pointed out.

Claude Scott left Sundridge to his son Samuel, who continued his father's business interests and also became a banker; they were very rich, with a London house in Mayfair and a house in the south of France. A large conservatory and vinery were added to the house, since demolished.[4] From 1869 till his death in 1883 the house belonged to Edward Scott and his wife Emilie, who embellished several of the rooms in an Adam Revival style – an early example of a style that was to become more popular in the 20th century. He developed the estate for pheasant shooting, made a private golf course and had house-parties there for the Prince of Wales; he also had a yacht at Cowes. But all this cost money and he began selling off parcels of land, as the arrival of the railway meant that land values had risen as Bromley and Chislehurst expanded. His son Samuel put the estate on the market in 1901 and again in 1904, but it was unsold. Instead part of the park was leased in 1903 to a golf club,

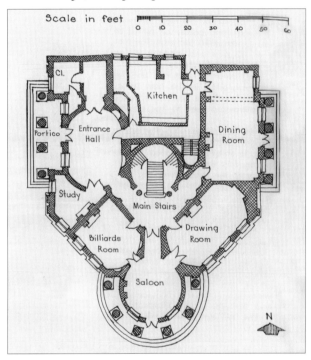

65 Bromley, Sundridge Park. Plan of the ground floor as originally built, *c*.1795.

which bought the freehold of the land in 1976. Scott finally sold the house and 200 acres in 1920 to a hotel group which advertised it as 'a magnificent well-preserved Adam mansion … within 12 miles of London'.[5] In 1953 the hotel was closed down and the house and 16 acres was bought as a management centre in 1955.[6] In the 1990s it changed hands and since then a considerable amount has been spent on restoring the buildings, improving the grounds, removing unsightly earlier additions and adding well-designed residential accommodation.[7]

BROMLEY-BY-BOW

THE OLD PALACE

This Jacobean house, interesting in itself, became a *cause célèbre* in 1894 when it was demolished by the London School Board. The campaign to save it was led by C.R. Ashbee and the Society for the Protection of Ancient Buildings (hereafter SPAB) founded by Ashbee and William Morris in 1877. Although it was not successful it did save one room and also meant that the building was recorded in detail before demolition. The report was published as the first volume of the *Survey of London* in 1900, and a monograph on the house followed.[1] In spite of research the original owner of the house has never been discovered, and the name itself is erroneous: the royal coat of arms over a fireplace led local people to think it had been a royal palace or hunting lodge, when it was simply a mark of loyalty to the new Stuart regime.

Bromley-by-Bow in the early 17th century was a fashionable village close to the City, with several good houses belonging to City families along the River Lea. This house was built in 1606 on St Leonard's Street as a double-pile brick house with two corner towers; it had four rooms per floor, with corner towers on the street front providing small closets. It was a substantial but compact three-storey house with attics and a façade 74 ft wide. To

66 Bromley-by-Bow, The Old Palace, entrance front. Record drawing before demolition by Ernest Godman, 1898.

88

the south and west lay the gardens, and to the north was a service courtyard. When it was demolished it had 25 rooms, but by the mid-18th century these large houses were no longer wanted in the increasingly industrial area of Bromley-by-Bow and it was divided in half and sash windows replaced the earlier mullioned windows. Later it became a school and by the mid-19th century was being used as a colour works, and later a club and lodging house. In spite of these changes of use it was in remarkably good structural condition, as Ashbee pointed out in his battle to save it.

The two *Survey* volumes describe the house. It probably had a screens passage and hall with the kitchen to the north, where a substantial fireplace remained. On the garden front were two panelled parlours, and at the south end of the house a wide wooden staircase led up round an open well to the first floor. The plasterwork ceiling of the great chamber on the first floor was particularly fine, similar to a ceiling made for Sir John Spencer at Canonbury House. But The Old Palace was unusual in having fine ceilings in the two parlours on the ground floor as well. These are typical of the work being done by top London plasterers in the late 16th and early 17th centuries; it was expensive, and points to the owner being a well-off City man. Only one ceiling has survived, which, together with the panelling and chimneypiece from the same room, is now in the British Galleries of the V & A. How did this come about?

In 1893 the London School Board bought the site to build a school, and found itself in the centre of a conservation battle when it sold the house for £250 to a firm of house-breakers. SPAB became involved and sent a strongly worded letter to the Board, saying that 'the house, which from a date recorded in stone in one of the towers, appears to have been built in 1606, was a magnificent Elizabethan [sic] mansion … in admirable preservation.'[2]

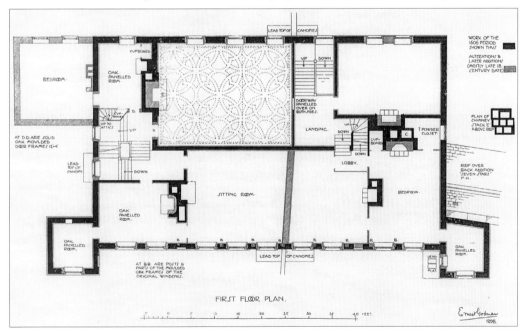

67 Bromley-by-Bow, The Old Palace. Plan of first floor, drawn by Ernest Godman in 1898. The ceiling of the great chamber also had elaborate plasterwork.

68   Bromley-by-Bow, The Old Palace. View of the ground-floor parlour, removed to the V & A. The overmantel has the royal arms in carved wood.

By then it was too late, the house-breakers had sold the internal fittings to a dealer for £167, and all the Board could do was to buy back a chimneypiece to be installed in the new school. The South Kensington Museum (now the V & A) bought the panelling for £75, and had the ceiling carefully removed, as well as buying the fireplace and overmantel from the London School Board. The finely carved stone fire surround has a splendidly showy overmantel with the royal arms of James I topped by strapwork decoration and flanked by figures of Peace and Plenty. The overmantel was probably originally coloured, and the panelling had many layers of paint on it, all of which was stripped off. So the museum had enough fittings to reconstruct the ground floor parlour of the Old Palace, where it is still today.[3] Ernest Godman managed to acquire some of the plaster fragments from the great chamber on the first floor and some pieces of the original oak mullioned windows; some 18th-century fittings were bought by a Chelsea pub; otherwise the house has disappeared.[4] But its lasting legacies are our system of listing historic buildings, first set up by Ashbee and his associates, and the *Survey* volumes which they instigated.

CARSHALTON

CARSHALTON HOUSE

The village of Carshalton is even today a watery place. Defoe described 'the innumerable springs of water which altogether form a river in the very street of the town' which joins the River Wandle. There were mills on each side of the village and 'houses of the citizens of London; some of which are built with such a profusion of expence, that they look rather like seats of the nobility, than the country houses of citizens and merchants'.[1] Carshalton House was just such a house. Before the Civil War the former house on the site was owned by Sir Edward Herbert, Attorney General to Charles I. It was confiscated when he went into exile and was later sold to another lawyer, Dixey Longe. His widow and her second husband, Edward Arden, kept the house which was known as The Old Farm; it had 10 hearths when it was rated for tax in 1664.[2] It stood in about 12 acres of grounds, with the usual barns and outbuildings. Mrs Arden died in 1686, and about ten years later the house was rebuilt.

What we see today is a triple-pile brick house of two main storeys with an attic and a semi-basement, nine bays by seven, so more substantial than many of these suburban houses; it was probably designed by a London builder rather than an architect. It looks rather top-heavy, due to the attic being turned into a full second storey in the 18th century; the deep wooden

69 Carshalton House from the south, built by 1710, with the second storey replacing dormer windows in the 18th century. The narrow windows on the outer corners light closets.

cornice between the first and second floors suggests this. It is given a sense of movement by the projecting centre bays and the rhythm of the windows: closely spaced in the centre, with tall narrow windows on the south front reflecting corner closets. The original entrance was on the east front, later moved to the south, and the service area was to the west, where later buildings have been added. The most celebrated interior is the Painted Parlour, the N–E corner room, which led off the original entrance hall. The panels are painted with large landscape views; the stiles have delicate *chinoiserie* scenes in *grisaille* on a brown background. The overdoors and even the dado panels and the insides of the shutters are painted. The work appears to be by several hands, with the large panels mainly attributed to Robert Robinson. It is a dazzlingly rich interior, typical of the rather flashy style which appealed to the rich merchants of London, and a remarkable survival.[3]

Arden died in 1707, and the house was bought by Edward Carleton, a City merchant with local connections: his first father-in-law owned the nearby gunpowder mills and his second wife also came from Carshalton. We know a lot more than usual about the interiors in Carleton's time due to his disappearance and bankruptcy. He was a tobacco merchant in partnership with his son, importing from Virginia and Maryland and selling in the Baltic. In 1713 he was pursued by Customs & Excise for large outstanding sums of tobacco duty; he was unable to pay and fled. As a result his assets were seized and put up for sale, and thanks to this we have a detailed inventory of his smart new house. It was full of valuable furnishings: chairs and settees, card tables, pictures and lots of expensive imported china in the ground floor rooms. The first-floor rooms were even more richly furnished: the 'wrought room' with a needlework bed, a chintz room with fashionable Indian hangings, a blue damask room and a red damask bedroom. The beds had matching suites of seat furniture and the rooms were furnished with 'japan' and lacquer pieces. Clearly Carleton had furnished his new house with expensive and fashionable pieces. His wife died in 1713, his son is never mentioned again, but Carleton reappeared at a bankruptcy hearing in 1714 and died in 1732, living modestly in Newington Green.

The house was sold in 1714 to Dr John Radcliffe, a well known physician, who paid the large sum of £7,163 for the house and its contents, the latter valued at £3,000.[4] He died within a year and in his will left money for building the Radcliffe Camera, Observatory and Infirmary in Oxford. So the house was again on the market with its contents and was bought by Sir John Fellowes.[5] He had a house in the City and was a director of the South Sea Company and from 1718 the Sub Governor. When its share price collapsed in 1721 he went bankrupt, was imprisoned in the Tower and forced to sell his City house. Yet again a bankruptcy provides us with detailed information, and a comparison of his inventory with Carleton's shows that many of the same things were in the house.[6]

The grounds of Carshalton House are enclosed by a high brick wall and we can still see traces of the alterations made by Fellowes. He added wrought iron gates with his crest of a lion's head in stone on the gate piers, and asked Charles Bridgeman to landscape the grounds. He planted many trees including an elm avenue south of the house, and made the canal (now almost dry) facing the east front of the house. At the far end of the canal is the Water Tower, a dramatic brick building with its pinnacled tower. It was built by Henry Joynes who worked with Vanbrugh at Blenheim, and is very much in the latter's style. The chalky ground round Carshalton was full of springs. Watts described 'the remarkable clear spring … rising at a little distance from the house'.[7] This was below the Water Tower, and the water was pumped to a lead cistern in the tower by a waterwheel and 'engine' in the pump chamber at the base of the tower. Remains of a slightly later waterwheel are still *in situ*.[8] This gave enough natural pressure for it to be piped to the house, a great luxury at this date. Round the pump chamber were grouped other rooms: an orangery, a saloon and a bathroom with an adjoining dressing room.[9] The bathing room had a plunge bath with its own supply of piped water, a floor of black and white marble and walls lined with panels of blue and white tiles framing plain white ones. The orangery and saloon were both rooms with high ceilings and tall arched windows. It was clearly a luxurious place of entertainment away from the house.

70 Carshalton House, the Water Tower, built by Henry Joynes *c*.1718. The cistern is at the top of the tower. The ground floor has the orangery on the right and the saloon on the left.

71 Carshalton House, the early 18th-century Painted Room. This may have been painted by Robert Robinson.

From his large fortune Fellowes was allowed to keep £10,000 and his younger brother Edward bought Carshalton from him. He managed to remain at Carshalton, as he died there in 1724 and his brother commissioned a monument in the parish church to him. A cousin inherited the house from Edward but promptly sold it. The house had various 18th-century owners: from 1732-40 Sir Philip Yorke, Lord Chief Justice and later of Wimpole Hall; the MP William Mitchell; the MP and merchant Sir George Amyand; and from 1767-82 the Hon. Thomas Walpole, nephew of Sir Robert. Like Carleton he was a tobacco merchant and lived in Lincoln's Inn Fields. It was either Amyand or Walpole who made various changes, raising the roofline, moving the staircase and rebuilding it on a smaller scale, and altering the hall. The Blue Parlour in the S-W corner of the ground floor was redesigned, probably by Robert Taylor. With its vaulted ceiling, delicate Rococo plasterwork and arches supported on Ionic columns it has similarities to the dining room vestibule at Arnos Grove.

The house was sold in 1887, when it was described as 'a fine old Queen Anne mansion' with 26 acres of gardens and meadow. The gardens included the lake 'well stocked with trout' and three walled kitchen gardens and two 'vineries'. The Water Tower was fully described but surprisingly also had 'a licensed chapel'. This had been installed when the house became a school in 1863. The sale particulars suggest continuing institutional use, as the land could be used for building 'leaving the mansion and the remainder of the grounds intact'.[10] This is what happened after it was bought in 1893 by the Daughters of the Cross. A chapel and many other large buildings were added to the west end of the house, leaving the main house comparatively unspoilt. It is now thriving as St Philomena's Catholic High School for Girls, with the Water House leased by the Carshalton Water Tower & Historic Garden Trust; the latter is occasionally open to the public.

CHARLTON

CHARLTON HOUSE

Charlton is a remarkable Jacobean house, of a quality unsurpassed in the London area, and one that deserves to be better known. It is also representative of the role played by Scots who came south with James I in 1603; indeed the earlier house on the site belonged to three Scottish courtiers in as many years. They were favoured at court, and wanted suburban houses in addition to their lodgings in royal palaces or London houses. We know very little of the earlier manor house. It had belonged to Bermondsey Priory from *c.*1095, and became royal property at the Reformation. James I gave it to the Earl of Mar in 1604, who sold it for £2,000 to Sir James Erskine. He made a quick profit, selling it in 1607 for £4,500 to his fellow Scot Adam Newton, who had come south as tutor to Prince Henry, the heir to the throne. Newton rebuilt it 1607-12, giving himself a surprisingly large and impressive house with 70 acres.[1] His origins are obscure, but he was not a landowner, instead rising to his position because of his classical learning; he had travelled in France before teaching law at Edinburgh University. Once in England he made a good marriage to Katherine Puckering, daughter of the Keeper of the Great Seal; possibly this marriage in 1605 persuaded him to buy this small estate conveniently placed two miles from Greenwich Palace and not far from Whitehall by river. The little village of Charlton is on a hilltop east of Greenwich; even

72   Charlton House, entrance front. The house was built 1607-12 for Sir Adam Newton.

95

today the house seems large, looming over the modest brick church (itself rebuilt just after Newton's death, probably with money from him).[2]

The house is uncommonly interesting in design, and it is possible that John Thorpe was the architect.[3] It is certainly a sophisticated house, symmetrical externally and with an ingenious plan, one of the earliest of a group of houses where the hall is placed axially, allowing a symmetrical façade to be combined with a double-pile plan.[4] It is an H-plan house, built of plum-coloured brick with stone dressings, and still has its mullion and transom windows. The projecting wings have bay windows running through all three floors, and slender ogee-capped towers at each side. Tall chimneys symmetrically arranged punctuate the balustraded roofline.[5] The house is austere externally, apart from the highly-decorated frontispiece with its crowded classical decoration. Now there are lawns all round the house but it was approached from the west through an enclosed forecourt, so the frontispiece would have been even more striking; the entrance arch survives, sitting isolated on the west lawn. As at Hardwick the double-height hall runs through the house from front to back; a staircase each side connects to the upper floors, although a gallery was added across the west side of the hall in the 19th century. A chapel was included in the plan, tucked into the N-E corner; unusually, this was consecrated, implying that Newton had high church sympathies. The hall itself is plain, with a ceiling given low-relief strapwork decoration.[6] It is on the upper floors that we can see remains of the richness of the original decoration. The first floor has comfortable low-ceilinged family rooms, and again like Hardwick it is the high-ceilinged top floor which contains the state rooms. An oak staircase with an open well leads up to the top floor and into the long gallery, which with windows on three sides has magnificent views north

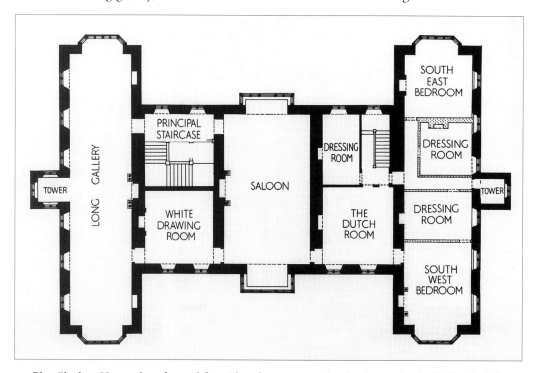

73 Charlton House, plan of second floor. The saloon or great chamber is over the double-height hall.

to the Thames valley. John Evelyn, visiting the house in 1653, wrote that 'the prospect … is doubtless for city, river, ships, meadows, hills, woods and all other distinguishable amenities the most noble the whole world has to show.'[7] The gallery, 90 ft long, has a fret ceiling with Newton's arms and a simple alabaster and black touch chimneypiece. Beyond is the White Room, with an original plasterwork frieze and ceiling, and a fine overmantel with a relief of Pegasus. This is an anteroom to the splendid great chamber directly above the hall, which has huge windows looking east and west. This allows light to ripple across the plasterwork ceiling, which has relief decoration of fruit and flowers on the ribs and shallow strapwork decoration in between; and there is a deep frieze below. The chimneypiece is of highest quality, with finely carved alabaster figures of Venus and Vulcan supporting a restrained alabaster and black touch overmantel. The bays of the east and west windows have the arms of Prince Henry and James I in plasterwork, repeated in stained glass below and reflecting Newton's loyalties. It is a magnificent example of a Jacobean state room, where Newton could have entertained in style. Beyond are two apartments, that in the S-E corner having more fine plasterwork. Here the overmantel has a relief of Danaë, linking it with the story of her son Pegasus in the anteroom. A service staircase leads from this side of the house to the service rooms on the ground floor.

After Newton's death in 1630 the house passed to his young son Henry, aged 12 at his father's death. He probably commissioned in the late 1630s the brick gazebo which still stands N-W of the house and which has tentatively been attributed to Inigo Jones or John Webb. It is certainly a fine little building, with its red rubbed brickwork, pilasters, arched windows and sweeping roofline. (Much of the brickwork has been renewed, not very carefully. The building is looking rather dilapidated and is in need of attention.) In 1636 Henry inherited the Warwickshire estates of his maternal uncle, as a result of which he changed his surname and was known as Sir Henry Puckering. As a royalist he suffered financially during and after the Civil War and in 1656 gave up living at Charlton and retreated to Warwickshire. Three years later he sold it to Sir William Ducie, a rich merchant and son of a Lord Mayor (who later became Viscount Downe). He did some repairs, putting in rainwater heads dated 1659 with his crest and installing in one of the first-floor rooms an elegant black and white marble chimneypiece with his arms. He also brought over an Inigo Jones chimneypiece from the Queen's House, Greenwich. Dating

74 Charlton House, great chamber. Venus and Vulcan support the alabaster and black touch chimneypiece, with the original frieze and plasterwork ceiling above.

from the 1630s, this is very different in style from the alabaster chimneypieces installed by Newton: it is of stone, based on the French prints so admired by Henrietta Maria, and decorated with caryatid figures rising from strange auricular masks.[8]

Ducie died childless in 1679 and his executors sold Charlton to Sir William Langhorne Bt. and it remained with his family until it stopped being a private house in 1925. Langhorne was a well-off East India merchant who had returned from India, where he had been Governor of Madras. He seems to have left the house largely unchanged, although he probably added the Venetian window to the east front of the hall, providing direct access to the gardens. He left the property to a relative, an elderly widow called Mrs Margaret Maryon. She let it to the 1st Earl of Egmont in the 1730s, whose diary shows typical use of these suburban houses: his wife and children spent several months there in the summer, while he hoped to be there at least for July and August. Asked by George II whether he used it in the winter, he replied that it was 'cold and would be inconvenient to go'.[9]

The house descended via descendants of Mrs Maryon to Sir Thomas Spencer Wilson, who married the heiress in the chapel at Charlton in 1777. Lady Wilson installed her large natural history collection of fossils and insects in the gallery, but they seem to have made few changes. At some point the Jacobean panelling was removed from many of the rooms; in the 19th century the main staircase walls were decorated with rather heavy plaster panels and drops of fruit and flowers in mid-18th-century style; otherwise the house remains remarkably unaltered. In 1877-8 Sir Spencer Maryon-Wilson added a billiard room to the south by Norman Shaw, but the family could not afford for much longer the upkeep of such a substantial house near London, as well as their country house. In 1909, the year in which *Country Life* photographed the house, part of the grounds was presented to the council to make Maryon Park, and more was added soon afterwards.[10] During the First World War the house was used by the Red Cross and the family remained on their Warwickshire estates after the war. The contents of the house were sold in 1920 and in 1925 the house and surrounding land were sold to Woolwich Borough Council for £60,000. The gardens were inevitably simplified and the Victorian terraces removed, although the two parallel 17th-century service wings with their shaped gables remain to the south of the house. The billiard room was demolished after bomb damage to the north end of the house in the Second World War, so much of the north wall has been rebuilt. The house is currently used by the LB of Greenwich as a community centre and although reasonably well maintained and much used by local people it is hardly recognised as the architectural masterpiece it is.

CHELSEA

BEAUFORT HOUSE

In the winter of 1739-40 one of the most historic houses near London was demolished on the orders of its owner, Sir Hans Sloane, the founder of the British Museum. This was a curious decision, as he was a leading antiquarian and it had been built *c.*1522-3 by Sir Thomas More, both Holbein and Erasmus had stayed there, and it had associations with many other famous people. Kip's bird's-eye view shows the house set back from the river behind two walled forecourts, with a long gabled façade, formal gardens to the east with a banqueting house on a mount, and service buildings to the west. (More seems to have built an H-plan house, not the courtyard house still usual at that date.) These included stables and outhouses and in More's time had also included a farm close to the river, where he had lived before he built the new and much larger house nearby. Originally known as The Farm, this was rebuilt in the 17th century as Lindsey House. On the river to the east were several small houses and a wharf, a reminder of the commercial possibilities of a property on the Thames.

'The Great House' as it was known was the most celebrated house in Chelsea but in spite of its prominence few people owned it for any length of time. It is an extreme example of the changes in ownership of these suburban houses. When More was disgraced and executed in 1535 his estate was forfeit and given to Sir William Paulet, 1st Marquis of Winchester. He died in his Chelsea house in 1571 at a great age and it passed via his son to Lady Dacre, who left it in her will to William Cecil. He had no need of it and passed it on to his second son, Robert. A series of plans at Hatfield shows the various ideas for improvements which were made by at least two surveyors around 1595, which may or may not have been carried out.[1] In 1599 Robert Cecil sold it to Henry Clinton, Earl of Lincoln, but it did not remain in his family for long, being sold in 1619 by his son-in-law to Lionel Cranfield, a City merchant and owner of Copt Hall in Essex. He commissioned a gateway from Inigo Jones, for which a drawing survives. Cranfield (1575-1645) was an astute businessman who became an adviser to the Crown and was made Lord Treasurer in 1621. He was created Earl of Middlesex and seemed set for a glittering career; but his attempts to reign in James I's profligacy made him many enemies, especially George Villiers, 1st Duke of Buckingham.

Cranfield's attempts to reform public finances ended in public disgrace and Beaufort House was forfeit once again. Ironically it was immediately given by Charles I to Buckingham. He was a great art collector, and an inventory of his possessions lists the sumptuous furnishings and works of art at Chelsea in 1635, which included Old Master paintings and antique gems and sculptures.[2] The Giambologna of *Samson & the Philistine* now in the V & A was one of the highlights of his collection, and stood on the mount in the garden.[3] Buckingham was assassinated in 1628, and his widow and family remained at Chelsea until it was seized by Parliament in 1649 and given to Bulstrode Whitelocke. It was repossessed by the 2nd Duke of Buckingham at the Restoration, but he was so indebted that he had to give it up in 1664. After more rapid changes of ownership it was bought for £5,000 in 1682 by Henry, Marquis of Worcester, who later became the 1st Duke of Beaufort – hence the name it has acquired.

His wife was Mary Capel (1657-1715), brought up at Cassiobury and a keen botanist whose gardens at Badminton and Chelsea became famous. Her 15-acre Chelsea gardens were full of rare plants and were much visited: it was so much easier to visit these gardens near London than to make the arduous journey to Badminton. She was particularly interested in the 'exoticks' which were being brought into England as a result of trading voyages and

75 Chelsea, Beaufort House. A detail of Kip's bird's-eye view shows the house built by Sir Thomas More's house *c.*1522-3, with its stables top left and Lindsey House lower left. The large gardens are to the right and behind the house, with the Inigo Jones gateway leading to the lane beyond the gardens. The gardens of Danvers House, with the circular bowling green, are on the extreme right.

76 Chelsea, Beaufort House. The garden gateway designed by Inigo Jones and moved to Chiswick House in 1738. Burlington added the short walls with ball finials.

was especially keen on plants from South Africa. Her tender plants were mainly in Chelsea because of its gentle climate compared with Gloucestershire, and the supply of clean piped water which was brought from springs in Kensington.[4] Her plant lists tell us exactly what was growing there in 1691.[5] She employed artists to record some of her plants, and these albums still exist. When she was widowed in 1708 her son took over Badminton but as was usual she retained the suburban house till her death in 1714.

In 1736 the 3rd Duke of Beaufort sold the house to Sir Hans Sloane (1660-1753) for £2,500. Sloane was a leading physician, who had used the fortune he had made to collect books, manuscripts, coins and curiosities. He had been a friend of the Duchess of Beaufort, but probably bought her house more as a land speculation than because he wanted it, as it was soon demolished. Edmund Howard, the caretaker, clearly had a low opinion of his employer and describes rather bitterly the demolition he had to arrange of the roof over his head. 'In vain did I plead that I was a gardener, and as such not likely to have sufficient skill in such matters … for there is more danger in pulling down than in building … I proceeded with much caution and circumspection on this hazardous business … for there were many stacks of chimneys of large size and great height, very thick brick walls, and wide piers between window and window. No accidents happened worth notice – only hurt two or three men …'[6]

The house gave its name to Beaufort Street which straddles the site; otherwise only two fragments remain of this great house. One is the Moravian Burial Ground, tucked behind World's End on the King's Road, where the nine-bay stables of Beaufort House were converted into a chapel in the mid-18th century; the walls of the burial ground seem to reflect the garden walls seen in Kip's engraving. The other is the Inigo Jones gateway, built for Sir Lionel Cranfield, which Sloane gave to Lord Burlington in 1738. It was re-erected in the grounds of Chiswick House, where it stands today.

Lindsey House

On the traffic-infested Embankment of the Thames in Chelsea stands a distinguished looking stucco building with a tiled mansard roof, at first glance appearing to be a group of terrace houses; but a closer look hints at a more interesting history. The earlier house on this site was part of the Chelsea estate of Sir Thomas More, Chancellor to Henry VIII. When More built his house c.1522 (later called Beaufort House) it was set well back from the Thames, with walled forecourts, large gardens and a service courtyard to the west. In addition to these there was a farm on the western boundary, and Lindsey House stands on the site of that modest 16th-century building, which soon became a desirable separate property.

In 1567 William Paulet, 1st Marquis of Winchester let his 'mansion or farm-house in Chelsey, nigh unto the said Marquis's mansion there' with 130 acres to 'Nicholas Holborne of Chelsey, Gent.' for an annual rent of £13 6s.8d. It seems not at that stage to have been used as a suburban retreat, but after Holborne's lease expired in 1617 The Farm was taken on by Sir Edward Cecil, later Viscount Wimbledon. He was the third son of Thomas Cecil, 1st Earl of Exeter, and made his career in the army, fighting in the Netherlands and France; he had a London house in the Strand, and later inherited his father's house at Wimbledon. When he took on The Farm in 1618 he had just remarried, and he chose to spend most of his time at his Chelsea house until his death in 1638.[1]

The next owner was the distinguished Huguenot, Sir Theodore Mayerne, physician to both James I and Charles I, who may have altered or rebuilt Cecil's house.[2] (As foreigners were not allowed to own property, it was held by trustees on his behalf.) It was much visited, as his numerous non-royal patients consulted him at home. But the present appearance of

77 Chelsea, Lindsey House seen from the Thames in 1935. It is the large white house with the mansard roof, partly hidden by trees.

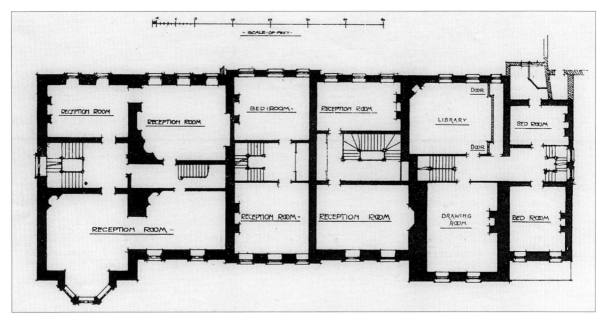

78 Chelsea, Lindsey House. Plan of first floor, showing the later division into four separate houses.

the house is due largely to Robert Bertie, 3rd Earl of Lindsey, who took on the lease in 1671 and may have rebuilt it *c.*1674; there was a date stone of that year, since lost. It was a three-storey house with a central pediment, built of brick with a high hipped roof and attics, and was assessed at 26 hearths, making it one of the largest houses in Chelsea. Kip's bird's-eye view of Beaufort House, published in *Britannia Illustrata* in 1715, clearly shows Lindsey House, as it was now called: the 13-bay house set back from the riverside road behind a small forecourt, with a small service courtyard to one side. Immediately to the east are the much larger gardens of Beaufort House. Behind the house are formal gardens, with a vegetable garden and fruit trees behind the service court.

The house remained in the Bertie family till 1750, by which time it was probably fairly dilapidated. It was sold to the leader of the Moravian movement in England, Count Nikolaus Ludwig von Zinzendorf, but the freehold was held by an English Moravian, as the law against foreign ownership still applied. Zinzendorf intended the house to be the headquarters of the Moravians in London, with accommodation for men and women and a great hall for meetings, as well as rooms for himself and his wife. He also acquired part of the grounds of Beaufort House, which had recently been demolished by Sir Hans Sloane. The old stables (which can be seen in Kip's print) were converted into a chapel, with a Moravian burial ground in front of it. Both these still exist, tucked away below the King's Road. Plans and drawings examined by Kroyer in the Moravian Archives at Herrnhut near Dresden provide the best evidence for the changes made by Zinzendorf.[3] It was a double-pile house of irregular plan, perhaps showing that Lindsey had kept at least parts of the earlier house. The Moravian's architect, Sigismund von Gersdorf, was asked to survey the old house and propose changes. Two designs showing minor changes were rejected, but his third elevation shows the impressive entrance front of the house, very similar to what we see today except with a balustraded roof platform and two cupolas. Zinzendorf's time as head of the Moravians was stormy and he left London in 1755, but the Moravian Brethren held on to the house and land for another nine years.

By the mid-18th century Chelsea was becoming a popular place to live, and Lindsey House with its curious internal arrangements for the segregation of the Brethren and Sisters was ripe for redevelopment. In 1774 the house and part of the grounds were sold for £3,000 to a consortium of builders, who sub-divided it into five terrace houses with a smaller house each side; they removed the pediment to provide the central house with dormer windows, and changed the roof to the mansard we see today. These alterations meant that the original staircase and many of the original fittings were destroyed. The rendering of the brickwork may have taken place at this date, or in the 1750s.

By the late 19th century the old houses and river views of Chelsea appealed to artists, and Whistler lived in 96 Cheyne Walk, the easternmost house, from 1867-78, and Isambard Kingdom Brunel lived in no. 98. In 1909 a leading art dealer and collector, Sir Hugh Lane, bought two of the houses, nos. 99 and 100. He added a covered porch designed by Devey leading from the road (since removed) and commissioned Lutyens to redesign the gardens.[4] Lenygon and Morant were asked to redecorate the house, restoring its 17th- and 18th-century appearance when possible. Lane filled the house with paintings, including one of the versions of Holbein's *Sir Thomas More & Family*, a suitable choice with the More connections to the site.[5] Augustus John was asked to paint three large canvases for the entrance hall, but this was not a happy commission. John was dissatisfied with his work, painted over one of the canvases, and left another unfinished when Lane was drowned in 1915; only one, *The Mumpers*, was completed, and is now in the Detroit Museum of Art. The National Trust now owns the house and although it is not open to the public it is the most important surviving early house in Chelsea, a village which once had so many fine houses.

CHEVENING

CHEVENING HOUSE

The high brick house seen across the park, with a tiny village and ancient church huddled at the gates and the North Downs beyond, seems the archetypal unchanged English country house. As usual the reality is different, and the house we see today has been enlarged, turned round, and adapted by different generations of the Stanhope family. Many architects and designers have been involved here: Inigo Jones, John Webb, Thomas Fort, Nicholas Dubois and James Wyatt and, more recently, Donald Insall and John Fowler. Although the Stanhope family no longer lives in it, this important house is not an institution: at present the Foreign Secretary has the use of it at weekends.

79 Chevening, north front. A bird's-eye view painted recently by Marcus May, showing the grounds and farmland round the house. The restoration of 1980 restored the roofline to its original height and refaced the house in red brick. The two pavilions were added in 1718 for the 1st Earl Stanhope.

105

The estate was bought by John Lennard in 1551, but the only trace of the 16th-century house is a small area of brick wall with mullion windows in the vaulted cellars. The present house was built by Richard Lennard, 13th Lord Dacre (1596-1630) and has been attributed to Inigo Jones – making it one of a very small group of houses designed by the Surveyor of the King's Works for a private client. Colen Campbell illustrated the house in the second volume of *Vitruvius Britannicus* in 1717, referring to Jones as the architect, but because of the sophisticated nature of the design and plan, and the lack of comparable contemporary houses, a later date was proposed by some architectural historians. However two recent articles by Andor Gomme present a convincing case for the reattribution to Jones.[1] The house as built was a compact three-storey house with stone detailing, raised on a semi-basement which contained the service rooms. The high hipped roof had dormer windows and a balustraded platform between two high chimneystacks. All this can be seen in a perspective view dated 1679, which differs in some ways from the elevation in *Vitruvius Britannicus*.[2] Campbell gives the seven-bay house five dormers instead of six, modifies the cornice, removes the stringcourses and decorates the roof platform with tall vases. Could these be proposals by Campbell, trying to tempt a new owner into employing him? The plan of Chevening as shown in *Vitruvius Britannicus* is apparently simple but most ingenious. The centre of the house has a wide staircase hall leading to a saloon, and transverse spine walls (with all the chimneypieces in them) separate these rooms from the smaller parlours, dining room and withdrawing room at the sides. The same plan on the upper floors would have provided bedchambers on each side of the more public central spaces. This suggests Palladio's villa plans, where the public rooms run through the centre of the house from front to back, with family rooms each side. It has usually been assumed that the present north-facing entrance hall is the original one, but careful study of various early views of the house shows that the entrance was moved from the south front to the north, possibly in 1679 when the view was drawn. This important change was made by Thomas Lennard, 15th Lord Dacre; otherwise, Campbell's plans reflect the house as originally built.

80 Chevening, south front. Early 20th-century view, before Wyatt's attic storey and stone-coloured mathematical tiles were removed. The conservatory on the left has also gone.

John Webb's contribution to the house is well documented but was never completed, possibly because the 14th Lord Dacre went abroad in 1655 to get away from his wife. Webb proposed a double-height saloon above the original south-facing entrance hall; had this been built it might have been an improved version of the Belisarius Room at Raynham Hall in Norfolk. Two of his drawings for the wall elevations survive, showing pedimented doorcases and carved drops derived from the Double Cube Room at Wilton, and similar to the Music Hall he was designing at Lamport for Sir Justinian Isham.[3] Roger North in his late 17th-century comments on Chevening – a house he knew well, as his aunt was the widow of the 13th Lord Dacre – describes 'the chief room above' as not finished, and so it remained until the house changed hands.[4]

In 1717 – the same year as the publication of Campbell's illustrations of the house – the house was sold for £28,000 to General James Stanhope, grandson of the 1st Earl of Chesterfield and a military man who was a strong supporter of the new Hanoverian dynasty. In 1717 he was made Chief Minister to George I, created Viscount Mahon and the next year became 1st Earl Stanhope. He immediately set about making changes to the house, employing Thomas Fort, who had worked as a master joiner at Het Loo and whom Wren had made Clerk of the Works at Hampton Court. Fort enlarged the house by an addition on each side containing closets on all three floors. He also added the quadrant colonnades and the substantial pavilions which enclose the courtyard today. The east side contained the kitchen, laundry and rooms for female staff, with the stables and male staff in the other. The pavilions are nine bays by five, with long sash windows above brick arcades. The hipped roofs have *oeuil-de-boeuf* windows flanking the pediments and rusticated central chimneystacks. There is a touch of Vanbrugh's style here, and more in the interiors, where Fort added some muscular marble chimneypieces similar to those designed by Vanbrugh for the apartments being completed at Hampton Court for the Prince and Princess of Wales. Fine ironwork made by Zachariah Gisbourn enclosed the forecourt, with the new Earl's cipher and coronet. South of the house formal gardens were laid out, with a central canal ending in a basin flanked by *allées* with denser planting between, replacing the earlier axial approach. (This canal was made into a picturesque lake in the late 18th century, and survives today.) The new owner died in 1721, and his widow made the next change, replacing the original stone staircase with an extraordinarily daring oak 'geometric stair' designed by the Huguenot architect Nicholas Dubois, similar to one she had seen in his own house in Soho.[5] This was inserted into the north entrance hall, where it sweeps up to the top of the house apparently without support.

Her son Philip, 2nd Earl Stanhope, was a child when he inherited, so it was only in 1736 that he commissioned new work at Chevening. His father had been given a fine and very rare set of Berlin tapestries by Frederick I of Prussia, and he decided to make a single-storey tapestry room in the lower part of Webb's great room. This room had already been divided horizontally by Fort, who had installed a simple chimneypiece on the upper floor, and a fine marble one below. The room is quite low-ceilinged, so the tapestries, unusually, hang from cornice to skirting. The whole room was furnished and decorated by William Bradshaw, who was paid £1,200 in 1737. He provided the elaborate frame to a portrait of the 1st Earl flanked by carved giltwood drops (which recall Webb's designs) as well as having sections of tapestry made up to fit the room. He also supplied pier tables and a set of upholstered giltwood chairs, all of which are still at Chevening.[6] At the same time the large and interesting collection of arms which the 2nd Earl had bought from Lord Londonderry were arranged decoratively in the hall, giving it the appearance of an ancient armoury. The dining room on the south front (originally the entrance hall) may have been altered about this time, its panelling incorporating some late 17th-century woodwork, with pilasters and arched panels; but this room remains puzzling.

81   Chevening, entrance hall in 1920. The 'geometric stair' was designed by Nicholas Dubois in 1721.

82   Chevening, the Tapestry Room in 1920. The Berlin tapestries were a gift to the 1st Earl Stanhope from Frederick I of Prussia.

The next major changes were made by James Wyatt in 1786-96 for Charles, 3rd Earl Stanhope. The house was given four Ionic pilasters on each front, topped by a delicate neo-classical frieze. The hipped roof disappeared, replaced by an attic storey. The whole house was faced in mathematical tiles, meant to protect and preserve the brickwork beneath while giving it a cool colouring, closer to stone. Minor changes were made over the 19th century, but the major alterations were due to the transfer of the house to a trust in 1967. James Stanhope, 7th Earl, also inherited the Earldom of Chesterfield and substantial estates in Devon & Derbyshire, which he sold, keeping his 3,500-acre Chevening estate. He had no children, and worked hard to find a solution for the future of the house and estate. The Chevening Estate Trust was set up by Act of Parliament, and took over the house at his death in 1967. The house was to be used by members of the royal family or members of the government, and was to be supported by the estate. From 1974-80 the Prince of Wales used the house, until he acquired his Highgrove estate; since then it has been used at weekends by the Foreign Secretary. The trust began a major restoration, with Donald Insall & Partners as architects. The mathematical tiles were removed from everywhere except the quadrant colonnades, revealing the warm red brick; the hipped roof was reinstated; the plate-glass windows were replaced by sashes, and the glazed porch removed from the entrance front. John Fowler was called in as decorator, and – perhaps unwisely – chose to remove the dark staining from the oak staircase, leaving it a pale colour out of keeping with the dark arms on the walls and ceiling. Today Edward Bulmer is continuing a programme of redecoration and conservation of the interiors with their fine furniture and paintings.

CHISWICK

CHISWICK HOUSE

Today the Palladian entrance front of Chiswick House looks as if it is one of the most perfectly preserved of London's 18th-century villas, but its history is much more complex than it appears. It is in reality only a fragment of a much larger house and its present appearance is due to a drastic mid-20th-century restoration. The gardens are at least as important as the house, and are a fascinating mixture of styles from the early 18th to the early 19th centuries. Also, the house now appears to be the only major house in Chiswick – but this is due to the disappearance of every other country house within the parish; only Hogarth's little house nearby survives.

Chiswick, with its river transport and its position on the way to Windsor and Hampton Court, was well placed to appeal to the upper classes. Chiswick House was built in the early 17th century as a good-sized brick courtyard house of two main storeys with shaped gables; it was assessed at 33 hearths in 1664. There were other properties each side but formal gardens extended behind the house and there were views of the Thames across the water meadows in front. The road was then much closer to the house, with a walled forecourt (it was moved back in 1828). This house changed hands many times in the 17th century; in 1664 Charles II bought it for his illegitimate son, the Duke of Monmouth; by 1677 it belonged to Richard Jones, Earl of Ranelagh and in 1682 it was bought from Edward

83   Chiswick House, entrance front in 1936. The two wings added by John White in 1788 were demolished 1956-7.

109

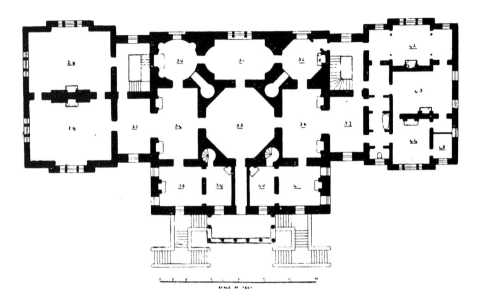

84   Chiswick House, plan of the main floor showing the 1788 wings.

Seymour by Richard Boyle, 1st Earl of Burlington and 2nd Earl of Cork, Ranelagh's uncle; it belonged to his descendants for over 250 years. Burlington had substantial Irish estates and his wife substantial Yorkshire ones, so they needed a house within easy reach of Burlington House, their London home. His major building project was at Londesborough in Yorkshire, where Robert Hooke rebuilt his country house. At Chiswick he only added the L-shaped stable block and service rooms (demolished in 1935). His great-grandson built the house we see today, as a small but exquisite addition to the older house.

Richard Boyle, 3rd Earl of Burlington (1694-1753), had come into his vast inheritance as a child, and was a well-travelled amateur architect by the time he designed this. He had already employed Colen Campbell and James Gibbs at his London house, had himself designed some minor changes to the old house at Chiswick, and had probably commissioned a garden building from Campbell (now demolished). He had a large collection of architectural books, a superb collection of architectural drawings including many by Palladio, and had in his household William Kent who was rapidly becoming a leading architect, interior decorator and garden designer. The villa – and for once this word is appropriate – was built 1725-9 and contained a splendid central reception space with two suites off it, one of which had a bedchamber, the other a study. It was never meant to replace his existing house, with its kitchen, service rooms, dining room, gallery and lodgings for the Burlington family and their household; it was instead a place to entertain in or to retreat to. So Burlington was free of many of the usual constraints on architects, and he designed a highly original little building, drawing on his knowledge of the classical past and the Italian Renaissance.

The house is 70ft square with an octagonal stepped dome over the central hall, which is lit by thermal windows in the drum. It is built of brick, stuccoed and painted stone colour, but is enriched to a remarkable extent with Portland stone details: the Corinthian portico, the deeply rusticated stone of its base, the string course, window surrounds and bold double stairs to the *piano nobile*. The sides have Venetian windows and three more Venetian windows set in recessed arches light the gallery on the north front, a detail which could have been taken from one of Palladio's drawings in Burlington's own collection. It is often said that the design is loosely based on Palladio's Villa Rotonda near Vicenza, but it seems closer to Scamozzi's Villa Rocca Pisani; even more, Burlington seems to be trying to recreate an ancient house. One very odd feature is the narrow passage leading from the portico directly into the central saloon; this unsatisfactory entrance can only be an interpretation of Vitruvius's description of the passage leading into a Greek house. Here Burlington is being purist rather than practical. Another curious feature is the use of obelisk chimneys on the side walls, a vernacular type seen in the Veneto, but with no classical or English precedent; fireplaces on outer walls are anyway an oddity in 18th-century England. So disparate sources were being quarried by Burlington, and fused, rather surprisingly, into an harmonious whole.

In the interior the richness of the exterior is repeated, but with many references to the style of Inigo Jones; Burlington owned many of his drawings. The coffering of the dome and of the apses in the gallery may be antique in inspiration, but the marble chimneypieces are based on designs by Jones for Henrietta Maria at the Queen's House in Greenwich. The compartmented ceilings are also Jonesian. William Kent painted some central panels for the ceilings, and much of the decorative work round these, giving a richness of colour that is lacking in many Palladian houses.[1] In many of these decorative details there is Masonic symbolism, and it has recently been proved that both Burlington and Kent were Freemasons. It has also been suggested that Burlington was a crypto-Jacobite, and that clues to this are also hidden in the decorative scheme; this remains a possibility.[2] Around 1732 the new villa was connected to the old house by a two-storey passage known as the Link Building, constructed of Bath stone. Here the first-floor Link Room has a ceiling based on a drawing of an antique ceiling from Burlington's collection. On the ground floor this connected the

85 Chiswick House, north front. The Link Room on the left used to connect Lord Burlington's addition to old Chiswick House.

new villa to Lady Burlington's Summer Parlour overlooking the gardens, which were to evolve slowly from the 1720s till *c*.1740.

Chiswick House has one of the best preserved 18th-century gardens in the London area, still containing some of Burlington's garden buildings and some of his extensive sculpture collection. Burlington's original land holding was only 15 acres and Kip's bird's-eye view shows the formal lay-out with an avenue to the north and parterres to the west. Possibly Charles Bridgeman was called in *c*.1715 to update the gardens: a *patte d'oie* with its avenues ending in various architectural features; the Orange Tree Garden with its temple designed by Burlington, overlooking a circular pond with an obelisk in the centre; and the formal sheets of water below the west side of the house. These are all fairly formal features, very

86 Chiswick House, interior of the first-floor Link Room.

different to the enlarged gardens to which William Kent contributed. These included the exedra made in 1736, giving a view from the gallery of the cedar avenue with its sphinxes, lions and classical statues. The old garden was bounded to the west by the Bollo Brook, with the gardens of Sutton Court beyond. In 1727 Burlington managed to acquire this property with its 237 acres. The house itself was let with only six acres, and the rest of its gardens incorporated into his grounds. This allowed Burlington and Kent to loosen up the design, making a small serpentine lake out of the Bollo Brook, and adding a cascade designed by Kent at its foot. But the low-lying site made it difficult to achieve a steady flow of water, and it was never as impressive as its designers hoped. Burlington also made a new gateway in the boundary wall, leading to an obelisk with a classical relief from Lord Arundel's collection, and from here another *patte d'oie* radiated to the lake. The gardens continued to evolve: in 1738 Burlington acquired the Inigo Jones gateway from Beaufort House in Chelsea which was being demolished. This nicely displayed his admiration for Jones, whose statue by Rysbrack was paired with that of Palladio at the entrance front. The gate was reconstructed north-east of the house, near to the Deer House designed earlier by Burlington, a small stuccoed building with Egyptian overtones in its tapering entrance. Luckily Burlington's gardens are well recorded in prints and paintings, and to some extent still exist, because major changes were to take place in both house and gardens over the next century.[3]

After the deaths of Lord and Lady Burlington his properties in Ireland, Yorkshire, London and Chiswick were inherited by their son-in-law, the 4th Duke of Devonshire. The 5th

Duke and his beautiful wife Georgiana were far too involved in London society to spend much time at Chatsworth, and instead they enlarged Chiswick House. The Jacobean house was demolished in 1788 and the surveyor John White (who had also worked at Buxton for the Duke) attached substantial wings each side of the villa, making into a large, practical but less elegant house, better equipped with large reception rooms, bedrooms and service rooms. Thus it remained until the mid-20th century. The gardens were also updated with the help of Samuel Lapidge, a pupil of 'Capability' Brown. The *patte-d'oie* from the obelisk was reduced, and softer planting introduced on each side of the remaining avenue. A raised walk was made from the cascade to the obelisk, giving river views, and a fine stone bridge, possibly designed by James Paine, was built across the head of the lake.[4]

Their son, the 6th Duke of Devonshire, also spent a lot of his time at Chiswick; his major change was the enlargement of the gardens to the east. In 1811 he bought the adjoining property, Morton Hall, a fine house by Hugh May which he promptly demolished. Keeping some of its walled gardens as kitchen gardens he commissioned a conservatory from Samuel Ware which he later filled with rare camellias, and in front of it. Lewis Kennedy laid out the Italian Garden with its geometric beds and colourful flowers. Buying more land enabled him to make a new drive approaching the house down what is now Duke's Avenue, and in 1828 an Act of Parliament allowed him to move the road away from the front of the house. From 1821 he also leased 30 acres to the Royal Horticultural Society, which had its gardens in the northernmost grounds of Chiswick House. As one of the richest landowners in England, he could afford to entertain splendidly at Chiswick. His 'breakfasts' which were in fact afternoon entertainments became famous: the Emperor of Russia visited in 1814 and again in 1844, Queen Victoria and Prince Albert in 1842. Guests could wander in the grounds which were dotted with tents, bands played and the house was decorated with banks of flowers. The house was more celebrated and more visited than in Lord Burlington's time.

With the death of the 6th Duke in 1858 Chiswick's days of splendour were over. The arrival of the railways meant that travel to Chatsworth became easier and quicker and later Dukes of Devonshire divided their time between London and Derbyshire without needing a suburban house as well; this also saved money, when the agricultural depression of the 1880s hit landowners. Chiswick was let to a succession of tenants, including the Prince of Wales from 1869-77 and the Marquess of Bute from 1881-92.[5] Part of the estate was sold off for development: street names such as Duke's Avenue, Edensor Road and Chatsworth Road refer to the ownership of the Devonshires. In 1892 it was leased by Dr Tuke and became a mental institution run on progressive lines.[6] There was pressure to develop the land for housing, so in order to try to preserve it the 9th Duke sold a 999-year lease of the house and 66 acres of gardens to the Middlesex County Council in 1929 for £81,000. As so often, the house was not the purpose of the purchase: it was the land which could be used as public open space in a now densely inhabited district of London. The house, ignored and neglected, provided tea rooms and caretakers' flats and gradually deteriorated. By the end of the Second World War it was in a poor state, and the local council was unwilling to spend large sums on repairs. But the Georgian Group, founded in 1937, was a pressure group for the preservation of 18th-century buildings. Public opinion was activated, Queen Mary was taken round the building and lent her support, and the house was given to the Ministry of Works. (Queen Mary had visited the house in 1929, just after the Council took it over, and was therefore aware of its deterioration.) A young architect, Claude Phillimore, suggested taking down the 1788 wings and allowing Burlington's villa to stand alone, and in 1956-7 this was done, entailing major recreation of the sides of the house, which was opened to the public in 1958.[7] The gardens were also restored to an approximation of their appearance in Burlington's time, but a low level of maintenance over the last few years has left them looking decidedly forlorn.

Today the house is no longer run by English Heritage (who took it on from the Ministry of Works) and the gardens by the LB of Hounslow. Instead the Chiswick House and Gardens Trust has been set up to run both as an integrated whole. A successful Heritage Lottery Fund application in 2008 meant that a programme of garden restoration has begun, to be followed by work on the house, with the aim of allowing this historic house and its gardens to be better presented and maintained in the next decades than they have been in the recent past.

MORTON HALL

Hugh May designed few houses and fewer still survive, but he was very successful at providing post-Restoration owners with exactly what they wanted: affordable, compact houses with good accommodation. Sadly it has long gone, but Morton Hall was one of these, described by Defoe as 'the flower of all the private gentlemen's palaces in England'.[1]

Sir Stephen Fox, who had been in the service of the exiled Charles II, continued as an able administrator of the royal finances after the Restoration. He had apartments in Whitehall Palace, and in 1663 was able to buy a house on the edge of the village of Chiswick, adjoining what we now call Chiswick House. It had only two acres, but in 1666 he was able to buy a strip of land next door from the Duke of Monmouth, which allowed him to build a new stable block. Having made a substantial fortune as Paymaster-General of the Armed Forces, Fox was wealthy enough to commission a new house in 1682 from Hugh May. This was a compact five-bay brick house with a pedimented centre and tall chimneys; it cost about £7,000 to build.[2] Fox chose the King's architect, and used artists and craftsmen who were also working for the Crown, such as Verrio and Grinling Gibbons. It had an entrance hall leading into an oak-panelled parlour with an 'exquisitely wrought plaster and carved ceiling' which opened onto the gardens. 'The handsome oak staircase with painted walls' led to a saloon which also had a rich plasterwork ceiling.[3] In the corners of the house were apartments, the attics had ten bedchambers, and the basement had vaulted service rooms. There were additional service rooms in a low wing between the house and stables.

The gardens were also reordered, possibly with Hugh May's help. Evelyn was not impressed by the site, writing 'the garden much too narrow, the place without water, neere an high way … little land about it … so as I wonder at the expense'.[4] There was a central gravel walk with yew hedges each side, leading to a pair of fine brick gate piers. The second enclosure was a kitchen garden, one side with high walls set diagonally to maximise the south-facing aspect. There was also a large greenhouse or orangery with a sheltered garden in front of it for 'exoticks' which can be seen in Kip and Knyff's view of Chiswick. Fox had superb fruit, including orange trees, lemons, limes, melons and pineapples.[5]

The house passed through many hands before being rented in 1807 by Lady Mary Coke, who had previously lived at Aubrey House in Kensington. When she died in 1811 the house

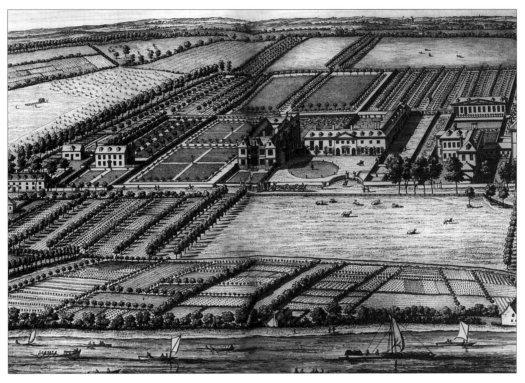

87   Chiswick, Morton Hall. Print from *Britannia Illustrata*, 1714. Part of Morton Hall just appears on the left, with its L-shaped service buildings and a large orangery behind. The stableblock of Chiswick House adjoins it, with old Chiswick House on the left and Sutton Court beyond it, across the Bollo Brook.

was put on the market. The 6th Duke of Devonshire, owner of the adjoining house, was interested in buying it and sent his surveyor to inspect it. The 1812 sale document gives a detailed description of the house and grounds, which with grazing across the road totalled 18 acres. The Duke's agent reported that houses like this were hard to sell and that their value was dropping and he was right. The asking price was £9,350 but the Duke bought the whole property for £7,402 and promptly demolished the house, selling the materials and incorporating Fox's gardens into his own.[6] This allowed him to make a new approach to Chiswick House from what is today Duke's Avenue, to lay out the Italian Garden, build the conservatory and turn the formal gardens behind Fox's house into a walled kitchen garden to supply his London and Chiswick houses with produce. Today only the brick gate piers with their iron gates and parts of the angled walls in the kitchen gardens survive to remind us of this once fine house.

CROYDON

CROYDON PALACE

Croydon today is a crowded, bustling place with a cluster of high-rise office buildings in the centre, and is trying to get city status; even in medieval times it was a large and prosperous village with a market and an important ecclesiastical property. Like Fulham Palace, the history of this site goes back to Anglo-Saxon times; but unlike Fulham Palace it is no longer a property of the church. Croydon Palace belonged to the See of Canterbury, and was one of the manors where the archbishop and his entourage would stay when going to London. Travel was painfully slow in medieval times; they would stay first at Charing, then Maidstone and Otford, moving on to Croydon and from there taking one more day to reach Lambeth Palace (which was acquired in the 12th century). The archbishopric held land in Surrey, Middlesex and Hertfordshire, and Croydon also became the centre for the administration of these estates. The Palace was almost encircled by water, having the River Wandle to the south and a tributary of it on each side. The enclosed area contained the manor house, fishponds and the parish church, where six archbishops were buried. There was also a deer park nearby, so the archbishop could entertain his guests with a day's hunting; a small fragment of open space, known as Park Hill, is a remnant of this. The earliest records date from 871, when the land was acquired by the see; a mill was recorded in Domesday Book, and there are traces of 12th-century masonry in the undercroft. Otherwise the remaining buildings date from the 14th century onwards, and in spite of many vicissitudes during the 19th century they form a picturesque group of hall, chapel and lodgings.

The great hall is on a modest scale (56 x 38 ft) but full of interest. It was probably built *c.*1390 by Archbishop Courtney, with walls of flint rubble and a steep tiled roof; the brick parapet is later. Today the two-storey porch is the best preserved part of this first phase, as the hall was remodelled by Archbishop Stafford in the mid-15th century. The fine timber roof of arched brace construction was installed by him, the timbers resting on finely carved stone corbels, some decorated with angels, some with armorials. The roof needed strengthening by the mid-18th century, and Archbishop Herring added the rather utilitarian tie-beams in 1748. There is no fireplace, but traces of a louvre can be seen in the roof. The screen has gone as the east end of the hall collapsed in 1830, and the wall was rebuilt in simplified form. Unusually there is no dais end to the hall; instead there is a stone pulpit at the west end with the arms of Henry VI, above which are leaded windows, installed in the 17th century to light the internal spaces above. The original solar, now known as the guard room, is approached up a wide mid-17th-century oak staircase, and has an undercroft below. It has been suggested that this exceptionally large room (51 x 21 ft) was originally a hall, remodelled as an audience chamber by Arundel (Archbishop 1397-1414). The roof, 24 ft high in the centre, is partly plastered but with the main timbers still visible. These are supported on eight carved stone corbels, some decorated with angels and the arms of the see of Canterbury and of Arundel. An oriel window on the south side was added in Tudor times. It looks into South Court, and its weathered stonework was replaced in 1910. The dining room beyond was made by Archbishop Morton, as part of his improvements to the Palace, as was a withdrawing room at the top of the stairs, facing south over the gardens, now known as the library. This leads to his long gallery, now divided into two classrooms. From outside its homely red brick south front and sash windows give no hint of its early Tudor origins.

The chapel (now about 70 x 24 ft) was probably built by Archbishop Bourchier (who added Knole to the archiepiscopal estates in 1456). It was a free-standing brick building over a flint-walled undercroft, the east end with a fine seven-light east window, now with glass by Clayton & Bell. It was extended westwards to connect internally to the first-floor lodgings by his successor, Archbishop Morton. There is no clear documentary evidence for this, but the work is very similar to the gatehouse he added to Lambeth Palace c.1495. The woodwork in the chapel is mainly 17th-century. Archbishop Laud (1633-45) added the altar rails, an organ and some of the panelling and stalls. 'Queen Elizabeth's Pew' is a gallery now set diagonally at the S-W end of the chapel, nothing to do with Elizabeth I but also dating from Laud's time.[1]

Croydon Palace was confiscated in 1640 after Laud's impeachment and was surveyed for sale. In 1646 it was bought by Sir William Brereton, a general in the Parliamentary forces, for £7,959. Most of the palace was used as his house, but he found the chapel with Laud's high church additions unacceptable: the organ and stained glass were destroyed and the altar rails removed. Brereton died there in 1661, by which time ownership of the palace had reverted to the church. Archbishop Juxon concentrated his efforts on Lambeth Palace, but he did restore

88 Croydon Palace, print after Joseph Nash. The great hall is on the left and the east window of the chapel on the right.

the chapel and his arms can be seen on some of the stalls and roof timbers. His successor, Gilbert Sheldon (1663-77), spent much time at Croydon, but the last archbishop to take an interest in the palace and to lay out funds on the building was Archbishop Herring (1747-57). He wrote, 'I love this old house, and am desirous of amusing myself with the history of its buildings; for the house is not one, but an aggregate of buildings of different castes and ages.'[2] As well as strengthening the hall he laid out fashionable gardens and it was possibly he who added the orangery south of the hall (demolished). He also arranged for Ducarel, his librarian at Lambeth, to research the history of the buildings.[3] But his successors disliked the old buildings and the low-lying situation and hardly used it; roads had improved, and they did not need to stay in Croydon when going to London. In 1780 Archbishop Cornwallis got an Act of Parliament allowing him to sell it and to build a new house on higher ground near Croydon, more appropriate for his fashionable wife. He never did build the new house but in 1807 Addington Park was bought by Archbishop Manners-Sutton as a replacement.

89   Croydon Palace, interior of the mid-15th-century chapel of the archbishops of Canterbury.

After 1780 the palace was no longer ecclesiastical property, Croydon was expanding and areas close to the River Wandle were becoming industrial. Abraham Pitches, a merchant from Streatham, bought the site for £2,520 and let it.[4] The various buildings, ponds and streams became the home of the three separate calico works, so printing and bleaching were carried out in what had been outbuildings and gardens, the vats in the brewhouse were used for dyeing and the hall was filled with lengths of material hung from inserted beams to dry. The next owner converted the old gatehouse on the Wandle into a mill; it was demolished in 1806, but was recorded in watercolours.[5] Small areas of land were sold off, and parts of the palace not in industrial use were lived in by managers of the various businesses or poorer tenants. Unsurprisingly the fabric suffered. The kitchen and service rooms adjoining the hall were demolished, weakening the east wall of the hall which collapsed in 1830. Various drawings and watercolours record this phase of the building's history, the contrast between the ancient buildings and modern industrial use appealing to artists. Soon after this the property was sold in several lots, some of which were bought by Benjamin Helps Starey, whose relatives had lived in the palace for some time and had owned some of the businesses there. It was largely due to him that the palace survived, although he did not live there.[6] The hall was described as part of a 'great washing and bleaching establishment, and steams with soapsuds … [it is] divided into floors of rafters from which to suspend blankets etc., for drying in wet weather'.[7] The orangery was converted into a four-bedroom house; other parts were let as tenements. The increasing population and the rise of industry in Croydon were leading to pollution and serious health problems, with sewage making the streams noxious. Around 1850 the ponds were drained and the streams put into culverts. After Starey's death in 1874 his widow began to sell off land for development, and it seemed likely that the palace itself would go too.

90 Croydon Palace, print after Joseph Nash. In 1830 the east end of the great hall collapsed.

The key to the rescue of the building was the meeting held in the palace in 1883, when the Rev. Cave-Brown read his paper on the history of the palace to the Surrey Archaeological Society; this led to efforts to find a more sympathetic use for it.[8] Anne Starey put the palace up for sale in 1886 but its poor state and jumbled buildings put off purchasers. It was saved in 1887 by the 7th Duke of Newcastle, who stepped in to buy it and presented it to the Sisters of the Church to use as a school. It remains in their possession today and is a successful girls' school; since they have had grants for building repairs there is occasional public access to this very interesting group of buildings.

DENHAM

DENHAM PLACE

Denham Place, 18 miles from central London, is one of a small group of houses – Chevening, The Grove, Moor Park – which were almost country estates. Their villages were not fashionable, pressure on land was less and the owners were able to buy more land than was available closer to the capital. Even so, their owners usually had close ties to London. Like many of these houses on the edge of London, Denham stopped being a private house in 1959 and became offices. Today it is being expensively converted back into a private house.

The River Colne winds down towards the Thames flanked today by a series of lakes and the Grand Union Canal. The attractive little village of Denham is on the River Misbourne close to its junction with the Colne, and Denham Place stands just to the west of the village; it can be seen across its grounds from the busy A412 from Rickmansworth. The entrance front faced west with an axial approach from the road; there was an entrance for family and servants on the south side. Today the entrance is from the east side in the village.[1]

91 Denham Place. Buckler watercolour of entrance front, 1806. Since then the balustrade on the roof has been removed and the dormers have lost their pediments.

The old manor house of Denham had belonged to the Peckham and then the Bowyer families. In 1673 part of the manor was bought by Sir Roger Hill (? – 1725), High Sheriff of Buckinghamshire that year and MP for Wendover. He came from a Puritan gentry family in Somerset and only began building the house, on a new site, in 1688. Might this have been because of the change of regime in that year? It was built slowly, not being completed till 1701. A lively bird's-eye view of the house painted soon afterwards shows its red bricks contrasting with a crisp white cornice and balustraded roof platform. The gardens are shown in fascinating detail: wrought iron gates and railings on the road allow passers-by to see into the gardens with their clipped yews, parterres and copious sculptures. A wall topped with putti separates the garden from the stables, the farmyard and a drying ground. We can see a hay cart in the yard, a horse being watered at the pond and a sheep pen crammed with animals. A canal divides the gardens in two, with an extraordinarily elaborate domed building acting as a bridge. The gardens across the water are laid out in geometric shapes with canals – there was no shortage of water in this area – and the whole is enclosed with a brick wall, much of which still exists today.

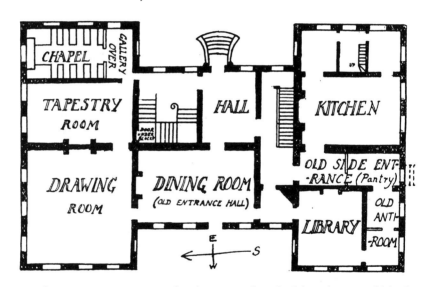

92 Denham Place, plan of ground floor.

In plan it was a typical post-Restoration H-plan house with a double-pile central block, not dissimilar in scale and plan to Fawley Court, also in Buckinghamshire. It is an 11-bay house of two storeys over a semi-basement, with dormers in the attics. This is a brick house with stone used sparingly; the quoins and string course are of brick and the deep modillion cornice is of wood; only the steps and entrance are of Portland stone. The house was designed by William Stanton, one of a large family of masons and sculptors in London. Payments to him between 1689 and 1694 were presumably for the design and for visits to check the building's progress. It was a finely finished house which cost just over £5,500 and from the building accounts we know a great deal about the craftsmen involved.[2]

Originally the west entrance led into a hall with the main staircase (since replaced) behind. The parlour and service rooms were to the south, as was the secondary staircase, a good example of sturdy late 17th-century joinery. The main reception rooms were on the north side, with a chapel in the N-E corner. This has earlier fittings: linenfold panelling with a carved frieze in Renaissance style and pews with both late Gothic and 17th-century woodwork, which must all have been brought in from elsewhere. The liturgical east window (actually facing north) had heraldic glass which has since been removed, and the plasterwork ceiling is dated 1691. There was a gallery at the upper level for family use, with an ante-chapel below. Private chapels were quite often included in house plans at this date, and probably Hill's interior was simpler. The early woodwork was brought in from an unknown source in the early 19th century and were not, as had been thought, fragments from an earlier house on the site.[3]

The interiors are what one would expect for a house of this date, with bolection moulded panelling in oak or painted deal and bolection moulded chimneypieces. Some rooms have simple plasterwork ceilings, but two are more unusual. The drawing room has a fine plasterwork ceiling with musical trophies in the central compartment and cornucopias spilling flowers around it; this was made by a London plasterer, William Parker. This is

93 Denham Place, the Tapestry Room in the early 20th century. The coving has village scenes in plasterwork and Cupid above the overmantel.

conventional enough, but the coved frieze has lively scenes of field sports after mid-17th-century prints by Francis Barlow. These are charming rustic scenes of men with dogs or fishing rods or hunting on horseback, against a backdrop of trees and cottages. The adjoining tapestry room has a similar frieze, dated 1693, of homely village scenes – except that Cupid unexpectedly appears over the chimneypiece, ready to fire his arrows at guests below.[4] The covings are unlike any other surviving examples, and are close in spirit to the much earlier hunting scenes in the frieze of the high great chamber at Hardwick Hall. Unlike many houses of this date, there do not seem to have been any ground-floor bedrooms. The first floor had suites of bedrooms with closets in each of the corners, and two rooms over the hall, later opened up into one space as offices.

After Hill's death the house went to his daughter, then to her niece Abigail Lockey. Her daughter, another Abigail, married Lewis Way and it was their son Benjamin Way MP who made important changes to the house and grounds after 1771. The formal gardens were swept away and the canals converted into a lake. He removed the cupola and possibly replaced the balustrade on the roof, as can be seen in Buckler's watercolour. The entrance was probably moved from the west to the east front to give the new dining room an uninterrupted view over the landscape, and he rebuilt some of the service buildings. The stone door surround was moved to the west front and possibly the stone busts which adorn it came from the formal gardens. The exceptional amount of sculpture in the gardens was removed, and some may simply have been buried in the garden. Christopher Hussey reported that 'a great number of bustos, fragments of capitals, mouldings and balusters … have been found buried in a mound by the lake.'[5] The main stairs were probably rebuilt at this time in the same space as the 17th-century stairs, and the drawing room was given a neo-classical chimneypiece of white statuary marble.

The Way family retained the house until the 20th century.[6] It was bought with 100 acres after the First World War by Basil Fothergill, and was recorded by *Country Life* while in his ownership. This provides a good record of its appearance before institutional use took its toll.[7] The next owner was Robert Vansittart (1881-1957), whose father owned Foot's Cray in Kent. He was a diplomat with a Mayfair house and an enormously rich second wife, Sarita.[8] They carefully did up the house, filled it with fine antiques and entertained lavishly at weekends, supported by a staff of 12 indoor servants. A formal garden was laid out north of the house based on the sunken garden of Hampton Court; the gardens were kept in perfect condition by their five gardeners.

After Lady Vansittart's death the house was put up for sale with 42 acres, but a period of decline began.[9] It remained empty for some years, and by the 1970s was on the Buildings at Risk register. In 1978 it was bought by the property company Housetrend, which carried out major works 1978-9, destroying parts of the fabric and evidence of early interiors. For instance, the basement with its brick vaults was stripped out, making it impossible to know how it was used; and the attics now have no original interiors, although a fine oak chimneypiece of 17th-century date was recorded there previously.[10] Dry rot had damaged some of the panelling, which was replaced insensitively, and rooms were subdivided. The house was in office use for many years and seemed likely to remain so. However when it came up for sale in 2000 with 55 acres it was bought by the present owner, who applied for planning permission to turn it back into a private house. He commissioned a report on the fabric, and has carried out a great deal of work to reverse the damage done during the 1970s.[11]

EALING

GUNNERSBURY PARK

The history of this site concerns two completely different phases: the early Palladian villa designed by Webb, and the large stuccoed mansions which belonged to the Rothschilds. And of course there had been a house at the centre of the estate before that.[1] Not many houses were built during the Commonwealth, so Gunnersbury was unusual in being a major house built in 1658-63 by a top architect. The estate, seven miles from London and in the parish of Ealing, belonged to Sir John Maynard (1604-90) a lawyer and MP who also had a London house and an estate in Devon. He had prosecuted Strafford and Laud, but had resigned from Parliament in 1648; by 1660 he was a supporter of the Restoration, so was able to complete the building and live there undisturbed.

John Webb had trained with Inigo Jones and had a deeper understanding of Palladian design than any of his contemporaries.[2] He produced a most impressive villa for Maynard, the entrance front dominated by the Corinthian pediment over a recessed five-bay loggia; it was built of brick with stone dressings. The three-storey house had a parlour and service rooms on the ground floor with cellars below, a *piano nobile* and a bedroom floor above, and a high hipped roof with servants' rooms. Since the house stands on high ground this gave views southwards to the Thames with Surrey in the distance. In lay-out it was most original,

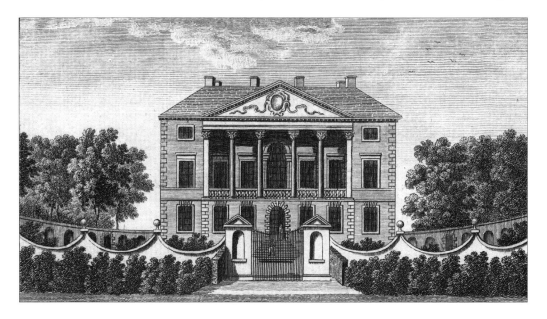

94 Ealing, Gunnersbury Park. Print showing the house designed by John Webb in 1658 for Sir John Maynard.

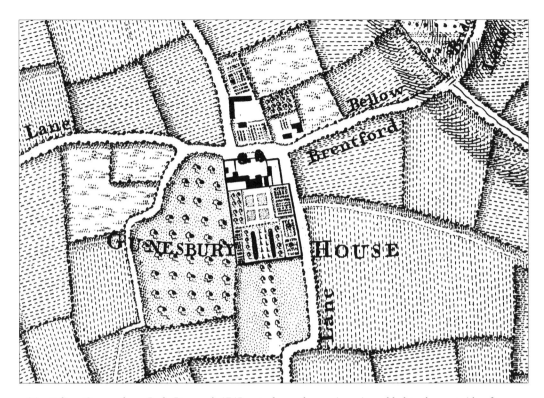

95 Ealing, Gunnersbury Park. Rocque's 1745 map shows the service wing added to the west side of Webb's house. Formal gardens are laid out south of the house with parallel canals. The orchard to the west was laid out as gardens by William Kent soon after this plan was made.

the plan being a development of the through hall which we see in earlier houses such as Charlton and Eagle House, Wimbledon and which was also a feature of Palladio's Veneto villas; Webb was presumably drawing on both the Italian and English traditions here. On the ground floor there was a stone-paved entrance hall with four pairs of columns supporting the great room above. They were more widely spaced in the centre to allow access to the staircase, a magnificent imperial stair in the centre of one side leading to the first floor only. (Secondary oak staircases from top to bottom were tucked away on either side of the hall.) The great room was a double cube with a coved ceiling, opening onto the loggia at the one end. In practice this was not enough light for such a deep room. Roger North's comment that 'the dining room hath no light but from this portico' is not quite correct, as it had windows at both ends; but for a room over 50 ft long it must have been rather dark.[3] Opposite the staircase was a drawing room, and both this and the staircase had three closely spaced windows. In the corners of the house were apartments with closets. This too was disapproved of by North, who thought that an enfilade of rooms would have been more impressive; but it produced a house 'equally grand and convenient'.[4]

The house was approached from the north across a walled forecourt set back from the Brentford road behind a scalloped wall with ball finials – a very Palladian touch. The gardens were to the south, and Rocque's map of 1745 shows a formal lay-out with two parallel canals roughly where the lake is today, with an avenue beyond and fields on either side. This lay-out was probably little altered from Maynard's time, as his widow remained in possession of the house till her death in 1721; then it was inherited by his great-grandson John Hobart, later Earl of Buckinghamshire, who did almost nothing to the property. In 1739 he sold it to Henry Furnese, MP and art collector. Loveday records some of the pictures he saw on his visit in 1746, which included paintings by Rubens, Maratta, Bassano, Sacchi and Guido Reni.[5] He employed William Kent to lay out the grounds. Part of his scheme is still there, although overlaid by 19th-century and municipal changes. Kent's changes consisted of loosening the garden design by removing the formal enclosures: the avenue and canals went and the gardens were enlarged to the west, taking in land that had previously been orchards. A two-acre round pond was made which is still there, and a crescent-shaped pond close to the south front of the house, which has gone; and trees were planted round the perimeter of the gardens. It was altogether a much freer design than the earlier lay-out.[6]

Princess Amelia (1710-86), third daughter of George II, bought the Webb house in 1761 from Furnese's executors. She had previously been using the two lodges in Richmond Park as her suburban houses, but on inheriting £130,000 from her father she bought Gunnersbury as her own house. She then spent about £20,000 on the grounds, buying more land to increase the estate and adding garden buildings, most of which have gone. She may have asked Chambers to design the Doric portico for the earlier temple on the north side of the round pond. She used the spaces behind it as her dairy, and the sale document at her death describes the 'cream room set with galley tiles and marble sideboards, a churning room, china room, kitchen and two chambers'.[7] Princess Amelia entertained at Gunnersbury in considerable style, so there are many reports of her parties. It was close enough to London for visitors to come down for an event and return that night, and Lady Mary Coke reported a reception for the King of Denmark in 1768. He was received 'in the great room upstairs … The Princess asked him to go into the portico [loggia] where immediately the signal was given for the fireworks … When they were over, the company came back into the great room, and the King of Denmark began the ball.'[8] After her death in 1786 the house and 129 acres were sold, and the sale document describes the mahogany staircase and her sumptuous furniture. It remained as a private house with its estate till 1800, when it was bought with 83 acres as a speculation by John Morley, a Chelsea 'floor cloth manufacturer'.[9] He immediately demolished the house and sold off the land in 13 lots. Two houses were quickly built cheek by jowl on the site of Webb's, with a wall dividing the grounds. Lot 1, the N-E part of the site, was bought by Stephen Cosser, and he built the Little Mansion, as his house is now known. It is a two-storey stuccoed house with a three-bay centre and bowed ends, not architecturally distinguished but taking full advantage of its position facing south over the gardens. Its long ground-floor windows give access directly onto the terrace under a pretty *chinoiserie* Regency verandah. To the east is the little Gothic building known as Princess Amelia's bath house, what we see today probably designed by William Fuller Pocock for Thomas Farmer, a later owner.[10]

The other lots were bought by Alexander Copland (1773/4-1834), a successful London builder in partnership with Henry Holland, who built himself a new house on the western end of the site. This is known as the Mansion today, and was bought after Copland's death in 1834 by Nathan Mayer Rothschild. He died almost immediately, but his son Lionel took it over. Robert Smirke was called in to embellish the house, which is much larger than the Little Mansion. It is a wide double-pile stuccoed house, with a seven-bay central block of

96 Ealing,
Gunnersbury Park,
south front of the
house built by
Alexander Copland
in 1800 and enlarged
by Smirke in 1834 for
Lionel Rothschild.

three storeys flanked by two-storey wings. The entrance is on the north side and three very large reception rooms face south over the grounds, the central room opening onto a loggia and the terrace of Webb's house. Smirke's richly carved chimneypieces and *scagliola* columns survive in the rather battered interiors.

Smirke also added the classical stables below the house, which were then masked by the owner of the Little Mansion, Thomas Farmer. He commissioned gothic ruins which still stand, designed by W.F. and W.W. Pocock. Smirke also designed a fine orangery with a high glazed roof facing the Horseshoe Pond (which has been drained), its severe façade reflected in the water. More land was bought in 1861 to the south, where the Potomac lake was made and a Gothic ruin built, doubling as a boathouse. Lionel was an MP, philanthropist and keen gardener, and entertained lavishly at Gunnersbury. In 1889 his son Leopold was able to buy the Little Mansion, so the dividing wall in the gardens could be demolished and there was more accommodation for guests. The terrace, now extending undivided across both houses, was covered with sumptuous pots of flowering plants. Leopold also took on James Hudson, the very talented gardener from the Little Mansion, as his own head gardener. By this time the lavishly-run gardens at Gunnersbury were famous, with their exotic hot-house plants and wonderfully productive kitchen gardens. In 1901 Japanese gardens were laid out near the stables, with Japanese trees and shrubs, ferns, water lilies and bamboo bridges; but these disappeared due to high maintenance after the Second World War.[11] By the time of Leopold's death in 1917 rail links had brought housing and commuters, and Ealing was no longer the quiet village it had been. His son Leopold de Rothschild sold Gunnersbury, to concentrate his gardening efforts at Exbury in Hampshire. 190 acres were bought from the Rothschilds in 1925 to make a public park, and the houses became a local museum and arts centre. Although this has preserved them, both houses and gardens have been fairly neglected; in 1971 the temple was almost demolished, and remained locked up and unused until in 1995 The Temple Trust carried out essential repairs. More work needs to be done on this historic landscape, and ways found of preserving the remaining historic buildings while preserving public access and enjoyment of the open spaces.

PITZHANGER MANOR

Ealing was a large parish, stretching from the Thames in the south to the River Brent in the north, with the village of Ealing in the middle. Pitzhanger Manor, famous as the country house of Sir John Soane, was in the northern part of the parish on a different site from the original manor house, which has been demolished. The history of the present house begins with Thomas Gurnell (1725-85), a Quaker and member of a successful banking dynasty. He lived mainly in London, but his family had owned a house and land in Ealing since 1722.[1] In 1768 Gurnell commissioned alterations to their house, known as Pitshanger Place, using George Dance the Younger as his architect. Dance had just been appointed Clerk of the City Works, so this was probably through their City connections; and in 1772 he married Gurnell's daughter Mary. It was an early work by Dance, who added a two-storey wing to the plain earlier brick house; it passed to Gurnell's son Jonathan and his wife, Susannah Swinden. After Gurnell's death she married Captain Peyton, and it was Peyton who sold the house and its land to Soane in 1800. Soane was by then a prosperous and successful architect with a wife and two sons, who he hoped would follow him into architectural careers. He was looking for a plot of land to the west of London at this time, and had just bought some land in Acton when he heard that Pitshanger was up for sale. He had gone to work in Dance's office in 1768, so would have been familiar with that building project. He made an offer of £4,500 for the house and 28 acres, and immediately started making ambitious plans for rebuilding it. Most of the old house was pulled down, leaving only the wing added by Dance with its two large reception rooms, which became the southern end of the new house. It was an expensive project: as well as paying a high price for the house and grounds, he spent at least as much again on rebuilding.[2]

The house faces east and Soane made an intriguing entrance, a vernacular version of a triumphal arch built of rubbed red bricks with vertical bands of flint. Tucked away nearby

97 Ealing, Pitzhanger Manor. Print showing Dance's wing on the left, Soane's addition with lower service wing and ruin garden on the right.

are the inconspicuous stables and a small lodge. From here there is a picturesque view of Soane's dramatic new entrance front. This also plays on the triumphal arch theme, with its brick façade dominated by crisp Portland stone Ionic columns topped by almost life-size Grecian figures in Coade stone. It has arched windows below and an attic storey above with only lion reliefs in roundels to break up the wall surface.[3] This announces itself as the house of a man fascinated by antiquity, and one in which sculpture is to play an important part. The garden front is gentler, Soane's new block here revealed to be of three storeys. Tripartite windows light the semi-basement and the wide windows of the main floor open onto a deep balcony. In 1802 this was altered and a conservatory with coloured glass infilled the balcony (removed in 1901). The north end of the house had a colonnade of primitive columns linking it to a new service wing to the north. John Haverfield was employed immediately after the purchase of the house to redesign its surroundings. The new drive has already been mentioned, but Gurnell's gardens were completely swept away apart from one or two ancient trees, a walled kitchen garden was made to the south of the house and landscaped gardens with a lake and a bridge were laid out to the west, taking in some of the land which had been fields. Beyond the kitchen wing Soane made a ruin garden, with columns buried in the ground as if only partially excavated and the earth partially covered with fragments of tessellated pavement: a typical Soane concept, blurring the boundaries between old and new.

Internally, Soane kept Dance's south wing as his dining room below and drawing room above, both on a much larger scale than the more intimate family rooms of the new house. The front door leads into a narrow vestibule with rusticated walls and incised decoration; at the upper levels are two over-sized reliefs after Thomas Banks of the chariots of the sun and moon, which are all bathed in golden light from his favourite top-lighting with coloured glass. The vestibule leads into the small drawing room, a comparatively plain room opening onto the balcony. It has double doors into the slightly larger library, also overlooking the gardens; this opens into the little breakfast room on the entrance front, so a miniature circuit of rooms was achieved. All these rooms have mirrors, and the library with its mirrored alcoves had Etruscan vases from his collection. These two rooms have characteristic Soane marble chimneypieces and gently domed or vaulted ceilings, recently redecorated after his designs; modern carpets have

98 Ealing, Pitzhanger Manor. In 1801 John Soane added this entrance front, based on a Roman triumphal arch. The wing on the left is part of the earlier house by Dance.

been made for these rooms from Gandy's watercolours. Soane's little dressing room flanked the vestibule, and as at his London house in Lincoln's Inn Fields this had a water closet off it. The two reception rooms in Dance's wing are much larger, the eating room down half a flight of stairs, and the drawing room on a level with the bedrooms in the new house. As Soane explains, 'the interior of these rooms have undergone very little alteration, and afford a specimen of the taste of that day.'[4] Both have neo-classical plasterwork by Dance on the ceilings, picked out by Soane in various colours.[5] The Soanes intended to entertain at Pitzhanger, and these were rooms with plenty of space for guests and for the display of their growing art collection: 'valuable pictures, antique marbles, Etruscan vases, and a very large collection of casts from antique objects.'[6] Some of the furnishings for Pitzhanger came from Lincoln's Inn Fields, but new furniture and carpets were ordered from John Robins, a cabinet maker, furniture supplier and auctioneer who was a friend of Soane.[7] The staircase is top-lit, an austere

99   Ealing, Pitzhanger Manor. Soane's breakfast room, designed 1801 and recently restored.

cantilevered stair with iron balusters which may have been reused; they are not a typical Soane pattern. It awaits redecoration in Soane's colour scheme of dark marbling. In the new house were four bedrooms, so it was not large; but the Soanes were able to come down for the day, and did not often have guests staying the night.

By 1810 it was clear that Soane's hopes for his sons were not being realised, and he decided to sell Pitzhanger. The contents were taken back to Lincoln's Inn Fields and somehow squeezed into their house, which took on the crowded appearance it has today. Christie's sold the house and grounds, which changed hands rapidly over the next decades, until it was bought in 1843 by Spencer Walpole. His four sisters-in-law, the unmarried daughters of the assassinated prime minister Spencer Perceval, lived there till 1900; it was partly because of them that few changes were made to the house. By that time Walpole had decided to sell Pitzhanger, and after the last of the sisters had died it was bought by Ealing District Council to provide a park, named Walpole Park.[8] The house was destined to be the public library and a substantial wing was added to the north, replacing the colonnade and service wing. After the library moved out in 1985 the council turned the library into exhibition space and decided on a programme of research and restoration of the house, helped by the vast Soane archive at Lincoln's Inn Fields. There is still work to be done but the restored interiors with their rich colouring and mirrors give an impression of Soane's taste, even without the objects with which they were once filled.

ELTHAM

ELTHAM LODGE

The history of this house is closely linked to that of Eltham Palace nearby. Charles I was the last monarch to have used it as a royal residence; it suffered badly during the Civil War and was restored to the Crown at the Restoration but Charles II had no intention of using it. He leased the palace and its three parks to Sir John Shaw (*c*.1615-80), who had helped him with loans and other services while he was in exile.[1] Shaw's exile in the Netherlands – and that of the architect Hugh May – helped define the style of the new house he built about half a mile away, possibly on the site of an earlier lodge.

Shaw came from a gentry family in Cheshire, was a member of the Vintners' Company in the City, where he lived; and he became an MP. He was knighted in 1661 and made a baronet in 1665; he was a farmer of the Customs, and in 1663 married as his second wife Bridget Drury, the widowed Lady Kilmorey. Both of them already had children, and were to have several more, so they needed a house near London, and the lease of Eltham must have been ideal. Hugh May was the Paymaster of the Works and must have known Shaw from their time in the Netherlands; the style of the house is strongly influenced by the compact Dutch houses they would have known, such as the Mauritshuis.

100   Eltham Lodge from the N-W. It was built in 1664 by Hugh May for Sir John Shaw.

131

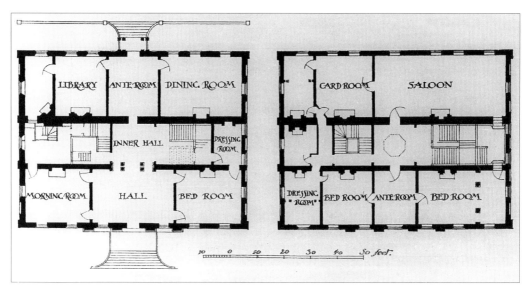

101 Eltham Lodge. Plans of the ground and first floors, showing the triple-pile plan.

Eltham Lodge is the archetypal Restoration house. It is a triple-bay house of brick, of two main storeys over a basement and with attics in the hipped roof. The tall panelled chimneystacks are placed to each side of the house, possibly to accommodate a balustraded roof platform, though there is no record of this. The entrance front to the north has a pediment supported by Ionic pilasters, while the south front is astylar with blank arches flanking the central window. It is an austere design, relying for its effect on the proportions, the subtle placing of the windows, and the deep modillion cornice which runs all round the house. The house is remarkably well-planned, a development from Jones and Pratt's Coleshill. The hall opens into a wide central corridor with the two staircases; on the south front is a central room with steps into the garden, flanked by a small winter parlour and a larger great parlour. The main bedroom and closet were to one side. The first floor had an impressive saloon in the S-W corner and two suites of bedchambers and closets on the east side.

The house was begun in 1664, and John Evelyn described going to see 'Sir John Shaw's new house now building'.[2] But he was not impressed, especially disapproving of the kitchen being in the basement. Perhaps the main staircase was not yet built, as that he surely would have approved of that. It has shallow steps and a wide handrail and the newels are capped with draped vases full of fruit. The balustrade has pierced panels with superbly carved acanthus scrolls and *putti*, each one different. This type of balustrade was highly fashionable post-Restoration and had developed from the heavier designs of the 1630s in houses such as Ham and Cromwell House. The staircase was stained in the 19th century, but has now been cleaned and painted as it should be. The ceiling over it has an oval compartment richly encrusted with flowers, fruit and leaves, a foretaste of the richly decorated saloon on the first floor. Here the oval ceiling compartments are framed with tightly-packed flowers, while the central rectangle has looser acanthus scrolls round it. The walls were hung with a superb set of six Brussels tapestries showing the story of Theodosius, after designs by Jacob Jordaens. These were later covered with wallpaper, and were only rediscovered in the 19th century.

They have now been removed from the house.[3] Typical of its date is the restrained bolection moulded chimneypiece in purple marble, with a painting of a classical landscape inset over it and Shaw's cypher above, framed with festoons and ribbons.

In 1752 Shaw's great-grandson, also Sir John Shaw (4th Bt.) married for the second time. He renewed the Crown lease and some elegant rococo work was introduced to update parts of the house for his bride. The N-E corner room on the ground floor had its panelling replaced by plaster walls which were decorated with crossed palm branches, flowery drops and a panel framed with festoons of flowers, while an oval mirror between the windows has a flowery plasterwork frame. The small room above this was given a new chimneypiece, but the finest one, a florid *chinoiserie* chimneypiece with a painted Chinese scene in the overmantel, was later ripped out and destroyed. This room had fine 18th-century Chinese wallpaper, fragments of which are now in the V & A.[4] Later the entrance hall was opened into the

102 Eltham Lodge. The main staircase has pierced panels carved with foliage scrolls.

corridor, the wall replaced by a screen of paired *scagliola* columns. Otherwise surprisingly few changes have taken place, in spite of the change of use from a private house to a golf club.

The Shaw family kept the house but it was let to a succession of tenants in the early 19th century. When the lease ran out in 1839 it reverted to the Crown. Eltham Golf Club took it over the lease in 1892, and in 1923 merged with the Royal Blackheath Golf Club. It was not in good condition then, when Tipping was writing his articles for *Country Life*, but has since been restored.[5] It is now used as their clubhouse, and their coat of arms replaced Shaw's in the pediment.

ELTHAM PALACE

Of the great medieval palaces round London little remains apart from Windsor, so the surviving fragment of Eltham Palace is a precious reminder of the scale and quality of royal building. Added to that is a 1930s house built for a member of the Courtauld family with striking Art Deco interiors. These buildings are in a remarkably beautiful moated site, making an unforgettable group. The palace was built on high ground with views over the Kent countryside and had three parks nearby; although the roar of the A20 can be heard nearby it is still surrounded by 30 acres of gardens, grass and trees.

Eltham was a royal manor in Saxon times and was given by William I to his half-brother Odo, Bishop of Bayeux after 1066. In 1295 it became the property of Anthony Bek, Bishop of Durham, who used it as his suburban house when he was on business in London. He built the moat we see today, with an inner wall of flint, brick and rubble, small areas of which are still visible. It enclosed a three-acre site on which he built his house, with his hall at right angles to the present one. When Bek died in 1311 it was taken over by Edward II (who had been given it by Bek in 1305 while he was Prince of Wales) and has been Crown property ever since, although last used as a palace by Charles I. The whole site was enlarged around the late 14th century as households became more elaborate; a further five acres was taken in beyond

103　Eltham Palace. The garden front of Stephen Courtauld's 1933 house seen above the medieval walls of the moat. These were built in the 13th century of flint, brick and rubble.

134

the moat and a large outer court constructed, with a gatehouse, service rooms and lodgings, with a tiltyard beyond. The timber-framed Lord Chancellor's House, one of a small group of old houses on the approach to the palace, is the only notable building remaining from this outer court, its name recording his lodgings close to the moat. The sturdy 4-arched limestone bridge over the moat was probably built *c.*1475 by Edward IV, and has later brick parapets.

What we see today is a magnificent great hall, one of the largest in England: 101 x 36 ft and 55 ft high to the apex of the roof. Edward IV demolished Bek's hall, and the new hall, designed by the royal master-mason Thomas Jurdan, was built 1475-83. Brick was becoming a fashionable material by this date, but Eltham was built in brick then faced in stone, Reigate stone on the north side and rougher Kentish ragstone on the south side. Although this front overlooking lawns and the moat provides visitors with their best view of the hall it was not always so: when built the kitchens were to the south, so it was not worth using the finer Reigate stone here. The walls are buttressed, with pairs of tall windows between each, and originally the parapet was battlemented and the roof leaded; the present tiled roof dates from the early 20th century. The dais is at the west end, and unusually has a bay each side, lit by a pair of tall windows. These must be an afterthought, as the windows are uncomfortably close in the angles. Each bay has a vaulted ceiling, contrasting with the magnificent hammer-beam roof of the hall itself, designed by Edward Gravely, King's Carpenter, with its massive pendants.[1] This must have looked even more splendid when partially gilded – traces were found during the Courtauld restoration. There was a louvre over the central hearth, since removed. The brick-built royal lodgings have gone, but lay parallel to the moat at the dais end of the hall, the king's to one side, the queen's to the other. A long gallery off the queen's apartments was placed to give fine views N-W towards London. The area which is now lawns between hall and moat was densely built up with lodgings, little courtyards and service areas.

104 Eltham Palace. South front of the medieval great hall, built 1475-83. This was originally obscured by kitchens, so the stonework of the wall is roughly finished.

105 Eltham Palace. Interior of the great hall with its magnificent hammerbeam roof, looking towards the dais end.

Eltham was much used through the 16th century. Visitors crossed the moat, passed through the gatehouse (demolished) and found themselves in Great Court, its open space dominated by the exceptionally large chapel (also demolished). This was rebuilt by Henry VIII, who made it as large as the hall. He connected it to the high end of the hall by a wide corridor, giving him a processional route to mass. He was also rebuilding the chapel of Greenwich Palace at this time, and used Eltham – which is only three miles away – as an annexe. The king would be at Greenwich, his guests might be at Eltham; they could be entertained with hunting in the parks of both palaces. Sometimes Cardinal Wolsey would be in residence, while attending the king at Greenwich; ambassadors might stay at Eltham, close to the route from Dover.

The 17th century saw the end of Eltham as a royal palace. John Thorpe made a survey in 1603, valuable for showing us what the medieval and Tudor palace then consisted of.[2] James I added towered royal lodgings, possibly intended for Anne of Denmark; then turned his attention to Greenwich and commissioned the Queen's House

for her instead. Charles I did use Eltham, but it was poorly maintained and parts were reported to be collapsing in 1631-2. Like other royal properties it was confiscated under the Commonwealth, Parliamentary troops were quartered there from 1648, and the 1649 Parliamentary Survey reported a building in very poor condition, the materials with a scrap value of £2,753.[3] The 1,652 acres were split up into lots and sold off, the palace going to Nathaniel Rich in 1651, who was buying up properties and asset-stripping them. The Eltham oaks were felled and sold to the Navy, the deer killed, the buildings left to decay. At the Restoration Charles II had no need for it and gave the lease to Sir John Shaw, who chose to build himself a new and much more convenient house half a mile away, Eltham Lodge.

Decline continued through the 18th century. The service ranges were gradually dismantled and Rocque's 1745 map shows a much emptier moated site. A tenant farmer put up a simple house at the service end of the hall, known as Court Farm; the hall was used as a barn, the screens passage converted into sheds. Increasingly the palace became admired for its antiquity and its air of picturesque decay. Buck and Grimm made prints of it, Sandby, Turner and Girtin painted watercolours of it. In 1827 Hunt published designs based on the bargeboards of the remaining timber-framed buildings – today the main early survivals apart from the hall, visible only from the first floor.[4] This was fortunate in the battle to preserve the building which was just about to break out. Storm damage to the hall gave the Treasury the excuse to propose demolition. Wyatville, busy on the transformation of Windsor Castle for George IV, suggested removing the roof of the great hall and installing it at Windsor for the new St George's Hall. This idea was rejected after a public outcry. In 1828 there was a debate in the House of Lords, the Society of Antiquaries objected and the Office of Woods & Forests reluctantly carried out repair work.[5] In 1831 A.C. Pugin published his drawings of the hall, with architectural details and compared its architectural magnificence with its present condition, 'its windows stopped up, its sculptural ornaments mutilated, the roof broken and obscured by dust and cobwebs, the whole fabric dilapidated'.[6] Court Farm, renamed Eltham Court, became an irregular group of buildings lived in by gentlemen, one of whom laid out gardens c.1860 between his house and the moat; the hall was his real tennis court. Major restoration work was done on the roof by the Office of Works in 1911-14, supervised by Sir Charles Peers, Chief Inspector of Ancient Monuments. It was taken down, strengthened with steel braces, and reconstructed.

After the First World War Eltham had become a commuter suburb and pressure to build more houses was growing: it was against this background that the Crown Estates decided to allow a private owner to take out a lease, on certain conditions. In 1933 a new phase began for Eltham Palace when Stephen Courtauld (1883-1967), a younger son of the textile manufacturer, took on a 99-year Crown lease. He and his Italian-Hungarian wife wanted a house within easy reach of central London but with gardens and grounds. The architects John Seely and Paul Paget had heard that Eltham Palace was on the market and persuaded them to look at it; it was not easy to negotiate a lease with the Crown Commissioners which suited both sides. Eventually their lease stipulated that they use Sir Charles Peers as their adviser, restore the hall at their own cost, incorporate the 15th-century gables with bargeboards, and demolish the 18th- and 19th-century additions. On that part of the site a new house could be built, and they had 30 acres of grounds, thus saving that area from unsympathetic development close to the historic buildings. Seely and Paget designed the house with two wings set at an angle; one for the Courtaulds was a continuation of the great hall, which thus became a vast reception room attached to their living quarters. A service wing was built at an angle to this new wing, close to the bridge. So visitors would cross the moat, come into the courtyard and enter the house through a convex colonnade in the angle between the two new wings. A semi-circular relief by Atwood over the entrance has a figure of Plenty with a cornucopia suggesting hospitality. The exterior is in a rather weak Wrenaissance style, built of brick with Clipsham stone detailing; the high tiled roof of the family wing reflects the hall roof. Seen across the moat the house appears more dramatic, the recessed angle between the wings being banded in brick and stone and with a high slate roof, although it simply housed a corridor connecting the family and guest wings.

Inside the house was much more modern, with many different designers at work. The triangular entrance hall is suffused with light through openings in the shallow concrete dome and is lined with an Australian wood with marquetry panels of Venice and Florence; this room is the focal point of the house. A loggia leads into the gardens, designed for them by Andrew Mawson. To one side is the dining room with service rooms beyond. On the other side are the drawing room and studies for the owners, with the great hall beyond. It is a neat plan, taking advantage of the moated site and providing up-to-date accommodation not just for the owners and their staff, but also for Mrs Courtauld's pet lemur, who was given

106 Eltham Palace. Entrance hall of the house added for Stephen Courtauld in 1933. It is toplit from the concrete dome.

a centrally-heated frescoed space off the bedroom corridor. The restoration of the hall was exemplary, with the careful recreation of the screen from surviving fragments; a Courtauld fabric was hung below the windows, the room was furnished with simple oak furniture, and Seely designed torch-like light fittings. Queen Mary came to see the work in progress in 1935, and the hall was opened to the public on Thursday afternoons throughout the year.[7]

However, running this house during the Second World War without the indoor staff and 15 gardeners they were used to became difficult; and there was some bomb damage to the hall. In 1944 the Courtaulds gave up their lease and moved to Scotland, then after the war to Zimbabwe. The remainder of their lease was taken up by the Royal Army Educational Corps, which remained there till 1992. The Courtaulds left their furniture in many of the rooms, and insisted that the hall remain open to the public; but their smart Art Deco interiors were virtually unknown. In 1995 English Heritage took over the site and carried out a notable restoration of the Courtauld house which was then opened to an astonished public.[8] There is very little Art Deco to be seen in England, and the stylish interiors were much admired. One of the most striking interiors is the dining room, designed by the Italian Peter Malacrida working for White Allom; it has pale wood walls contrasting with the smooth lines of the black and white marble fireplace and the black and silver of the door panels, all with Greek key pattern inlays. The recessed ceiling is of silver and the seating upholstered in rose-pink leather. Upstairs the bedroom and bathrooms are equally stylish: the Venetian bedroom with its marquetry panels, Virginia Courtauld's bathroom with its gold mosaic niche and marble bath. The Mawson gardens were restored where possible and new gardens were designed by Isabelle van Groeningen. It is a most successful restoration of both house and grounds, and has given a new lease of life to the medieval hall, the Courtauld house and the wider landscape.

ENFIELD

FORTY HALL

Forty Hall is one of a group of houses built on the royal park of Enfield Chace as it slipped from use for hunting. It is also one of a group of interesting early 17th-century houses which were experiments in a new type of planning. The high ground of Enfield Chace, north of the small town of Enfield, had a large house belonging to the Lovell family called Elsyng (or Elsings) close to the site of Forty Hall. This had been a royal property since 1539, but it was reduced in size after James I took over Theobalds nearby from Robert Cecil, and was sold by the Crown in 1641. By 1656 it was united with Forty Hall, although described as 'a very ancient house' and never lived in by the Raynton family.[1]

Sir Nicholas Raynton (1569-1646) was a City merchant, importing the luxury textiles from Italy which were used for clothing and furnishing: velvet, taffeta and satin. A portrait of him hangs in Forty Hall today showing him richly dressed in a fur-lined gown and

107 Enfield, Forty Hall, built in 1649. Seen from the N-E in 1933.

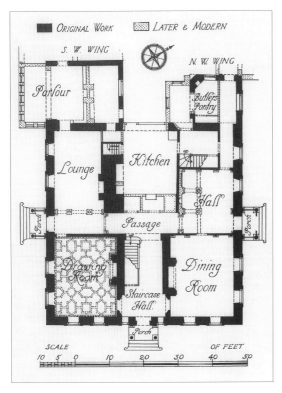

108   Enfield, Forty Hall. Plan of ground floor. The dining room was the original hall.

silk doublet. He became very rich and was a member of the City establishment: Master of the Haberdashers' Company, a governor of St Bartholomew's Hospital, an alderman and Lord Mayor 1632-3. But he was also a Puritan, and refused a loan to the king in 1639, as a result of which he was briefly imprisoned in the Tower. After this he retired to Forty Hall where he died soon afterwards, and was buried in Enfield church. In 1616 he had bought the manor of Worcesters and Lysons records that the land had belonged to Hugh Fortee – hence the name of the house.[2] Raynton did not build his new house until 1629; there is a dated brick of that year. It was complete by his mayoralty. He was aged 60 but chose an innovative design, one of the compact brick houses going up round London. (The Enfield area had good supplies of London clay for brick-making.) Unfortunately no building accounts survive, nor are there clues as to the builder or architect involved. Forty Hall is a triple-pile house of three storeys under a high hipped roof, slate today but originally tiled. The roof is atypical in that it has a central leaded well, through which the tall brick chimneys rise. This is original, so it never had a central roof platform like many of these houses. The three main five-bay fronts are almost identical, although the fourth or service side to the west has later additions. Below the roof a heavy wooden modillion cornice wraps round the whole house; this was added 1700-08, when the present sash windows with their eared surrounds were also installed. Recent research has shown that originally the east front had slightly projecting bays, similar to those at the later Thorpe Hall, Peterborough; these were removed when the sash windows were put in.[3]

The original entrance front was to the north and opened into a screens passage. This continued through the house to the gardens on the south side, and separated the main rooms on the east side from the kitchen and service rooms to the west. The hall has a good plasterwork ceiling of geometric design, but it is typical of a slightly earlier date – Raynton's taste was more adventurous in the design of his house than in its decoration. The chimneypiece has an overmantel with strapwork and pierced obelisks, slightly overscaled for a fairly low-ceilinged room. The fine wooden screen is still *in situ*; it has inwardly tapering columns topped with coarsely carved male and female figures. The wide central arch was filled in the 18th century with Gothick detailing: it is a house where later owners have responded to the style of the original house. The staircase hall, in the centre of the east front, has another fine strapwork ceiling with a deep frieze. The main parlour, beyond the stairs, has its original wooden chimneypiece, its paired columns embellished with curious rustication for one-third of their height. The walls retain their panelling, and the plasterwork ceiling has delicate floral sprays within geometric bands. Two bedrooms on the first floor also have plasterwork ceilings; the one in the S-E corner is dated 1629, and was probably the great chamber. It is a house rich in plasterwork of early 17th-century style, with no sign of the innovations being introduced by Inigo Jones.

Raynton died in 1646 having outlived all seven of his children, so the house went to his nephew, another Nicholas Raynton. He bought more land, including Elsyng next door, which he demolished. Possibly it was he who built the service courtyard to the west with its dramatic brick gateway, buttressed, battlemented and topped with a shaped gable and stone ball finials. His grandson, Sir Nicholas Wolstenhome, made the changes noted above: the cornice and sash windows. His two daughters then jointly inherited the house, and the Rococo plasterwork frame to Raynton's portrait must date from their ownership, as well as the embellishments to the hall screen. When Mary Wolstenholme died her married sister Elizabeth Breton became sole owner, but she lived in Northamptonshire. She decided to sell the estate, which was now very large: 1,440 acres. It failed to sell in 1773, but was offered for sale again, this time as 65 lots.[4] This was more successful, and the house and grounds were bought by Edmund Armstrong in 1787. The warm red brick was no longer fashionable, so the house was limewashed, and an early watercolour records this.[5] In 1800 it was bought by a merchant of Dutch origin, James Meyer. The date and his initials are on one of the

109 Enfield, Forty Hall. The screen in the dining room dates from 1629, embellished in the mid-18th century.

rainwater heads on the north front. He gradually built up his land-holding, and the house remained in the Meyer family till 1894.

Henry Bowles, the local MP, took over the house, which had been bought for him by his father. Various changes were made, both externally and internally. On the east front the pairs of narrow closely spaced first- and second-floor windows were replaced by tripartite openings on both floors, their eared stone surrounds sympathetic to the early 18th-century window surrounds. The warm red brick panel in which they are set has a terracotta cartouche round the coat of arms, its strapwork reflecting the plasterwork inside the house. This panel does not disguise the traces in the wall of the earlier windows. These new windows lighted the staircase, which was rearranged for greater effect. A new sitting room with a large bay window was added to the S-W and more servants' accommodation provided in an enlarged west wing. In 1951 the Parker-Bowles family sold the house and 273 acres to Enfield Urban District Council, to whom

110 Enfield, Forty Hall. The plasterwork ceiling over the staircase is original, although the stairs have been altered.

it still belongs. The house is now a local history museum; the brick gateway to the stable yard leads to low buildings rebuilt in the 1960s to provide space for a café and offices. The 273 acres of grounds are now part farmland, part public park.

Many of these suburban houses were recorded in prints or described in travellers' accounts, especially if they were the home of famous people or were on an admired stretch of the Thames. Enfield Chace was more remote, and in spite of its architectural interest Forty Hall was not recorded in watercolours or drawings till the late 18th century, no prints were made of it, and few visitors mention going there. In 1937 it was surveyed for the RCHM, but otherwise little research was undertaken even after it came into public ownership.[6] Partly as the result of an architectural study day held there recently, English Heritage has begun a programme of research, and it is hoped that archaeological investigation will reveal more of the complex history of this house.

ESHER

CLAREMONT HOUSE

To most people today Claremont means a historic garden, carefully maintained by the National Trust and not connected with a house. But that garden belonged to a house by Vanbrugh, demolished long ago; and the present house of Claremont, invisible from the gardens, is much less widely known, although it was a favourite retreat of Queen Victoria.

Vanbrugh built the first house for himself, taking a 70-year lease on a 60-acre farm called Chargate in 1709. The site was low lying, with rising ground close to the house which Vanbrugh was to take full advantage of in the gardens. Might Vanbrugh's house have been inspired by the ancient Esher Place nearby? In many ways Chargate could have been built a century earlier: it was a two-storey H-plan house with the hall in the centre flanked by corridors and a loggia, the cross wings with lodgings, and closets projecting like miniature staircase towers. Drawings for it show an early essay in the castle style, with arched windows, battlements and towers – ideas which he was to repeat in his house at Greenwich.[1] But Vanbrugh was not a rich man, and the house was on a small scale: the hall only 13 x 15 ft 6 ins and the bedrooms only 10 ft 6 ins square. Possibly the house was built more for Vanbrugh's widowed mother than for himself: he was not yet married, and soon after his mother died at Chargate in 1711 he put it on the market. It was bought by Thomas Pelham-Holles (1693-1768) later 1st Duke of Newcastle and twice prime minister. It was his elevation as Earl of Clare in 1714 which gave the house its name, combining his title with the hill in the grounds.

Newcastle's London house was in Lincoln's Inn Fields and his country estates in Sussex and Nottinghamshire; he needed a house near London to use for political entertaining and for family life, hence buying Chargate. But it was far too small, so he invited his friend Vanbrugh to enlarge it. The result was curious, Vanbrugh's house becoming the unlikely centrepiece for an immensely long façade. Its battlements were removed and replaced by a pediment and parapets, and the long wings each side had arcades below and arched windows above, the roofline broken by towers. One wing had a huge reception room with a clerestory rising above the roofline. A massive double staircase led up to the front door, the ground having been excavated to form a basement storey. But Newcastle also dramatically altered the garden, and possibly building on an earlier garden by Vanbrugh, he set about acquiring more land and laying out ambitious gardens. Three great garden designers of the first half of the 18th century were involved here: Vanbrugh, Charles Bridgeman and William Kent. In 1717 Vanbrugh crowned the hill behind the house with the Belvedere, a chunky whitewashed brick tower with arched windows, set at an angle to the house. The platform between the corner towers had magnificent views out over the surrounding country, and the room below could be used for entertaining.[2] (This is outside the National Trust gardens, but survives, no longer whitewashed.) The plan in *Vitruvius Britannicus* shows a winding walk through dense woodland on the hillside, echoing Vanbrugh's Ray Wood at Castle Howard.[3] Beyond

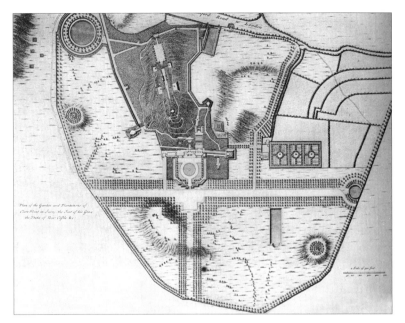

111 Esher, Claremont. Plan of the Duke of Newcastle's grounds, from *Vitruvius Britannicus*, 3, 1725. The steep hill behind the house is crowned with Vanbrugh's Belvedere.

the Belvedere was the bowling green, that essential feature of 18th-century entertaining, and the original grassy walk with earthworks which connected them still exists. The hill was surrounded by a bastion wall – another reflection of Vanbrugh's military preoccupations – which also enclosed the circular pond. The house was approached from the Guildford road down a tree-lined drive, off which was the vast kitchen garden, Vanbrugh's massive brick walls enclosing nearly four acres. A wide avenue was laid out parallel to the house, which had a deep forecourt in front. It was on a massive scale, and designed to impress.

Bridgeman contributed to the landscape, adding the striking grassy amphitheatre which overlooked Vanbrugh's round pond with its central obelisk, features copied on a smaller scale by Lord Burlington in his gardens at Chiswick. William Kent, who was also working for Newcastle's brother at Esher Place, then softened parts of the garden, breaking the avenue in front of the house to give views into the park and removing Vanbrugh's bastion wall on one side of the hill so the park and woodland merged, with only a ha-ha to divide them. The round pond was enlarged into an irregular lake, and the obelisk replaced by an island with a rusticated pavilion. These changes are recorded in Rocque's map of 1738, with its vignettes of the house and garden buildings, and in a painting based on a Rigaud drawing. Five rather naïve anonymous paintings show the gardens *c.*1740: grassy walks between high clipped hedges, the island with Kent's little pavilion, the crisp outlines of the amphitheatre, and views out from the hilly garden over the Surrey landscape.[4] Around the mid-18th century the cascade bringing water to the lake (pumped from Epsom Common) was replaced by a grotto, possibly made by Josiah Lane of Tisbury, the leading grotto maker of the time.

Lord Clive's Claremont

By the end of Newcastle's life his house was becoming dated. Henrietta Pye described the house as 'an old-fashioned ungraceful building … all the apartments are very small, and very ill furnish'd. The best rooms in it are a handsome saloon and a ballroom, supported by Corinthian pillars and surrounded by a gallery.' She was slightly more impressed by the grounds: 'The garden contains 360 acres and is extremely magnificent … but in my opinion it falls far short of Esher, both in richness and variety.'[5] After Newcastle's death in 1768 his widow sold it for £40,000 to Lord Clive (1725-74), recently returned from India and fabulously rich, though in trouble with Parliament over his administration there.[6] He demolished Newcastle's house and asked Lancelot 'Capability' Brown to design him a smaller one on a new site.[7] Henry Holland went into partnership with Brown at this time, as well as becoming his son-in-law, and the entrance hall in particular shows Holland's refined taste. The house sits on a hilltop facing S-E over parkland. It is a compact two-storey house over a semi-basement, the nine-bay entrance front broken by a massive

112   Esher, Claremont, entrance front. It was designed in 1768 by 'Capability' Brown and Henry Holland for Lord Clive.

Corinthian portico approached by a wide flight of steps, the whole impressive if slightly dull. It is built of white Suffolk bricks with stone enrichments, and the garden front has a double flight of steps connecting house and garden. The main floor provided a circuit of reception rooms round a top-lit central staircase, with a suite of apartments on the west side for Clive and his wife. The first floor had ten well-planned bedrooms, most with dressing rooms. In the basement were the kitchen, pantry and servants' hall, connected by a tunnel to service areas outside the house. The grounds were landscaped by Brown with lawns sweeping right up to the house, the amphitheatre planted over and loose groupings of trees in the park. But Clive did not live to enjoy his new house. The strain of the Parliamentary investigation of his finances and administration brought on depression and he took his own life.

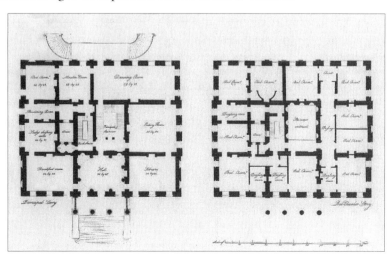

113   Esher, Claremont. Plans of the ground and first floors from *New Vitruvius Britannicus*, 1, 1802.

This newly and expensively built house and its 469-acre demesne was put up for sale and changed hands several times before being sold for £66,000 to the Commissioners of Woods & Forests in 1816, after which it remained in royal use till 1922. It was bought for Princess Charlotte and Prince Leopold of Saxe-Coburg-Gotha, who married in 1816 and needed a country house; it was settled on them for life. In fact it was so close to London, and the roads so much better by this date, that it was their main residence. The Princess made some alterations, employing Hiort and Papworth; her main addition was a little Gothic tea-house in the gardens, soon converted into a chapel in her memory: for Princess Charlotte died in childbirth in 1817 at Claremont. (Neglected for years, it fell down during the Second World War.) Leopold was left in possession of the house, with a pension of £50,000 *p.a.* Since he became king of the Belgians in 1831 he spent less time in England, and allowed his widowed sister, the Duchess of Kent, to borrow it. She and her daughter Princess Victoria often made use of it, so that when Victoria became queen it was a house she knew and loved.[8] She and Prince Albert often stayed there with their family, and her diary records her pleasure in relaxed country life, going on expeditions to Painshill and Hampton Court, or enjoying the gardens while Prince Albert went shooting on the estate. Princess Charlotte's apartment remained untouched after her death, so the queen used first floor rooms.[9] She commissioned a series of watercolours to record the house and grounds and some of the rooms; the formal 18th-century appearance of Clive's relatively unaltered dining room contrasts with the cosy clutter of their private rooms.[10]

114   Esher, Claremont House. Clive's Great Room was used as a dining room when the house was in royal use in the 19th century. Watercolour by Joseph Nash, commissioned by Queen Victoria in 1848.

But this was short-lived: in 1845 Victoria and Albert built Osborne for seaside holidays and in 1848 Leopold offered the house to his son-in-law, the exiled Louis-Philippe, who lived there as the Comte de Neuilly. He died in 1850 but his widow stayed on till her death in 1866. With the death of King Leopold the house reverted to the British government, and Victoria was under pressure to allow development of the estate. Instead she bought it herself from the Commissioners of Woods and Forests.[11] Her haemophiliac son Leopold, Duke of Albany was by now married and in need of a country house, so gave them use of it, but kept tight control of it. The best rooms were reserved for her own use, he was not allowed to make changes, and he had to pay the bills. After his death his widow stayed on, but it was officially the property of their son, the Duke of Saxe-Coburg-Gotha who lived in Germany. During the First World War he was treated as an enemy alien and his property confiscated, so at his mother's death in 1922 it reverted to the government. It was sold to Sir William Corry, and at his death was again sold, but this time part of the park was developed with housing. The 49 acres of the main historic gardens were in separate ownership, and disregarded, until in 1949 the National Trust bought them. But the restoration of the gardens did not happen at once: garden history was in its infancy, and it was only c.1975 that serious efforts were made by the NT to investigate the historic gardens and to recreate some features, such as the amphitheatre, which had almost disappeared due to a combination of later planting and neglect. The gardens were opened in 1979, so there is now public access to the restored amphitheatre, lake and grotto. Clive's house was bought in 1930 with 33 acres of parkland and became Claremont Fan Court School; the grounds include part of the kitchen gardens, the 19th-century stables and Vanbrugh's Belvedere, to which access is occasionally allowed.

Esher Place

Two buildings remain from a long and complicated history: a large 19th-century house on a splendid hill-top site and an old tower on the riverbank below, a fragment of a much larger episcopal property. This is all that survives of the old Esher Place. The c.1460s brick gatehouse known as Wayneflete's Tower gives us an idea of the age and interest of this exceptional property, which is now beautifully restored as a private house. The site on the River Mole, with water meadows in front and a hill behind, made it a sheltered and easily accessible spot. This made it particularly attractive to its medieval owners, the Bishops of Winchester, and it became a staging post on their journeys to London. The building was a rambling courtyard house close to the river, and after William Wayneflete became Bishop of Winchester in 1447 he set about rebuilding it.

Brick was becoming a fashionable material for major buildings in the South East and East Anglia at this time, and Wayneflete was in the forefront of this in his numerous building projects. At Esher he rebuilt the bishop's lodgings close to the river, as well as adding the gatehouse as an imposing entrance to the courtyard from the land side. At Farnham he also rebuilt parts of the palace employing Flemish brick makers, and probably used the same craftsmen at Esher.[1] Here octagonal towers with moulded brickwork flank the central archway and there is diaper brickwork remaining on large areas, but the fenestration and battlements are due to William Kent's embellishments of the 1730s.

Cardinal Wolsey became Bishop of Winchester (as well as being Archbishop of York) in the spring of 1529, and added a gallery to Esher Place. It was while Wolsey was at Esher that Henry VIII took his London palace of York Place, and added insult to injury by removing the new gallery to his palace at Whitehall.[2] Wolsey's successor was forced to relinquish Esher to the King, who used it as a hunting lodge while at Hampton Court. Queen Mary returned it to the See of Winchester, but Elizabeth I reclaimed it. In 1582 she granted it to Lord Howard of Effingham, and from that date it has been in private ownership. One of its more curious uses was as a prison for three distinguished commanders from the Spanish Armada, who were captured in 1588 and housed at Esher Place, as it was then owned by Richard Drake, a cousin of Sir Francis. During their four years there they were much visited by the local gentry.[3]

Major changes took place in the late 17th century. Captain Christopher Colborne had bought it in 1663, but 15 years later his business failed and he reduced the house to what we see today: just the gatehouse, known as Wayneflete's Tower. He sold it to Sir Thomas Lynch, who had a West Indian fortune and had been Governor of Jamaica, and who was succeeded by his son-in-law Thomas Cotton. One or other of those men made it habitable by adding a wing on each side as high as the tower; it is this house which we see in the Kip engraving of 1707.[4] This print also shows the walled gardens to the river which are on the site of the old courtyard house, and the stables and other outbuildings set back towards the road. Several enclosed gardens extended along the River Mole and were on the site of earlier gardens which can be seen in Treswell's survey of 1606.[5] In 1720 the house was sold for £7,000 to a South Sea Company director, Peter Delaporte. But this was just before the crash, and the house and its 115 acres were seized and sold to pay off some of his liabilities. The owner from 1723-9 was Dennis Bond, and it was he who first leased, then sold it to one of its key owners.

This was the Hon. Henry Pelham (1695-1754) a Whig politician and later prime minister, younger brother of Thomas Pelham-Holles, 1st Duke of Newcastle, who in 1720 had bought the nearby estate of Claremont. The purchase of Esher Place in 1730 gave Pelham the opportunity to rebuild the house and redesign the garden, and for both these projects he chose William Kent, who also worked at Claremont and later designed Pelham's London house, 22 Arlington Street. Important drawings by Kent for Esher turned up in the 1950s and 1980s, which have thrown new light on the development of the now-vanished house and gardens.[6] Kent, like Vanbrugh, was very aware of the picturesque possibilities of ancient buildings, and in one proposal suggested taking down the late 17th-century wings to leave the tower isolated near the river, and building a Palladian house on the hill to overlook it, safe from the risk of flooding.[7] The final building was more interesting: lead-covered cupolas were added to Wayneflete's Tower, which was embellished with battlements and quatrefoil windows in its upper stages. The three-storey wings may have been adapted rather than completely rebuilt, but as seen in the drawings they have the stamp of Kent's taste for the Jacobean, which we can see also at Rousham. On the west front to the river there were three-bay, three-storey wings with ogival windows; on each side were low extensions making a symmetrical composition and masking the entrance forecourt. On the eastern entrance front the wings project boldly in canted bays, imitating the towers.

Kent's lay-out of the 29-acre gardens and 44-acre park was much admired, and described by Horace Walpole as 'Kentissime.' Rocque's map of 1737 shows the avenue leading down the hill to the entrance forecourt, part of the existing lay-out shown in Kip's print. The formal gardens beside the house to the north had open grassy areas beyond, leading to the Black Pond, possibly a vestige of Wolsey's garden which is still there today. Here Kent designed a Fishing Temple, now demolished.[8] Kent's highly original plans for a Chinese temple were not carried out, nor probably was his Turkish tent, similar to the one he was later to design for Painshill. To the south was the wilderness with its winding paths and dense planting, and beyond that a bastion wall separated the grounds from the surrounding farm land, and would have given views across the river to the water meadows.

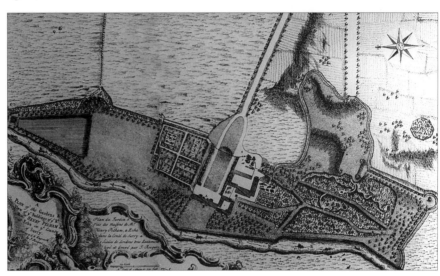

115 Esher Place, detail of Rocque's map of 1737. The house is parallel to the River Mole, with service and stable courtyards on the right.

When Pelham died in 1754 Esher was inherited first by his unmarried daughter Frances, who lived till 1804. Her nephew, Lord Sondes of Lees Court in Kent was the next owner, but immediately decided to sell it. It went to a City stockbroker, John Spicer in 1805 and yet another turn of fortune awaited Wayneflete's Tower. Probably due to the risk of flooding, and perhaps partly to its eccentric appearance, Kent's wings were demolished and only the tower remained as an eye-catcher from the new house – the idea which Kent had first proposed to Pelham. The Belvedere on the hill was demolished and sold for scrap and a new house built on the site.

John Spicer's Esher Place

Spicer chose Edward Lapidge as his architect, the son of a landscape gardener at Hampton Court and later Surveyor to the County of Surrey. He designed a substantial but plain two-storey house with bowed corners, and a long service wing behind it. The house passed from Spicer to Sir Money Wigram, a ship owner, who does not seem to have appreciated his inheritance. In 1863 and again in 1864 the house was offered for sale by auction. The estate was split into 27 lots, and although the house remained unsold, much of the farmland and small houses in Esher went. In 1864 the same agents enthuse over the 161 acres and 'noble park' only forty minutes by train from central London. The Lapidge house with its Ionic portico had fine views of 'Windsor Castle, Eton College and Hampton Court' and the two drawing rooms 'were elegant and lofty rooms with columns in imitation of the Verde Antique, and statuary marble chimneypieces'. There were the extensive service rooms

116   Esher Place, 1759 print showing the River Mole with a Chinese bridge. The 15th-century Wayneflete's Tower is in the centre of the castellated house. On the hill behind it is the Belvedere, the site of the later house.

required by the early 19th century as well as 'stabling for eight horses … and standing for six carriages'. However, it was being offered in six lots, one of which was the tower with 13 acres of gardens, 'a beautiful freehold property of extreme interest … the residence of Cardinal Wolsey … mantled with ivy, replete with historic associations, and capable of being converted into an excellent residence'. But the sale document also mentions the possibility of laying out a road behind it, therefore opening up the site for the development which was eventually to happen.[9]

In 1893 the main house was again offered for sale by Wigram's executors, valued at £29,000; but it was unsold.[10] It went soon afterwards to Sir Edgar Vincent, Viscount D'Abernon, a diplomat and financier who had made a fortune in Turkey and Egypt. He employed G.T. Robinson and Achille Duchêne to rebuild the house in French Renaissance style. Spicer's house was kept as one wing but masked in red brick with stone dressings to match the main house, completed in 1898. Lutyens was asked to design a sunken garden. Here the D'Abernons entertained in great style, with the Prince of Wales as a frequent visitor. But after the First World War the area was changing, with Esher growing rapidly. In 1930 they gave their house to the Shaftesbury Society, and the large house with its extensive servants' quarters became home to 180 girls; it has since become a residential college for a trades union and is surrounded by the usual car parks and modern additions. A development company bought much of the land, new roads were laid out and lined with suburban half-timbered houses. Today these provide an unlikely setting for the French-style château on the hill and the ancient tower below, which has been immaculately restored as a private house.

FOOT'S CRAY

FOOT'S CRAY PLACE

This large domed house, demolished in 1949, was one of a group of 18th-century houses based on Palladio's Villa Rotonda near Vicenza. Most of them were built in the heyday of the Palladian movement but Foot's Cray was not built till 1754, a generation after the others. The estate was about two miles south of Bexley in Kent and had belonged to Sir Francis Walsingham. There was a substantial 16th-century house built on low ground close to the River Cray. Like many houses reasonably close to London it had changed hands several times after Walsingham sold it in the late 16th century.

In 1752 George Smith sold the estate to Bourchier Cleeve (1715-60) a pewterer in the City who lived in Cornhill.[1] He was a successful businessman and a writer on finance and taxation, well enough off to buy more land in the Limpsfield area as well as his Foot's Cray estate. He rebuilt the house on a new site *c.*1754 at a cost of about £8,000. His architect was

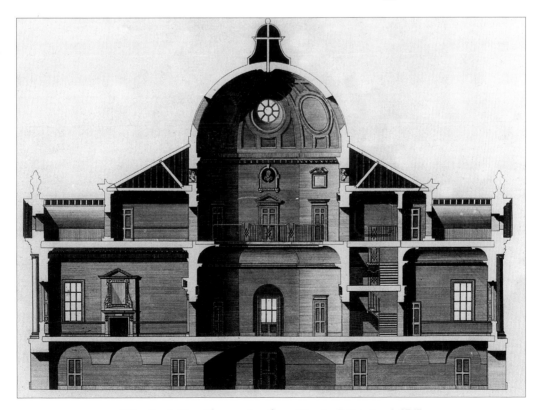

117   Foot's Cray Place, section from *Vitruvius Britannicus*, 4, 1767.

probably Isaac Ware (the architect also of Wrotham Park) although there are no surviving drawings or accounts to prove this. Ware was one of the younger generation of architects in the circle of Lord Burlington, and in 1738 had published a translation of Palladio's *Quattro Libri dell'Architettura*; this could be the clue to Cleeve's choice of architect. The site of the new house was on rising ground so a design based on the Villa Rotonda would be appropriate, giving fine views all round. The house was built of stone and had four massive Ionic porticoes, although like Mereworth Castle only two have steps down to ground level. The semi-basement had the service rooms, the reception rooms were on the *piano nobile* and there was a bedroom floor above. The section in *Vitruvius Britannicus* shows the stone-paved octagonal hall, domed and toplit, with a gallery running round at first-floor level to give access to the fairly low-ceilinged bedrooms.[2] On the main floor a gallery filled the whole of one side, with the portico giving access to the gardens down the second great flight of steps. Perhaps as a critique of Burlington's Chiswick the stairs were much more spacious at Foot's Cray, with good-sized main and secondary staircases to one side of the hall. The interior detailing was good, with pedimented overmantels, eared doorcases and crisp egg and dart mouldings. The unhappiest feature of the house is the placing of the chimneys which appear to clasp the dome, and like the chimneys at Chiswick House are based on a vernacular Veneto type. Pococke described them as the 'four ugly chimneys round the dome'.[3] A canal was laid out in the park, fed from the River Cray.

Cleeve died in his new house in 1760 and his only child, married to Sir George Yonge, inherited in 1765 after the death of her mother. His estates were in Devon and in 1772 they sold Foot's Cray to Benjamin Harenc, a citizen of London who became High Sheriff of Kent in 1777. In 1792 he employed Henry Hakewill to make some alterations and Hakewill was also called back by the next owner, Nicholas Vansittart, 1st Lord Bexley. He was a politician of Dutch origin who had been a not very successful Chancellor of the Exchequer from 1812. The promise of a peerage and a substantial pension persuaded him to resign in 1822, the year he bought Foot's Cray, and he devoted the rest of his life to philanthropic work, especially the Bible Society. He later employed J.W. Hiort on changes to both Foot's Cray and his house in Westminster. His nephew inherited in 1851, and his great-nephew in 1886, when the estate was over 2,000 acres. But the family moved west, buying Denham Place in Buckinghamshire, then a more rural location than near Bexley as well as being a very fine house. The estate was sold to S.J. Waring, head of the long-established furniture firm Waring & Gillow. Some excellent photographs taken by Bedford Lemere in 1905 show the house in his time. It remained in his family until after the Second World War, although they moved out in 1936 and it was requisitioned for naval use 1939-45. In 1946 the Waring family sold it to Kent Education Committee which was planning to open it as a museum. Works were being carried out when a fire broke out on 18 October 1949 and the remains of the house were demolished in 1950. The grounds became Foot's Cray Meadows, a wide open space along the River Cray, still with some fine trees from its days as parkland. The walled kitchen gardens and brick stable block show that there was once a large house here, but all trace of the house itself has gone.

FULHAM

FULHAM PALACE

One of the most ancient properties near central London, Fulham Palace was used by the Bishops of London for more than twelve hundred years and its large grounds still give it the appearance of a country house. The Bishopric of London was not nearly as rich as many of the provincial dioceses, but there were country estates, mainly in Hertfordshire. Waytemore Castle in Bishop's Stortford was little used after the 15th century, and Much Hadham, a timber-framed courtyard house, went out of use after the Civil War. So although Fulham Palace was originally a truly suburban house – one that could be easily reached while the bishop was on business in London – it long ago became his main country residence, although he continued to have a London house until 1919.

118   Fulham Palace, largely rebuilt *c*.1500. View through the arch of the gatehouse into the main courtyard. The great hall with its diaper brickwork is left of the porch.

It is easy today to ignore the River Thames, which is hidden by an embankment and mature trees, but its riverside site was ideal for travel to Westminster. The manor of Fulham belonged to the bishops of London from 704, and a moat enclosed 37 acres, making it the largest domestic moated site in England. By the 13th century there seems to have been a timber-framed courtyard house on a slightly different site to the present palace. Many bishops were upgrading their houses in the early Tudor period and Fulham Palace was no exception. Although the accepted date for the present entrance courtyard was thought to be *c*.1500, recent dendrochronology suggests that the hall was built *c*.1480, in the time of Bishop Kempe (1450-89), who ordered shingles for the roof; the great oak doors to the courtyard are of the same date. The diaper brickwork, still visible in parts of the courtyard, was probably a refacing of earlier work by Bishop Savage (1496-1501) or Bishop Fitzjames (1506-22). In spite of many alterations in later centuries, this courtyard with its well still suggests an early Tudor building on a domestic scale. The hall across the courtyard, entered through a brick porch, is also modest in size and no longer medieval in appearance: the roof timbers are hidden by a later ceiling, and the woodwork was brought in from other buildings. The south range had a passage through it towards the river, which was probably the main entrance for the bishop and his visitors. There were service rooms and lodgings in the ranges round this courtyard; today some have early interior fittings possibly moved from other parts of the palace. Lysons observed the arms of Bishop Fitzjames on the south range, although they are now too weathered to be legible; the bishop also placed them in the hall and on a garden arch, so he may have made major alterations which have been obscured by later changes.[1]

Dial Court lay beyond the hall. The higher status rooms on its east and north sides were all demolished over the 18th century, but we know from the Parliamentary Survey of 1647 and various 18th-century plans that the state and private rooms were in this part of the palace, as were the two long galleries added in the 16th century.[2] The chapel, obviously an essential part of a bishop's residence, has been on four different sites, but in the 16th century extended eastwards from Dial Court. Parallel to it was a loggia with 'a great gallery matted and wainscotted' above and another gallery at right angles to it, leading to the bishop's lodgings: both would have overlooked the private gardens. The *Survey* shows that the gardens within the moat were extensive, with a walled kitchen garden near the service rooms, a walled orchard, plum garden, rose garden and 'great garden'. Also within the moat were various ponds as well as the 17-acre Warren, originally for rabbits but later arranged as a wilderness garden with trees, shrubs and winding paths. And there were in addition all the appurtenances of a country house: stables, coach houses, a brewhouse and bakehouse, as well as a laundry, cottage, dovecot and barns.

During the Civil War Bishop Juxon retired to Fulham (another function of these suburban houses was as a place of retreat from awkward situations), but was expelled in 1647 and the manor and estate were bought for £7,617 by Colonel Edmund Harvey, a supporter of Cromwell and a Commissioner of the Navy. He bought additional land and built a timber-framed barn west of the palace, which survived until bomb damage in the Second World War. At the Restoration the palace was reclaimed by the church, but the Fire of London in 1666 further impoverished the diocese, and it was only with Bishop Compton (1675–1713) that improvements were made, and then to the gardens rather than the house.

Henry Compton, brought up at Compton Wynyates in Warwickshire, was a soldier before turning to the church; he was also a loyal supporter of the princesses Mary and Anne, whom he instructed in the Anglican faith. From 1686-88 he was suspended by James II and retired to Fulham, but was rather more in favour under William III, and remained as Bishop of London until his death. His main passion was botany, where 'he joined to his taste for gardens, a real and scientific knowledge of plants'.[3] As well as his London diocese, Compton was also responsible for the church in all the American colonies, and sent a botanically minded chaplain, the Rev. John Banister, to the West Indies and then to Virginia.[4] Examples of the new trees and plants being discovered there were regularly sent back to Fulham, and were lovingly tended in Compton's gardens and glass houses, where they could be examined by other plant enthusiasts. He shared his taste for 'exotics' with Queen Mary, and employed George London as his gardener, till he moved in 1689 to Hampton Court to tend the queen's collection of imported plants, as well as becoming a leading garden designer and nurseryman. Of the thousand or so plants established at Fulham Palace by Compton, only two trees possibly survive today, but many other plants were sent to the Botanic Garden at Oxford when he died.[5]

Compton concentrated his efforts on the gardens, and by his death the palace had become seriously dilapidated. Major changes took place over the 18th and 19th centuries, which form the basis of the building we see today. Bishop Robinson (1714-23) requested permission to demolish the early state rooms and the extensive kitchen offices, claiming the palace was 'old

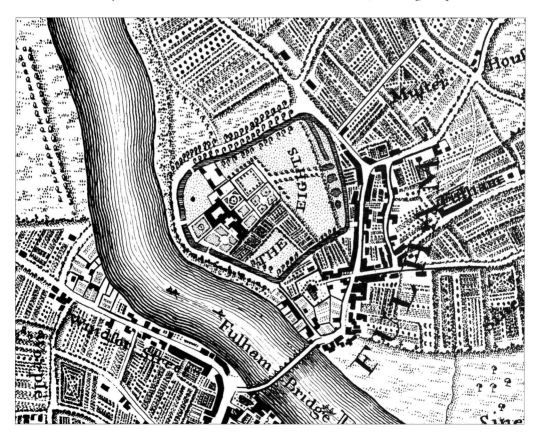

119 Fulham Palace. Rocque's 1745 map shows the moat enclosing the 37-acre grounds. The house was surveyed just before the large wing to the south was demolished by Bishop Sherlock.

and ruinous … and much too large for the revenues of the bishopric'.[6] Vanbrugh was among the commissioners asked to report on the palace before permission was granted to demolish some of the state rooms, the bakehouse and the pastry house. Even after that, the palace still consisted of some 50-60 rooms. Bishop Sherlock (1748-61) demolished the solar or winter parlour to the north of the hall, and replaced it with a Palladian dining room with delicate Rococo plasterwork on the ceiling.[7] (This room later became the kitchen, and is currently being restored to its appearance in Sherlock's time.) He also inserted a coved ceiling into the hall and used it as his drawing room.

Stiff Leadbetter made major and interesting changes to the palace, although very little trace remains of his work. From 1756 he was Surveyor of St Paul's Cathedral, which brought him into contact with the bishop and commissions for other work followed. Bishop Osbaldeston (1762-4) commissioned Leadbetter to provide plans for alterations to the palace, but died before these could be carried out; it was Bishop Terrick (1764-77) for whom Leadbetter built new ranges. These involved the demolition of the earlier chapel, which was used as rubble in the foundations; ironically, the style of the new work was Gothick. Although this work has now been obscured, it was a fine example of the taste of Anglican prelates for the Gothick, similar to the work carried out at the Archbishop's Palace at Bishopthorpe, and at Durham Castle and Bishop Auckland; Leadbetter himself worked on a Gothick interior at Hartlebury Castle for the Bishop of Worcester.

Dial Court became smaller, with a range to the north containing the new chapel, and the south and east ranges having the main reception rooms and bishop's lodgings. There were corner towers, and a canted bay window lit the 48-foot long library on the east front. All were battlemented, and while the main rooms had sash windows, the chapel was distinguished by its lancet windows.[8] Terrick sold London House in Aldersgate at the same time and moved

120 Fulham Palace, 1798 print by J. P. Malcolm. The north side of the palace, with Leadbetter's *c*.1765 castellated south range and Bishop Sherlock's Palladian dining room on the right.

156

to St James's Square; some of the chapel fittings, such as woodwork and stained glass, were removed to Fulham. The gardens were also opened up, with winding walks and shrubs replacing the walled enclosures; the kitchen garden was moved away from the house to the walled garden to the east – making it the only one of the walled gardens to survive.

121 Fulham Palace. Interior of the hall, *c*.1900. The timber of the early Tudor roof is hidden by the 18th-century coved ceiling. The late 17th-century overmantel came from London House in the City, where it had been a reredos.

Bishop Porteous (1787-1809) was a friend of Horace Walpole who often visited him, and 'was delighted with the palace, with the venerable chapel [*sic*] and its painted episcopalities in glass, and the brave hall'.[9] He would also have approved of the portrait collection of bishops and monarchs which Porteous bequeathed to the see, and of the 'Monk's Cell' which he made next to the library. In the gardens he planted a grove of trees, and made 'a retired walk behind, called the Nun's Walk'.[10] However all this Gothick work was swept away by Bishop Howley (1813-28). Just as Leadbetter as Surveyor of St Paul's had been architect to two mid-18th-century bishops, so Howley in 1814 went to his Surveyor, Samuel Pepys Cockerell, who was also a cousin. His brief was to enlarge the reception space and provide more bedrooms, which he did by bringing the east front forward to the level of the corner towers, which thus disappeared. Terrick's library was destroyed, and a range of plain interconnecting reception rooms was built overlooking the east gardens, with bedrooms above. Cockerell's south and east façades are austere to the point of dullness, but he did keep the Gothic windows of Terrick's chapel on the north front, which he turned into his library. (This, named the Porteous Library in honour of the books bequeathed by that bishop, is now the Museum.) He converted the hall into his chapel, even though the altar was on the north wall; demolished the original kitchen south of the hall, and put his new kitchen into Sherlock's dining room.

The only major changes made by his successors were the reinstatement of the hall and the building of a new chapel. These were carried out by Bishop Tait (1856-68), using William Butterfield as his architect. The hall was restored, with large mullion and transom windows replacing the 18th-century sashes; the screen was reinstated using late 17th-century woodwork brought in from Doctors' Commons in the City; this matches the reredos moved previously from Aldersgate, which became an overmantel. Butterfield also rebuilt the well in the courtyard as a fountain, and added a lodge with pretty bargeboards and hoodmoulds by the bridge over the moat, and new gate piers. But his great love was ecclesiastical architecture, and the most important part of his commission was to build a chapel which fulfilled the High Church aspirations of mid-19th-century churchmen. It would be more seemly to separate it from the everyday life of the palace, so it was built near the site of the old kitchen and connected to the hall by a passage; otherwise it was a free-standing building. Bishop Tait bore the cost of £1,849 himself, and if the exterior with its diaper brickwork is fairly plain, the interior was almost as rich as Butterfield's other churches: the walls were of polychrome brickwork, the reredos was a mosaic of the Adoration by Salviati, and the stained glass was by Clayton & Bell. The black and white marble floor came from the hall, and is still in situ, but bomb damage in the Second World War destroyed the glass, and the reredos was dismantled; part of it is now at the west end. In 1939 the firm of Seely & Paget had been appointed as surveyors, and it was Lord Mottistone, one of the partners, who carried out the post-war restoration. Under Bishop Wand (1945-55) the High Victorian style of the interior was toned down, the polychrome interior covered with murals of the life of Christ and the apostles by Brian Thomas, and new stained glass was designed by Ninian Comper.

The village of Fulham was becoming a residential suburb by the late 19th century, and public open space was urgently required. Some of the land outside the moat was given up to the Fulham District Board of Works in 1884 and 1889, making the 12-acre Bishop's Park along the Thames. A narrow strip of land between the palace and the river was sold in 1894, destroying the last remains of the bishop's landing stage but providing land for the LCC to embank this section and lay out a tree-lined walk, replacing the earlier footpath, from Putney Bridge and All Saints church to the new park.

The cost of maintaining this extensive palace as well as the town house was becoming unrealistic by the early 20th century, and in 1919 the house in St James's Square was let, making Fulham Palace for the first time in its history the only residence of the bishop.

Soon further economies were required, and Bishop Winnington-Ingram (1901-39) chose the cheapest option in dealing with the moat: in 1920 it was let for the sum of £1,500 for use as a rubbish tip, in spite of local protests and questions in Parliament. Its form can still be traced in many parts of the grounds, but only a very short section by the bridge at the entrance to the palace still has water in it, and the sluice connecting the moat to the Thames became obsolete.

By 1956 it was recognised that the modest lifestyle of a modern bishop meant changes had to be made, so apartments for Bishop Campbell (1956-61) were made in the east front. His chaplain was given a flat in the south range, and an 18th-century staircase was brought from Peckham House to provide access to it. A fine chimneypiece from Appuldurcombe House in the Isle of Wight replaced a bomb-damaged one in the drawing room.[11] Part of the entrance courtyard was let as offices, and its future seemed secure. But Campbell's successor, Bishop Stopford (1963-73) still found the palace large and inconvenient, and campaigned for a central London residence. This was finally agreed, and since 1973 the palace has been leased to the LB of Hammersmith & Fulham.[12] The Fulham Palace Trust has set up the Museum in the north-west corner, and it is hoped that the current lottery application will allow restoration of Bishop Sherlock's room, and of other parts of the palace and grounds.

HACKNEY

*B*ALMS

Balms or Baumes was one of a group of brick houses built in Anglo-Netherlandish style in the early 17th century. The City merchant who built it, Sir George Whitmore, had a house in Lombard Street and was Lord Mayor in 1631-2. Had he perhaps travelled in the Netherlands and brought back ideas from there? He was related to Lord Craven, whose Berkshire hunting lodge, Ashdown House, has some similarities with Balms. Whitmore replaced an earlier house on the site, which took its name from the Bamme family of goldsmiths who had owned it in the 14th century. His father had rented Balms, as did Sir George before buying it in 1634; this probably prompted the rebuilding.[1]

A print of 1707 shows the house set in a walled enclosure, bounded on two sides by canals, which may be the remains of an earlier moat. A gatehouse leads to the house which is set back behind two walled forecourts, with the pleasure gardens to one side of the house. There are kitchen gardens, a large orchard, a stable block and farm buildings; cows and horses graze in the fields. It is the picture of a pleasant and productive little estate, with London only a short ride away. The house was compact, its most striking feature being the exaggeratedly high hipped roof with two storeys of dormer windows. There may have been a balustraded roof platform between the high brick chimneys, which would have given fine

122　Hackney, Balms. Watercolour by Toussaint, *c.*1852, shows the 1630s house just before demolition.

159

views to the spires of the City and over the formal gardens which surrounded the house. Its Dutch features included the deep eaves cornice and the paired pilasters which punctuated the five bays of the entrance front, and were more widely spaced on the corners. The garden front had only single corner pilasters, and here the original mullion and transom windows had not been replaced with sashes. The house had a semi-basement and door surround of rusticated stonework, but was otherwise brick with a tiled roof.[2]

No plan is known, but a group of watercolours made just before the house was demolished in 1852 give us some idea of the interior, which combined traditional features with some influence of the style of Inigo Jones. Whitmore, a Royalist, entertained Charles I at Balms in 1641, so we can assume he was aware of Jones's style even if he chose to introduce only some elements into his own house. There was a traditional hall and screens passage, but the woodwork and ceiling compartments were in Jones's style. Detailed drawings record the plasterwork ceilings of two other rooms, one of them probably the great chamber upstairs; both have deep compartments with foliage scrolls on the beams, with none of the sinuous geometry of Jacobean plasterwork. The main staircase was of wood, rising round an open well, with a balustrade of heavy pierced woodwork, similar to the stairs at Cromwell House, Highgate.[3]

Whitmore died at Balms in 1654, leaving the house to his widow. In 1687 his son sold it to Richard de Beauvoir. By the mid-18th century the house was too close to London to be a suburban retreat and it was rented by Meyer Schomberg, a German doctor who set up a lunatic asylum; this continued till the mid-19th century. By that time it was run very badly, and when questions were asked about the regime it was closed down and the house demolished. The land could more profitably be built on, and the de Beauvoir estate was developed in the grounds. But its unusual appearance, combined with a growing interest in old buildings, meant that an artist recorded it, giving us detailed views of three sides of the house and showing how little it had changed since it was built. The area was badly bombed in the Second World War, and the site of Balms is now covered by post-war housing.

BROOKE HOUSE

There are very few houses in the London area which date back to the late 15th century, so the loss of Brooke House on Upper Clapton Road, demolished after serious bomb damage in 1940, is all the sadder. Fortunately it was carefully recorded in its damaged state, and the results published in a *Survey of London* monograph.[1] The house was on slightly raised ground with Hackney Brook marking the boundary of the gardens to west and south. In 1476 it was bought and rebuilt by William Worsley, who became Dean of St Paul's in 1479. It was a timber-framed courtyard house, with a brick porch and hall on the east side close to the road. The hall was a two-storey room with a central hearth and an open timber roof, but it was destroyed in the 18th century. Most houses had a parlour off the dais end of the hall; instead Worsley's had a two-storey chapel with a floor of Purbeck marble. Wall paintings of ecclesiastics were discovered during the demolition, one of which was possibly a portrait of Worsley. The kitchen was in the north range, with further service buildings loosely scattered to the north. Worsley gave up the house after twenty years, selling it to a London goldsmith, Sir Reginald Bray. The house changed hands constantly after his death, with Thomas Cromwell being the next owner to leave his mark on the house.

Cromwell made major alterations although he only had the house about a year. In the courtyard brick walls were carried up to the jettied upper floor, enlarging the ground-floor rooms. He added to the service rooms, making a second courtyard to the north with a carriage entrance. In 1535 the house became the property of the Crown, and was used by Henry VIII for his reconciliation with Princess Mary. Edward VI granted the house to Lord Herbert in 1547 and a surviving document describes it at this time as having, as well as the usual extensive service rooms, 'A Fayre Hall and a parlor … many Fayre chambers a Faire long Galerye a proper Chapell and a Closet coming out of the great Chamber over the Chapell a proper lybrarye to lay bokes in many other proper Roomes within the same Place.'[2]

The next significant owner was Henry Cary, Lord Hunsdon, a leading courtier and a cousin of Elizabeth I. He bought it for £1,550 from the Carew family, and spent large sums on the house and gardens. He embellished the long gallery which overlooked the gardens to the west, where he installed Serlian panelling and a fine plaster ceiling with his arms surrounded by the Garter. Although the gallery was later partitioned into bedrooms and a corridor, much of it survived and was recorded before demolition. However he lived extravagantly and had financial problems so in 1583 he sold it to a City merchant, Sir Rowland Hayward. (This house changed hands frequently between City and aristocratic families, suggesting that their requirements were similar.)

The gardens of Brooke House were celebrated, and visited by both Samuel Pepys and John Evelyn. In 1666 Pepys records 'the house not so good, nor the prospect good at all – but the gardens are excellent; and here I first saw oranges grow … Here were also great variety of other exotique plants, and several labarinths [sic] and a pretty aviary.'[3] The creator of these gardens was Fulke Greville, 1st Lord Brooke, who bought the house with 270 acres in 1609. He already had a London house and had recently acquired Warwick Castle, where

123 Hackney, Brooke House, *c.* 1750 print after Chatelain. The timber-framed house on Upper Clapton Road had a mid-17th-century brick addition on the S-E corner, seen on the left.

he also made famous gardens. Brooke House was inherited by his nephew who added 'The Cottage', a projecting wing at the S-E corner of the house, built of brick and presumably providing a set of apartments in a more fashionable style, with a pergola on the first floor from which to look at the gardens. (This was demolished for road widening in 1909.) The widowed Lady Brooke stayed on in Hackney, so Pepys's visit is a good example of the accessibility of some of these houses and gardens to curious Londoners. After her death in 1676 the house was let and split into tenements, becoming increasingly shabby. In 1759 William Clarke took a 99-year lease in order to establish a lunatic asylum. He repaired the courtyards and rebuilt the east wing for the superintendent to live in, thereby destroying the great hall. From the road the house now appeared to be a conventional nine-bay Georgian building with a simple pediment. This change of use probably saved the house but did entail many changes over the years, such as the partitioning of the long gallery, the addition of a passage round the courtyard, and many small additions.

Although the Brookes sold the house in 1820 it remained an asylum till 1940, when the north courtyard was destroyed by a bomb; and there was further bomb damage in 1944. At this stage it was bought by the LCC along with 5½ acres, with the intention of building houses on the land and restoring the house for some sort of community use; but the cost was prohibitive, and it was demolished in 1954-5. During demolition the house was thoroughly investigated and recorded; some excavation of the site followed, and the result was the definitive history of the building in the *Survey*.

SUTTON HOUSE

Sutton House belongs to the National Trust, but has a very different recent history to great houses owned by the Trust such as Osterley or Ham. A modest Tudor house in a poor area with inner-city problems, it was not open to the public and was let as offices. It was local pressure when it was under threat which alerted the Trust to its importance and led to its recent renaissance.

The builder Ralph Sadleir (1507-87) was typical of the men who were rising under the Tudors: clever, well-educated, useful servants to the Crown. His father was well connected enough to arrange for his son to join the household of Thomas Cromwell; he rose to become his private secretary and agent, and married a young widow also in his household. By 1535 he had joined the King's service, being made a Gentleman of the Privy Chamber. Henry VIII entrusted him with some business relating to the Dissolution and with delicate negotiations in Scotland; he was clearly effective and trustworthy. His father had a house in Hackney, Thomas Cromwell also had property there and Ralph decided to build himself a new house nearby. In the 16th century Hackney was a fashionable parish, only a mile or so north of the City. There were several large houses and gardens (all of which have gone) most of which were timber-framed. Sadleir's house was built *c.*1535 but of brick – a material unusual enough for it to be called 'the bryk place'. His grounds extended to Hackney Brook, and there was a service range with stables and a brewhouse behind the main house. This was well-planned but not large, an early example of the H-plan house which was to become usual by the end of the century. The north front has the hall in the centre with slightly projecting wings, but the site was small and the longer wings behind the house are set a slight angle to the hall. The screens passage on the east side led to the service wing, with the kitchen at the back. Unusually the room off the screens passage appears not to have been the buttery or pantry, as a stone Tudor chimneypiece and traces of painted decoration were discovered behind panelling. Fine linenfold panelling and an original stone chimneypiece survive in a parlour on the other side of the hall. The main staircase in the west range led to the best rooms on the first floor. In a neat piece of planning the hall is only one storey high, allowing the great chamber to be directly above it, an idea which is developed in some later houses. The great chamber still has oak panelling, partly dating from Sadleir's time, and his stone chimneypiece with a four-centred arch. The upper part of the house had four gables (since removed) and provided rooms for his household and growing family.

We do not see much of Sadleir's house today, as it has changed hands many times and been used for many purposes. Sadleir did not keep it long, being rewarded by the king with the estate of Standon in Hertfordshire about ten years later.[1] This was easily reached by the main road to Cambridge, so in 1550 he sold Sutton House to John Machell, a successful City wool merchant and alderman.[2] He died in 1558 just before he would have become Lord Mayor, leaving the house to his son John who remained there till around 1605. It was at this time that Sir Thomas Sutton, who set up the Sutton Foundation in the Charterhouse, owned the adjoining property and whose name erroneously became attached to this house.[3] The house passed to John Milward, a silk merchant in the City, who added some flamboyant decoration. The doors on the main staircase were given painted strapwork overdoors, and the panelling in the ground-floor parlour was painted cream, red and green. But he went bankrupt before the Civil War, and in 1670 the house became a school, as did many other houses in Hackney.

124 Hackney, Sutton House. Entrance front, showing the division of the 16th-century house into two houses in the 18th century. There is some Tudor diaper brickwork on the right.

125 Hackney, Sutton House. Interior of the first-floor great chamber, with a portrait of Sir Ralph Sadleir, who built it *c.*1535.

Today the house is largely 18th-century in appearance with its brick parapet and sash windows, only some traces of diaper brickwork pointing to its Tudor origins. The gables with their bargeboards were cut back and the fenestration completely altered.[4] The wide windows of the hall and great chamber were replaced by evenly spaced sashes; only one original window survives in the courtyard. Panelling replaced some of the earlier wall-coverings and fireplaces were adapted for burning coal; a wrought-iron gate with an overthrow separated the house from the road. These major changes were probably due to a local man, Daniel Stacey, who took a lease on the property in 1700. By this time Hackney was respectable rather than fashionable, and he probably updated it to live there all the time. After his death in 1719 the house reverted to school use, and by *c.*1750 it had become two separate houses, with an additional front door cut into the entrance front and part of the hall becoming an entrance passage. However the two staircases and wings made subdivision comparatively simple, and much of the structure was left in place. The west wing became Picton House and the east wing was known as Ivy House – old photographs show that so many of these houses were covered in ivy a century ago. The cement render on Ivy House, with its quoins and heavy window surrounds, was probably added *c.*1870, further disguising the original appearance of the house.

By the late 19th century Hackney had become a poor and overcrowded parish, close to the polluted industrial areas of the River Lea. Sutton House was saved by the rector of Hackney, the well-connected Arthur Lawley, a royal chaplain and later Lord Wenlock. In 1890 he bought both houses and turned them into St John's Institute, a place where working men could relax and be educated. But preservation of the old house was not one of his priorities; interiors were whitewashed and many of the old outbuildings and the garden were destroyed to clear a site for a school. After further fundraising in 1900 things improved: the Wenlock Barn, a large hall open to a timber roof, was built behind the house for meetings and events. SPAB principles were followed in later works in the house, where additions were made by Lionel Crane, son of Walter.

By 1936 the Institute wanted to move and the buildings were offered for sale for £2,500. The LB of Hackney was not interested but the involvement of men such as Lord Esher, chairman of SPAB, meant that its fate became a matter of public concern, and in 1938 the National Trust bought it.[5] With war imminent there was no obvious use for the house and it was let as offices until 1982, by which time it was virtually unknown to architectural historians and Londoners. When the tenants left the Trust failed to find a replacement, squatters took over and the house deteriorated rapidly. Burglars broke in and removed fittings, such as the carved wood panels in the overmantel of the great chamber and the linenfold panelling. The vigilance of local people, concerned at the damage to the house, led to these items being recovered from a local architectural salvage firm. The Trust then proposed dividing the house into flats, but the installing of fire escapes and modern plumbing would have been very disruptive, and there was strong local feeling against it. The Sutton House Society was set up in 1987, local opinion mobilised and research carried out, with the result that the Trust decided to open the house to the public. Unlike their country houses there was to be community use and opening for most of the year. A thorough research programme was carried out with English Heritage and the house was gradually restored between 1990-3 by Julian Harrap Architects. It is now a much-used and much-loved part of the community and a good example of how the preservation of a key building in an urban area can help regeneration.

HAMMERSMITH

BRANDENBURG HOUSE

Sir Nicholas Crisp (1598-1665) rebuilt *c.*1625 the riverside house in Hammersmith which he inherited from his mother. Like many City merchants he was quite rich enough to do so: he had a house in Bread Street, was an MP, farmer of the Customs and a leading member of the Guinea Company, which had a monopoly of the West Africa-Caribbean slave trade. It was probably a compact triple-pile house, but we know very little about it and have to rely on Bowack's 1705 description of it, 'very lofty, regular and magnificent, after the modern manner, built with brick, cornered with stone and has a handsome cupola at the top … The whole house in building, and the gardens, canals etc in making, is said to have cost near £25,000.'[1] Crisp as a royalist suffered during the Civil War; he sold his London house to raise troops for the King, had his Hammersmith house taken over by General Fairfax as his headquarters, and went briefly into exile. By 1650 he was back in Hammersmith, and in 1660 was sent to Breda as a representative of the City to request the return of Charles II. When he died his heart was embalmed and placed in an urn topped by a fine bronze bust of Charles I by Le Sueur, in the chapel of ease which he had paid for in Hammersmith.

126   Hammersmith, Brandenburg House. River front, from *Vitruvius Britannicus*, 4, 1767.

127 Hammersmith, Brandenburg House. Print from Neale, 1822, showing the Thames-side theatre and the river front of the house.

Crisp's grandson sold the house to Prince Rupert who passed it on to his mistress, the actress Margaret Hughes. But the most important later owner was George Bubb Dodington, 1st Lord Melcombe (1691-1762), an ambitious and extravagant courtier, diplomat and politician. He had a London house in Pall Mall, inherited Vanbrugh's Eastbury in Dorset, and in 1748 bought Crisp's house, renaming it La Trappe – an ironic reference to the noisy parties he held there. Roger Morris, who also worked on Eastbury and his London house, was asked to remodel it, and plans and elevations were later published.[2] He disguised his changes to the fenestration by covering the brickwork with stucco, made a tetrastyle entrance hall, with an alcove bedroom and two closets off it; the main and secondary staircases were top-lit in the centre of the house. On the *piano nobile* were two apartments flanking a saloon, which was decorated by Cipriani. A five-bay gallery with Venetian windows at each end was completed after Morris's death in 1749 by the Italian designer Servandoni, who worked mainly as a theatrical designer but occasionally as an architect. He made it into a splendid and richly decorated room with an *all'antica* coffered ceiling and an inlaid marble floor. The windows were framed with Ionic pilasters and antique sculpture was placed in the bays, their pedestals carefully lined up with the dado rail. The most important piece was a figure of Ceres, framed in the central Venetian window and flanked by columns of Sicilian jasper.[3] Melcombe died at La Trappe and was commemorated by his heir with a column in the grounds.[4]

Flamboyant and *outré* owners made up the last phase of this historic house. In 1792 the Margrave of Brandenburg-Anspach bought the house for £8,500, having sold his German principality to a cousin in order to escape the approaching wars. He had recently married his mistress – only days after she was widowed – the beautiful if notorious Elizabeth Berkeley, Lady Craven. They lived lavishly with 30 liveried servants and the Margrave kept a stud of 60 horses. In spite of her husband's royal and German connections the Margravine was never received at court and instead devoted herself to theatricals in Hammersmith. She built a little theatre disguised as a ruined Gothic castle on the banks of the Thames, and connected to the house by a 150 ft long conservatory. It was described as 'one of the most elegant and convenient private theatres ever built in this kingdom'.[5] Her husband died at their Berkshire estate in 1806, and she eventually went to live in Naples; the contents of the house were gradually sold.[6]

Her son, Keppel Craven, was Vice-Chamberlain to Queen Caroline of Brunswick and in 1820 suggested that she rent his mother's house during her 'trial' in the House of Lords. The year of her tenure of Brandenburg House was a tumultuous one, with crowds of her supporters besieging the house. It was to Hammersmith that she retreated after being refused admission to Westminster Abbey for George IV's coronation on 19 July 1821.

She was already ill, and died there on 7 August 1821. Her funeral procession left from the house with a huge crowd following the bier, which was augmented as it crossed London for Harwich and her eventual burial in Brunswick. Queen Caroline was the last tenant of the house: her belongings were taken to London to be auctioned in February 1822, and in May the house was demolished and sold for scrap. Today there is no trace at all of the house and its grounds; only the name of the post-war Queen Caroline Estate recalls its last and most controversial inhabitant.

HAMPSTEAD

KENWOOD HOUSE

Kenwood is one of the best known houses round London and famous for its Robert Adam transformation in the 1760s, but its later history and additions are also interesting and important. Its position was and is still spectacular, on a ridge of high sandy ground between the hill-top villages of Hampstead and Highgate, protected to the north by Cane Wood and facing south with views down to the City. The house overlooks a picturesque lake fed by the springs along the ridge, so it also had a supply of pure water.

The land had belonged to the Priory of Holy Trinity, Aldgate, before the Reformation but there was no house on the site till *c.*1616 when John Bill (1570-1630) bought about 460 acres of land, making it one of the largest estates near London. Bill was a successful stationer who was made King's Printer. He lived and worked in the City, so this was a retreat for his family to enjoy. It is a rare example of a new house on a new site, but we know very little about it. His son, also John Bill, inherited it and in 1664 it was rated at 24 hearths, making it one of the largest houses in the area.[1] His son Charles Bill sold the house and a reduced estate in 1690 and it was rebuilt soon afterwards by William Brydges, Surveyor-General of the Ordnance. His house, smaller than that we see today, nevertheless remains encased in the

128   Hampstead, Kenwood House, garden front. Robert Adam altered the house for Lord Mansfield in 1764. He added the low wing on the right to match the existing orangery on the left.

later alterations. The 2nd and 3rd Dukes of Argyll were owners in the early 18th century: John, 2nd Duke of Argyll owned it from 1712-15, then built Sudbrook in Petersham. He sold out to his brother and brother-in-law, the 2nd Earl of Bute. The house was let until 1746, when John Stuart, 3rd Earl of Bute took over his father's half-share and bought out the 3rd Duke of Argyll (who lived at Whitton). Bute had large Scottish estates but was tied to London by his position at the court of Frederick, Prince of Wales, so a house nearby was ideal for his family and allowed him to indulge his passion for gardening. He probably built the orangery on the west side of the house for his exotics.[2]

In 1754 Bute sold the house to a fellow Scot, William Murray, later 1st Earl of Mansfield (1705-93). He was a younger son of Lord Stormont of Scone Palace in Perthshire and was a brilliant lawyer, a judge and eventually Lord Chief Justice. He and his wife lived in Bloomsbury, and a house near London would have been an advantage socially and as a place to relax. Choosing fellow Scots as his architects, he invited Robert and James Adam to alter and enlarge Kenwood in 1764. This proved to be one of their most successful commissions, perhaps because they were given a comparatively free hand. Mansfield was a busy man and does not seem to have been over-concerned with the details of the work. They maximised the publicity they could get from a job near London for a well-known figure by illustrating plans, interiors and details in their publication.[3]

The house is approached from the north, but in the 18th century Hampstead Lane was close to the house with just a forecourt between the house and the road. The seven-bay north front of the old brick house was of two storeys with attics, with the kitchens and service wing on the west side – the opposite side to their later position. There is still a mid-18th-century plunge bath, marble-lined, close to the present service buildings. The south front had a series of medium-sized family rooms overlooking the view. The main reception room was the north-facing saloon on the first floor, perversely overlooking the road not the view. The Mansfields wanted a new and more imposing reception room on the ground floor, an impressive entrance front and the updating of some interiors. Robert Adam provided all this brilliantly: he matched the existing five-bay orangery with the library,

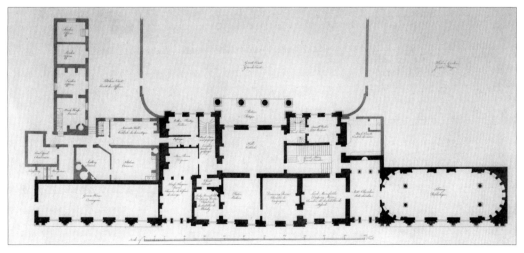

129 Hampstead, Kenwood House. Plan by Robert Adam, showing the orangery with service rooms behind on the left, and the new library on the right.

which doubled as a splendid reception room. A new staircase led to the revamped saloon, and the ground-floor rooms were given new chimneypieces and cornices. Externally an enriched Ionic portico was added to the recessed north front, and the whole house was raised a storey to provide more bedrooms, as by this time the childless Mansfields had two young nieces living with them. All these alterations meant a patchwork of new and old brickwork which was disguised by a stucco finish. On the south front this was given up-to-date neo-classical decoration in Liardet's cement, made by a company which the Adam brothers had bought up.

The route through the house began with the old entrance hall, given an Adam ceiling and new chimneypiece. It doubled as a dining room, so Adam designed a set of furniture for this which he illustrated in his book. The staircase hall opened into a new ante-room which made a link between the old house and the magnificent library. This, with its apsed ends screened by Corinthian columns, its coloured and decorated ceiling, sumptuous mirrors and furniture, has become the epitome of the Adam style. Its three great windows which overlook the Claudian landscape have huge pier glasses between them which reflect the

130 Hampstead, Kenwood House. Interior of Robert Adam's library with its apsed end and screen of columns.

mirrored alcoves opposite with their settees made by William France.[4] These flank the marble chimneypiece over which hung a portrait of Mansfield in his peer's robes.[5] The plasterwork of the ceiling was done by Joseph Rose and paintings by Zucchi inserted, but the present colouring is a fairly crude version of Adam's 'light tints [which] created a harmony between the ceiling and the side walls'.[6]

Mansfield died at Kenwood in 1793 and was succeeded by his nephew, David Murray, who became the 2nd Earl of Mansfield and also inherited Scone Palace. He intended to use Kenwood as his main house and immediately began making changes, consulting Humphry Repton about landscape designs and Robert Nasmith about architectural changes. But Nasmith soon died and was replaced by George Saunders, who edged Repton out. His changes were carried out 1793-6, and are often downplayed in comparison with Adam's work, but actually form an interesting contrast as well as demonstrating the changes in social life which were taking place. The house still lacked a series of large reception rooms which were a requirement by the end of the 18th century, so a large dining room and music room were added in wings projecting from the entrance front. Saunders was severely rational in his designs and did not attempt to relate them to the Adam front; they are of white brick not stucco; and of two storeys not three. The end of each wing has a Venetian window in a depressed arch, otherwise they are completely plain. Internally they are plain high-ceilinged rectangular rooms, a contrast to the highly decorated Adam interiors, and they rely for their effect today on the superb paintings which fill them. The music room was linked with the existing house through a lobby with an elegant screen of Ionic columns, the dining room with a lobby which led to the new service passage. The service wing was unsightly and old-fashioned, so Saunders moved the kitchens from west to east, placing them in a sunken area beyond and behind the Adam library. He designed a most attractive group of plum-coloured brick buildings, the three-storey centre pavilion topped with a weathervane, the two-storey wings set at an angle with a Tuscan colonnade filling the triangular space. In 1796 the 3rd Earl inherited as a young man, and later made further changes at Kenwood, following on from his father's alterations. He employed William Atkinson, who was mainly restoring the fabric and overseeing redecoration, unlike his work at Twyford Abbey and Titsey Place.

The 1st Earl of Mansfield had increased the size of the estate to 232 acres, and he commissioned some features of the present landscape. The view from the new library was obviously of prime importance, and the views S-W towards the City were less obscured by trees than today. The lake was made for him with the sham bridge at the eastern end as an eye-catcher. When Repton was asked by the 2nd Earl to rethink the grounds several major changes were made, though Saunders' critical comments about Repton imply a spirit of unfriendly competition and Repton's plans were superseded.[7] Repton in his 'Red Book' suggested making a new drive through the grounds from the S-E, so the south front would be seen as one approached.[8] This was not done and instead Hampstead Lane was moved north, making the entrance front more secluded and allowing a winding approach from the N-W. Following this a flower garden was laid out west of the house, linked by a verandah with the music room. The head gardener had a new house designed by Saunders just beyond the kitchens, conveniently close to the new walled garden; new stables were built close to the new line of the road; and Saunders designed cottages, a dairy and a model farm west of the house, partly hidden in trees. This group of buildings still stands although rather neglected, and is an intriguing example of the scientific interest in agriculture as

131   Hampstead, Kenwood House. George Saunders designed a new service wing, which was built in a sunken courtyard on the east side of the house 1793-6.

well as the increasing interest in the provision of picturesque improved housing for estate workers.[9] Lady Mansfield was as interested in the dairy as her husband was in his agricultural improvements, and a spirit of competition existed between them and their neighbours, Lord and Lady Southampton, at Fitzroy Farm.

The Mansfields owned Kenwood until 1922, although it was let. Its large estate bordering Hampstead Heath was clearly a valuable asset, and with public pressure mounting to preserve open space the 4th Earl sold 201 acres (mainly Highgate Ponds and Parliament Hill Fields) to the Metropolitan Board of Works in 1889 to be added to the Heath. Just before the First World War the 6th Earl began to negotiate the sale of the remaining estate for building. This prompted intense public protest and the Kenwood Preservation Council raised enough money to buy the woods opposite the house for the public; they were opened by George V in 1925.[10] In 1922 he decided to sell Kenwood and a sale of the contents took place at which much of the original Adam furniture was dispersed.[11] The house was under threat and had it not been for the philanthropic gesture of Edward Guinness, 1st Earl of Iveagh the house and gardens would probably have disappeared. In 1925 he bought the house and 74 acres and in 1928 the house opened with his collection of furniture and paintings: the Iveagh Bequest. For Iveagh died in 1927, before he could see his collection opened to the public. The house is now administered by English Heritage and over the last 20 years the curators have managed to buy various pieces of Adam furniture, so Iveagh's superb British and Old Master paintings are now displayed in rooms with a few pieces of appropriate furniture.

HAMPTON

BUSHY HOUSE

Bushy Park in Middlesex was a group of three royal deer parks, the Lower, Middle and Upper Parks, which had developed between the late 15th and early 17th centuries. Bushy House, also known as Great Lodge or Bushy Lodge, was originally for the keeper (or ranger, as he came to be known) of the 370-acre Middle Park.[1] The present house stands on the site of an older lodge which is recorded in the Parliamentary Survey after the Civil War when it was described as 'a large dwelling house or lodge with the barns, stables, outbuildings and other appurtenances'.[2] These lodges were early examples of compact houses, similar in type to suburban houses. It was used during the Commonwealth by James Challenor, brother of one of the regicides, who wisely disappeared at the Restoration. The parks were restored to Charles II who appointed General Monck, Duke of Albemarle as Keeper of all three parks with a deputy in each; he was succeeded by Barbara Castlemaine, Duchess of Cleveland. One of the deputies was Edward Proger (1621-1713), appointed in 1663 for life. He was an MP, Groom of the Bedchamber and a friend of the king, who asked him to build a new lodge for royal use. The king seems never to have used it and Proger lived there when not in his Whitehall Palace apartments or on his Suffolk estate.

The architect of the new house was William Samwell, a gentleman architect who produced only a few buildings, but all of interest; he was later to be responsible for the alterations to Ham House. He designed a triple-pile brick house of two storeys with a semi-basement, almost square in plan with seven-bays both on the main fronts and the sides. It had a hipped roof with dormer windows and a balustraded roof platform with a cupola, which would have given views to the Thames and Hampton Court Palace to the south and to Hounslow Heath to the north. Later alterations removed the roof platform and cupola and raised the attics into a full second storey with a brick parapet, as we see today. It was a good example of the type of compact Restoration house which was being built in the country and round London at this time. Proger seems to have paid for the house himself in the expectation that he would be reimbursed by the King, and one of his petitions for payment survives, stating that he had paid about £4,000 for the building – a huge sum at this date, even if it included the new stables, barns, outbuildings and elm avenue. He died aged 92 and was buried in Hampton church.[3]

The association of the Montagu family with Bushy Park began c.1708 when Charles Montagu, made Earl of Halifax in 1714, became ranger (as it was now called) for all three parks, which had been merged into one by the removal of fences. He lived in the Upper Lodge but his nephew George Montagu, also created Earl of Halifax, took over Proger's house after his death and carried out some major rebuilding, including refacing the house and replacing the mullion and transom windows with sashes. His son, George Montagu Dunk, 2nd Earl of Halifax took over as ranger, and it was he who built Hampton Court

173

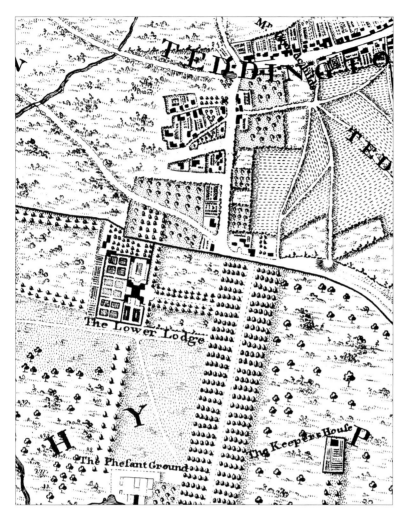

132 Hampton, Bushy House. Rocque's 1745 map shows the house with its four corner pavilions. The formal gardens lie west of the main avenue of Bushy Park.

House nearby for his mistress in 1757. He may also have added the four pavilions, linked to the house by quadrant wings, which enlarged it considerably.[4] His death in 1771 brought to an end the link with the Montagus, for the rangership now reverted to the Crown. George III appointed Lady Anne North, wife of the prime minister as ranger, and they moved in that year. Possibly it was they who altered the roofline and added the attic storey, although the first direct evidence of this is the set of plans drawn up by John Soane for the Office of Works in 1797.[5] These plans show that the original service rooms in the basement had been augmented by the N-E kitchen pavilion and the N-W housekeeper's pavilion; the two pavilions on the south side of the house contained a ballroom and a greenhouse. But the main house still appears to have some of the 17th-century arrangement of rooms. The deep entrance hall has a marble bolection moulded chimneypiece which may be original and the plasterwork ceiling in the small closet in the S-E corner of the ground floor, with its heavy foliage frame enclosing a wreath and cherubs' heads must date from Proger's time. The first floor had two main reception rooms in the centre of the house divided by a corridor, and four corner apartments with closets; two small staircases gave access from basement to attics.

With the death of Lord North's widow in 1797 the house again reverted to the Crown, and George III made his third son, William, Duke of Clarence (1765-1837) ranger of Bushy Park with use of the lodge. This is the best known phase of the history of this house, as he lived there with his mistress, the actress Dorothy Jordan and their many children, seven of whom were born at Bushy.[6] In 1811 their liaison came to an end and in 1818 he married Princess Adelaide of Saxe-Meiningen; their wedding took place in front of Queen Charlotte in Kew Palace. While living with Mrs Jordan he had been short of money, but now that he had made a royal marriage he required more formal rooms and could ask for government funds for improvements. The two service pavilions were considerably expanded and more service rooms were added on the north side of the main house. On the east front the approach to the house was flanked by two new wings with bowed ends; one had service rooms but the other had a large new dining room, even if it was a considerable distance from the kitchen. The two south pavilions became the Duke's library and the Princess's morning room, connected by a long drawing room which was opened up on the south side of the old house.[7] They continued to live at Bushy until William became king in 1830, after which they moved to Buckingham Palace and Windsor; but Queen Adelaide was made ranger in place of her husband and retained the house.[8] So when she was widowed in 1837 she lived partly at Bushy till 1848, then moved for the last few months of her life to Bentley Priory.

In 1865 Queen Victoria offered Bushy to the Duc de Nemours, a member of the French royal family in exile. As a Roman Catholic he required a chapel, which was made out of the morning room in the S-W pavilion. He kept the house even after returning to France in 1871, in case he had to go into exile again. In 1897 it reverted to Queen Victoria who did not want it; Hampton Court was no longer in use as a royal palace, and both the palace and its various parks were open to the public. The Commissioners of Woods and Forests arranged

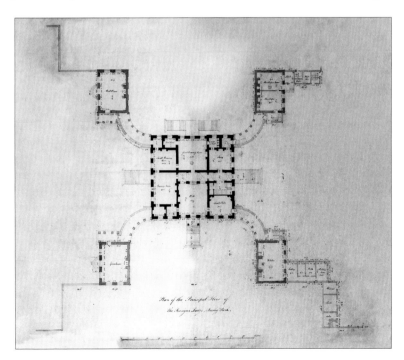

133 Hampton, Bushy House. Plan of main floor by John Soane, 1797, with Samwell's house in black and the mid-18th-century pavilions in grey. The service pavilions are on the right.

134   Hampton, Bushy House. Print of garden front by Neale, 1822.

an exchange with various properties in Pall Mall and in 1902 Bushy House became offices for the National Standards Laboratory, part of the Royal Society. This was not a very suitable use for a historic building, with parts of the house being changed into laboratories. It has since become the National Physical Laboratory, and over the 20th century research buildings have been added nearby. During the Second World War research for the Spitfire was carried out in a windtunnel, a water tank was built for the development of the 'Dambuster' bomb and experiments with radar were carried out in the park.[9] All this has disfigured what were once fine gardens and parkland crossed by the Longford River, and the landscape could do with further research.

GARRICK'S VILLA

Formerly known as Hampton House, this Thames-side house owes its fame to David Garrick (1717-79), actor-manager and playwright, who altered and embellished both house and grounds. The earlier house on the site was probably a more modest 17th-century building, and the land included gardens, fields and some cottages. Lacey Primatt inherited it in 1751 and let it to Lady Furnese; David Garrick took on the £60 *p.a.* lease in 1754 and bought the property the following year. He had recently married the Viennese dancer, Eva Maria Veigel, and they moved in fashionable circles. Hampton, only 14 miles from London and on the Thames, provided a convenient retreat.

The three-storey house is of brick, and the seven-bay entrance front has a portico over an arcaded entrance; there is a canted bay on the east side overlooking the gardens. The house was not large and architecturally it is slightly unsatisfactory, but provided elegant rooms for entertaining. Robert Adam's name is associated with the house, but he cannot have been responsible for the early improvements as he was still in Italy, although he did come down to visit the Garricks as soon as he was back.[1] He definitely carried out improvements in 1775, by which time Garrick's London house was in Royal Terrace, the best street in the Adam brothers' Adelphi development.[2] His work at Hampton may have included the Ionic capitals on the portico, the paired pilasters on the corners of the façade and the delicate fluted frieze. He certainly covered the brickwork with Liardet stucco, which was so unsatisfactory that Mrs Garrick later had it removed and the façade refaced in brick. Inside he possibly redesigned the staircase and added neo-classical plaques on the first-floor landing; but there are no surviving drawings for any of this work. Mrs Delany described Mrs Garrick as a woman of taste, and the interiors were furnished in a fashionable but comparatively informal way. Hogarth was a friend whose works they admired and his *Election* series hung in the house, as well as many portraits of Garrick in various theatrical roles. They were especially keen on *chinoiserie* decoration, and in 1757 Jean Pillement painted panels in the drawing room in this style for them; in 1775 a bedroom was hung with Chinese wallpaper. For both the Adelphi and Hampton houses Thomas Chippendale supplied the furnishings and his invoices list the new furniture, upholstery and curtains, as well as repairs to existing pieces. Several pieces of furniture are in the V & A: a clothes press and a pair of small bookcases made for Garrick's dressing room were made of deal, with japanned decoration in green on a cream background; and a pretty painted bed, the Indian chintz hangings for which were confiscated by Customs & Excise as illegal imports while being made up in Chippendale's workshops.[3] The best bedroom had a blue and white colour scheme, and some of the japanned furniture for that room has also been traced.

The gardens were one of the attractions of the house, and Garrick added the Green House which housed 16 pots of orange trees over the winter; there was a mount in the N-E

135 Hampton, Garrick's Villa, also called Hampton House. The road separates the mid-18th-century house from its riverside garden.

corner overlooking Bushy Park. There was one disadvantage: the road to Staines separated the riverside garden from the house. As soon as Garrick had acquired the copyhold of the house he demolished a riverside cottage and like Pope's Villa a tunnel was made beneath the road, incorporating a grotto. The Shakespeare Temple was built beside the Thames, celebrating Garrick's acting in and promotion of Shakespeare's plays. It is an octagonal domed building 21 ft in diameter with a portico supported on four Ionic columns.[4] It was well-lit and comfortably furnished with a suite of mahogany chairs and a matching sofa, and in 1758 Roubiliac carved a life-size statue of Shakespeare (now in the British Museum) which dominated the interior.[5] Zoffany painted two views of the riverside garden in 1762, one showing Garrick and his wife outside the Temple with their dogs, the other showing them taking tea on the lawn with Dr Johnson, while Garrick's brother fishes in the Thames – two paintings which sum up the pleasures of suburban life.

When Garrick died the contents of the house were recorded in an inventory.[6] His wife remained there until her death in 1822 when her solicitor, Thomas Carr, bought it and renamed the house Garrick's Villa. In the 1823 sale he bought some of the contents which remained in the house until 1864, when Silvanus Phillips auctioned them. He added a discreet west wing, then let the house. A threat to its future came with the growth of public transport: in 1902 the London United Tramway Company bought the house in order to demolish it, and it was only saved because the manager of the company decided to live there himself. Part of the front garden was lost to road widening but the house survived. After the First World War the house was made into flats and the orangery which Garrick had added was enlarged to turn it into a house. The riverside garden was sold, and an ugly extension added to the Shakespeare Temple to convert it into a dwelling. Hampton Council bought this in 1932, demolished the extension and made the garden into public open space. Gradually the Temple deteriorated through a combination of vandalism and neglect; in 1998-9 a major restoration project was carried out and a replica of the Roubiliac statue placed inside. The Temple and its garden now belong to the LB of Richmond upon Thames and can be visited, although the house remains in residential use.

HAMPTON COURT HOUSE

The history of this house is closely linked with that of Bushy House in the middle of Bushy Park, and with George Montagu Dunk, 2nd Earl of Halifax (1716-71), who was made ranger of Bushy Park in 1739. It was not an onerous post as most of the work could be carried out by deputies, and with it came the use of the ranger's lodge, Bushy House, which served as Halifax's suburban house. In addition he had a London house and an estate, Horton, in Northamptonshire. His wife had brought him a fortune in return for which he had to take her uncle's name of Dunk, but she died in 1753 and from then onwards he was living more or less openly with his mistress for whom this house was built in 1757. Anna-Maria Faulkner was an Irish singer who first appeared at Marylebone Gardens in 1747 and was soon talent-spotted by Garrick, also of Hampton. The following year she married William Donaldson, a Londoner who had a job in the Customs House; but as soon as Halifax was a widower she was appointed 'governess' to his children and Donaldson was packed off to a well paid post in the West Indies. Mrs Donaldson and Halifax remained together till his death.

The house was built on a 3½-acre plot which Halifax acquired, which had been part of the common land of Hampton Court Green. Its northern boundary was that of Bushy Park, so it was only a few minutes from his own house. Halifax employed Thomas Wright to make alterations to Horton (demolished) and to build the menagerie in the park.[1] He probably chose the same architect to design the new house for his mistress, and the design has Rococo features and a sense of movement across the façade which are typical of Wright's work. Hampton Court House is of two storeys over a semi-basement, the centre being a canted bay with a dome above and the two outer bays projecting forwards. The house is of brick with stone enrichments, although the window surrounds seem to combine both original and later stonework. Two pyramid-roofed pavilions flank the entrance and were linked to

136 Hampton Court House. Entrance front detail, from 1912 sale brochure.

the house by colonnades. The house was unusual in being only one room deep so it was not large. It has had major alterations and additions and not much of the original interior remains, but there is some fine Rococo plasterwork on the ceiling of the octagonal entrance hall. The house was finished in 1757 but from 1761–2 Mrs Donaldson accompanied Halifax to Dublin while he was Viceroy. She moved into her new house on their return with her two children by Halifax and remained there until his death.

The north front of the house overlooked Bushy Park so it was conveniently close to Halifax, and a gate led directly from the gardens into the park. In 1767 Halifax helped himself to a further three acres of unenclosed land to the west which allowed him to extend the gardens to about the same size as they are today. He created a Rococo garden which has lasted better than the interiors of the house. A heart-shaped pond or lake was made S-W of the house, fed by the Longford River which had been built by Charles I to supply Hampton Court. Overlooking this is an ice-house given a casing of rough stonework and tufa, linking it visually with the grotto across the lake. Both must be designs by Thomas Wright, the architect, astronomer and mathematician who had published his *Six Designs for Arbours* and *Six Designs for Grottoes* in 1755 and 1756.[2] The splendid grotto has all the hallmarks of his work. The basic structure is of brick with a slate roof, as can be seen from the back, but outwardly it is faced with tufa and fragments of blue coke (a residue from the iron smelting process) as well as '*pierres antidiluviennes*' which were large rough pieces of rock drilled to

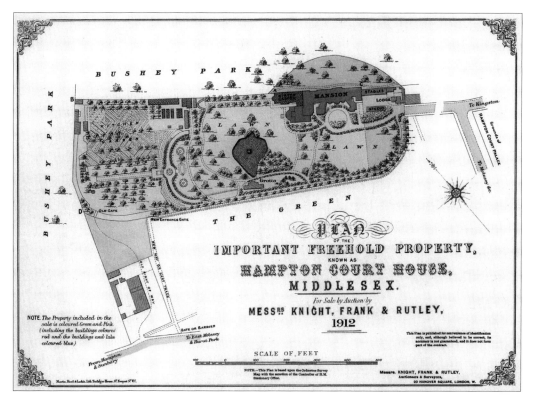

137 Hampton Court House, estate plan from 1912 sale brochure. The north side of the house overlooks Bushy Park, the large kitchen garden and greenhouses are on the left and the lake and grotto in the centre.

138 Hampton Court House. Interior of grotto looking west, after restoration.

give an ancient appearance. The high central chamber has a columned apse at each end with small leaded windows, and the walls were lined with shells and branches of coral. The whole has been meticulously restored by Diana Reynell, who also worked on the grotto at Painshill.[3]

Mrs Donaldson's son died young but her daughter Anna Maria had been adopted by Halifax. At his death in 1771 the house was left to Mrs Donaldson and Anna Maria was left a comfortable sum, conditional on her marrying with the approval of her trustees. Her mother returned to London and Hampton Court House was let, first to the 12th Earl of Suffolk, then to the 12th Earl of Sandwich. She was still married to Donaldson but after his death she married Colonel Charles Lumm. They lived mainly in London and the house continued to be let. After her death in 1797 the house was Lumm's for life, and was then inherited by Anna Maria, who married Richard Archdall, and then by their son, also called Richard. The tenant at one time was Admiral Lord Keith, Comptroller of the Household to the Duke of Clarence at Bushy House, so there was again a link between the two houses.

Richard Archdall the younger owned the house until 1807, after which it changed hands several times. In 1871 it was bought by Marmaduke Blake Sampson, the City correspondent of *The Times*. He was also a classical scholar and art collector and added a gallery for his pictures, later converted for concerts and theatrical performances by the de Wettes. He also added the winter garden on the west side of the house. This survives in truncated form, the glazed tiles of its full extent now flanked by tall palm trees which used to be grown indoors. He died five years later, tainted by financial misdealings, and his widow tried unsuccessfully to sell the house. She finally did so in 1883, when Thomas Twining bought it for his daughter and her husband, Augusta and Augustus de Wette. They used the house as their home and were deeply involved in local affairs, opening the house and gardens for charitable events as well as entertaining lavishly and using the art gallery as a room for concerts.[4] In 1903 they decided to sell and the sale document records the plan of the gardens, but it remained unsold for several years – a sign of the move away from these houses near London to ones further afield.[5] By 1912 the possibility of demolition was being discussed, but fortunately the house was finally bought in 1915 by Hubert Gore-Lloyd. His alterations to the house destroyed the sequence of original rooms: he opened up three rooms on the north side of the house on both the ground and first floors to make a large hall with a first-floor gallery looking into it. His son sold the house in 1945 to the Middlesex County Council and it was made into an old people's home and later a children's home, which it remained till 1991. During that time the fabric of the house and grotto deteriorated considerably, and it was only when it was sold by the LB of Richmond in 2001 to Hampton Court House School that the house and grounds have been restored.

HARROW WEALD

GRIM'S DYKE

This masterly example of Norman Shaw's Old English style was built 1870-2 for the artist Frederick Goodall (1822-1904). Born in north London, and living in Camden Square with his wife and children, he longed for some land on which to experiment with plants and trees. In 1856 he was successful enough as a genre painter to buy 100 acres from the Marquis of Abercorn's Bentley Priory estate. This hilly land, sandy and gravelly in type, had been part of Harrow Weald Common, but its history went back much further, as the name of the house suggests. Over three miles of a pre-Roman tribal boundary – a dry ditch and bank – are still visible today, and part runs through the land which Goodall had acquired.[1]

The land was sub-let and Goodall did not build a house at once; instead he 'made nurseries of choice conifers, having them moved from time to time to prepare them for their final planting'.[2] After his 1858-9 visit to Egypt he began painting biblical scenes, which were very successful, and after the death of his wife in 1869 he returned there, buying a flock of Egyptian sheep and some goats which he sent back to his farm at Grim's Dyke; these featured in various Old Testament paintings. It was during this second Egyptian visit

139   Harrow Weald, Grim's Dyke. Drawing of the entrance front of Norman Shaw's house soon after completion, from *The Builder*, 1872. The studio is on the left.

that Norman Shaw started work on the house. The site had already been chosen, close to Grime's Ditch, renamed by Norman Shaw Graeme's Ditch and later given its present name. The house is an asymmetrical composition, long and low but punctuated by half-timbered gables and by tall brick chimneys breaking through the tiled roofs, a perfect example of Shaw's taste for a picturesque English style suitable for domestic buildings, rather than the Gothic Revival of an earlier generation.[3] It is built of brick with Bath stone dressings, the wide windows framed in stone or wood mullions, their leaded lights catching the sun. The upper storey is partly tile-hung, and originally had small areas of pargetting in some of the gables.[4] The result was a house both attractive and comfortable, which was to be Goodall's main residence; he moved here in 1872, the year of his second marriage.

The house has a Gothic porch leading into a modest entrance hall, with the main reception rooms – drawing room, dining room and breakfast room – facing south over the gardens. An oak staircase leads to the bedrooms above, its panelled ceiling still with its 1890s Japanese wallpaper. Studio space was essential and Norman Shaw was an expert in this, having designed London studios for himself, Luke Fildes and others. At Grim's Dyke the studio was vast (47 x 27 ft with a curved ceiling about 22 ft high), set at an angle to the main house and with a different floor-level, subtly differentiating it from the family accommodation. It was mainly north-facing, with one window to the south, and service rooms below.

Grim's Dyke itself was incorporated into the gardens: a stretch of the ditch nearest to the house was dammed to allow rainwater to collect, giving a glimpse of water from the house; this has recently been restored. Goodall also cleaned out the fosse, finding Roman coins and pottery. His friend Thomas Blackwell, who bought many of his pictures, gave him a statue of Charles II by Cibber which had been in the centre of Soho Square. This was placed on a plinth in the water of the ditch, so that it looked 'very mysterious and weird with its reflection in the water'.[5] His carefully nurtured trees were moved to their final places in the gardens, and the house is still screened from the outside world by some of his tall conifers and giant redwoods. Here he could entertain his artist friends, such as Alma Tadema and Val Prinsep. But he found it difficult to get models for his paintings outside central London, and his large biblical scenes were going out of fashion. He gave up the house in 1883 and moved back to north London, but his reputation continued to decline and he died bankrupt in 1904.

The new owner was a banker with Hambros, Mr Heriot, who kept it for only a few years. He added a billiard room, designed by Arthur Cawston, but made no other changes. In 1890 it was bought by W.S. Gilbert, the librettist of the Gilbert & Sullivan operettas. In 1883 he had commissioned a large house in Kensington from Ernest George & Peto, so this was to be his suburban house for weekend use. He employed Irish navvies to excavate a large lake in the woods; it had an island tennis court approached by a drawbridge, and his boat was kept in a pagoda-style boathouse. He kept monkeys in an octagonal thatched monkey house, and also built the little bridge over the ditch, using flints and stone from the recently demolished church at Stanmore. Ernest George & Peto were commissioned to enlarge the house for his lavish entertaining. The studio was converted into a magnificent music room, and they designed an elaborate alabaster chimneypiece in French Renaissance style, with leering satyrs supporting a massive overmantel. Possibly the satyrs hinted at Gilbert's taste for young girls, as he drowned in 1911 in his lake in mysterious circumstances, possibly pursuing two young girls whom he had invited to swim there.

Lady Gilbert had the lake drained after his death, although there are now plans to restore it. She remained in the house till her death in 1936, when it was left to their adopted daughter, Lindsay Mackintosh. She could not afford to keep up the large house and grounds, so sold the contents and donated the house and grounds to Harrow Council, which still owns part of the 100 acres bought by Goodall. In the Second World War the house was requisitioned and housed a replica of the Enigma machine at Bletchley, in case that should have been damaged. After the war it became a clinic for TB sufferers, then a hotel, but was becoming increasingly dilapidated. In the 1990s it was bought by the present owner, who has restored it as a luxury hotel with the advice of English Heritage, keeping the main interiors as unaltered as possible. The gardens are also being restored to their late 19th-century design, and the house, secluded in its woodland setting, keeps its sense of being a retreat from London.

HAVERING-ATTE-BOWER

BOWER HOUSE

The royal palace of Havering stood close to Bower House. It was a much-frequented medieval palace on the edge of Hainault Forest, and remained in use into the 17th century: James I used it often, Charles I less so. In 1650 it was sold, by which time the house was described as decayed. Although returned to the Crown it was not in royal use after the Restoration. By 1719 it was reported to be 'run to ruin' and in 1796 Lysons noted that 'some remains of the palace are still to be seen' but by 1816 'not a vestige' remained.[1]

Bower House, originally called Monthavering, was built in 1729 on a new site, possibly using some of the fabric of the old palace. The builder was John Baynes (*c*.1676-1737), a successful lawyer who was appointed Serjeant-at-Law in 1724. With his busy career he was mainly in London, living in Russell Square: this was his suburban house, to escape to for 'ease' and 'leisure'.[2] The village of Havering-atte-Bower and the Round House are built on the top of the hill, as was the palace, but the site of Bower House is slightly lower. So it is sheltered from the north and has magnificent views to the distant Thames, about 13 miles to the south. Beyond the river can be seen the North Downs. Even today, with a much-reduced garden and Romford sprawling below, the house has a comparatively unspoilt view.[3] The architect was the young and comparatively inexperienced Henry Flitcroft, while the gardens were laid out by Charles Bridgeman. It is possible that Bridgeman chose the site, and the inscription over the hall fireplace records Flitcroft as 'architect' and Bridgeman as 'designer'.

140 Havering-atte-Bower, Bower House. Entrance front designed by Henry Flitcroft for Serjeant Baynes.

The house is a really good and well-preserved example of a compact Early Georgian country house, described as 'a neat seat' on Baynes's monument.[4] The approach is from the west and leads past the stables, also built by Flitcroft. They are of warm red brick with depressed arches with bold brick voussoirs, above which is a tiled roof crowned by a clock tower. The north front of the house is a simple and well-proportioned composition of 1-3-1 bays, the centre projecting slightly and crowned by a pediment. A plain brick parapet almost hides the dormer windows set into the hipped slate roof. There is a semi-basement on the far side of the house due to the fall in the ground, but only cellars on this side. The front door is given a pediment supported on consoles, but there is otherwise no decoration apart from the string course below the ground-floor windows and the modillion cornice below the parapet. This design is echoed on the south front, except that the garden door is given a Gibbs surround and bold keystones; and the string course has been clumsily lowered when the ground-floor windows were enlarged. All the sashes of the south front have the thin glazing bars of early 19th-century type, while some of the basement windows and those on the north front keep their thicker original glazing bars. The south front also has two wings projecting in front of the façade, probably added c.1800.[5] These, probably providing a new and larger dining room and drawing room, are built in matching brick and have canted bays with long arched windows which give access directly into the gardens, although the east wing is a much deeper room than that on the west. They hardly enhance the appearance of the house, but the smaller rooms of the original house were no longer suitable for entertaining by this date, and this inter-connection of house and gardens was highly desirable.

The house has a double-pile plan: the hall leads directly into the great parlour, and there are two rooms on each side, divided by the main and secondary staircases. The decoration throughout is in muscular Early Georgian style, its style established in the entrance hall. The walls have plaster panels above the dado, there is a rich dentil cornice and the doors have eared surrounds, while the chimneypiece is of the Jonesian type with a pedimented overmantel flanked by drops. Above it is the royal arms, a reference to the palace nearby. The saloon (also called the great parlour) beyond is even more richly decorated, its window surrounds topped with swags of drapery enclosing masks, and the splendid chimneypiece with an overmantel enclosing a portrait of Baynes's daughter Lucy, his only surviving child. This room still has a set of portraits of the Baynes family inset into the panels, a remarkable survival when the house has not had continuity of ownership and is now an institution. The main staircase is approached from the hall, with *trompe-l'oeil* decoration of rusticated masonry on the lower walls. The stairs are as splendid as the saloon, made of mahogany with sturdy balusters and plain panelled newels; it is reminiscent of the stairs at Marble Hill, but more spacious. The plaster ceiling is Jonesian: Flitcroft as a protégé of Burlington was well aware of Jones's style. In contrast the walls have rich Baroque decoration. Sir James Thornhill was commissioned to decorate the walls with scenes of drunken Silenus and the Judgement of Paris, painted in oil on plaster as life-size figures. It must have been one of his last works but has been largely ignored by art historians, as for many years it was covered over and forgotten; perhaps the Bacchanalian scenes so close to anyone walking up the stairs were too much for Victorian sensibilities. Now, uncovered and conserved, it looks superb.

When Baynes died in 1737 the house was left to his widow, on condition that she did not remarry.[6] Lucy Baynes predeceased her mother so the house went to her husband, Francis Lee, who let it to a City merchant.[7] From 1776 it was let to Sir John Smith (later

John Smith Burges), a director of the East India Company. He must have added the two wings and lowered the windows on the south front, as well as covering the brickwork in white-painted stucco.[8] After his death in 1803 his widow remained there until her remarriage, after which it was let to Edward Robinson 1819-46. It was probably Robinson who installed the oak panelling and the carved oak chimneypiece dated 1659 in the east wing. During his tenancy it was sold to John Barnes, the owner of the Round House, and continued to be let. It was possibly empty from 1886-1915.

In 1915 Sir John Smith bought the house (the second John Smith to do so), partly as a suitable place to house his wife's very fine collection of 17th- and 18th-century furniture and objects, which Queen Mary came to see in 1934.[9] He was the last private owner and in 1948 the property was bought by the photographic company Ilford as offices. From 1959-2003 it was owned by the Ford Motor Company (Dagenham was not far away) who ran training courses there. They maintained the house well, and removed the coverings from Thornhill's wall-paintings. By this time the house was listed Grade 1, so the additional residential accommodation required was added fairly unobtrusively in low blocks east of the house, just outside the walled kitchen garden. Since 2006 it has belonged to the Anana Trust which continues to use it as a residential college.

141 Havering-atte-Bower, Bower House. The great parlour in the early 20th century. The portrait in the overmantel is of Lucy Baynes.

142 Havering-atte-Bower, Bower House. Sir John Smith's drawing room in the east wing was added in the late 18th century, and the 1659 oak chimneypiece installed in the early 19th century.

HESTON

OSTERLEY PARK

Osterley and Syon are both magnificent 16th-century courtyard houses on the west side of London which were rearranged and redecorated by Robert Adam in the 1760s. In both cases he provided a series of sumptuous state rooms, so perfect in their way that they have been little altered since. Even critical Horace Walpole was enchanted, describing Osterley as 'the palace of palaces … so improved and enriched that all the Percies and Seymours of Sion must die of envy'.[1]

A farmhouse stood on the site of Osterley until Sir Thomas Gresham (*c.*1518-1579) bought it by 1565 with about 200 acres.[2] He was an enormously successful City merchant, a member of the Mercers' Company and with business interests in Antwerp, where he lived for several years. He saw business opportunities in his new estate and built mills, described by Norden as 'paper-milles, oyle-mills, and corne-milles'.[3] He also had a London house and estates in Norfolk and Sussex, so this was a house for occasional use, especially in the spring. He rebuilt the old farmhouse *c.*1565, at the same time as he was rebuilding his Bishopsgate house and helping pay for the Royal Exchange which he established in the City – which gives an idea of his resources.

The 'faire and stately' brick courtyard house which he built is the core of the house we see today, although Adam cut through the east range to make his portico. Moses Glover's 1635 map showed it as a high building with four towers, set in a large walled enclosure and approached across two forecourts.[4] There was also a large courtyard to the N-E which included the surviving stables as well as having the laundry, brewhouse and probably some farm buildings. The park was impaled and had a series of ponds, one of which has a tall lodge beside it. (Lodges were rare in these houses round London, and it would be nice to know more about this one.) Some of the ponds were converted into the present lakes in the 18th century. By the time Gresham died in 1579 his only son had predeceased him, so he left his wealth to his wife, his step-son William Reade (who lived at nearby Boston Manor, Brentford) and to Gresham College, which he founded. His wife remained at Osterley till her death, after which Reade let it to Sir Edward Coke, the Lord Chief Justice, till his death in 1634. In 1655 the Osterley estate was sold by Gresham's heirs to Sir William Waller, a moderate Parliamentarian who continued to live there peacefully after the Restoration. When he died in 1668 an inventory was taken, with Francis Child among the valuers.[5] After several other owners it was bought for £9,500 in 1684 by the notorious builder and speculator Nicholas Barbon, whose ruthless methods allowed him to develop many streets in the Holborn area at great profit to himself. He seems to have carried out some work at Osterley, probably replacing the staircase towers on the inner sides of the courtyard with two of the present corner towers with their ogee lead domes; and he smartened up the stables with a Tuscan doorcase in the centre of the range. But why did he want Osterley? Perhaps

143   Heston, Osterley Park. The entrance front, redesigned by Robert Adam in 1764. He encased the much-altered house in red bricks and punched a screen of Portland stone columns through one side of the 16th-century courtyard house. The ogee roofs on the corner towers are of lead.

he had ambitions to own a country estate, or perhaps it was just another asset to mortgage as part of his complicated financial dealings. When he died in 1698 he had mortgaged it for more than it had cost him, and because that mortgage could not be repaid it became the property of the Child family.

Sir Francis Child (1642-1713) was a successful goldsmith who established Child & Co. as a bank at 1 Fleet Street, where it still has premises; he was Lord Mayor in 1698-9. He married well and lived with his large family in London, with a suburban house in Fulham. He had loaned money to Barbon but was not interested in Osterley as a house for himself; taking it on was simply a way of redeeming his debt. So the family who were to be such important owners of Osterley over several generations acquired it by chance. Three of his sons, Robert (1674-1721), Francis (1684-1740) and Samuel (1693-1752) were to inherit Osterley and Child's Bank, and from 1720 onwards it became their occasional home. Francis carried out some work there, probably raising the two-storey house with a hipped roof into the three-storey house we see today. No major architect was employed, Child using the City carpenter Matthew Hildyard as builder and Boulton Mainwaring as surveyor. His brother Samuel probably added the two other corner turrets to match those on the garden front, a curiously old-fashioned project for the mid-18th century; and he may have raised the courtyard to the level of the *piano nobile*, thus making the ground floor into an inconspicuous service floor. He also ordered the exquisite and highly fashionable statuary marble chimneypiece designed by Chambers and made by Wilton which is in the gallery. It was Francis Child III (1735-63) who asked Robert Adam in 1761 to sort out the various changes that had been made and to pull the whole together into a more unified design. But he died on the eve of his marriage and before the work had really begun, so the next part of the project was overseen by his brother Robert and his wife. They turned Osterley into a centre of social life, spending the autumn at Upton in Warwickshire, the winter in London, and the summer at Osterley.

Adam was at the start of his career, and this was a valuable commission from a prominent and very rich family. Many of his drawings are still in the house, so his long association with it can be followed in detail.[6] The house had been much altered and like most courtyard houses was not convenient. He redesigned the entrance front, removing the rooms in the east front to give it a superb open portico with a wide flight of steps. The other fronts were refenestrated and refaced in warm red brick. His work was a brilliant combination of elegance and practicality: no wonder the Childs continued to employ him for two decades.[7] Guests entered through the impressive new portico, then across the courtyard into the new apsed entrance hall. The west-facing gallery linked the family and state apartments, and was little altered by Adam; but the suites of rooms on each side were completely redesigned by him.

The state rooms of dazzling richness faced south towards the lake, with the traditional enfilade of withdrawing room, anteroom, bedchamber and dressing room. This was fairly old-fashioned for the 1760s, but was transformed by Adam in the most up-to-date manner. The ceiling of the damask-hung drawing room was based on one of Robert Wood's designs from Palmyra; the Gobelins tapestries in the ante-room were designed by Boucher; the state bedroom had a splendid domed bed designed by Adam; and the

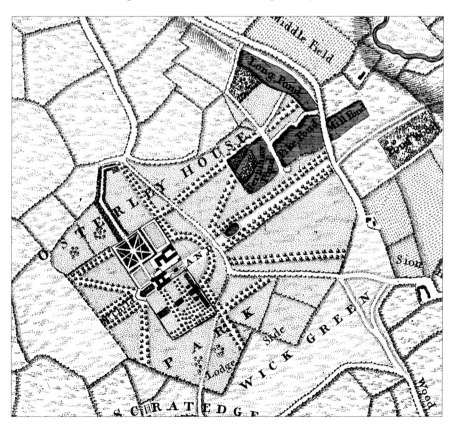

144 Heston, Osterley Park, from Rocque's 1745 map. The courtyard house has a *patte d'oie* to the west and formal gardens to the north and south, all swept away soon after this map was made. The ponds which Gresham utilised are close to the River Brent.

191

145 Heston, Osterley Park. The library, restored to its original white, designed by Robert Adam.

Etruscan Room beyond was a clever variation on the Greek or 'Etruscan' vases, newly fashionable after Sir William Hamilton's collection had been bought by the British Museum. Behind these he added a corridor so the servants could discreetly access the rooms. The family had a modest private entrance into the ground floor on the north front. The main stairs led up to the ground floor, where Adam designed a library for Mr Child and the eating room; they left unaltered the pre-Adam breakfast room. The staircase continued to their bedrooms and dressing rooms upstairs. On the top floor were guest bedrooms with their own dressing rooms, decorated with fashionable Indian chintzes and wallpapers. Inset in the ceiling over the staircase was Rubens' *Apotheosis of the Duke of Buckingham*, which was moved from the Child's London house.[8] New furniture was commissioned for most of these rooms, some key pieces designed by Adam, others by John Linnell, a leading cabinet-maker who was perfectly capable of designing furniture suitable for Adam's interiors. Remarkably, most of that furniture is still in the house.[9]

The Childs had only one child, Sarah, who eloped with John Fane, 10th Earl of Westmoreland, in 1782. To the dismay of her father they got married in Gretna Green and Child died not long afterwards.[10] In his will he ensured that Osterley (and all his other property) went first to his widow and then to the Fane's second child.[11] So in 1793 it was inherited by Sarah Fane, then a child. She married George Villiers, 5th Earl of Jersey, who added the name of Child to his own. They divided their time between his Oxfordshire estate, Middleton Park, Osterley and their house in Berkeley Square. Their extravagant lifestyle meant that after their deaths Osterley was let. The family was also hit by the late 19th-century slump and in 1885 the contents of the library were sold.

The grounds were clearly shown in two maps, Moses Glover's of 1635 and Rocque's of 1741.[12] The latter shows the formal avenue and *patte d'oie* east of the house and the lodge south of the house. The Doric Temple by John James closed one of the vistas, but now stands in the less formal lay-out introduced by Robert Child while the house was being refashioned by Adam. The only Adam garden building to survive is the bow-fronted Garden

146 Heston, Osterley Park. The main staircase, with the original lanterns designed by Robert Adam, leads from the family entrance at the side of the house to their rooms on the first and second floors.

House with its painted Windsor chairs, which were such a common feature of garden rooms but so rarely remain in them. The flower gardens were close to the house, the vast walled kitchen garden, said to cost £1,400 *p.a.* to run, was to the north, and a belt of lakes replaced the ponds. A Chinese sampan was kept on one of the lakes and the menagerie with its exotic birds made a delightful visit. But like many of these houses near the Thames the ground was flat and dull and water and trees were essential to make it interesting.[13]

The expense of keeping up a house on this scale became too much after the Second World War and in 1949 the 9th Earl of Jersey gave the house, most of its contents and its very large park to the National Trust. When the M4 was constructed in 1965 the Trust was forced to give up some of the land, so the motorway sliced across the park and between the lakes most insensitively. However, the house retains a sense of its almost rural setting, and with its superb rooms and contents remains one of the greatest creations of Robert Adam.

HIGHGATE

CROMWELL HOUSE

Cromwell House is a fine example of a pre–Civil War suburban house, its good brickwork making it stand out on Highgate Hill. Highgate was already a fashionable place to live, easy to reach from the City, perched on a hilltop, with good air, spring water and wonderful views over London to the hills beyond Greenwich. Distinguished houses had already been built there, although Cromwell House is the only important one to survive.

Richard Sprignell (*c*.1602-1659) built the house in 1637-8 on land which his father had owned.[1] They were a City family, his father and grandfather belonging to the Barber-Surgeons' Company, and like many City families they owned land scattered through various counties without having a major country house. He had married Anne Delaune, whose French father was Apothecary to Anne of Denmark; they were well-off, well-connected and royalist. Sprignell was a Captain of the Trained Bands (linked to the Honourable Artillery Company) and was made a baronet by Charles I in 1641.

147   Highgate, Cromwell House. Entrance front of 1637-8 with cut and moulded brickwork. The mansard roof was introduced after a fire in 1865.

194

His house was typical of City taste with its showy façade in virtuoso English bond brickwork, similar to Kew Palace. It is of two main storeys, the seven-bay south front breaking forward in the three centre bays, and again in the centre bay. It has a heavy cornice and a less emphatic string course, and there are brick quoins on the corners and the projecting bays. The wide windows (sashes instead of the original mullion and transoms) have eared surrounds, with bold scrolls framing the central first-floor window. This is all carried out in moulded or cut brickwork of a warm red. The parapet is later, rebuilt after a fire in 1865 which destroyed the attics and original roof, so its form is unclear. Unlike Kew it did not have shaped gables, instead a cupola gave access to a balustraded roof platform giving spectacular views.

The interior is laid out on that familiar plan of four rooms to a floor, although its irregularities may relate to an earlier house on the site. The entrance today is into a passage, but was probably originally into a hall, leading to the magnificent oak staircase beyond. This has wide shallow steps and a triple-moulded handrail, as well as pierced panels of florid strapwork with military trophies; the work is slightly coarse, but vigorous. The walls may have been painted with the same design, as at Boston Manor. The chunky newels are carved with lions' masks, but most striking of all are the nine carved military figures, about a foot high, which adorn the newels. Sprignell was a member of the Trained Bands, and the figures are of a drummer, musketeers, an officer etc. These became so celebrated that they were carefully drawn in 1849, which proved invaluable when some were stolen a century later.[2] Usually these impressive staircases lead only to the first floor, but here the stairs reach from basement to roof, and appear tower-like on the north front of the house.

The plasterwork at Cromwell House is also outstanding. The panelled hall, now slightly truncated by the partitioned entrance hall, has a simple but elegant ceiling of narrow ribs in a quatrefoil design. The carving on the stone fireplace has military references: a trophy of armour, a helmet, a cannon and a basket of cannon balls. The parlour behind has a corner fireplace with a stone Tudor chimneypiece, re-used from an earlier house. The doors on the first floor landing have flamboyant woodwork echoing the brickwork of the façade, with open pediments and eared

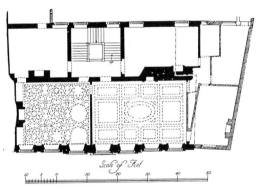

148   Highgate, Cromwell House. Plan of first floor, with later addition on the right.

surrounds with scrolls below. The five-bay great chamber also has a plasterwork ceiling, but here the influence of Inigo Jones's Banqueting House can be seen in the heavy oval compartment with its surrounding rectangles, all with guilloche ornament. Low-relief strapwork designs fill the panels, with Sprignell's arms in the centre. It is comparable with the plasterwork in the hall at Swakeleys, of the same date.

His son spent more time on his Yorkshire estates and in 1664 sold the house and its 19 acres. In 1675 it was bought by Alvares da Costa, a Portuguese merchant with court connections who was the first Jew to own property in England.[3] He added the long service wing behind the house and also the side addition with rooms above a carriage entrance,

149 Highgate, Cromwell House, in 1923. The staircase with military figures on the newels. The doors on the first-floor landing have elaborate pediments and carved decoration.

150 Highgate, Cromwell House. Plasterwork ceiling of geometric pattern in the ground-floor parlour.

one of which has a fireplace with his monogram delicately carved in the keystone. His widow remained in the house till her death in 1727, after which their son Anthony took it on. Defoe notes that 'the Jews have particularly fixed upon this town [Highgate] for their country retreats ... also, I am told they have a private synagogue there.'[4] As the first and most prominent Jewish family there, it is possible that this was either in Cromwell House or established by them nearby.

The house changed hands many times after Abraham da Costa sold it in 1749, and in 1843 became a school. By this time it had acquired its present name; there is no connection at all to Cromwell, although his son-in-law Ireton did take over Lauderdale House opposite in 1649. In mid-winter 1865 fire destroyed the top floor, damaging the rooms below. The great chamber ceiling and that in the adjoining room were both damaged by the 1865 fire but were repaired to their original appearance.[5] The cupola on the roof was also reconstructed, as a clause of the lease insisted that an exact restoration be carried out; Thomas Harris was the architect in charge. From 1869-1923 the house was a convalescent home for patients from the Great Ormonde Street Children's Hospital, the healthy Highgate air making it more suitable than central London. In 1924 the Mothercraft Training Society bought the freehold and added some unsympathetic low buildings in the garden (since removed). From 1953 it belonged to missionary societies, but it was expensive to maintain and was becoming dilapidated. It was sold to developers and restored 1988-9; it is now part of the Ghanaian Embassy. There is no public access to this interesting and important house.

ICKENHAM

SWAKELEYS

Swakeleys was one of the more distant areas of Middlesex, only a mile from the Buckinghamshire border and barely two miles from Denham Place. Now its remoteness has disappeared and it is close to the centre of Ickenham and the busy A40. But it is a well-preserved house and is still surrounded by gardens and trees, giving it a semblance of its original setting. The old house on the site was moated, and had changed hands many times. Robert Bromley bought it *c*.1596 and sold it in 1606 to Sir John Bingley, who sold it in 1629 to Edmund Wright (1573-1643), the builder of the house we see today.[1] London and its environs were having a building boom in the early 17th century, and houses such as Kew Palace and Cromwell House demonstrate the flamboyant style which seems to have appealed strongly to the City élite; Swakeleys is a far more splendid house than either of those. It, too, was built by a City man, Wright being a member of the Grocers' Company from 1599, an alderman from 1629 and Lord Mayor in 1640-1, not an easy time to be in office. The house was begun in 1629 and has rainwater heads dated 1638, so that is the assumed completion date.

151   Ickenham, Swakeleys. The entrance front in the early 20th century. Apart from changes to the windows, this has hardly been altered since it was built in 1629.

The house is a large and impressive example of an H-plan house with a double-pile central block. It has two main storeys and attic rooms set into the shaped gables. The centrepiece on the entrance front and the east front rises into a niche with a segmental pediment, there is a high tiled roof and tall chimneys; so the roofline is dramatic, and would have been more so when its cupola was still *in situ*.[2] The house is built of brick laid in English bond and enriched with window surrounds and quoins of plaster, coloured to resemble stone. There were strapwork enrichments which can still be seen below the staircase windows. With its bay windows and its cheerful disregard of the classical rules in the placing of pediments it is not a classically correct house of the type Inigo Jones was designing at the same time; but it has a forceful presence, and some interior details do suggest a familiarity with Jones's work. Wright must have spent lavishly on it: one of the extravagant touches is the use of Purbeck marble for the window sills and round the doorways. Even the back door, the original door studded with nails, has this surround.

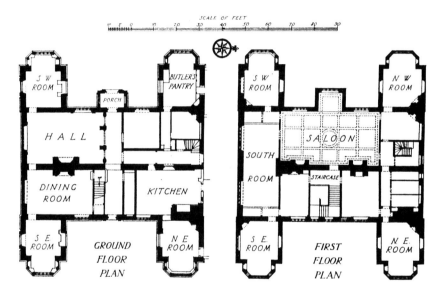

152 Ickenham, Swakeleys. Plans of the ground and first floors. It is a double-pile H-plan house.

The house is entered from the west through a porch into a screens passage leading into the hall, a conventional plan at this date. But the screen itself is not conventional, with its triple arches and a large segmental pediment squeezed in below the ceiling with a pair of almost life-size lions peering into the hall from it. In the pediment is a bust of Charles I, possibly by Besnier. The floor is paved in stone, and the wide marble chimneypiece is very much in Jones's style.[3] Behind the hall lay the everyday parlour with a small room in the S-E bay, both of which have simple panelling of early 17th-century type. The north side of the ground floor has a corridor leading to the service courtyard and dividing the pantry and secondary stairs from the kitchen, which still has its wide stone fireplace.

The main staircase has been rebuilt but the walls have decorative paintings of Dido and Aeneas dating from *c*.1700. They were attributed to Laguerre, but do not seem of good enough quality; possibly they are by Lanscroon or Streater.[4] On the first floor the great chamber, over 40 ft long, extends through the central range and into the space over the porch.

It is a splendid room, with a fine and restrained plasterwork ceiling with compartments, the beams decorated with guilloche ornament and a central wreath; even the projecting space over the porch has its own wreath, the spandrels filled with cherubs energetically puffing towards clouds. Leading off the great chamber was the south-facing gallery, but this has been partitioned into several rooms. The rooms on the north side, probably the family rooms, have corner fireplaces, as do the corner rooms below. This is a feature mainly found in late 17th-century houses, but clearly practical and space-saving in these small rooms. The attic used to have 16 bedrooms, but has been opened up into large and fairly featureless spaces.

Swakeleys was left to Wright's daughter Katherine, who had married Sir James Harrington, one of the Commissioners who had tried Charles I. He risked punishment in 1660, and after a spell in the Tower went abroad, but his wife was able to remain in England.[5] Swakeleys was sold in 1665 to another Lord Mayor, Sir Robert Vyner, made a baronet in 1666 and Lord Mayor in 1674-5. He was a goldsmith and banker, and made the regalia for the coronation of Charles II. Pepys describes a visit to Swakeleys soon after Vyner had bought it, which makes the point that even these distant houses could be visited inside the day. He describes being shown

153 Ickenham, Swakeleys. The hall screen seen from inside the hall. The two lions flank a pediment with a bust of Charles I.

'the house and grounds … a place not very modern in the gardens nor house … And now he lives no man in England in greater plenty, and commands both King and Council with his credit he gives them.' He was amused by the juxtaposition of the bust of Charles I with that of Fairfax on the hall screen, which he attributes to Harrington.[6] The family portrait painted by John Michael Wright shows him outside Swakeleys, but his riches did not last, and the King's cancellation of his debts eventually bankrupted him in 1683. Vyner's son, another Robert Vyner, lived to be 94 and it was only after his death that the house changed hands again. It was sold to Benjamin Lethieullier in 1741 and resold in 1750 to the vicar of Ickenham, Thomas Clarke, in whose family it remained till 1923.[7]

By that time London was easily accessible and the land was sold for development. The detached houses in a bewildering variety of styles which one passes on the approach to Swakeleys were built from this time. The house was to be demolished, but was saved by Humphrey John Talbot who bought it in 1924, together with the 11 acres which still surround it. With the help of SPAB he managed to find a new buyer, the Foreign Office Sports Association, which opened it in 1929. It remained a sports club until 1986, when it changed hands. It is a Grade 1 listed house which by then was in need of attention and it was carefully restored for office use with the help of architects Kirby Adair Newson. They added a glazed entrance to the north front, thus allowing the original entrance front to remain clear of cars and the paraphernalia of a reception area. The restoration and future of the house were financed by discreetly building a low courtyard of offices north of the house, and the house now looks better than it has for decades.[8]

ILFORD

VALENTINES

The high ground near Epping Forest was always an attractive place for City men to retreat to, close to their business interests and healthy in summer. The land round Valentines is now heavily built up and close to industrial areas, but the house and the substantial remains of its park and formal gardens remind us how it once looked. Valentines was built 1696-7 on a ridge to the east of the River Roding in Essex by James Chadwick, the son-in-law of Archbishop Tillotson of Canterbury. It was a double-pile brick house facing south, of two storeys with dormer windows in the roof. The kitchen may have been in the N-W corner, as there was no basement but only beer and wine cellars below the house. It has nine bays today, but was probably slightly smaller when built.[1] Externally the north front with its irregular fenestration is probably little altered, although there is not much evidence internally of Chadwick's house.[2] The main staircase with its three twisted balusters to a step probably dates from the 1690s, as well as the upper flights of the secondary staircase. Many changes were made by Robert Surnam, the man who created the remarkable formal gardens.

Surnam was a City banker and, more importantly, was Cashier of the South Sea Company. He had bought various Essex properties which he sold in order to buy Valentines in 1724, where he remained for the next 30 years. Several of the ground- and first-floor rooms have good early 18th-century panelling and box cornices and simple marble or stone chimneypieces without mantelshelfs, all typical of the 1720s. He probably also added the canted bay running through both storeys on the east front of the house, which would have given him a glimpse of his new gardens. West of the house he built a south-facing five-bay orangery, converted in the early 19th century into a service range. It is an agreeable house, but it is the gardens which make it special. Very few formal gardens have survived the changes in taste of the last 300 years, but Surnam's garden was not destroyed and is now undergoing a complete restoration.

He built two walled kitchen gardens north of the house, with an unusually large tripartite dovecot with ogee windows at one end. The formal gardens are to the north of the walled gardens and so were not integrated with the house, and would not have been seen from the south- and east-facing main rooms. They were approached by a walk beside the garden walls which had a ha-ha to the east, allowing uninterrupted views into the park.[3] The main feature is the brick-lined canal running from west to east, fed from the horsepond beyond. The water flowed into the canal through a grotto, carefully faced with flint, fragments of earlier masonry, shells and spar. At the east end there was another flint-faced grotto through which the water flowed into a pond at a lower level. This area was planted more naturally and flanked the park. North of the canal and parallel to it was 'Bishop's Walk' from which a *patte d'oie* reached back towards the canal. One vista ended in the lower grotto, another was aligned on the approach path, and the third ended in an alcove seat built into the kitchen garden wall; all these garden features are now being carefully restored.

When Surnam died in 1754 the estate was bought by Sir Charles Raymond Bt., a banker and ship-owner who owned other properties in the area. He, too, made alterations to the house, giving it its present appearance. The most important change was the rebuilding of the south front, removing the dormers to make it a three-storey façade. This provides good-sized but very low-ceilinged rooms on the top floor. The present roof structure with its internal drainage must also date from this time, and lead rainwater heads have Raymond's crest and the date 1769. He also added bows running through the full height of the house on the south front. This is a similar updating to that carried out at Water House in Walthamstow at about the same time, and the details of the woodwork of the new windows in the bows are almost identical, suggesting that the same builder may have been involved. The fine statuary marble chimneypiece in the S-E room, with fluted decoration in coloured marble inset, was added at this time.

After Raymond's death in 1788 the house was sold and changed hands several times until bought in 1808 by Charles Welstead, who made further changes. He moved the entrance from the south to the north front, and in order to mask the service rooms on that side of the house he built a wide semi-circular Doric colonnade to provide a covered approach to the new entrance vestibule; its white stucco and asymmetrical position do not enhance the north front of the house. The orangery was converted into pantries and a dairy, and a new

154 Ilford, Valentines, in 1799. The late 17th-century house is shown from the S-E, showing the bows added in the late 18th century.

kitchen was built linking it to the house. Inside he made a secondary staircase at one side of the staircase hall and added a neat cornice to the hall and south-facing drawing room. After his death in 1832 the house belonged to Charles Holcombe, whose daughter Sarah Ingleby was the last private owner of the house. In 1870 she added a room to the N–E on the two main floors, which may have meant further changes to the staircase hall; the rather coarse Restoration-style plasterwork on the staircase ceiling was put in at this time, as was the stained glass in the Venetian window on the main staircase.

In 1898 Mrs Ingleby sold 47 acres at the south end of the parkland to Ilford Urban District Council so they could make a park, which opened the following year with a boating lake, bowling green, bandstand and cafe.[4] She died in 1905 and her son sold the house and a further 37 acres to the council in 1907 and gave them a further 10 acres. In the First World War Valentines was used to house Belgian refugees, after which it became council offices. Little was done to it, so the interiors survived remarkably intact. The house is now owned by the LB of Redbridge which has recently begun a major restoration of the house and historic gardens, funded partly by the Heritage Lottery Fund. When completed the house will be open to educational groups and the restored gardens will be open to the public.[5]

ISLEWORTH

SYON HOUSE

Syon is the only large house on the outskirts of London which is still a private house and used as suburban houses traditionally were. The owner is the Duke of Northumberland who lives at Alnwick Castle in Northumberland, and Syon was the suburban retreat the family used when based in London. Until 1874 they owned the early 17th-century Northumberland House in the Strand, one of the largest and finest town houses in London. After that was compulsorily purchased for road improvements the family had a central London house or flat and continued to use Syon for weekends and in the spring and summer. The house is under the flightpath to Heathrow which gives this ancient house an almost surreal air. Planes come in low overhead but from the house one sees a landscape little changed since the 18th century: the unbroken greenery of Kew Gardens across the Thames, the water meadows beyond the gardens with cattle grazing, the 'Capability' Brown landscape in the park.

In 1415 Henry V founded an order of Bridgettine monks and nuns in England, giving them premises close to Richmond Palace. They moved to Syon in 1431, taking over a 30-acre site north of Isleworth. Over the next 30-40 years they built a church, cloister, dormitories and a refectory and enlarged their estate. Recent excavations have revealed fascinating evidence of the scale of the church, which has proved to be one of the largest abbey churches in England. It had always been assumed that, as in so many other conversions of monastic buildings, the courtyard was on the site of the cloister; below the present entrance hall there are remains of what was long thought to be the undercroft. Both these assumptions have been proved wrong.[1] The east end of the church was in the present gardens towards the river, but it stretched westwards to the entrance front of the present house.[2]

155   Isleworth, Syon House, 1737 print by Samuel & Nathaniel Buck. The river front with the mid-17th-century loggia, formal gardens and flood defences.

Syon was dissolved with difficulty in 1539. Powerful families had daughters there, and many of them became leading recusants: Scropes, Stricklands, Treshams. It became royal property but Henry's revenge was to use it as a munitions factory. After his death he lay in state there on his journey to Windsor. In 1547 the Duke of Somerset was given the property and he demolished the church, keeping its footings as foundations for part of his new house and presumably reusing the stone.[3] The house we see today is basically Somerset's house. Under Queen Mary the Bridgettines were re-established at Syon, though suppressed again when Elizabeth came to the throne. She only used the house occasionally and in 1594 leased it to Henry Percy, 9th Earl of Northumberland, who acquired the freehold in 1604 from James I. It has remained in the Percy family ever since.

156 Isleworth, Syon House. Watercolour of the courtyard, before the refacing of the house in the 1820s.

The house could be approached by river or by road; a barge from London was the most convenient method. The river front had a high wall as flood defences and the main entrance was to the west with a walled forecourt in front of the house, which is now marked only by two lodges. This forecourt had a kitchen wing on the north side and a range of lodgings to the south, both of which have disappeared. The three-storey house was built of stone and had four corner towers, as it has today. The great hall was on the site of the present entrance hall, and the courtyard had a range of state rooms on the south side with service and family rooms to the north. The whole of the east or river front was taken up by the long gallery, just as it is today. The 9th Earl of Northumberland (1564-1632) carried out extensive and expensive work on the house after 1604, refitting many of the rooms with new panelling and chimneypieces. He also demolished the gatehouse and built the pair of crenellated forecourt lodges, rebuilt the laundry and brewhouse and added new coach houses, bought more land and planted avenues.[4] His son, the Parliamentarian 10th Earl, was a great art collector and bought some of the finest pictures in the Northumberland collection.[5] The loggia on the east front was made for him and he added some rich furnishings; the house was being used to house the royal children while Charles I was in captivity, so it needed to be splendid. He also embellished the gardens, possibly employing André Mollet from Paris. Otherwise little was done to the house until the arrival of Sir Hugh Smithson, a highly intelligent and business-like Yorkshire landowner who inherited the house through his wife, Lady Elizabeth Percy, in 1748.

Smithson (1714-86) was made first Earl (in 1750) and then 1st Duke (in 1766) of Northumberland. He and his wife transformed Syon which they used frequently, especially in the spring and summer. In 1753 they employed 'Capability' Brown to open up the landscape, demolishing the wall between the house and river and replacing it with a ha-ha. Brown landscaped the park and made a lake, for which James Paine designed a bridge (now gone). He also created a new drive from the London Gate, for which Adam later designed new gates with a screen and a pair of lodges. In the botanical gardens to the north of the house the Duke and Duchess added to the rare trees already planned by the 10th Earl, built the tall column with Flora on top which still stands and laid out the narrow lake, although the delicate iron bridge which spans it was added in 1790.

157 Isleworth, Syon House. The main entrance, designed by Robert Adam. The Percy lion is over the arch, with metal holders for lanterns above the screen.

Having updated the gardens they turned their attention to the house, dropping James Paine who had worked at Syon and Alnwick and choosing Robert Adam as their architect. (They were so pleased with his work at Syon that they later employed him to transform both Alnwick Castle and Northumberland House.) Adam's task was not easy: Syon was a single fairly narrow range of rooms round a courtyard, there were various changes in level, and some of the ceilings were quite low. He triumphed over all these, making a magnificent series of state rooms. Somerset's double-height great hall became the entrance hall with the front door moved to the centre. Doric columns flanked the doors and windows and the strong design of the black and white paved floor was reflected in the deep ribs of the ceiling.[6] Sculpture was arranged along the walls and Wilton's copy of the *Apollo Belvedere* filled the apse which led to the private apartments; at the other end a double flight of steps led through a screen of columns into the anteroom. James Adam sent a set of *verde-*

antique marble columns from Rome to line the walls and to disguise the irregular shape of this room. Their richness is matched by the *scagliola* floor (relaid 1830s), the gilt lead sculptures above the columns and the panels of gilded trophies on the walls. The next room in the sequence was the dining room. Adam was ever practical and he made a pantry in the basement below the anteroom, so food could be warmed up before going upstairs. The long narrow dining room was given apses at both ends with screens of Corinthian columns to disguise its length, and the windows on the courtyard side were converted into niches for sculpture. The drawing room was next, with a high coved ceiling made by taking some of the height from the floor above. This room is now hung with faded 19th-century red silk damask and some of the fine collection of family portraits. The original red damask had a bold design of white, green and gold and was left bare of paintings. The room has remarkably rich decoration: the ceiling was decorated by Cipriani with painted roundels of neo-classical subjects, the chimneypiece is of white statuary marble with a delicate overlay of gilt-bronze decoration, and the door surrounds are veneered with ivory with gilt-metal overlay. No wonder visitors were impressed.

The last state room was the 136-ft long gallery overlooking the Thames. The walls and ceiling are painted in soft and subtle colours with low relief plasterwork and small inset paintings.

158   Isleworth, Syon House. The long gallery of the mid-16th-century house was redesigned by Robert Adam as a library, with delicate low-relief plasterwork and painted decoration.

Adam broke up its great length by dividing the walls into pilastered sections with bookcases, and flanking the several doors and two chimneypieces with niches for vases and sculptures (later converted to more bookcases). At each end the tower rooms are treated differently, one square with painted silk hangings, the other circular with niches and a domed ceiling from which hangs a birdcage. In 1768 the Northumberlands entertained the King of Denmark at Syon and had a spectacular circular tent constructed in the courtyard. This led to Adam's scheme to make this permanent, and a plan by him shows the domed 'Rotonda' he proposed. This did not happen, but descriptions of the event allow us to see how these houses were used for wonderful parties. Mrs Delany described 'the entertainment that beat all others … [with] a temporary pantheon erected in the court … which was illuminated with four thousand lamps in variety of pretty forms; the King of Denmark's cypher on four parts of the building.'[7]

Following the Duke's death not much was done at Syon apart from the addition of two minor buildings: the charming fishing pavilion and the dairy. The former was added by Robert Mylne in 1803 and is a small stuccoed building overlooking the Thames. It has a domed circular room flanked by low wings, one with a boathouse. The dairy was built 1797-8 near the farm buildings, and was more efficient than elegant.[8] Not much of it survives as it was rebuilt c.1850 by Decimus Burton for the 4th Duke. It was given a Minton tiled floor and marble-topped shelves on cast-iron legs and the walls had relief roundels by Gott, one of Flaxman's pupils. In the 1820s the 3rd Duke, who lived and entertained splendidly, carried out some major works in house and gardens. These tend to be down-played in comparison with Adam's work though they are impressive; Thomas Cundy was his architect. The house was completely refaced in Bath stone, the kitchens were rebuilt behind the north wing and a corridor made on the north side of the house, allowing easy access for family and staff to the new family dining and drawing rooms, the only rooms today which overlook the courtyard. He also had a much larger staircase installed at the north end of the entrance hall. The first-floor bedrooms were updated, some of them for the visit of Princess Victoria and her mother, the Duchess of Kent, in 1831. Outside he commissioned new stables and rearranged the gardens on the north side of the house, making a formal setting for the superb conservatory designed by Charles Fowler and built 1827-30. This has a great glazed dome, a façade of Bath stone broken by immense vertical windows and fully glazed curving wings leading to pavilions. The approach from the house leads past rockwork mounds which disguise the existing ice-house to a round pond, in the middle of which is a copy of Giambologna's *Mercury*. From there radiating paths lead to the conservatory. The gardens continued to be filled with rare and interesting plants and the gardens were opened to the public in 1837.

The 4th Duke swept away Adam's interiors at Alnwick and employed Montiroli to redesign them a High Renaissance style. He was also asked to work at Syon where his changes were confined to the print room, private dining room and private drawing room, where he installed rich Italianate ceilings.[9] More Adam fittings were brought in when Northumberland House was demolished. The private dining room now has an exquisite chimneypiece from the glass drawing room, and furniture was divided between Syon and Alnwick. In the 20th century the house was little altered although the 10th Duke opened it to the public, making it one of the first private houses to be opened commercially. He also employed John Fowler to redecorate the hall and some of the other rooms. The house and its very fine collection of paintings and furniture are now undergoing restoration.

ISLINGTON

CANONBURY HOUSE

Islington was not a fashionable village for suburban houses in the 16th century, nor later: it was too close to the City and with its hilltop site, fresh air and good views had a reputation as a place of resort, so it was full of dairies, pubs and possibly rowdy Londoners enjoying a day out. But in the N-E part of the parish there was one splendid house, secluded in large gardens; much of it has gone, and what remains today is a group of buildings of various dates, but is still of great interest.

Canonbury House was built on land gifted to the prior and canons of St Bartholomew the Great in Smithfield in 1253, hence its name. William Bolton, Prior 1509-32, replaced the earlier manor house with a large single courtyard house for his own use and laid out extensive gardens. St Bartholomew's had been dissolved by the time Bolton died and its properties transferred to the Crown. By 1529 Thomas Cromwell had been given the manor and by 1532 he was owner of Bolton's house (as well as many other properties) and was carrying

out some work on it. After his downfall it changed hands many times, with the next notable owner being Sir John Spencer (?-1610), who bought it for £2,000 as a property investment in 1570.[1] He was an immensely rich City merchant, a member of the Clothworkers' Company and Lord Mayor in 1594-5. For his mayoralty he bought Crosby Place in Bishopsgate, one of the finest late medieval houses in the City.[2] Around 1599 he began to use Canonbury as his own suburban house, and carried out considerable work there.

Spencer's work remains most visibly in the wing adjoining Canonbury Tower. The tower, now on Canonbury Place, was probably built before Spencer's time and is 66 ft high with a viewing platform on the roof. The wooden staircase with its closed well fills the whole tower. The adjoining gabled building, originally part of the west range, has two fine panelled rooms installed by Spencer. The first-floor Spencer Room has simple panelling with fluted pilasters

159   Islington, Canonbury House. Canonbury Tower, a 16th-century prospect tower giving views over London. The adjoining wing contains Spencer's Oak Room.

and an elaborate carved overmantel. The more opulent Oak Room on the second floor is not large, but with its Serlian panelling, pilasters decorated with relief ornament, carved frieze and rather crude female figures representing Faith and Hope in the overmantel, it is a wonderful example of the exuberance of late Elizabethan decoration. The east range, now split into various private houses, has two rooms with excellent plasterwork ceilings. One was probably Spencer's first-floor great chamber and has a splendid ceiling with a flowing geometric pattern. It is dated 1599 and has the royal arms in the centre and sailing ships in roundels within the compartments, referring to Spencer's trading interests and to the East India Company, of which he was a founder-member. The other ceiling is in a ground-floor room of the same range and has pendant bosses and moulded flower ornament. All this is high quality work by top London craftsmen, which Spencer could easily afford. Spencer also laid out or embellished the large gardens to the south of the house, and a print of 1811 shows this with gazebos in the angles of the walls – rare London examples of 16th-century garden buildings which remarkably both still exist.[3] They are hexagonal brick buildings of two storeys over a semi-basement, each now linked to semi-detached early Victorian houses.[4] One is stuccoed, but the other still has some diaper brickwork and the rebus of Prior Bolton, a tun with a bolt through it, which must have been moved from another part of the site.

Spencer had only one child, Elizabeth, who was therefore a considerable heiress. In spite of his best efforts she married William, Lord Compton in 1599. He owned Bruce Castle in Tottenham as well as Compton Wynyates in Warwickshire and Castle Ashby in Northamptonshire. He was a wildly extravagant and idle courtier, not at all the sort of

160   Islington, Canonbury House. The Oak Room dated 1599.

son-in-law for Spencer. Sir John Spencer and his wife both died in 1610 and Compton and his wife inherited the bulk of his enormous fortune.[5] William was made Earl of Northampton in 1618, by which time he had let Canonbury House to Francis Bacon, who had it from 1616-25. Northampton and his wife spent their time either in London or Castle Ashby which they enriched with their newly-inherited fortune, for she was as extravagant as her husband. The Compton family retained Canonbury, but apart from 1649-60 when the 3rd Earl lived there quietly under the Commonwealth it was let. By the 18th century it was sub-divided, with the Northampton's bailiffs living in the Tower from 1684-1826. James Boswell records a visit in 1763 when he 'walked out to Islington and went to Canonbury House, a curious old monastic building, where Dr [Oliver] Goldsmith stays'.[6]

161 Islington, Canonbury House. Plasterwork ceiling dated 1599, with ships in roundels representing the East India Company.

In 1770 John Dawes leased the whole building and demolished the south range of the courtyard house in order to build a terrace of new houses. At the same time the east side was sub-divided into three separate houses, making numbers 6-8 Canonbury Place. These are now stuccoed and have sash windows, but the gables with their mullion and transom windows betray their earlier origins. (The two rooms with plasterwork ceilings are in these houses.) The 16 acres of walled gardens were still unbuilt on and could be used by the residents of these houses.[7] In 1795 the later five-bay Canonbury House was built on the site of part of the west range, and in the mid-19th century Alwyne Villas and Alwyne Road were developed along the line of the garden wall of the old house, incorporating the garden buildings described above. In 1865 three richly carved chimneypieces with overmantels were removed from the remaining fabric of the old house and two installed in Castle Ashby, where they still are today. Unfortunately it is not clear which rooms they came from as our information about the lay-out of the original house is scanty, but with their lavish carving and heraldic ornament they must have been in important rooms.[8]

In 1907 the 5th Marquess of Northampton commissioned C.E. Dance to restore the tower, which had been badly damaged by rampant ivy and dry rot. The brick parapet which we see today replaced the iron railings, and the hall adjoining it was built as a communal space for tenants on his estates. After the Second World War the hall was taken over by the Tavistock Theatre Company, and for many years was known as the Tower Theatre. Since 1998 it has been the home of the Canonbury Masonic Research Centre. Part of the Compton estate was sold to property companies in the 1950s, and gradually the 'rather insalubrious surroundings' with large houses and big gardens has become an area of desirable family houses.[9] Remarkably the Compton family still owns the area immediately round what is left of Canonbury House, and without this history of ownership by one family it is unlikely that the remains of Canonbury House would have lasted to this day.

KENSINGTON

HOLLAND HOUSE

The most important suburban house to be destroyed in the Second World War was Holland House in Kensington, hit by a bomb on the night of 27-28 September 1940. Until then it had been a private house, one of the last great houses to be lived in. A photograph of the library, charred and roofless, with local residents leafing through books, is a vivid image of the result of that air raid. Today part of its grounds make up Holland Park and only a fragment of the house remains: part of the entrance front and the east wing, restored post-war and in institutional use. Why does its loss matter so much?

The house was built 1605-6, and was the only remaining one of the three great houses built on the ridge of high ground north of the village of Kensington at that time: Nottingham

162 Kensington, Holland House. The south front today, with only the east wing restored post-war.

House became Kensington Palace and Campden House was burnt down in 1862. These houses had excellent sites, with good views and gardens on the south-facing slopes and supplies of fresh water from springs along the ridge. They were close to London, and closer still to Hyde Park, originally enclosed by Henry VIII.[1] Sir Walter Cope, the builder of Cope Castle (as it was nicknamed), was a landowner, courtier, and collector. His London house was in the Strand, close to that of his friend Robert Cecil, who was building Hatfield House at the same time. Both produced innovative houses, Cope's house being a fascinating example of the new ideas in planning which were being experimented with in suburban houses. It was possibly designed by John Thorpe, whose drawings do so much to illuminate the architectural scene of the early 17th century. A plan of his showing it more or less as built identifies it as Cope's house and has inscribed on it 'pfected p JT' implying that he was the designer.[2]

The entrance front faced south. It was of three storeys below shaped gables with attics, and had a semi-basement with service rooms. The central feature was a canted bay which formed a porch and was topped by an ogee roof. It was flanked by bay windows on the ground and first floors. The east side had a loggia facing the gardens; this survived the bombing and has been restored. There were also loggias in front of the wings, enclosing the terrace in front of the house. The north front also had projecting bay windows below shaped gables and a small stair turret in the centre. The design had a sense of movement and drama yet was tightly controlled. It was also highly decorated, with the stonework of the loggias, porch and bay windows carved with Serlian ornament and pierced strapwork.

It was an H-plan house. There is nothing unusual about that, but Holland House was also a double-pile house with a new type of hall. This was not a through hall as at Charlton or Eagle House, Wimbledon; instead it was a rectangular room, its front wall broken by the

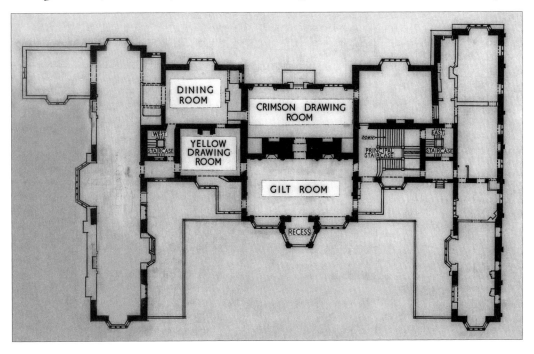

163   Kensington, Holland House. Plan of first floor.

porch and the pair of bay windows, its inner wall by a pair of fireplaces. It was not especially large, and its two fireplaces meant that the traditional arrangement of a high end with a dais was impossible; it was a new type of entrance hall. Behind it were parlours and a passage leading to the small staircase. The wings were extended slightly soon after the house was completed. On the west side were the family rooms, including a winter parlour tucked in cosily beside the kitchen; there were other service rooms and a secondary staircase. On the east side were the state rooms, approached by the principal staircase. This was wide and well-lit, its carved balustrade picking up the theme of the external decoration with its arches and rusticated newels. The great chamber was above the hall, also with a pair of chimneypieces. It was a most successful piece of planning, and was much admired by contemporaries.

Cope did not have long to enjoy his new house, as he died in 1614. It was inherited first by his widow, then their daughter Isabel. She had married Sir Henry Rich, a younger son of the Earl of Warwick and a courtier. He was soon made Baron Kensington then in 1624 Earl of Holland, thus giving the house the name it still has today. His ambitions for preferment at court and in politics were not fulfilled and he turned to improving the house he had inherited. Around 1625 he decorated the great chamber, known from then onwards as the Gilt Room. The overmantels had large allegorical figures and the wall panels were painted with grotesque ornament and the *fleur-de-lys* of the Holland arms.[3] The walls needed some restoration by the 19th century, which was carried out by Watts in 1847-8.

164   Kensington, Holland House. The Gilt Room, with early 17th-century painted decoration.

The ceiling collapsed in the late 18th century and there is no reliable source for its original appearance. Apart from those changes the Gilt Room kept something of its early 17th-century appearance until 1940. A set of *sgabello* chairs must have been bought at this time for the house, one of which is now in the V & A.

Recent research has shown that Holland added a large wing to the west side of the house in 1638-40, which was demolished in 1704. Not much is known about this three-storey wing, but it contained a new dining room and great chamber, as well as a stone staircase. He also built impressive new stables west of the house, fragments of which still exist. These were very expensive and up-to-date, with stalls for eight horses and space for several carriages. The design appears to have been by Inigo Jones, whom Holland would have known through his court connections. All that survives today of this restrained and elegant design are brick arches in English bond, some of the original openings for the coach house and stables.[4] He commissioned stone gate piers from Nicholas Stone, which now stand in front of the remains of the house.

Holland supported Parliament when the Civil War began, more from bitterness at his lack of success at court than from conviction. General Fairfax used the house in 1649, but it was

165 Kensington, Holland House. Gate piers designed and built by Nicholas Stone *c.*1630, moved to the front of the house after the Second World War.

given back to the widowed Lady Holland for her use under the Commonwealth. In the later 17th century the house was let from time to time. In 1716 Joseph Addison married the widowed Charlotte, Countess of Warwick and Holland, so in his middle age Addison went to live at Holland House, where his wife was bringing up her young son. He died there five years later, and his step-son in 1721. The house then went to another branch of the family, was leased to Henry Fox in 1726 and bought by him in 1768. This was the beginning of the important association between the Foxes and Holland House.

Henry Fox (1705-74) was a fairly unscrupulous politician and the son of Sir Stephen Fox, builder of Morton Hall in Chiswick. Like his father he was Paymaster-General during the Seven Years' War, but unlike him was corrupt enough to be investigated by Parliament. He was made 1st Baron Holland of Foxley in 1763. In 1744 he eloped with Lady Caroline Lennox, and they bought Holland House which they used as their London house; they later built a country house by the sea in Kent.[5] They loved the house in spite of its being unfashionably old and very cold. Their most famous son, Charles James Fox, was born and brought up there, but it was inherited by his elder brother Stephen, 2nd Lord Holland and later 1st Earl of Ilchester, who let it in an effort to retrench.

In 1874 Lady Holland, the elderly widow of the 4th Lord Holland, was in serious financial straits and the house was increasingly dilapidated. She decided to pass on the house and the Kensington estate to Lord Ilchester, a descendant of Sir Stephen Fox and therefore with a family connection to the house. His country estate was at Melbury in Dorset. He would give her an annuity and she could remain there for life. He was a practical and business-like man, who started to develop part of the grounds with large houses. One of the new streets was Melbury Road, named after Ilchester's Dorset estate. Here Norman Shaw designed houses for two leading artists and William Burges and Lord Leighton built themselves houses; the area became a favourite one for artists. His widow remained at Holland House after Ilchester's death for a further thirty years. When she died in 1935 Kensington was densely built up and Holland House seemed a timewarp. It inspired Giles Fox-Strangways, the 6th Lord Ilchester, to write a history of the house, *The House of the Hollands, 1605-1820* which he published in 1937. In order to raise funds to repair the house he also began the development of Abbotsbury Road, named after his other Dorset estate. The road was hardly built when the Second World War broke out, and building was not resumed till after the war.

When the house was bombed in 1940 some of the contents had been removed to Melbury for safety. The fire took hold in the centre of the house and only the east wing was saved. In 1943 SPAB inspected the ruins and wrote a report, proposing that after the war it might be restored for use as their own offices.[6] Probably at this stage the house could have been repaired for some such use, but nothing was done. Instead Lord Ilchester offered the grounds and house to the LCC on certain conditions, and in 1952 this came into effect.[7] The grounds became Holland Park, with the stables and service buildings becoming a cafe and a restaurant. A decision had to be made about the house. The ruins were largely demolished, only the hall remaining of the central block, flanked by the loggias. The east wing with its bay windows, shaped gables and loggia was restored. It became a youth hostel, with low and fairly unobtrusive extensions to the east designed by Hugh Casson and Neville Conder.[8] This is still in use today as a hostel, the park around it is a haven of wildlife in what is now a fashionable part of London, but the house is a sad reminder of what was lost.

KESTON

HOLWOOD HOUSE

Keston is a small village about three miles south of Bromley with high wooded ground to the S-E. This was an ancient site with evidence of inhabitants going back 5,000 years and Iron-Age earthworks, as well as evidence of a Roman cemetery and possibly traces of a villa. All these were merged in the popular imagination to make it known as Caesar's Camp. The earliest mention of a large estate called Holwood was in 1484 and by the 17th century this was owned by Sir Stephen Lennard, whose family owned Wickham Court at nearby West Wickham. The most celebrated owner of Holwood was William Pitt the Younger (1759-1806). His father, the 1st Earl of Chatham, had his country house at Hayes only a mile or so away and Pitt was born there so he was familiar with the country. He bought the Holwood estate of about 500 acres with its modest house in 1785 and used it as a retreat from the cares of office. Pitt's house has been replaced but the site, on high ground with extensive views across Kent to the S-E, is the same.

Pitt immediately summoned John Soane to make alterations, and in 1795 Soane was asked back to make fairly minor improvements. Although that house has gone Soane's drawings give us a clear idea of the compact and convenient house which he proposed.[1] The house was a late example of the triple-pile plan with the entrance on the nine-bay north front into an oval vestibule. On the east side were the service rooms, on the west the main reception rooms: a breakfast room, an eating room with a bow, the withdrawing room beyond. Separating the service and family rooms was the largest room of all, Pitt's library, with a canted bay overlooking the view. The centre of the house had a small lightwell and a main staircase, lit at upper levels by thermal windows.[2] The house was of two main storeys with some attic rooms, and all the reception rooms had long windows down to the ground. The main bedroom in the bowed west front had a balcony of delicate ironwork in an S-pattern. Not all these works were carried out, but from Soane's point of view it was prestigious commission and led to work for others in Pitt's circle. After Soane's first phase of building works was under way Humphry Repton was called in to make proposals for the grounds. He found the prime minister so busy that he didn't meet him at once, but when they did meet Repton was 'delighted with the clear and decided manner in which he explained his wishes' and even more so by 'the readiness with which he acquiesced to my suggestions'.[3] Repton tactfully brushes over Pitt's partial destruction of the Iron-Age earthworks of Caesar's Camp in order to open up the views from the hill behind his house.

Pitt sold the house in 1803 due to his crushing debts and after his death it was burnt down. In 1823 the new owner, John Ward, set about rebuilding it with Decimus Burton as his architect.[4] This was a much larger and more impressive house in fashionable Grecian style. The two-storey house is built of white brick with stone details, with a long entrance front 2-2-3-2-2. The three central bays have a shallow pediment and the recessed front door is flanked by Greek Doric columns. On the garden front the centre is dominated by a bow running through both storeys with Ionic columns supporting a deep entablature. It thus echoes one feature from Soane's design, a bowed front with long windows overlooking the wooded view. The entrance hall opened into a top-lit atrium with four Ionic columns, beyond which was the bow room flanked by the other reception rooms. These were plain and relied on their proportions and fine views for their effect. It was an impressive house, praised by Neale as 'one of the most ornamental, convenient and substantial mansions in the county [of Kent]. The scenery is very varied and extensive, owing to the elevation of the site.'[5]

Ward sold Holwood in 1852 and by 1876 it was the suburban house of the 15th Earl of Derby, in whose family it remained till 1953. Its decline began after that. In 1953 it was put up for sale and was bought by Seismograph Ltd., which converted the stables as office and laboratory space without making major changes to the house itself. It also applied successfully for government grants to plant conifers as a commercial crop in the Repton landscape. In the 1970s it was allowed to massively expand the office space in the grounds even though it was in the Green Belt, building additional office space and laboratories close to the entrance front and in a large circular development beyond the stables; some of this was on the remains of Caesar's Camp. In 1983 there was a fire after which the company applied for planning permission to expand the site still further, but by this time the house was listed Grade 1 and the application was called in by the Department of the Environment. When permission was not forthcoming Seismograph sold it to a consortium which planned to make a golf course in the grounds and convert and expand the house as a hotel. A long planning battle ensued which generated a lot of interest locally and has only recently been resolved. The house has been sold and will become a private house again with about 40 acres of grounds, while the office and laboratory space is being rebuilt as modern housing. It is perhaps the best solution in the circumstances.[6]

166   Keston, Holwood House. Designed by Decimus Burton in 1823 for John Ward.

217

KEW

KEW PALACE

Today Kew Palace is part of the royal enclave of Kew Gardens, isolated from the village which clusters round the green by Kew Bridge. This was not always so: the green once extended further west and the house had a public road in front of it leading to the Brentford ferry. There were cottages nearby and the stables and service buildings were across the road. It was only in the 18th century that Kew became a royal preserve. Another name for the house, the Dutch House, hints at its earlier existence as a riverside house for a City family of Flemish extraction. This was built about 1631 by Samuel Fortrey (1567–1643), whose grandfather, de la Forterie, came over to England in 1567. Fortrey was a merchant who in 1620 leased the earlier house on the site from Sir Hugh Portman, a Somerset landowner. The Earl of Leicester had had a house in this area in the 1550s, and it is just possible that the brick vaults below part of the present house are part of that, although the evidence is poor.[1]

The house is one of many examples round London of a compact brick house with florid brickwork, the design probably by a London bricklayer not an architect, and one that with its showy qualities appealed to City taste. (Other surviving examples are Cromwell House, Highgate and Forty Hall, Enfield, but there were many more which have disappeared.) The date and the initials of Fortrey and his wife Catherine are in cut and moulded brickwork over the entrance, so the date is secure even if there are no known building accounts. It is a particularly good example of its type, with a symmetrical entrance front facing S–E and three shaped gables which light the attics. It is a three-storey seven-bay house with paired windows projecting below the outer gables. The central frontispiece projects slightly in the centre, with banded brickwork suggesting the Doric order at ground level, Ionic pilasters above and Corinthian columns on the second storey which all frame arched windows. There are groups of tall diagonally set chimneys, and all this verticality is countered by the heavy string courses and cornice across the façade. The sides are simpler with plain gables and no cornice, and the river front has a recessed centre and three shaped gables, with pedimented windows at the upper level.

Until recently one could see the Flemish bond brickwork, the uneven shapes of the bricks requiring thick mortar joints. Recent investigation has shown that there was originally limewash over the brickwork; this has recently been reinstated, giving the house an even red-ochre colour.[2] It would originally have had oak mullion and transom windows, all of which were replaced by sashes in the 1730s. The tiled roof is still partly in its original state with three parallel ranges, although the inner valleys were filled in to provide more servants' rooms in the 18th century.

The house is a compact block of 70 x 50 ft, an example of the double-pile plan which was considered so suitable for merchant and gentry houses in the London area. It has a thick spine wall across the middle of the house, and has four rooms to a floor, a common type. The

167 Kew Palace. The garden front before the limewash was applied. The loggia was possibly designed by William Kent. The formal gardens were laid out in 1970.

entrance led into the screens passage with the hall on the east side, and the winter parlour and kitchen to the west; the cluster of chimneys this side of the house marks the kitchen. The main parlour was on the river front, and the stairs led up to the great chamber and family lodgings above. As at Cromwell House, the open-well staircase went right up to the top of the house, making it a very impressive feature. (Later stairs are often only to first-floor level, with a secondary staircase continuing to the top.) The stairs have been replaced, but the fragment of painted decoration recently found in the attics at dado level must reflect the design of the original staircase. (This is similar to the remnants of painted decoration at nearby Boston Manor, which also reflect the design of the carved balustrade.) Not much remains of Fortrey's decorative schemes, though the overmantel and the strapwork overdoors in the hall suggest bold and fashionable decoration. Only one plasterwork ceiling survives from his time in the queen's boudoir, and a low-relief strapwork frieze can still be seen in the great chamber (or queen's drawing room) and suggests that this room, too, had a ceiling of decorative plasterwork. After Fortrey's death the house remained in the family but was let. In 1697 it was leased by another City man, Sir Richard Levett, a tobacco merchant and Lord

Mayor 1699-1700, who repanelled the great chamber without destroying the frieze above it. Otherwise little was done to the house until it became part of the group of royal houses at Kew in the reign of George II, which has defined its history ever since.

From 1719 the favourite retreat of George II and Queen Caroline (as they became in 1727) was Richmond Lodge, also known as Ormonde Lodge, originally a hunting lodge built for William III in the Old Deer Park opposite Syon House and therefore close to Kew Palace.[3] Here the queen laid out celebrated gardens with the help of Bridgeman and Kent. In 1729 she took a 99-year lease of Kew Palace from the Portman family, not for herself but for her daughters the Princess Royal and princesses Amelia and Elizabeth. (Princess Amelia later lived in White Lodge, Richmond Park and Gunnersbury.) About the same time her son Frederick, Prince of Wales, took a lease on the Capel's house and rebuilt it from 1731-5 as The White House, using William Kent as his architect.[4] This much enlarged house therefore stood opposite Kew Palace so the royal children were effectively at the far end of the gardens created by their mother.

Various changes were required at the Dutch House for the princesses. The kitchen was moved outside the house to a new west wing with more service rooms (demolished in the 1880s). All the original windows were replaced with sashes and new internal shutters; the

168   Kew Palace. The first-floor boudoir after its recent restoration. The ceiling still has its 1630 plasterwork, although the rest of the room reflects Queen Charlotte's taste *c*.1800.

staircase was replaced by the present one, but only to the second floor; more space was made in the attics; and new stone chimneypieces were installed in the hall and the small parlour opposite. These are bold and simple and point to William Kent as the designer. It is possible that the loggia on the river front was also part of these building works, but since it was completely rebuilt in the 1930s its earlier history is unclear.

By 1754 the Prince of Wales (the future George III) lived there with his brother Edward, Duke of York and a succession of tutors. His widowed mother lived opposite with his sisters and his other brothers stayed in a house on Kew Green, so the family was scattered through the area and many courtiers chose to live nearby. When George III married he often came to Kew with his growing family, using Richmond Lodge. His mother died in 1772, after which he moved to the White House and demolished the lodge so he could lay out new gardens and experiment with farming. He and Queen Charlotte also spent more time at Windsor, and it was only when George III's madness set in that Kew Palace came into its own again.

In 1799 the White House was demolished and James Wyatt's new Castellated Palace was under construction nearby. Queen Charlotte spent some time at Kew Palace, which had become – temporarily, it was hoped – the only royal house at Kew in a good state of repair. When the king had another bout of madness in 1804 it was decided to move him to new lodgings in the west wing, where his rooms could be shut off from those of the queen. He later moved to Windsor where he died in 1820; his half-built Castellated Palace was blown up by George IV in 1827. Queen Charlotte spent much of her old age with her unmarried daughters at Kew Palace, where fashionable decoration was carried out for them – but how curious that they should be using a modest 1630s house, having demolished all the other royal houses at Kew. The double wedding of William, Duke of Clarence and Edward, Duke of Kent took place in the Queen's Drawing Room at Kew Palace just a few months before the queen's death in November 1818.

After 1818 Kew was rarely used by the royal family: better roads made Windsor easier to reach, the railway arrived in Brentford across the Thames and it became industrialised and polluted. Queen Victoria in her early married life preferred Claremont with its large estate and greater privacy and rarely visited Kew. It was opened to the public as a museum in 1898, administered by the Office of Works and from 1970 the Department of the Environment. In 1969 the Director of the Royal Botanic Gardens at Kew redesigned the gardens on the river front using only plants available before 1700, bringing in some Tijou ironwork from Hampton Court and a set of terms commissioned by Frederick, Prince of Wales. The present appearance of the house is due to the major restoration carried out 1996-2006 by Historic Royal Palaces. With so little remaining of its original appearance it was decided to present it as in Queen Charlotte's old age, and the research carried out for that project has built up a history of the house in considerable detail.[5] Particularly successful is the contrast between the redecorated rooms on the first floor with the almost untouched 18th-century paintwork and bare interiors on the second floor.[6]

LALEHAM

LALEHAM ABBEY

J.B. Papworth, author of architectural books as well as a competent architect and designer, designed this Thames-side villa for the Irish peer Richard Bingham, 2nd Earl of Lucan (1764-1839). In spite of the usual changes of ownership, a period in institutional use and then conversion into flats, it is still an elegant Regency villa set in comparatively rural surroundings. Only its picturesque lodge, Thatched Cottage in Abbey Drive, shows Papworth's interest in vernacular buildings: the roof is thatched, and a thatched verandah is supported on tree trunks, it has Tudor chimneys and its small windows have elaborate glazing.

Lucan owned Castlebar House in Co. Mayo as well as a London house, so this was his suburban retreat. Being well outside London land was more easily available, and it had a farm of 338 acres.[1] He bought the land in 1803, at which time he had been married for almost ten years and had a large family. Papworth produced a well-planned house in a restrained Grecian style. It was an almost square house of stone (although it is now painted stone colour) on two storeys, over a deep basement containing cellars not service rooms; these were discreetly hidden to the north, so the main block of the house contained a suite

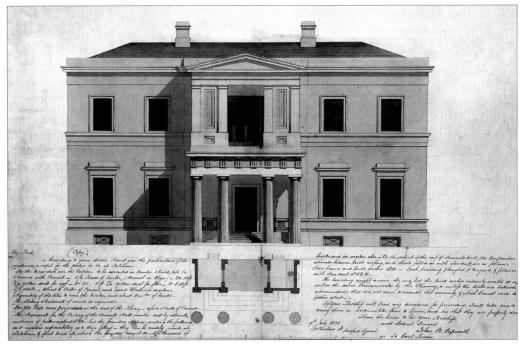

169   Laleham Abbey. Elevation of entrance front by J.B. Papworth dated 1828, with proposed changes.

of fine inter-connecting reception rooms on the ground floor, with bedrooms above. The exception was a suite of bedroom, dressing room and gunroom in the N–E corner, which was probably Lucan's own apartment, with his wife's on the first floor. By the time the house was built his marriage was in trouble, and his wife left soon after they moved in.

Papworth cleverly varied the room shapes, with the small oval entrance hall opening into a much larger D-shaped staircase hall. This is top-lit, with a cantilevered stone staircase; a black fossil marble chimneypiece contrasts with the plasterwork frieze of the *Triumphal Entry of Alexander into Babylon* above it. This was by Thorvaldsen, a sculptor much admired by Lucan after his travels in Europe as a young man. The dining room with apsed ends overlooked the grounds to the west, while the south side was taken up by a large drawing room and library, both opening onto a verandah – a nice example of the integration of house and garden which is such an important feature at this date. The library contained more sculptures by Thorvaldsen, including a relief of the Three Graces above the chimneypiece and an aedicule on the end wall with a life-size figure of Venus.[2] All the details of the house, from the plasterwork cornices to the double doors, are of high quality, although Barratts ripped out most of the original chimneypieces when they converted the house into flats in 1981.

A number of Papworth's drawings for Laleham survive and show his later schemes for the house.[3] The Greek Doric portico on the east front and the Greek key pattern frieze which

170   Laleham Abbey, Lord Lucan's library. The figure of Venus and the Three Graces overmantel panel were both by Thorvaldsen.

wraps round the house below the parapet were added *c*.1828. Several drawings relate to his design for a conservatory which was added as an extension to the south front; this was later converted into a chapel, so has been very much altered. A thatched ice-house was built in the park, although today only a mound remains. Lucan died in 1839 and his son the 3rd Earl immediately commissioned new stables, again from Papworth. These were rebuilt close to the service wing, providing stabling for 12 horses as well as coach houses, a laundry and bakehouse. Built in white brick, the thermal windows and deep eaves give it an Italianate look.

171 Laleham Abbey. The thatched lodge designed by Papworth.

Although the family remained at Laleham after they sold their Irish property they made no major changes, and increasingly were unable to afford the upkeep of the house. It was unsuccessfully offered for sale in 1899, and in 1922 a sale of the contents took place. The Thorvaldsens were sold, and the fine Savonnerie carpet woven for the library in 1803 went to the V & A.[4] The land-holding had shrunk by then to 85 acres, which was offered in various lots, some being 'ripe for early development'. Again both house and grounds remained unsold. The family went to live in London and the house remained empty for six years. Two private owners briefly lived there 1928-31, till it was bought for £7,500 by the Community of St Peter the Apostle, an Anglican order of nuns who ran it first as a school, then as a home for the elderly. This entailed various changes, and low buildings of indifferent quality were added to the north; the stable yard was converted into a cloister by the addition of a covered walkway, which remains; and a school chapel was made in one corner. A smaller chapel was made in the conservatory. However the upkeep of a historic house became too much for the nuns, and in 1980 they sold the house, its outbuildings and nine acres of grounds to Barratts Developments for conversion into flats. The outbuildings and stables were converted into small houses or apartments, and the house itself divided up, leaving the entrance and stairs unaltered. Recent research has led to a fine restoration of the original colour scheme here. The water meadows below the house have become a country park along the Thames, so the house remains in a sylvan setting.

MITCHAM

EAGLE HOUSE

This beautifully restored house stands at a busy junction in the centre of Mitcham, surrounded by schools, industrial premises and blocks of flats. It is a most unlikely survivor among the suburban houses round London, and a particularly unaltered example of a compact Baroque house built for a rich Londoner. It was built *c.*1705 by Fernando Moses Mendes (1647-1724), a Portuguese who had studied medicine in France before coming to England in 1669. He came from a family of well-off Jewish merchants, and his uncle had bought Cromwell House in Highgate in 1675. Fernando was a Roman Catholic and he became physician to Queen Catherine of Braganza. As such he had apartments in Somerset House, and probably also had a house in the City. He married in 1675, and his daughter Catherine da Costa went on to become a well-known portrait painter.[1]

172   Mitcham, Eagle House, entrance front. The balustraded roof platform gave views over the gardens and surrounding country.

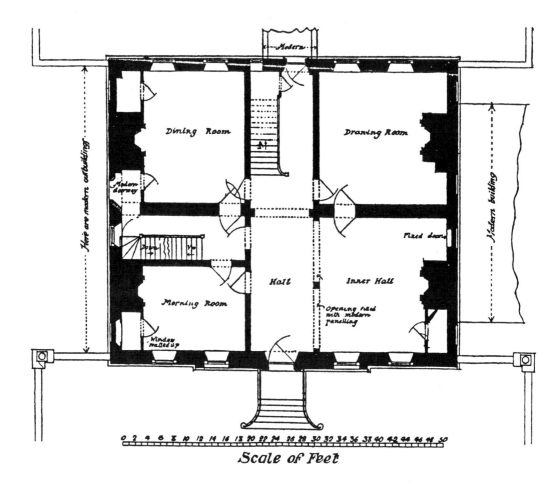

173   Mitcham, Eagle House. Plan of ground floor, showing the four rooms per floor and the deep chimneybreasts which allow for corner closets.

The house can be clearly seen from the road behind fine wrought-iron gates and high railings which end in brick piers with flamboyant eagles on top, so we still get a sense of the formal axial approach it would have had.[2] It is tall, with two equal storeys over a basement and a high hipped roof with tall chimneys, a cupola and a balustraded platform. The south-facing entrance front has a slightly projecting central section with a steep pediment, and a deep dentil cornice. There is no decoration other than the segmental porch over the half-glazed front door and the string course, which ends abruptly just before the corners of the house. It is built of stock bricks with rubbed red brick detailing round the windows and on the angles. The chimneybreasts are all on the side walls, so the roof is flanked by tall brick chimneystacks with stone capping, and the dormer windows have segmental pediments. The design is assured if not advanced for its date; when it was built Mendes was no longer young and perhaps conservative in his taste; and we have no idea who the architect or builder was. The north front is similar but lacking the pediment, and enlivened instead by the immensely long staircase window in the centre.

The interior has a simple plan with the two main floors almost identical.[3] It is of the common four rooms to a floor type. The wide hall runs from front to back with the staircase on the north side, and access to what was once the garden at the back. On each side are two high-ceilinged rooms, those on the west side being smaller to allow for the secondary staircase, which runs between them from basement to attics. The service rooms were in the basement, with doors leading into it on both sides of the house. Remains of the wide kitchen fireplace can be seen in the N-W corner room, and the everyday parlour was probably the room above. The main rooms seem to have been on the east side of the house, with finer panelling and more elaborate chimneypieces on both the ground and first floors. None of the rooms has a decorative plaster ceiling, although every room on the ground and first floors retains its original panelling, shutters and box cornice; and although only some of the simple stone and marble chimneypieces are still *in situ* every room has its deep chimneybreast. In some of the rooms this was used to provide a small closet; the room in the N-W corner of the first floor still has tall narrow sash-windows with window-seats on each side of the chimneybreast, although the panelling partition has been removed; on the east side of the house some of these windows have been blocked.

The wide main staircase, lit by the exaggeratedly tall window, runs from ground to first floor only and has twisted balusters, three to a step. The newels are most unusual, with four of these twisted balusters grouped into a cage; this is repeated on every landing. The walls here are lined in wood as if they were to be covered with textile hangings. The secondary staircase has simple panelling and balusters, but even here the newels are made up of four balusters tightly grouped. Even the attic floor is little altered: the rooms are quite high-ceilinged and well-lit with their tall dormer windows, and the sloping walls are simply panelled. From the landing a tight spiral staircase leads up to the cupola which gives access to the flat leaded roof. The wooden balustrade is uncomfortably low by today's standards, like the one at Cromwell House. Perhaps it was memories of the magnificent views from his uncle's North London house which inspired this one; certainly the views are extensive, from the North Downs visible to the south to the ridge of Wimbledon Common to the N-W.

In 1711 Mendes let the house to Sir John Doliffe, a director of the South Sea Company, and his monogram is on the gates. It changed hands many times before becoming a school in 1855, after which additional buildings were built behind the house. By the late 20th century it was owned by the LB of Merton and was in a very poor state. A local surveyor offered to convert it into offices, and carried out an exemplary restoration of the Grade 1 listed house, completed in 1991. He built additional office accommodation in a new 'stable block' behind the house on the site of the earlier school buildings, designed to English Heritage specifications. The house now has only small grounds front and back and a sliver of approach road beside it; it is leased to a school, and has been successfully adapted to its current use without impairing the historic fabric.[4]

PETERSHAM

HAM HOUSE

Ham House is one of very few houses which can still be approached from the River Thames, even if one can only cross from the Twickenham bank in a small ferry. It is a foretaste of the time-warp that Ham is today, surrounded by gardens and water meadows and with hardly a house in sight. The approach from the river leads to an avenue and a walled forecourt, still with the tall iron gates and piers designed by Sir William Bruce in 1671. The axial approach has gone; instead there is a carriage sweep round a Coade stone statue of a river god.

The north front has been little altered since it was built for Sir Thomas Vavasour from 1608-10. He was a Yorkshire landowner and courtier, made Knight Marshal by James I, so this was a place of retreat from his duties in the royal household. His unknown architect designed a three-storey entrance front of brick with stone dressings with a hipped roof, the earlier tiles replaced with slate. From this side the original H-plan with deeply projecting cross-wings can be seen. Linking these to the central range were corner towers topped with lead ogee domes which were removed in the 18th century, leaving a continuous roofline below a deep cornice. Most of this front still has its leaded mullion and transom windows

174   Petersham, Ham House. Nineteenth-century print of entrance front. The loggias originally had towers with lead-covered ogee domes.

with later sash windows in the canted bays. Between the ground and first floors and in the walls of the forecourt are inset ovals with lead busts of Roman emperors, which may have been rearranged from elsewhere. The centrally placed entrance led into a hall, which in advance of its time did not have a screens passage. There were service rooms on the west side, and the kitchen in the N-W corner of the basement still has its big stone fireplace and spits. Beyond the hall lay the parlour and stairs up to the first floor with its two apartments and the great chamber above the hall. This led to a withdrawing room and a long gallery in the west side of the house. It was a competent plan, and the house and its formal gardens were interesting enough to be recorded by Smythson when he was in London in 1609.[1]

After Vavasour's death in 1620 the house passed to John Ramsay, 1st Earl of Holdernesse, one of the Scottish courtiers who came south with James I in 1603. In 1626 it passed to another Scot with whose descendants it remained until given to the National Trust in 1948. It is this remarkable continuity of ownership which has helped preserve the house and its contents. William Murray (c.1600-55), later 1st Earl of Dysart, and his daughter were to transform the house into what we see today. Murray was brought up with the future Charles I, sharing his lessons as his 'whipping boy.' He became a Gentleman of the King's Bedchamber in 1625 and shared the King's taste for art collecting. In 1637 he made a series of changes to the interiors at Ham, creating a state apartment impressive enough for royal visits. Much of this survives: the reconstructed main staircase, the North Drawing Room and Green Closet, the pilastered gallery. The designer of these changes was Franz Cleyn, director of the Mortlake Tapestry Factory nearby and a man Murray would have known through his court connections.

175 Petersham, Ham House. The North Drawing Room on the first floor, made in 1637 by William Murray.

The staircase was built round an open well, the richly carved panels with military trophies; the newels are carved with weapons and topped with baskets of flowers. The undersides of the flights are decorated with simple oval wreaths of plasterwork and the walls are still hung with some of Murray's art collection. His great chamber for formal dining was painted deep blue like the cabinet room in the Queen's House at Greenwich. It was destroyed in the

18th century, although the withdrawing room and the Green Closet which opens off it are little altered. Their decoration has a Continental Baroque feel that is rare in England and points to Cleyn's European background. The ceiling in the drawing room has restrained Jonesian decoration, unlike the chimneypiece. This has gilded Salomonic columns supporting wild foliage decoration while *putti* frame the overmantel painting. Tapestries hang on the walls and the doorcases are elaborately carved. The closet is similar, with richly carved doorcases and dado and a coved ceiling decorated by Cleyn with scenes of *putti* painted in tempera on paper.[2] Here Murray hung green material as a background for his collection of cabinet pictures and miniatures.

Murray was rewarded for his loyalty to the king with an earldom, which under Scottish law could pass to his daughter. He died during the Commonwealth and his family managed to keep a low profile through those difficult years and to continue living at Ham. In 1648 the eldest daughter, Elizabeth, married Sir Lionel Tollemache of Helmingham Hall in Suffolk; she was highly educated, quick, very strong-minded and ambitious. After her father's death she became Countess of Dysart in her own right and at the Restoration played a lively part in court life. Her husband died in 1669 and she began an affair with John Maitland, Earl of Lauderdale, a Scottish landowner with Thirlestane Castle near Lauder as his country seat and official lodgings at Whitehall Palace and Holyrood. He was a highly intelligent but violent-tempered man who was made Secretary of State for Scotland by Charles II and was rewarded with a dukedom in 1672. His first wife (who lived in Lauderdale House, Highgate) died in 1671 and only six weeks later he married Elizabeth Dysart. So it was as the Duke and Duchess of Lauderdale that they embellished her property at Ham, turning it into one of the most splendid of the suburban houses round London.[3] Due to the remarkable survival of many of the furnishings which can be checked against a series of inventories the house still appears today very much as it did then.[4]

William Samwell was the architect asked to enlarge the house, which he did by making the single-pile central range into a double pile. The space between the projecting bays of the south front was filled in, creating ground-floor apartments for the Lauderdales with a state apartment on the floor above. Roger North, often critical, wrote that the enlargement of Ham was 'the best of its kind I have ever seen … For I do not perceive any part of the old fabric is taken downe, but the wings stand as they were first sett, only behind next the garden they are joined with a strait range entirely new. And there are all the rooms of parade, exquisitely plac'd.'[5] The apartments for the Duke and Duchess on the ground floor flanked the central dining room which opened into the gardens. Her rooms ended in the White Closet with direct access to the east garden; his in his closet on the west side, though he also had a first-floor library which has early examples of fitted furniture with its fall-front desk and floor-to-ceiling bookshelves. The S-E corner room in the basement was converted into the Duchess's basement bathroom and connected to the ground floor by a private staircase. A chapel was made out of the parlour in the N-E corner, the bay window being blocked and panelled internally to make a simple recess for the altar. Unlike many private chapels the Lauderdales did not have a gallery but sat in box pews by the door. The furnishings in the other rooms were showy and colourful, but nothing to that in the new state apartment on the first floor. The gallery, its panelling embellished in 1637-8, became a showcase for their collection of royal and family portraits and led to the antechamber, bedchamber and closet, all designed for a royal visit by the queen. These rooms have their original rich plasterwork ceilings and bolection moulded fireplaces, grained and gilded decoration and even their original textile hangings. Apart from the bedchamber, which was rearranged *c.*1744 as a drawing room, all the rooms are filled with their original English, Dutch and French furnishings, and give an overpowering impression of luxury.

The gardens in their various phases are also well documented. Smythson's plan records the lay-out which Vavasour commissioned, with its parterres immediately south of the house with raised walks round the edge. In 1672 new gardens were planned for the enlarged house and drawings were made by the German engineer, John Slezer, who had worked for Lauderdale in Scotland.[6] His plan shows the axis of the gardens to the south aligned on the bedchamber in the state apartment, with a central *allée* with radiating paths cutting through a wilderness area. A painting by Danckerts in the White Closet shows this area with statues set on pedestals and fashionably dressed visitors. There was also a privy garden on the east side, an orangery and extensive kitchen gardens beyond the stableyard to the west. A dairy in the service courtyard to the west was added in 1672, and given an early 19th-century facelift: marble shelves were supported on cow's legs, with pretty Minton tiles with an ivy leaf design as a splashback. The discovery in the family archives of a later plan of the gardens shows that Slezer's design was still in place around 1730 and only later was the garden lay-out loosened up, the parterres swept away and the entrance forecourt altered.[7] The National Trust has been gradually restoring parts of the garden to its late 17th-century appearance.

176   Petersham, Ham House. Garden front drawn by John Slezer after Samwell had enlarged the house in 1672.

177   Petersham, Ham House. The ground-floor chapel, made in 1672 by the Duke and Duchess of Lauderdale.

These changes were very expensive and by the time Lauderdale died in 1682 he left his widow deeply indebted. She retired from court and lived quietly at Ham for another 16 years, mortgaging the estate and selling some items. Her son by her first marriage inherited Ham as well as his father's Tollemache estates; this preserved Ham as a little-altered secondary house. His main change was to create a two-storey entrance hall by cutting through into the great chamber above and making a gallery. His son, the 4th Earl, made more changes, largely as a result of the survey carried out by John James in 1730 which showed structural weaknesses. As a result the towers on the entrance front were lowered and the bays rebuilt with sash windows.[8] He also changed the first-floor state bedchamber into a fashionable drawing room with Soho tapestries and furniture supplied by Bradshaw.[9] His son married Horace

Walpole's niece, and Walpole described going to see her 'in her new principality of Ham …
It is so blocked up and barricaded with walls, vast trees and gates that you think yourself an
hundred miles off and an hundred years back. The old furniture is so magnificently ancient,
dreary and decayed, that at every step one's spirits sink, and all my passion for antiquity
couldn't keep them up … In this state of pomp and tatters my nephew intends it shall
remain.'[10] After a succession of Tollemaches with varying degrees of interest in the house
it was put into better shape by the 9th Earl of Dysart, who installed electricity and central
heating. In 1889-90 he employed Bodley & Garner to restore some of the rooms, with a
Watts wallpaper in the gallery and a new green damask chosen for the walls of the Green
Closet.[11] The house became well known as a time-warp and its interiors and furniture were
photographed for books such as Tipping's.[12] By the end of the Second World War the house
could no longer be maintained and Sir Lyonel Tollemache, 5th Bt., and his son gave it to the
National Trust in 1948. The Trust handed over its administration to the Ministry of Works,
while the rare and fascinating contents were bought by the government and passed on to the
Victoria & Albert Museum. Peter Thornton, curator of Furniture & Woodwork at the V & A
in the 1970s, pioneered the study of inventories and rearranged the house according to this
evidence (as he also did at Osterley). He recreated the historic interiors and had textiles

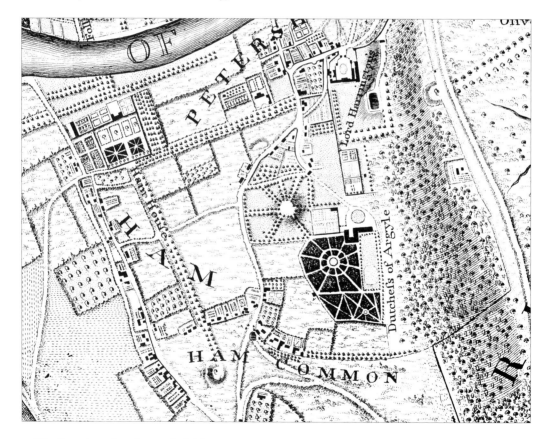

178 Petersham, from Rocque's 1745 map. Ham House is in the N–W corner close to the Thames, while
Sudbrook Park has absorbed part of Richmond Park into its grounds.

woven from original fragments to recreate the original colours where they had been lost: the strong colours shocked some people, used to the faded tones of old fabrics. The furnishings have been loaned by the V & A to the National Trust, which is now responsible for the whole site. Research continues into this most fascinating of houses and its grounds.

SUDBROOK PARK

This well-preserved early 18th-century house on the edge of Richmond Park is one that really can be described as a 'villa' in its plan and in its appearance. Built 1715-19 for John Campbell, the 2nd Duke of Argyll & Greenwich, it is an important early work by the Scottish architect, James Gibbs. The Duke of Argyll (1680-1743) was head of the Clan Campbell in the western Highlands, with Inveraray Castle as his main country seat. But he was born at Ham House in Petersham and was largely brought up in England. By profession he was a soldier, commanding a Dutch regiment for William III by the age of 17, and a commander of forces in Europe under the Duke of Marlborough. His most important contribution to the Hanoverian cause was his defeat of the Earl of Mar at Sherriffmuir, effectively ending the 1715 Jacobite rebellion.

In 1712 Argyll had bought the Kenwood estate in Hampstead but seems to have done nothing to the existing house before selling it on, and instead in 1715 bought the small estate of Sudbrook in Petersham. We know nothing about the modest existing house, only that James Gibbs, a leading architect recently returned from Rome, was sent down there at once to provide ideas for a new house. This was by no means Argyll's only house: apart from Inveraray, he had lodgings in the Palace of Holyroodhouse, a London house in Bruton Street, and in 1717 was to take a lease on the Oxfordshire estate of Adderbury, where both Gibbs and Roger Morris were to design improvements. During the building of Sudbrook the duke's first wife had died, and he had quickly married Jane Warburton, a Maid of Honour to the Princess of Wales. Their first daughter was born at Sudbrook in 1717, and it remained the family home until the duchess's death in 1767.

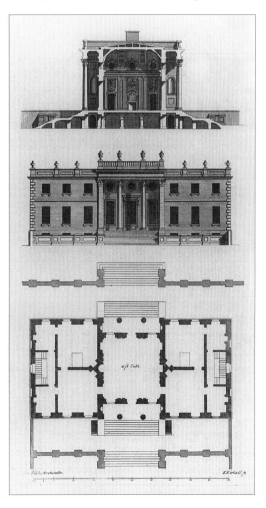

179 Petersham, Sudbrook Park. Section, elevation and plan from James Gibbs's *Book of Architecture*, 1728.

Gibbs designed a two-storey brick house with basement, only the centre being faced in Portland stone. This three-bay central feature with its Corinthian columns and balustrade is not a portico but a slightly recessed loggia, approached by a double flight of steps. The three outer bays of the house are simpler and more Baroque in style, the windows slightly arched and with brick aprons, and brick quoins. In plan the house is Italianate: the loggia leads directly into a central *salone* which rises through two storeys and has a coved ceiling. Each side of the *piano nobile* has an apartment of a panelled withdrawing room and bedchamber with corner fireplaces and two closets; a simple wooden staircase each side leads to both the basement and the upper floor, where there are four smaller apartments on each side of the *salone;* service rooms were in the basement. The house seems to have been built quickly, and the duke's account at Coutts Bank list some of the payments made to Gibbs and his craftsmen, such as the mason William Townesend and the bricklayer Thomas Churchill.[1]

The only remarkable interior is the cube room in the centre, but this is superb: a double-height space lit on each side by three long windows with *oeuil-de-boeuf* windows above; these are echoed on the side walls by blank roundels. The room is richly decorated: paired columns support a deep entablature below the groin-vaulted coving, and frame the chimneypiece, which has a Baroque marble surround with an inset overmantel mirror, etched with the duke's motto and crest. Above it is a large and splendid panel with the ducal crest and coat of arms, probably carved by Rysbrack. The four subsidiary doors, based on a design by Rossi, have finely carved trophies of arms both within and above the pediments, reflecting Argyll's military career.[2] This was probably designed as a dining room as well as the main reception room. A drawing by Gibbs shows the niche in the centre of the side wall with shelves, implying a buffet for the display of plate; but there is no trace of shelves now, and they may never have been executed.[3]

James Gibbs, Roman Catholic, Scottish and dependent in his early years on the Earl of Mar, might have found it difficult to make a career in Hanoverian Britain; the patronage of the Whig Duke of Argyll was therefore particularly important to him, and his 1728 *Book of Architecture* was dedicated to the duke, thanking him for his encouragement and protection. He included Sudbrook among his designs, describing it as 'a villa … Here is a Cube Room of 30 feet, handsomely adorn'd and lighted from two Portico's'. There are certain differences from the house as built. The arched windows became rectangular, the aprons were replaced by stone sills on brackets, the brick quoins became stone, and most striking of all, the complex steps to the loggias were replaced by a flight of steps the full width of the loggia, with a low wall masking the basement. These changes make the house more Palladian and in tune with the style of the late 1720s as promoted by Lord Burlington and Colen Campbell. But the plan and section are as built, showing the originality of Gibbs's conception.[4]

However this compact plan was not ideal for a growing family, and the duke's five wild daughters, known as the 'Bawling Campbells' were housed in an annexe, probably the separate building on the garden side of the house today, although that has been much altered. The duke was uninterested in their education, and they 'did what they pleased, nobody caring, and romped as much as they pleased' with their Bute cousins when they were out from Eton, according to Lady Louisa Stuart.[5] When the duke died in 1743 his widow inherited both Sudbrook and their London house for her lifetime, and her youngest daughter, Lady Mary Coke lived there with her after her formal separation from her husband, and as a widow after his early death. Her letters show that 'the great room' as they called it was used as a family living room; she describes playing cards and writing letters there. The house had a farm attached: when her mother died in 1767, a list was made of the stock belonging to it, which included two cows, nine pigs and fourteen ewes with lambs: these houses were run as small-holdings, able to provide at least basic food for the household.[6] The house was inherited by the eldest daughter, Caroline, who had married the Earl of Dalkeith, and it was probably she and her second husband, Charles Townshend, who altered the entrance front, replacing the loggia with a projecting portico to form an entrance hall. Other than this, the exterior has hardly been altered at all, apart from a small 19th-century side extension. Lady Mary Coke's regular visits to her sister show that she could reach Sudbrook from central London in about 1½ hours – not much longer than it would take today in heavy traffic.[7]

180 Petersham, Sudbrook Park. The saloon with the arms of the Duke of Argyll over the chimneypiece, probably carved by Rysbrack.

In 1784 the Crown lease on the property expired, but Lady Greenwich (as Caroline was known) was able to renew it and remain there until her death in 1794. Her son, the 3rd Duke of Buccleuch, inherited it, but at his death in 1819 his executors chose to auction it to provide for his daughters. The sale catalogue describes 'the beautifully wooded park of upwards of 130 acres' with a 'lodge … a gardener's house, capital walled gardens etc.' but in spite of this it did not meet its reserve at auction.[8] Only part of the land was sold, and the house was let. In 1825 Robert Horton, the tenant, bought it off the 5th Duke of Buccleuch, but let it again. In 1842 the estate was split: the house was sold with only three acres of garden, and the Crown bought back the rest of the land to re-unite it with Richmond Park. Like so many of these houses, it went to institutional use, becoming a 'Hydropathic Establishment' run by a Dr Weiss of Vienna. This closed in 1879, and the house reverted to private use, being leased by the Earl of Bute for a while before he moved to Chiswick House. From 1891-8 it was a private hotel, with Richmond Golf Club laying out part of the grounds as a golf course. In 1898 they took over the house and, fortunately for its survival, it has remained with the golf club ever since.

RICHMOND

ASGILL HOUSE

Richmond Palace, the riverside palace rebuilt by Henry VII after a fire in 1499, had fallen into disrepair and had largely gone by the early 18th century, and today only fragments of the old palace remain between Richmond Green and the river. But in the 18th century the brewhouse still stood in the S-W corner of the site and was leased to Colonel Cholmondeley in 1711, then in 1734 to his son, the 3rd Earl of Cholmondeley; he later mortgaged it, and sold the lease to Moses Hart in 1756. Hart died the following year, and his daughter and son-in-law immediately sold the lease to Sir Charles Asgill, a City banker. Asgill, a hard-working banker admired for his integrity, had already asked Robert Taylor to design his business premises at 70 Lombard Street, one of the earliest purpose-built banks. Like many successful City men in the 18th century he lived well away from his work, in a large house in Berkeley Square. In 1757-8 he was Lord Mayor and asked Taylor to design a new state coach, which is still in use. Taylor was also commissioned to design him a new house on the Richmond site, which was built 1761-2.

Asgill House, or Richmond Place as it was then called, is one of Taylor's most exquisite creations: a compact villa overlooking the river, austere outside but supremely elegant within. Like many of Taylor's houses, it avoids rectangularity: the three-bay centre is three storeys high, with half-pediments on the two-storey wings; a canted bay on each side of the ground floor

181   Richmond, Asgill House. The entrance front *c.*1972, after restoration.

each side again breaks the outline. There are deeply projecting eaves hinting at the Tuscan order, and the balustrades below the first-floor windows reappear as balconies above the side bays. It was built of warm Bath stone, rusticated on the ground floor and ashlar above, a choice of material which discreetly reflected Asgill's wealth.[1] The house, which had larger gardens than it has today, was approached from the N–E with the narrow vaulted entrance hall flanked by an elegant oval staircase and an oval vestibule (the hall and vestibule were altered in the 19th century). Three inter-connecting reception rooms occupy the ground floor, so the house is a progression through varied room shapes, an idea which is taken up by Taylor later at both Danson and Mount Clare. The first to be entered was the octagonal room 25 ft across with its superb views of the Thames. It had two chimneypieces, since replaced with just one, which today blocks access from the entrance hall. From this central room the drawing room and dining room could be entered, each lit by a canted bay and a splendid Rococo chimneypiece; that in the dining room was moved to the Octagon Room in the recent restoration. The cantilevered staircase leads to a curved landing with arched openings to the two main suites of bedrooms. A secondary staircase leads to the top floor. On the first floor there was another octagonal room which probably served as a dressing room or boudoir.

This now has the mythological paintings by Andrea Casali which were originally in the dining room; being oil on canvas they could easily be moved. In the 19th century they were given elaborate scrolled and gilded surrounds which have since been removed.

Asgill died in the house in 1788 and Sir Robert Taylor, a good friend of his, attended the funeral, where he caught a chill and died soon afterwards.[2] Asgill's son sold the house to James Whitshed Keene, MP and former Surveyor of the King's Works.[3] The house changed hands many times in the early 19th century, and by the later 19th century Richmond had grown into a populous village within easy reach of London by rail. So Asgill House became a main residence rather than an occasional retreat. As such the house was small, and Benjamin Cohen, J.P. and Deputy Lieutenant of Surrey, who lived there from 1836–67, raised the side wings to add bedrooms to the top floor. In spite of the care taken with the additions the house appeared top-heavy without the half-pediments.[4] Later a low service wing was attached to the N–W corner of the house, replacing the basement service rooms of the original house; a porch was added and the present square entrance hall was made out of the narrow hall and oval vestibule.

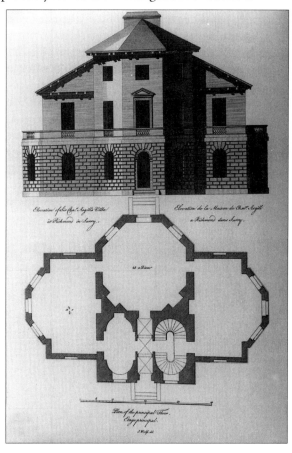

182 Richmond, Asgill House. Plan and elevation from *Vitruvius Britannicus*, 4, 1767.

183 Richmond, Asgill House, the first-floor boudoir *c.*1960. The Casali paintings were originally in the dining room.

A long-standing owner was James Hilditch, who took over the lease in 1882 and died there in 1920; his widow remained till the Second World War. In 1966 the house, by now rather dilapidated, was put on the market by the Crown Commissioners. At this point it would have been at risk but for their insistence that the house remain in private use and be sympathetically restored. Mr Fred Hauptfuhrer took on a new Crown lease in 1969 and with the help of Donald Insall as architect carried out an exemplary restoration, lowering the side wings to their original height, removing the service wing and restoring the fabric to its original 18th-century appearance.[5] It is a precious survival of Taylor's work: of his other villas near London, Mount Clare in Roehampton is in institutional use and Danson, although recently magnificently restored, kept its heightened side-wings and is not lived in. Even with the nearby road and railway Asgill House with its garden and views of the Thames is a reminder of the attraction of these riverside retreats. It is also an example of the superb architectural quality of some of these suburban houses, which has often been ignored in the 20th-century concentration on the history of the country house.

WHITE LODGE

Richmond and Kew were much favoured by the Hanoverians through the 18th century, and this accomplished Palladian villa was built as a hunting lodge for George I in the centre of Richmond Park. The Prince of Wales and Princess Caroline of Anspach used the Old Deer Park south of Kew Gardens and spent much of their time at Ormonde Lodge in the present Kew Gardens (demolished), where they had made elaborate gardens along the Thames.[1] Since relations between George I and his son were appalling, George I hunted in Richmond Park, the New Park created by Charles I, where the lodge was unimpressive.[2] He has little reputation as a patron but both at Kensington Palace and here he shows himself to be in the forefront of architectural fashion.

In 1726 the king commissioned a new lodge on higher ground, with views over the ancient oaks and herds of deer. He chose Roger Morris as his architect, a curious choice in that Morris was at this time building Marble Hill for the Countess of Suffolk, the ex-mistress of his son. The man behind both projects was Henry Herbert, later 9th Earl of

238

Pembroke, owner of Wilton House and an amateur architect who used Roger Morris as his professional assistant. The king took a close interest in the designs and approved them in the winter of 1726-7, after which they were sent to the Treasury for approval. In its usual way the Treasury tried to pare down the costs, in particular urging the use of oaks from the park for timber and brick rather than stone for the facades; but the royal will prevailed and it was expensively built in stone, hence its name White Lodge. Unusually, Morris was not yet part of the Office of Works and the post of 'Clerk of the Works at Richmond New Park Lodge' was created for him.

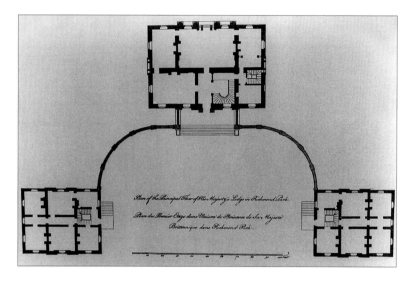

184 Richmond, White Lodge. Elevation and plan of main floor from *Vitruvius Britannicus*, 4, 1767.

George I died suddenly in June 1727, but building continued for George II and the carcase was finished in 1728. The entrance front faces east and has a raised walkway leading directly into the *piano nobile*. The five-bay front is pedimented over the central three bays with banded ball finials.[3] The ground falls away to the west, so that the garden front has a full basement storey. This has a rusticated loggia below the Doric frontispiece, and the pediment on both fronts is echoed in the pyramid roof, which was topped with a weather-vane. The whole house is faced in stone from the Hildenley quarries in north Yorkshire, so it cost £7,659 (instead of £5,780 for brick).[4] The accommodation was not large: the main floor had a stone-paved staircase hall leading to the double-height saloon in the centre of the west front, its Venetian window giving views into the park. The original chimneypiece is chunky and plain, with just a heavy festoon of leaves in the frieze with the crown and the initials GRC. The saloon was flanked by a dressing room in the S-W and a bedroom in the N-W angles, where the Corinthian columns of the bed alcove are still in place. In the alcove is a jib door leading to the secondary stairs. The house had no gardens at this date and the basement could be used as an entrance direct from the park: the king could come in muddy from hunting via the loggia into a stone-paved vaulted passage, leading to either the main or secondary stairs. The north side of the basement contained a large kitchen and a pair of smaller pantries, and the upper floor had plain bedrooms round the upper part of the saloon. It was the typical minimum accommodation required in a hunting lodge, with provision for simple food preparation, entertaining and sleeping, here built in a pure Palladian style.

It is not clear how much it was used by George II and Queen Caroline, although some internal finishing was done in the 1730s. When Sir Robert Walpole's son died in 1751 Princess Amelia was appointed ranger of Richmond Park in his place; she therefore had the use of both the old lodge and White Lodge. She was the third daughter of George II, unmarried and strong-willed. Her first act was to try to prevent public access to Richmond Park, both for pedestrians and people in carriages. This was very unpopular and she was eventually forced to concede access after a court case.[5] She carried out work on the house, immediately employing Stephen Wright to add pavilions which greatly increased the accommodation, and planned curving tunnels connecting them to the main house. After her father's death she gave up the rangership at Richmond and bought Gunnersbury, possibly tired of the lack of privacy and the friction with the local inhabitants which she had caused. George III appointed his friend and mentor the 3rd Earl of Bute as ranger, but he and the queen sometimes used it themselves as a retreat while their gardens at Richmond were open to the public.

In 1801 the arrangements changed. Henry Addington, later Lord Sidmouth, was offered it while he was prime minister; this was the personal gift of George III, who had reclaimed Richmond Park for various agricultural improvements and had not appointed a new ranger after Bute's death. Sidmouth kept it till his death in 1844, and transformed the surroundings of the house. Humphry Repton was brought in to design the surroundings of the house, which was at last provided with a five-acre plot. So the deer were pushed back from the

185 Richmond, White Lodge, garden front, from Repton's *Fragments*, 1816. He shows the deer in Richmond Park just outside the house, and proposed a garden here instead.

house and gardens and kitchen gardens were established.[6] James Wyatt was summoned to connect Wright's pavilions to the house by the two-storey quadrant wings we see today. These swept right round to the entrance, making a wide corridor with tripartite windows on the front of the house. At the same time the ground on the entrance front was raised so that a carriage could drive into the *porte-cochère* which was also added. It had become a comfortable updated house, with plenty of family and servant accommodation, easy access and greater privacy.[7] After Sidmouth's death at White Lodge it was used by members of the royal family, first the Duchess of Gloucester, then the Prince of Wales. When the Duchess of Kent died in 1861 Queen Victoria and Prince Albert retreated there for a period of mourning; a Leitch watercolour shows the house at this time, with figures in mourning dress in the gardens.[8]

186 Richmond, White Lodge. Bedford Lemere photographed the outer hall of the Duke and Duchess of Teck, decorated for Christmas in 1892.

The Duke and Duchess of Teck had apartments in Kensington Palace with very little garden, so in 1869 they were given use of White Lodge as well. As their extravagant lifestyle continued unabated and their debts mounted uncontrollably Queen Victoria forced them to give up Kensington for — she hoped — a more economical life at White Lodge, hence the future Queen Mary came to be brought up there. The Duke of Teck was noted for his decorative flair, and Lemere's 1892 photographs show how they arranged it, the fine interiors respected but filled with comfortable chairs, indoor plants and heaps of books.[9] The last major change to the house was carried out for the Duke and Duchess of York, later George VI and Queen Elizabeth, who took over the house in 1923 soon after their marriage. To make the garden easily accessible from the saloon a massive perron was attached to the west front; it was carefully matched to the existing stonework, but makes the attractive loggia a poorly-lit internal space. But Richmond Park was very public and they found that White Lodge lacked privacy, so they gave it up in 1927. It was given to Lord Lee of Fareham, who had given his own country house, Chequers, for the use of the prime minister.[10] Since 1955 White Lodge has not been a private house, but has become the home of the Royal Ballet School, with additional buildings discreetly tucked away round the 18th-century house.

RICKMANSWORTH

MOOR PARK

Four great houses were built in the early 18th century on the outskirts of London: Moor Park, Wricklemarsh, Canons and Wanstead. Of these only Moor Park survives, giving us an idea of the ostentation of the houses of the very rich at the moment when the Baroque style is beginning to give way to the Palladian. It has changed hands constantly, but always attracted the super-rich, who have employed many leading architects and designers. But its history goes back much further than the 1720s. The More was a brick courtyard house standing on slightly higher ground than the present house, built in the 1460s as his suburban retreat by George Neville, Archbishop of York (1432-76) when he was also Chancellor of England. It was seized by the Crown and later granted to Cardinal Wolsey, so when he fell from favour it again became royal property.[1] Sir John Russell, later 1st Earl of Bedford, was made ranger of the Park, the beginning of the connection of the Russell family with this house. Elizabeth I granted Francis Russell, 2nd Earl of Bedford, the manor and 830-acre deer park with 415 deer. But it was not an important residence of the Russell family until Edward Russell, 3rd Earl of Bedford and his wife Lucy Harrington took over The More in 1617. They may have reduced the old house in size and made alterations to it; they certainly remade the gardens, turning them into one of the most celebrated gardens near London.[2] They both died in 1627, but their gardens lasted through the 17th century. Sir William

187   Rickmansworth, Moor Park, garden front. The house was rebuilt 1720-28 by Sir James Thornhill.

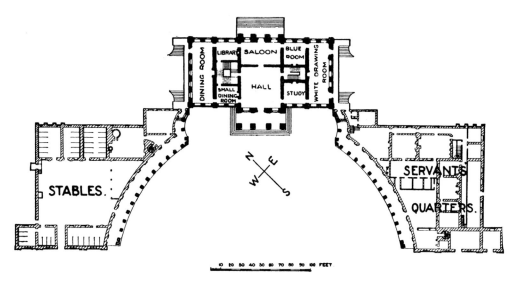

188   Rickmansworth, Moor Park. Plan showing the stable and service courtyards in the wings, which were demolished in the late 18th century.

Temple, whose cousin Sir Richard Franklin was then the owner, spent his honeymoon here in 1655. He was so impressed that he wrote a detailed description of the gardens and later named his own house at Sheen Moor Park. From 1663-70 it belonged to James Butler, 1st Duke of Ormonde, and the history of the present house starts with that 1670 sale.

James Scott, 1st Duke of Monmouth (1649-85) was the illegitimate son of Charles II and greatly in favour with his father, who arranged a splendid marriage for him with Anna Scott, Countess of Buccleuch in her own right and a great heiress. They were only children when married, but in 1670 they moved into The More and from 1679-84 built a new house nearby, which still forms the core of Moor Park today. There are no views of this house, but plans show that it was a compact triple-pile house of seven bays, built of brick and astylar.[3] The saloon was on the ground floor; the imposing main staircase was in the centre of the house, as was a small courtyard. An unusual feature was the easy access to the gardens, with no fewer than four rooms opening directly into the grounds. Hugh May was the architect, not surprising given Monmouth's royal links; he was building Cassiobury about two miles away at the same time. The work was carried out by craftsmen from the Office of Works.[4] The Italian decorative painter Verrio decorated the ceiling of one of the rooms, a painting which is still in the house; and Grinling Gibbons carved an exquisite marble overmantel with a relief of Neptune and Galatea. These tantalizing interior details are all we have of their house. When Monmouth was tried and executed in 1685 his wife was pardoned by James II and given full title to Moor Park, where she lived with her children. After the death of her second husband she returned to Scotland, taking the Grinling Gibbons chimneypiece with her to Dalkeith Palace where it remains.[5]

She sold the house in 1720 to Benjamin Styles, a City merchant who had invested deeply in the South Sea Company. Thanks to insider knowledge he was able to sell out in time to avoid the crash, and with the proceeds bought and rebuilt Moor Park c.1720-8. He was said to have spent £150,000 on turning it into one of the most flamboyant houses near London. The Monmouth's house was enlarged into an 11-bay house and entirely encased in stone.

James Thornhill, better known as a decorative painter, was the architect of these alterations. The west-facing entrance front was given a bold pedimented portico running through all three storeys, matched with a giant order of pilasters. Because the old house had the main rooms on the ground floor this remained the case, the tall arched windows set in channelled rustication reflecting the scale of the rooms behind; the two upper floors are of ashlar. The roofline has a deep entablature and a balustrade hiding the roofline. The garden front is similar, except that the projecting portico is replaced by attached three-quarter columns supporting the pediment. The house today stands rather starkly, but was originally balanced by quadrant wings and pavilions. The north pavilion provided lavish stabling, the south pavilion had kitchens and service rooms.

The house is particularly rich in painted decoration by many artists, some of them Italian. Lavish painted decoration was commissioned, much of which is painted in oil on canvas and then inserted into plasterwork frames, a very different technique from the oil on plaster of the previous generation. Thornhill was to be paid the huge sum of £3,500 for his paintings in the hall. The double-height hall, a 40 ft cube made out of several small rooms in the old house, was given a gallery supported on consoles and Thornhill was commissioned in 1725 to paint the ceiling and eight panels for the walls. Thanks to a disagreement with his client and a lawsuit, there are records to illuminate this.[6] The artist won the case and was paid in full, but his painted decoration did not last long. The wall panels of the Heroic Virtues were replaced c.1729-32 by the Venetian artist Jacopo Amiconi who painted canvas panels with the luscious scenes of Jupiter and Io which we see today. The upper level was painted by another Venetian artist, Francesco Sleter, whose *grisaille* figures of gods and goddesses (after classical sculptures) line the gallery. The ceiling has a dazzling *trompe l'oeuil* of a view into a dome by the Italian artist and designer Giacomo Brunetti.[7] The whole room was richly decorated with plasterwork by Artari & Bagutti, the arched frames of the paintings enriched with cherubs supporting festoons of foliage, the doorcases surmounted with reclining figures, and narrow panels on both levels filled with military trophies – which would have linked with the martial theme of Thornhill's decoration. The room is a fine example of that moment when the Baroque is being challenged by the Palladian movement, with the Venetian artists importing elements of the new Rococo style. Sleter and Amigoni may have also collaborated on the paintings in the staircase hall. The main staircase, less imposing than that in the earlier house, was given painted panels with scenes from the story of Pluto and Proserpine. *Grisaille* figures in the corners are signed by Sleter, but Amigoni has recently been suggested as the painter of the canvas panels. Sleter also added wall paintings to the saloon, a room unaltered in the rebuilding, where Verrio's painted ceiling of Aurora survives to this day. The walls have panels of the four seasons, given painted frames with cherubs, flowers and foliage. This Rococo decoration contrasts with the severe Palladian doorcase. Artari & Bagutti created a rich plasterwork ceiling in the White Drawing Room, a long room facing south, where almost life-size figures of Ceres and Bacchus in high relief fill the central panel, suggesting its use as a dining room.

Styles died in 1739 and his executors sold it in 1754 to another of the super-rich, Admiral Lord Anson, who had made his fortune in the navy. He employed 'Capability' Brown to landscape the park, creating a lake and building the Temple of the Winds overlooking it (demolished in the building of houses in Temple Gardens). Any surviving traces of Lucy Harrington's gardens were swept away in creating a natural landscape, which can be seen in the painting commissioned by Dundas and painted by Richard Wilson and Zoffany.[8] In 1763 Moor Park was bought by Sir Lawrence Dundas (1712-81), a Scot whose fortune was made through army contracts. He had profited particularly from the Seven Years' War, and bought this house for £25,000 just as the war ended. He already had a Yorkshire estate, a house in Arlington Street, and land in Scotland and Ireland, and was soon to employ Chambers to build him a smart new house in Edinburgh. At Moor Park he chose Robert Adam to carry out some work for him. The most spectacular interior alteration was the Tapestry Room, lined with a set of Gobelins tapestries ordered from Paris in 1766; but these were removed to Arlington Street in 1783.[9] The ceiling with its geometric ribs was perhaps designed not to conflict with the existing modillion cornice, and Adam commissioned painted decoration and panels from Cipriani, which are still *in situ*. A fine pair of marquetry commodes by

189
Rickmansworth, Moor Park. The double-height entrance hall of this 1720s house had scenes of Jupiter and Io by Amiconi on the lower level, *grisaille* figures by Sleter at gallery level and a ceiling in *trompe l'oeuil* by Brunetti.

Pierre Langlois was made for this room, their French style compatible with the Gobelins tapestries.[10] In the grounds Adam also designed a new south entrance with a Doric arch flanked by little lodges, and the charming Tea Pavilion. This little building combined a cottage with a central room where the family and guests could take tea after fishing in the River Colne. This had palm trees supporting the cornice; sadly the decoration was sold to the U.S. and has not been traced. It had a thatched roof and rough tree trunks supporting the gabled roof, and was a much more rustic building than the fishing pavilion at Syon. All that remains in Moor Lane today is a fragment of the pavilion with its leaded windows, the thatch replaced by tiles, incorporated into a 20th-century house.[11]

Dundas died in 1781 and his son sold the estate to Thomas Bates-Rous, a director of the East India Company. The main change effected by Rous was to demolish the wings and pavilions, moving the kitchen to the basement.[12] In 1828 the house was bought by Robert, 2nd Earl Grosvenor, who laid out fashionable formal gardens to the east of the house with a broad terrace

190 Rickmansworth, Moor Park. Plasterwork ceiling panel of Bacchus and Ceres by Artari and Bagutti in the White Drawing Room.

walk, urns and statues. His third son, later Lord Ebury, inherited the house in 1845. Around this time the stable block to the north of the house, loosely based on one of the earlier pavilions, was built. The area was still largely rural, although the population was growing and he encouraged the building of a railway linking Watford and Rickmansworth, which opened in 1862. Under the Grosvenors the house and estate were run lavishly: in the early 20th century there were about 20 indoor servants, four men in the stables, 18 gardeners and a gamekeeper. His grandson, the 3rd Baron Ebury, put the estate up for sale in 1919.[13] It consisted of the 400-acre deer park as well as a large amount of farmland to east and west, totalling about 3,000 acres. The buyer was the Lancashire industrialist Lord Leverhulme, who bought Lot 1 – the house, gardens and deer park – for £250,000. However, this was not for his own use but as a commercial venture. He saw the profit to be made out of providing a golf course in such a fine setting so close to London, and had the small private golf course of the Grosvenors replaced by a much larger one, opened in 1923. His property company sold out in 1937 to Rickmansworth Urban District Council, but the costs of maintaining a Grade 1 listed historic house and its paintings were too much for the Council. Today the house is owned by the Moor Park Golf Club, with the Moor Park Heritage Foundation responsible for the historic paintings and furnishings; there is occasional public access.

ROEHAMPTON

GROVE HOUSE

Roehampton, once a remote hamlet in the parish of Putney, still has several large houses near Richmond Park. Its development as a place of retreat for well-off Londoners began when David Papillon bought land there in 1620 and as a speculation built three large houses on the sites of Roehampton House, Elm Grove and Grove House; the latter concerns us here. (House names change frequently, and this house has also been known as Roehampton Great House, Roehampton Grove, and Upper Grove House.)

Papillon's house was an H-shaped brick house, just east of Roehampton Lane, built by Bartholomew Bennett.[1] It was the largest of the three new houses: in 1674 it was assessed at 56 hearths, much larger than anything else in the area. Papillon lived in it himself before selling it in 1625 to Sir Richard Weston, 1st Earl of Portland (1577-1635), Lord High Treasurer to Charles I. He was described by the Venetian ambassador as being 'most influential, and most signally favoured by his Majesty … a man of deep and sagacious intellect'.[2] This important post put him at the heart of Charles I's court, with appropriate perks. One of these was the gift of all the deer in Putney Park, which he transferred to his own 350-acre park at Roehampton.[3] His park adjoined the king's new Richmond Park, and he had a gate leading directly into it from his grounds. He shared the king's artistic tastes, and employed the Flemish Balthasar Gerbier as his artistic adviser. Perhaps with his help he commissioned a most expensive work of art for his grounds: a bronze equestrian statue of Charles I by Hubert Le Sueur, the French immigrant sculptor who worked mainly for the king. This is the famous statue now in Trafalgar Square.[4] In 1632 Portland added a private chapel at one end of his house. He was a High Anglican, possibly a crypto-Catholic, and the chapel, dedicated to the Holy Trinity, was consecrated by Laud, Bishop of London.[5] The antiquarian Daniel Lysons, who was Deputy Curate for the parish of Putney 1791-99, reported seeing the altarpiece of the Last Supper by Zuccaro.[6] In 1632 his son Jerome married Esmé Stuart in this chapel; the king was present, the bride being his cousin. Might the chapel have been built for this ceremony?

Portland died in 1635 leaving the house to his widow, then to Jerome, 2nd Earl of Portland. He sold it in 1640 for £11,300 to Abraham Dawes for his son Sir Thomas Dawes, owner during the troubled years of the Civil War. From 1653 it was leased and then owned by the staunch royalist Christian, Dowager Countess of Devonshire. Her town house was in Bishopsgate, from where she would process in state to Roehampton; she entertained lavishly and kept in touch with royalists both in England and Europe. After the Restoration Charles II often visited her there, and after her death her son and then his widow kept it on.

Through the late 17th and 18th centuries the house changed hands many times, mainly among City families. In 1768 the banker Alexander Fordyce bought it, and saw the advantages of splitting up the park into smaller lots: both Mount Clare and Parkstead were built on land

191   Roehampton, Grove House, west front from the gardens.

from Portland's park, but in spite of these sales Fordyce went bankrupt in 1772. Thomas Parker bought it in 1775 and two years later demolished the chapel, but the old house was rebuilt by Sir Joshua Vanneck, a rich merchant and MP, some time between 1779 and 1793. The Vanneck family, Dutch in origin, had previously owned a house in Putney, and Joshua rented the Roehampton house from Parker. Their new house was designed by James Wyatt and may have incorporated part of the old house, although it was smaller, an example of the switch to smaller houses from the mid-18th century.

The house is much altered, but the south front preserves elements of Wyatt's modest house, built of stucco with stone enrichments. The three-bay central block projects slightly and is crowned by a pediment. The decoration is pared to the minimum: there are no columns, the only decoration is a profile portrait in a roundel. Above the simple Ionic porch is a Venetian window is set in a depressed arch with fan decoration, and the two flanking windows have carved festoons set in panels. There are lower three-bay wings each side, and to the west a low wing extended to the west. This may have been the conservatory and aviary, although the blank wall to the south seems impractical. Not much remains internally of Wyatt's house, just the drawing room and staircase to the west. Like much of the house, these have been embellished *c.*1900, but the elegant plasterwork of the ceilings in both spaces and the finely carved chimneypiece in the drawing room appear original. The other rooms are overlaid with florid work in various styles, ranging from Wren Revival in the entrance hall to Louis XVI in the boudoir to the east.

The house was further altered through the 19th century, with William Burn asked to design a new wing in 1851, although all he seems to have built there was a mausoleum in 1862 for the dancer Yolande Lyne Stephens. This appears over the wall, close to Roehampton Lane. The Lyne Stephens family owned the house from 1843 until 1911, when it briefly belonged to Charles Fischer, a Swiss banker who absconded in 1913 leaving large debts. By that time the house had more than doubled in size, and from the north it now presents a confusing and asymmetrical appearance, united only by its stone facing. Behind the pediment is a three-storey centrepiece with a canted bay running through all three storeys and topped by a balustrade with urns. To each side are long wings, that to the east of two storeys with a ground-floor verandah, that to the west longer and higher. Both are pedimented, the west pediment being decorated with a carved trophy of rakes, hoes and scythes. A wide terrace extends across all three sections and there are French windows giving direct access from the reception rooms inside. The gardens, rather neglected, still keep a vestige of their appearance a century ago. The terrace overlooks a circular pond where a stone fountain is gently collapsing in the middle. Beyond that large old cedar trees frame a lake, and at one side vast sandstone blocks are piled up to form a rockery with a cascade (now dried up) feeding the lake. But this house was far too large to remain in private use; during the First World War it was used by the Royal Flying Corps, and in 1921 was bought by the Froebel Institute. The core of Wyatt's house may remain, but unlike Parkstead and Mount Clare it is no longer a fine example of a neo-classical villa. Like them it is now part of Roehampton University.

MOUNT CLARE

Roehampton, only seven miles from London, was a remote corner of the parish of Putney but with its own sense of identity. It had the advantage of high ground and proximity to Richmond Park, and still has several houses of architectural interest. Mount Clare, designed by Sir Robert Taylor, is one of these.[1] George Clive was a banker with a London house in Arlington Street; he was related to Clive of India, the builder of Claremont, and had been in India too. He bought 23 acres of the Putney Park estate in 1770 for which he paid a high price, but the place was fashionable and the site a good one.[2] Taylor, who was adept at designing compact villas, was asked to provide him with a small house on a new site; the result was an elegant house with well-planned accommodation.[3] It is a two-storey stuccoed house with a rusticated semi-basement lit by thermal windows; it has a five-bay pedimented entrance front and the garden front has a canted bay, a typical Taylor feature. There is very little decoration, just delicate ironwork on the double staircase to the entrance, and a fine cornice. The hall is a rectangular space with a shallow barrel-vaulted coffered ceiling, the walls with niches. Delicate plasterwork decorates the end walls and festoons frame the set of classical reliefs.[4] To one side is a cantilevered stone staircase, the iron balustrade of the same pattern as the exterior stairs; there is a study beyond. On the other side of the hall is the dining room, but the glory of the house is the octagonal saloon, 25 ft across, with views south over grounds landscaped by 'Capability' Brown, with Richmond Park beyond. There is a fine chimneypiece, and the ceiling has delicate neo-classical plasterwork of the highest quality. The main bedroom above is also octagonal with windows almost down to the floor; in the angles of the room are fluted Corinthian columns, partly gilt like the cornice to catch the sunlight. There were a further four bedrooms. Service rooms were partly in the basement, with kitchens and laundry in a separate wing to the east, with an ice-house beyond. The house is a perfect example of a villa in miniature, and not surprisingly was expensive: Clive claimed that it had cost him nearly £16,000.

192   Roehampton, Mount Clare, garden front. Robert Taylor designed this in 1770 for George Clive.

Clive died in 1779, and his widow sold the house the next year to Sir John Dick who had been British Consul in Leghorn from 1754-76. He made minor changes, employing the Italian designer Placido Columbani to add a wooden portico to the entrance front; this may be practical, but does not enhance the facade. In the hall Dick added a pair of marble relief portraits of two Russians, Counts Fyodor and Alexei Orlov, brothers who were friends of his; these had been commissioned by the Duke of York from Shubin in 1772, and were presumably given to Dick while the Duke was in Leghorn.[5] He also converted the octagonal bedroom into a library. He had made possibly £50,000 from victualling the Russian fleet in the 1770s, and was rich enough to buy more land. Watts in his *Seats* describes the improved 'plantations and grounds, which together form a *ferme ornée*' and he may have added the pair of cob cottages mentioned below.[6]

193   Roehampton, Mount Clare. The entrance hall has exquisite neo-classical plasterwork.

Dick died in 1804, and Mount Clare remained a private house through the 19th century, with Roehampton remaining leafy and prosperous. A few changes were made to the house: the south-facing windows were lowered to the floor, and ironwork balconies added; in the 1840s the service wing was connected to the house, and *c.*1900 the service range was further enlarged by Hugh Colin Smith, whose family owned Mount Clare from 1874-1954. They moved the temple from Parkstead nearby to their own grounds, where it remains, trapped between houses. The house was furnished with fine paintings and furniture, including the set of chairs designed by Adam for Moor Park when it belonged to Sir Lawrence Dundas.

It was still rural just before the Second World War, with cows grazing in the park and the picturesque cottages built in the late 18th century still in use. But this was not to last: the house was requisitioned by Wandsworth Borough Council during the Second World War, and the Smith family was reluctantly forced to give up Mount Clare in 1954. This was due to the development of the Alton Estate: after the war the LCC was greatly in need of new housing, and several large houses and their gardens were compulsorily purchased for this important development. Mount Clare was among these, and the house was gradually surrounded by the high-rise

194   Roehampton, Mount Clare, entrance front. The house was compulsorily purchased in 1954, and the Alton Estate was built by the LCC all round the house.

blocks we see today. A fine statue of Charity outside the house records the ownership of the Smith family. However the LCC carried out a major restoration of the house, removing the later additions and returning it to more or less its original appearance. Since then it has been in institutional use; it is now part of the campus of Roehampton University, and is used as offices. It remains remarkably unaltered internally, and is a fine example of Taylor's refined style.

PARKSTEAD

The Roehampton side of Richmond Park was dotted with substantial houses in the 18th century, and this is one of the finest surviving ones, also called Manresa House. It was an early work by William Chambers for William Ponsonby, 2nd Earl of Bessborough (1704-93). His wife, Lady Caroline Cavendish, had died in 1759 and he found their Kent home, Ingress Abbey, a sad place without her so he moved to Roehampton. His political career was slowing down in the 1760s, so he divided his time between here and London; he hardly ever visited his Irish estates in Co. Kilkenny, although his son was to spend more time there. His Roehampton house stands on high ground east of the park: it was a desirable site, and Bessborough had to pay Alexander Fordyce of nearby Grove House a very high price for the land, as did Clive of Mount Clare. Like that house its grounds abut the park boundary, and even today both houses have splendid views over the park with its deer and ancient oak trees. Bessborough, taking advantage of his position on the committee running Richmond Park, was allowed a ha-ha as the boundary of his land, 'all Richmond Park appearing to belong to it' as Creevey wrote.[1]

195
Roehampton,
Parkstead, designed
by Chambers in
1761. The west
front overlooks
Richmond Park,
and the wings
were added by the
Society of Jesus
after 1864.

The old house on the site was valued at 10 hearths in 1664, and had belonged to a succession of Londoners: an embroiderer, a fishmonger, a merchant.[2] In 1761 Chambers designed a compact house, which although now part of a much larger complex of buildings is remarkably unaltered, and is a fine example of the type of neo-classical villa which was going up round London. It was approached from Roehampton Lane through its own 100-acre grounds, the drive leading into a deep forecourt flanked by service pavilions; these have gone. There is a severe five-bay brick entrance front, the house looming three storeys high, and very austere. The west front is much more elegant: faced in stone, with a rusticated ground floor and curving steps with fine ironwork leading up to a modestly scaled Ionic portico. This is only one storey high, so the attic storey rises above it − a feature not seen in Chambers' other villas, and giving the house a rather heavy appearance.[3]

Chambers was not a master of varied room shapes, and compared to the planning of Robert Taylor or Robert Adam the sequence of rooms is a little dull. The staircase hall formed the entrance, and Chambers introduced a novel secondary staircase, winding up in the central space within the main cantilevered stone staircase, a design based on Webb's double staircase at Amesbury Abbey. The inner staircase has gone, destroyed in a fire in 1888, but it is shown in *Vitruvius Britannicus* and cuts in the handrail of the balustrade show where its 'bridges' connected to the landings.[4] The ground floor consists of everyday rooms − the service rooms were in the pavilions − and there is a door to the garden beneath the portico. The two small rooms each side of this passage may have been a bathroom and dressing room, since the symbolism on the garden door is of ewers, and the vaulted passage has bulrushes in its plasterwork. The second floor had six large bedrooms, some with dressing rooms. Many of these houses have a top-lit central staircase, so all the rooms face outwards, but not here, so the corridor and two small dressing rooms on the top floor have top-lighting only, evidence perhaps of Chambers' lack of experience.

The main rooms are on the *piano nobile*, a series of rectangular spaces, one with a coved ceiling, the rest with flat ceilings decorated with Chambers' designs in rich plasterwork. The dining room faced north over the forecourt and has plasterwork with vines and hops in the ceiling, and the old-fashioned feature of wood-panelled walls − for warmth perhaps.

Bessborough's bedroom and library – his own rooms – are on the east side of the house; the drawing room faces west. The hall or saloon opens onto the portico, so one could admire the view or to go down into the gardens.[5] It may also have served as an entrance on special occasions. The decoration in this room is typical of Chambers' heavy and slightly Palladian style: the walls have plaster panels with egg and dart borders, the dado rail has a Vitruvian scroll, the frieze and cornice are classically correct; only in the oval ceiling compartment is there a lighter touch, with scrolls of leaf ornament.[6] The finely carved stone chimneypiece has festoons of drapery above, and down the sides are Masonic insignia, referring to Bessborough's role as a leading Freemason.[7] This room has brackets over the doors for busts, which would have been framed by the plasterwork ovals. For Bessborough was a collector, his antique sculpture praised by Michaelis as 'a collection of some repute.'[8] He had bought some of his sculpture while on his extended travels in Europe as a young man, and added more later. When it was sold in 1801 pieces went to major collections: *Pan & Daphnis* to Petworth, the torso of Venus to the Ince-Blundell collection, a porphyry foot to Thomas Hope; Soane bought a Roman fragment which he incorporated into his 'Pasticcio' outside the dining room of 13 Lincoln's Inn Fields.[9] The paintings were also of very high quality: a van Eyck, a Poussin, a Salvator Rosa, the Rubens portrait of Sir Theodore de Mayerne (of Lindsey House, Chelsea), many Dutch cabinet pictures.[10] He also had an exceptional collection of antique gems, which was sold to the Duke of Marlborough. Lady Mary Coke

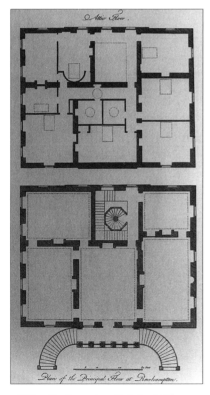

196 Roehampton, Parkstead. Plans of main- and bedroom-floor, from *Vitruvius Britannicus*, 4, 1767.

197 Roehampton, Parkstead. Plasterwork designed by Chambers in the saloon, with a bracket over the door to take one of the Earl of Bessborough's classical busts.

wrote in 1768 that 'the house is magnificent; I think I never saw one so crowded with fine things'.[11] This was the house of a connoisseur, a Trustee of the British Museum from 1768 till his death, and a member of the Dilettante Society.[12]

His son, the 3rd Earl of Bessborough, inherited; he had married the beautiful Lady Henrietta Spencer, whose sister Georgiana lived not far away at Chiswick House. After her death he spent more time at Bessborough House in Ireland, and from 1827-57 let Roehampton to Abraham Robartes, a banker and MP with interests in the East Indies. In 1861 the 5th Earl planned to sell the house with its land broken up into small lots, but the place was bought as a whole by the Society of Jesus to become their training college; Gerard Manley Hopkins was an early inmate. In memory of the Spanish town where Ignatius Loyola had composed his Spiritual Exercises it was renamed Manresa House. In 1864 the Chambers pavilions were demolished and over the next few years were replaced by the large wings we see today: a chapel by J. J. Scoles begun in 1864, a refectory wing by H. Clutton built 1869-71, and two further wings built 1877-86. Fortunately the main block of the Chambers house was left almost unaltered, and the main staircase was rebuilt to its original design after the fire of 1888. A temple, probably designed by Chambers, was moved to the grounds of Mount Clare *c.*1905; it is now islanded among modern housing near that house. Bomb damage in 1940 to the dining room was repaired post-war, and the original ceiling reinstated following Chambers' designs.

After the Second World War the Jesuits were unhappy about LCC plans to build the Alton Estate and the compulsory purchase of their land. In 1962 they sold up and the buildings became a training college. The Grade 1 listed villa is now Whitelands College, part of Roehampton University, and is used for conferences and events. A new entrance block was completed in 2006, and the historic house, renamed Parkstead, is maintained in excellent condition.

ROEHAMPTON HOUSE

London and its surroundings boasted several houses of the 17th and early 18th centuries with exceptional brickwork, of which only a handful remain; Roehampton House is one of these. This is the second house on the site: the Huguenot David Papillon had begun building large houses in the area as a speculation in 1620, and built one here. His other houses were all west of Roehampton Lane and therefore closer to Richmond Park, so his house on this site was probably one of the smaller houses. But what we see today, even in a somewhat mutilated form, is one of the grandest houses of its date, a fine Baroque house by Thomas Archer.

Thomas Cary, a merchant, took a 63-year lease of the old house in 1710 and asked Archer to design a new house, which was ready in 1713. Archer's Continental Baroque style, seen in all his designs, was evident here in the enormous broken pediment which crowned all seven bays of the entrance front, making the already tall house (three storeys over a high semi-basement) even more dramatic. This elevation was illustrated in *Vitruvius Britannicus*, with a plan.[1] It shows the house in its setting, which was equally dramatic: the house was approached from Roehampton Lane through gates of fine Baroque ironwork into a deep forecourt enclosed with curved walls. Large pavilions housed stables on one side, kitchens on the other; quadrant walls and a covered passage led to the main house.[2]

The house is of red brick with rubbed red brick detailing. It is astylar, with heavy brick quoins on the outer corners and slightly projecting central bays. There is a large proportion of window to wall, and a strong vertical emphasis, even without the pediment, which has gone.[3] Wide Portland stone steps with fine ironwork lead to the Doric entrance, and ingeniously part of the ironwork swings open so the lower steps can be used as a mounting block. Portland stone also emphasises the central feature, a blank niche running through the two upper storeys and topped by a balustrade. The garden front echoes the façade but in a plainer form.

The entrance hall has good original panelling, as do other lesser rooms, but the main room was destroyed by bombing in the Second World War. This was the magnificent first-floor saloon which rose through two storeys, lit by the tall window over the front door and a pair of *oeuil-de-boeuf* windows above. It was splendidly decorated by Sir James Thornhill with glimpses of landscape seen through fictive architecture on the walls and the Feast of the Gods on the ceiling; some of his designs survive.[4] These were appropriate themes for a country retreat, and for a room which would have been used for dining in state.[5]

Cary died in 1716, and the house changed hands many times over the

198   Roehampton House, elevation of entrance front. *Vitruvius Britannicus*, 1, 1715.

next century, and like so many of these houses was often let.[6] One Scottish family, the Lesley-Melvilles, remained there from 1837 till 1908; they added a north wing in 1859, since rebuilt. They were bankers and financiers, and were followed by another financier, Arthur Grenfell, who made substantial changes to the house after he took it on in 1910. Households were large by this time, so he invited an architect called Parker to provide more servant accommodation; Parker was replaced by Lutyens in 1911. The house was greatly enlarged by additional wings north and south, the pavilions were rebuilt and a new service wing was constructed behind the north pavilion.[7] This had all the staff rooms then considered essential: a large servants' hall, a room each for the chef, butler, housekeeper and maids, kitchen, pantries, scullery, still room, larder and safe. The south pavilion contained six loose boxes, as well as a kitchen and bedrooms for the grooms. All this was soon to become redundant, and cars and chauffeurs were to be better housed than horses and grooms. Lutyens also designed a pair of small lodges, but these were demolished in 1956 in order to widen Roehampton Lane, now a busy bus route. (They were rebuilt to a slightly different design, and Grenfell's wrought-iron gates placed between them.)

Grenfell, socially ambitious, also wanted lavish space for entertaining. Archer's fine oak staircase was removed from the central block and accurately reconstructed by Lutyens in the south wing. The undersides of the steps have a rippling effect, an example of the sense of movement which Archer gave to his buildings. Beyond the stairs was a suite of rooms for Grenfell and his wife, while the north wing had a series of interconnecting halls leading to

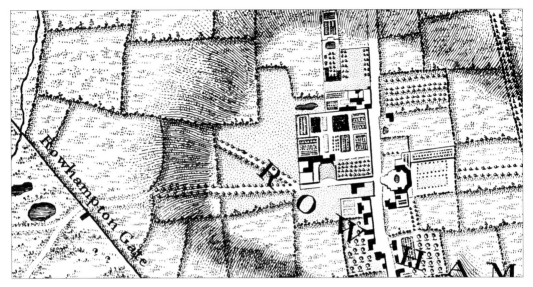

199   Roehampton, seen in Rocque's 1745 map. Roehampton House with its shaped forecourt and formal gardens is east of the road, with Grove House almost opposite. Parkstead and Mount Clare have not yet been built on the land adjoining Richmond Park.

the dining room and ballroom.[8] The main house was hardly utilised at all apart from the saloon. There were also suggestions that Lutyens redesign the garden, but Grenfell had over-extended himself and went bankrupt in 1914. The new wings were not finished internally at this point, and it was brave of Kenneth Wilson, a Hull ship-owner, to buy the house during the First World War. He hardly had time to enjoy it, as it was taken over in 1915 as Queen Mary's Hospital, looking after amputees from the trenches. The hospital has expanded ever since, with the house used first as a home for nurses and later as offices. Recently a new hospital has been built in the grounds, and the Grade 1 listed house is currently being converted into apartments, with new houses being built uncomfortably close on the gardens behind the house.

200   Roehampton House, garden front in 1915, showing the old house in the centre dwarfed by the wings added by Edwin Lutyens.

ROMFORD

HARE HALL

On the flat land 13 miles east of the City stands Hare Hall, a villa by James Paine, an architect whose practice was mainly in the north of England. It was built 1768-9 for John Arnold Wallinger, a subscriber to the first edition of Paine's book, *Plans, Elevations & Sections of Noblemen's & Gentlemen's Houses* of 1767. The Wallinger family of Essex had owned Goodwins, as it was then called, since at least 1744.[1] It was a modest house and a small estate, but John Wallinger, who inherited in 1763, possibly made contact with Paine about plans for the rebuilding. He died in 1767, leaving the property to his nephew John Arnold on condition that he take the name of Wallinger. Arnold was a cork and timber merchant with a London house, and he called his new house after Hare Street, the nearby hamlet where Humphry Repton was to live.

Paine designed a compact house, a smaller version of the Palladian country houses he specialised in. Wallinger's business provided the stone, although it is used only for the front and sides; the south front is of brick. It is a three-storey five-bay house, with the main rooms on the *piano nobile*. Paine wrote that he could not make a basement because of the damp ground, so the rusticated ground floor contains mainly service rooms. The upper floors are faced in ashlar, and unfluted Ionic columns support a pediment with Wallinger's coat of arms. The detailing is austere, with only a central arched window flanked by niches, and a dentil cornice wrapping round three sides of the house. A pair of pyramid-roofed pavilions is set back, connected to the house by a passage with a screen of columns, a not entirely practical arrangement. One pavilion contained the brewhouse, the other the kitchen, and a mezzanine and upper floor had servants' bedrooms. The planning here was a little clumsy, as the floor must have cut across the tall first-floor windows.

The entrance to the house is on the north front into a small and low-ceilinged hall. On the side nearest the kitchen was an occasional breakfast room, on the other side the 'cellar'. In the centre was the top-lit staircase; these are a dramatic feature of many of Paine's houses, and here he manages in a small oval space to fit elegant cantilevered stone stairs with a bowed balustrade leading to the first floor. The bedroom floor above is approached only by the secondary stair, and has a gallery looking down into the stairwell. The circuit of rooms on the *piano nobile* includes a drawing room running from front to back, 36 x 20 ft, with a small breakfast room in the centre; this used to be hung with a set of paintings by Angelika Kauffmann. On the east side was the dining room, not as large as the drawing room as it had a lady's dressing room behind it.[2] On the upper floor were five bedchambers, some with closets, which opened onto the top-lit gallery.

Hare Hall had a view north to the high ground of Havering-atte-Bower, but the grounds were flat and featureless until laid out in 1771 by Richard Woods. He was an interesting landscape designer, a friend and neighbour of Philip Southcote of Woburn Farm in Surrey;

201   Romford, Hare Hall. Print of the entrance front, seen across the park.

like Southcote he was a Roman Catholic. In 1768 he had moved to Essex and was living nearby.[3] No correspondence or plans of the garden survive, but Angus attributed the design to Woods and described the grounds.

'The piece of water has the appearance of a winding river, over which is a stone bridge at one of its terminations, and at the other end some remarkably fine weeping willows. On the opposite side of this canal is the Elysian Walk, raised with the earth which was taken up to form the piece of water, which has considerably added to the beauty of the grounds … There is … a serpentine terrace, near a mile in length, whose sides are planted with a variety of flowers, shrubs and forest trees, and extends to the lodges by the side of the great road.'[4]

This may have been suggested by Southcote's circuit walk at Woburn Farm, bounded by bulbs, flowering shrubs and native trees. A plan from the sale document of 1895 is the best evidence for the grounds, showing the roughly triangular site with the lake east of the house and planting round the perimeter of the park.[5] This has all gone, apart from a muddy fragment of the lake near the house and the little bridge, built of knapped flint not stone.

The builder died in 1792, dividing his properties among his three children. Hare Hall went to his son, unimaginatively called John Wallinger Arnold Wallinger. His younger brother inherited the family business, and the new owner struggled to maintain the house with its approximately 70 acres of land. He took out several mortgages, and when he died in 1805 left complicated financial arrangements which took years to sort out. The house had to be sold to pay his debts, and in 1812 went to a speculator, John Coape of Hanover Square, for

£15,999. He quickly passed it on to Benjamin Severn, but he too struggled maintain it and went bankrupt in 1830.

The house narrowly missed being demolished and the land entirely built on as the area became threatened by the Eastern Railway Company, who wished to extend their line eastwards from Romford. The ownership of the house is unclear through the 1830s, but in 1836 the railway company decided the only way to put the tracks where they wanted was to buy the whole estate; having taken what they wanted, they offered the rest of the land in six lots, but most remained unsold. The house sat empty until it was bought in 1852 by Robert Pemberton, related to the Pembertons at Havering-atte-Bower; he remained there until his death in 1895 when the future of the house, in an increasingly built up and industrial area, looked bleak. At that point it was photographed by Alfred Wire, recording its appearance just before major changes took place.[6] It was put up for sale as development land, but was bought as a private house by a cosmopolitan couple who had been living in Europe, Edward and Lucy Castellan.[7] The place was dilapidated, and they called in Howard Seth-Smith to modernise and enlarge it; we see his sensitive alterations today. The Castellans wanted their main rooms on the ground floor, so two large new rooms with gently canted bays were added to the south front, the brickwork carefully matching that of the house. These were the drawing room and dining room, so the new dining room and the original kitchen (still in use) were conveniently close. A semi-circular stone porch was added to the entrance front, and what had been Paine's cellar became a 'corridor hall' with a screen of columns leading to the sunny drawing room. Less satisfactorily the *piano nobile* with its very high ceilings became mainly bedrooms, with the great drawing room divided into a bedroom and dressing room and the central room as Mrs Castellan's boudoir. The pavilions were enlarged and the single-storey colonnade connecting them to the house raised and rebuilt. The kitchen pavilion had further service rooms attached to it, while the other became a billiard room below and bedroom suite above for Edward Castellan. He died suddenly in 1901, and in 1904 Seth-Smith designed Hare Lodge in the grounds for Major Charles Castellan so he could be near his widowed mother. She remained in the house till her death in 1912, and was the last person to use it as a private house.

During the First World War it was requisitioned by The Artists' Rifles, and in 1921 was sold to Essex CC to become the County High School for Boys, now the Royal Liberty School. The garden to the south was enclosed by brick ranges in 1929-30 by the Essex County Architect and other buildings have been added since; Richard Woods' grounds became playing fields. But the main block of Paine's house has lasted remarkably well and the interiors, although stripped of their original ornament, largely preserve his room lay-out.

SOUTHGATE

Arnos Grove

Today Arnos Grove is known mainly as the name of a tube station, with the house which is the origin of its name largely ignored. But it is a fine house and in spite of huge additions keeps much of its original 18th-century appearance. It stands in a commanding position on the edge of the hilltop village of Southgate, set back from Cannon Hill. The attractive Arnos Park, a long narrow strip with the Pymmes Brook and the New River flowing through it, is now dominated by a majestic brick viaduct carrying the tube line northwards. The park is now unconnected with the house, the west-facing slopes having been built over with suburban housing in the 1930s, but the print in Watts' *Views* shows the sweep of park up to the house in the late 18th century.

James Colebrooke, a City mercer and banker, bought the old house on the site in 1719 and rebuilt it 1720-23. There is no known architect, although Talman has been suggested.[1] The result was a tall seven-bay house, the three central windows topped by a pediment, the east-facing entrance front almost identical to the garden front, although a stone portico was added later. It is astylar, built of plum-coloured brick with rubbed red brick detailing and with a deep modillion cornice below the hipped roof. The only oddity is the small off-centre cupola, probably a later addition. It was a compact and practical plan, with service rooms in the semi-basement and a spine corridor running through the house from north to south.

202   Southgate, Arnos Grove. Print of garden front, with the Pymmes Brook and a *chinoiserie* bridge.

Like many houses of this date, the entrance hall is a large and impressive double-height space, dominated by the wide oak staircase with its twisted balusters and by the powerful Lanscroon painted decoration. (The staircase with its three balusters to each step has been altered slightly, and the elaborately carved newel posts are late 19th-century enrichments.) The Flemish artist Gerard Lanscroon was also working at Broomfield House in Southgate, although those paintings are not *in situ* until the house is repaired. Here the paintings, in oil on plaster, are in excellent condition, with the 'Triumphal Entry of Julius Caesar into Rome' on the walls, the panels divided by fictive architecture. Painted coving links the walls and ceiling, its central panel with the 'Apotheosis of Caesar' and the arms of Colebrooke and his wife, Mary Hudson, in the corners. Lanscroon dated his work 1723 beside his signature on the stairs. Colebrooke was a City man with no military connections so the subject matter did not relate to his career, but it certainly made an impressive ascent to the first floor. The best bedroom suite, with its three-bay anteroom, two-bay bedchamber and one-bay closet, had extensive views west into the park and across the valley. These rooms all have their original panelling and box cornices and the tall oak doors still have their brass box locks with the original handles, although the 1720s chimneypieces have been replaced.

203 Southgate, Arnos Grove. The entrance front today, with large additions each side.

The house was inherited by Colebrooke's third son, Sir George Colebrooke Bt. in 1752, who commissioned alterations from Sir Robert Taylor – a typical choice of architect for a City man. These were for the addition of a library and dining room on the ground floor of one wing, part of the move in the later 18th century towards having the main reception rooms on the ground floor. These were not finished when he sold it in 1762, in order to move to his father's country estate in Kent. Taylor's new wings were not completed till Sir William Mayne (later 1st Lord Newhaven) bought it in 1776. These three-bay wings were slightly deeper than the original house, and are now dominated by later and larger additions, but some of the interiors do survive. The new north wing had the library on the east front with a tripartite window (since removed). This room was given an Art Deco interior in 1935, so no trace of Taylor's work remains. His new dining room was connected to the old house by an apsed vestibule with a screen of columns. This elegant little space, with its vaulted ceiling and fine Rococo plasterwork, still exists although it no longer opens into the dining room; today it is used as a pantry. Its *serliana* would have visually linked the vestibule with the same motif flanking the chimneypiece on the north wall of the dining room. The spine corridor opened onto a north portico, leading to the gardens. The five-bay saloon in the centre of the south front was also altered by Taylor. It is lower ceilinged than the new rooms, and Taylor added a deep bow, supporting the outer wall of the old house on a pair of columns. The room was given fluted pilasters to increase its height and an imposing Sicilian jasper chimneypiece. The south wing seems to have had another dining room and possibly a bedroom suite as well, but it has

204 Southgate, Arnos Grove. The entrance hall with walls and ceiling painted by Lanscroon in 1723.

been much more altered than that on the north.[2] It was probably at this time that the park was landscaped and the *chinoiserie* bridge built over the New River.

In 1775 Mayne sold Arnos Grove to another City man, and in 1777 it was sold again, to the brewer Isaac Walker. It remained in the Walker family till 1918, and although they made few changes to the house they bought up various Southgate properties, adding the land to their estate; by 1870 this was 300 acres.[3] The last private owner was Andrew Weir, Lord Inverforth (1865-1955), a tough ship-owner from Glasgow who had become immensely rich. He bought the house at the end of the First World War, when he had been made Minister of Munitions; he was rewarded for this with a peerage. He rebuilt the drawing room bow, and redecorated the drawing room in the 'Adams' style which was so popular then. When he sold the house in 1928 he hoped to break up the estate for housing, but Southgate Urban District Council battled to buy some land as public open space. They managed to acquire 44 acres to make Arnos Park, and insisted that only low-density housing be built on the rest of the land; reluctantly Weir agreed. Arnos Grove became offices, renamed Northmet House, and was massively enlarged in 1929 and 1932 by the addition of long wings on the west side of the house; as a result the north portico was demolished and only a small area of garden remains round the house today, scattered with some 18th-century urns. In 1995 Beaumont bought the whole site and carefully converted it into a residential care home for the elderly, keeping the core of the old house as communal and office space while converting the wings into small semi-independent units. So it is now back to being lived in, even if as an institution.[4]

SOUTHGATE GROVE

Southgate Grove, or Grovelands as it was sometimes called, is one of John Nash's most exquisite creations and like Sundridge Park in Kent was the result of Nash's partnership with Humphry Repton. It was built in a fine stretch of country, high wooded ground at the southern end of Enfield Chace, which had been part of the Minchendon estate belonging to the Duke of Chandos. His daughter had inherited it, and her husband, Earl Temple, sold 231 acres soon after their marriage in 1796.[1] The new owner was Walker Gray, a Quaker brandy merchant, and he already knew Southgate, as his uncle, Isaac Walker, lived at Arnos Grove. It was a new house on a new site – this in itself is very rare, when nearly all houses had at least a farm or cottage on the plot of land. He may have chosen Repton as the landscape designer before deciding on Nash, who had recently returned from Wales and was barely re-established in London. Under their agreement Nash paid Repton a proportion of the fees he received in return for getting the commission.[2] His partnership with Repton was flourishing at this time and this seems to have been a most successful collaboration, although the partnership broke up soon after the completion of this house. Repton produced a 'Red Book' of his designs for the grounds, but it has disappeared.[3] The house is a lovely example of the compact smaller houses, which really can be called villas, which were being built around London (and other cities) in the later 18th and early 19th centuries for prosperous business and City families.

The house was built 'in the midst of a grove of timber trees beautifully scattered over the lawn, the ground falling gradually to a fine piece of water'.[4] This was a stream which was

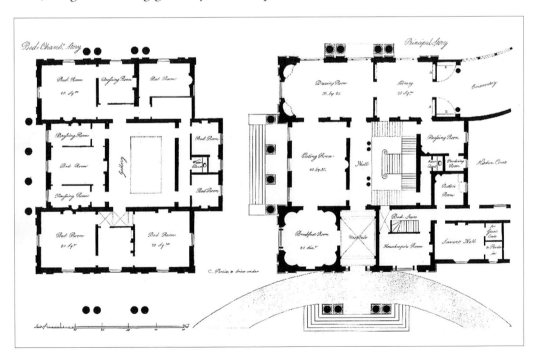

205 Southgate Grove, plans of ground and first floors. *New Vitruvius Britannicus*, 1802. The reception rooms are on the ground floor, opening into the gardens.

263

206 Southgate Grove. The Nash house from the N-E in 1982, before restoration.

dammed to form a lake, which is still there. The site had been carefully chosen by Repton for its picturesque views, each of the three main fronts having different views of the grounds, and in spite of later developments the house still preserves an area of parkland round it. The park was stocked with fallow deer (which remained there into the 20th century) which were kept away from the gardens by a ha-ha. The design of the house is a nice example of the asymmetry which Nash was to be among the first to introduce, with the three main fronts subtly different and the S-W façade with a sweep of conservatory attached.

The house is of two main storeys with an attic, which has oval windows lighting the low-ceilinged but large rooms behind. It is built of brick and stuccoed, the corners emphasised with paired pilasters, and contrasting stone used only for the three tall porticoes. These unpedimented porticoes were shown in the designs with rather French looking urns on the outer corners, and one has a sphinx in the centre, but these have all gone. The tripartite windows on the ground floor are set in recessed arches which are decorated with shell and fan mouldings. The entrance was from the north with the carriage drive conveniently sweeping under the Ionic portico. On one side of the hall was the breakfast room. This is a most enchanting small room, octagonal but with deep niches in the corners, and painted as if it were a

207 Southgate Grove, the elegant cantilevered staircase. Photographed in 1959.

264

birdcage, with flowers appearing to burst through and trail over the vaulted roof. The larger eating room faced east, its three long windows opening onto a shallow Ionic portico. The next room was the drawing room, again with long windows giving access to a portico with paired columns facing south. Nash could add theatrical touches: from here, with all the doors open, the mirrored overmantel in the Birdcage Room reflected the *enfilade*. The last room of the circuit was the small library, which with its double doors open could be linked with the drawing room. From the library mirrored doors led into the wide curving conservatory (72 x 25 ft) attached to the S-W corner, another example of the links between house and garden which were so essential at this time. Nash's planning was eminently practical. 'The end of the conservatory communicates with the hot-houses in the kitchen garden, at the back of which are the stables; to which a covered communication is thus provided.'[5]

The top-lit cantilevered staircase forms the core of the house, rising from the stone-flagged hall to the first floor with wide shallow stone steps. The simple S-shaped ironwork is reminiscent of Taylor's at houses such as Mount Clare, perhaps not surprising as Nash had worked in Taylor's office as a young man. The bedroom floor has a series of well designed bedrooms and dressing rooms, and even had a water closet at the back. A secondary staircase continued to the top floor, which had six good bedrooms. The service rooms were on the west side, with the kitchen outside the main block of the house. The kitchen court was flanked by low buildings, with the stables beyond. There were cellars and a dairy below the

208   Southgate Grove. The Birdcage Room, a breakfast room exquisitely painted with flowers and overlooking Repton's gardens.

265

house, and instead of the ice-house being in a distant part of the garden it, too, was placed in the cellars. It was in every way a house which combined elegant design and good planning with convenience.

Gray died in 1834 leaving the house to his nephew John Donnithorne Taylor, a brewer with Taylor Walker. He was opposed to housing development, so he bought more land as it came on the market and built up the already large estate to 600 acres. In 1876 Southgate could be described as 'flourishing; one of the pleasantest looking and least changed [villages] round London'.[6] When he died in 1885 the estate went to his son, Major Roger Kirkpatrick Taylor, who died in 1902. It was then offered for sale in several lots, some described as 'ripe for immediate development'. The Northern Line was about to be built and there was already a railway to Palmers Green and Winchmore Hill, so commuting to central London was possible. But 341 acres were reserved for sale with the house, and the sale particulars made clear that parts of the estate could be developed without interfering with the house.[7] In the end the house was retained by Taylor's son, although he did not live there after 1907. In 1911 he sold 64 acres to Southgate Urban District Council to make a park for the increasing local population. During the First World War the house was used as a hospital, and in 1921 Taylor sold it to the Middlesex Voluntary Aid Detachment; it has been a hospital ever since. By the 1980s the house was in very poor condition and was put up for sale; it was bought for use as a private psychiatric hospital. It has been carefully restored, but understandably it is therefore not possible to visit this example of a refined Nash villa set in the remains of an exceptional landscape.

TRENT PARK

Trent Park remained in use as a true suburban house far longer than most, due to its elegant and flamboyant owner between the wars, Sir Philip Sassoon. He had a London and a country house as well, each of them exquisitely furnished, and used Trent as a place for weekend and summer entertaining in an almost 18th-century manner. But its history goes back much further, and in the grounds are traces of a moated site with vestiges of ancient buildings. Even today its 1,000 acres are a remarkably rural landscape, once part of Enfield Chace. Various houses had been built on parts of this royal hunting park, and with the agricultural improvements of the late 18th century there was pressure to develop it as farmland; George III was interested in these farming developments himself. In 1777 an Act of Parliament allowed some parts of the Chace to be leased by the Duchy of Lancaster to farmers, retaining other areas for deer. The Trent Park estate was the king's personal gift to a physician, Sir Richard Jebb (1729-87). This successful London doctor had looked after the Duke of Gloucester when he became ill in Trento, and the name Trent Park derives from this. George III rewarded Jebb with a baronetcy and made him his Physician Extraordinary, as well as presenting him with a 99-year lease of 200 acres of Enfield Chace.

Jebb's London house was in Great George Street, Westminster. For his new house he went to William Chambers and they chose a site on high ground looking north over a valley with a small stream. This was dammed to form a lake, which is still there, and the park was stocked with deer. Jebb was unmarried so did not require a large family house; but he was musical, and the centre of the house was a high domed room with a bow, facing the lake. This was flanked by two-storey wings, so the garden front had three interconnecting reception rooms with a few bedrooms above; none of the rooms was large. This really was quite minimal accommodation, but the *Gentleman's Magazine* describes the additional buildings on the site of the present stable block. 'The offices form a large quadrangle at a proper distance from the house, including every accommodation for farming, besides bedchambers, library, billiard–room and other conveniences.'[1] There was also a three-acre kitchen garden and a melon ground.

209 Southgate, Trent Park, garden front. 1808 print of Jebb's house, designed by Chambers.

When Jebb died in 1787 he had spent the considerable sum of £19,000 on his new property, which was bought by the 4th Earl of Cholmondeley. He kept it for only six years, and it then changed hands several times before going to the Quaker family of Bevan in 1836. Robert Bevan, a banker in Barclay, Bevan, Barclay & Tritton, made various additions to the house in the 1860s. His son Francis largely rebuilt it before his death in 1894, producing a large but undistinguished three-storey house with a tower at the east end and a service wing to the west; but Jebb's house still formed the core of it. In 1909 Sir Edward Sassoon, Bt., took over the lease, but died only three years later. The Sassoons were a Jewish family who had made a fortune from trade in India and China, and had moved to London in 1876. Edward, MP for Hythe in Kent, had married Aline de Rothschild from Paris, a beautiful and artistic woman who collected French furniture; they had a vast house in Park Lane (since demolished) which she filled with her treasures. It was in this rarified atmosphere that their two children, Philip and Sybil, grew up. In 1912 his father died, leaving a fortune and several houses to his son Philip (1888-1939), a connoisseur and politician. He, too, became MP for Hythe, and in 1912 built himself a house near the coast at Port Lympne. This was no conventional country house: it was designed in Cape Dutch style by Herbert Baker, had one room painted by Rex Whistler, another with lapis lazuli decoration, and another with an Egyptian frieze. Outside there were formal gardens and a glamorous swimming pool designed by Philip Tilden, who was later to work at Trent Park; here he could entertain the great and the good in style during the summer.

By the 1920s Sassoon was becoming more interested in 18th-century English style; he was collecting conversation pieces, walnut furniture and English ceramics. He was now a member of the government, albeit a fairly junior one: from 1924-9 and 1931-9 he was Under-Secretary of State for Air, and 1937-9 was Commissioner of Works; he was also a

210   Southgate, Trent Park, entrance front. Rebuilt by Philip Tilden for Sir Philip Sassoon in 1926.

trustee of the National Gallery, the Tate and the Wallace Collection, and wanted to spend his weekends nearer London. Trent Park was a mere 14 miles from central London, near enough for guests to come for the day as well as staying for weekend house-parties. In 1923 he acquired the freehold of Trent Park and set about improving the largely Victorian house. His first alterations were tentative, but more radical changes were made in 1926 with the help of his architect Philip Tilden, giving the house the regularity and monumentality of an Early Georgian building. The Victorian tower on the east end was removed and Trent Park became a symmetrical three-storey house, the main fronts with 2-3-3-3-2 bays. Some of the great London houses were disappearing in the 1920s, and the Victorian brickwork was replaced by recycled bricks from the recently demolished Devonshire House in Piccadilly; the warm red contrasts with Portland stone window surrounds, also from Devonshire House. The high Victorian roof, slightly French in style, was lowered and almost hidden by a stone balustrade. A pair of stone lions by the entrance came from Devonshire House, the columned door surround from Chesterfield House. The main ground-floor rooms opened onto a terrace on the garden front, with fine views northwards over the lake; an avenue beyond has a hill-top obelisk brought from Wrest Park, Bedfordshire. The lawns were filled with fine French and English sculptures in stone and lead, some bought from the Stowe sale of 1921, some added later from the Milton Abbey sale of 1932.[2] Many of these are still there. But mixed with his love of the 18th century was a love of the new. On the east side a sunken garden was laid out with an orangery designed by Colonel Reginald Cooper – still there, but shrouded in trees. The swimming pool in front was reflected in the blue flowers of the flanking borders, described as 'two of the finest blue borders in England'.[3] He had a nine-hole golf course, and an airfield for his private plane. And like Port Lympne it had an exotic quality: the lake had not just ducks and geese but black and white swans, cranes, and penguins; some of the deer in the park had gilded antlers. No fewer than 18 gardeners looked after the grounds, and like houses in the 19th century his London house and Port Lympne were supplied with produce from his kitchen gardens in Middlesex.

Much of the basic lay-out of the house was unaltered in spite of the exterior changes: a wide spine corridor separates the main reception rooms from the smaller rooms on the south front. But the Victorian decoration was transformed into Sassoon's vision of the 18th century with the help of his architect Philip Tilden and the decorators Lenygon and Morant. The house has a columned entrance hall, with a 1778 door belonging to Jebb's house leading into the saloon with its Chinese wallpaper. The early 18th-century staircase was brought in, and an arched corridor runs through the house from east to west, dividing the main reception rooms on the north front from the more intimate rooms behind. The drawing room and library are panelled in Early Georgian style, and appear somewhat bland today, but photographs showing them full of his collection make a very different impression.[4] Sassoon sold his parents' furnishings, concentrating instead on buying English 18th-century works of art.[5] He bought *chinoiserie* including black and red lacquer furniture, giltwood pier glasses, mirrored sconces, walnut furniture, and fine English silver. He also bought paintings, particularly conversation pieces by Zoffany and others. Some of these were sent to his London house for two major exhibitions which he put on in aid of charity. One was on conversation pieces and helped to raise awareness of this very English type of painting. The other, 'The Age of Walnut', was one of the earliest to exhibit the decorative arts; both were very influential.

The result was a house in exquisite taste, run by a large staff and with every modern comfort. The Duke and Duchess of Kent were lent the house for their honeymoon in 1934, Mountbatten, Churchill, and Baldwin were visitors, Queen Mary came to look at the gardens; Rex Whistler added painted decoration to the Blue Room. Sassoon's many artistic and literary friends came to stay, with his sister Sybil acting as his hostess; his cousin Hannah Gubbay took over that role when Sybil married Lord Rocksavage. Osbert Sitwell described 'that state of luxury, imbued with the spirit of fun' which Sassoon provided, making 'a kind of paradise, touched with magic'.[6] But it was not to last: Sassoon died after a short illness in 1939, aged only 53; his ashes were scattered over Trent Park from his plane.[7] It was left to Hannah Gubbay, was requisitioned in the Second World War as the Combined Services Detailed Interrogation Centre and was never again lived in as a private house. After the war the house became a teacher training college, and Mrs Gubbay used the agent's house nearby. At her death in 1968 Sybil, by now the Marchioness of Cholmondeley, inherited it, thereby bringing a connection with the owner who had succeeded Jebb. Since 1992 the house has been the headquarters of the University of Middlesex and inevitably changes have been made. Some modern buildings have been added at the service end of the house, and the elegant cobbled forecourt has become a vast car park. The herbaceous borders have gone and the gardens are simply lawns dotted with sculptures, while part of the grounds have become a country park; but the house down its long drive retains an air of seclusion and its beautiful rural views.

211 Southgate, Trent Park. The 18th-century lead sphinx was placed in the grounds by Sassoon. Behind it are 20th-century university buildings.

STANMORE

BENTLEY PRIORY

This large but rather unsatisfactory house was an Augustinian priory whose origins go back to *c*.1170, and although John Soane worked here extensively the appearance of the house today is essentially Victorian. The priory is 12 miles from central London and is on high and well-drained ground between Harrow Weald and Stanmore Common. Even today the house is still surrounded by well-wooded grounds and has extensive views.

The priory was dissolved at the Reformation and went to the Colte family for about a century, then to the Coghill family till 1761. There is no evidence as to the appearance of their house, but it was on lower ground. The history of the present house starts with James Duberly, an army contractor who bought and rebuilt it. He chose a site 500 ft above sea-level facing S-W towards Harrow-on-the-Hill. (Most of the estate was in the parish of Stanmore, although the house itself was in the parish of Harrow.) He built a two-storey house with

212   Stanmore, Bentley Priory. Garden front with original house on the left and Soane's much larger additions on the right. The tower was added in 1852 for John Kelk.

a north entrance front, the L-shaped service wing at one side masked by screen walls. Due to the fall in the ground there is a semi-basement on the garden front. It was built of brick, its five-bay garden front having brick pilasters – not a sophisticated design, and there is no architect's name associated with it.[1] His house is now an incongruous wing of the larger house built by Soane and others.

In 1788 he sold it to John James Hamilton, later 9th Earl and 1st Marquis of Abercorn (1756-1818). He was to inherit Scottish and Irish estates, had a house in Grosvenor Square and in 1785 had asked John Soane to find him a house near London. Soane had inspected Bentley Priory and presumably thought the 466-acre estate so close to London was ideal, even if the house itself was too modest. The view of the hilltop church of Harrow-on-the-Hill also appealed to Hamilton, who had loved his time at Harrow School. Soane was asked to enlarge the house three times in quick succession: first when Hamilton bought it, second when he inherited the Earldom from his uncle in 1789 and thirdly when he was made Marquis in 1790. At no time was a complete rebuilding contemplated; instead piecemeal additions were made. This was not the recipe for a successful project, and the result was a mess. In the first phase of building a new range was added to the east, with a main staircase, library and breakfast room and a circular domed 'tribune' beyond. This room, toplit, still survives in the core of the house. As soon as he became earl he planned further enlargements, and Soane designed three large rooms round the tribune: a vast drawing room to the south, a dining room to the east and a music room-cum-entrance hall to the north; this last was demolished in the 19th century. To try to make a symmetrical garden front a secondary stair was added to the east to match the existing library. In the third phase a new entrance was made with a simple *porte-cochère* opening into a vestibule, creating a new axis through the house from W-E. These very expensive alterations produced a house which was large and impressive enough for entertaining, but which had odd proportions, particularly the contrasting scale of the old house and new drawing room.[2] By this time Soane was also remodelling his Irish house, Baron's Court in County Tyrone. But relations between the

213 Stanmore, Bentley Priory. The entrance hall, added by Soane in 1798-9.

two men deteriorated, and in 1802 Soane stopped working for Abercorn after an angry exchange of letters, to be replaced by Smirke. But he did design a poignant monument in the garden to Abercorn's three-year-old son, which remains there.

So what had Soane achieved? His earliest additions provided two rooms and the tribune, which at this stage had windows as well as a modest lantern, and niches for sculpture. In the second phase this lost its windows but gained a larger dome; it also served as the route to the new dining room. This had no views to the south, due to the insertion of the staircase on the south front. The music room with its organ acted as both an entrance hall and a link between the old and new parts of the house. The elliptical drawing room (50 x 30 ft) had three large windows opening onto a terrace as well as a window in each apse; it is a light-filled room with wonderful views, but its proportions are uncomfortable. There are interesting Soane chimneypieces in the drawing room and tribune. The most successful part of Soane's work is the entrance he created in 1798-9, where at last one gets a real sense of his abilities as a designer. The *porte-cochère* opens into a low dark vestibule with a stone floor and a vaulted ceiling, dominated by massive Doric columns; he designed a pair of most original stoves in the form of trophies of medieval armour.[3] In 1802 the vaults were painted by Crace with a Grecian scheme of ornament in red, blue and black on buff which is still in place. Crace also added blue sky and clouds on the drawing room ceiling and the dome of the tribune.

Abercorn died in 1818 and his grandson, created 1st Duke of Abercorn in 1868, used it. He was Foreign Secretary from 1828-30 and being so close to London the house was well-placed for entertaining; he could offer his guests pheasant and duck shooting on his land and there were two packs of foxhounds nearby. In 1839 he bought the adjoining estate of Stanmore Park, adding a further 300 acres. But by 1848 Abercorn, rich and landed as he was, was £400,000 in debt and decided to sell Stanmore Park and to let Bentley Priory.[4] The Dowager Queen Adelaide became his tenant for the last few months of her life. As widow of William IV she had the use of Bushy House but in 1848 had lent it to the exiled Duc de Nemours. She first rented Cassiobury from the Earl of Essex and quickly decided it was lacking in privacy so took Bentley Priory instead. She was not well, and arranged a suite of rooms for herself on the ground floor of the old house. Knowing she was not going to live much longer, Queen Victoria and Prince Albert visited her there and found the Priory 'a charming house' with beautifully kept grounds 'very fine trees, a piece of water and a pretty flower garden'.[5] They commissioned watercolours of the house: William Leitch painted a charming view of the garden front, showing the attractive creeper-covered verandah which opened from the drawing room, since replaced by heavy paired columns. James Stephanoff painted views of the bedroom and dressing room used by Queen Adelaide, who died there in December 1849.[6]

This was almost the end of Abercorn's tenure. In 1852 he found a buyer for Bentley Priory. This was a rich industrialist, John Kelk (1816-86), who had begun his career working for Thomas Cubitt and had gone on to build his own contracting business, building houses and churches in London as well as railways, docks and the Albert Memorial. He was very successful, later buying an estate in Hampshire as well as a house in Grosvenor Square and being made a baronet. So he could easily afford to 'improve' Bentley Priory. He built the tall clock tower near the entrance to the house, added a conservatory 126 ft long west of the house, and enriched the main staircase with gilt-metal panels in French style and tall gas-lights on bulbous carved pedestals. Kelk sold the house a few years before he died, and

214 Stanmore, Bentley Priory. Queen Adelaide's bedroom, where she died in 1849. The simply furnished room is decorated with strongly contrasting colours and patterns. Queen Victoria commissioned the watercolour by James Stephanoff in 1850.

the sale document has a detailed description of the 466-acre estate with its home farm and the four-acre lake. This was overlooked by a summer-house, where 'in the quiet seclusion of this charming spot Sir Walter Scott wrote Marmion'. The impressive kitchen gardens provided not just peaches and grapes but even bananas, orchids and stephanotis. The house was 'replete with every comfort and convenience' and included a covered tennis court with gas lighting.[7] The buyer, Frederick Gordon, wanted to turn it into a hotel and built himself a house in the grounds nearby, but it was not a success and in 1909 it was offered for sale. The sale brochure advises that it is 'half an hour by motor' to central London, surely quicker than today.[8] It became a girl's school, but this closed in 1922 and the estate was sold in several lots. Middlesex County Council bought 90 acres for a public park, about 240 acres were developed with upmarket suburban housing, and the house and remaining 40 acres were sold to the Air Ministry in 1926 for £25,000. With war approaching it was chosen as the headquarters for Fighter Command, which it remained till 1968. The surroundings of the house suffered under institutional use; huts sprang up in the grounds, the conservatory was demolished in 1939, and in the same year the RAF expanded, buying back Stanmore Park and immediately demolishing the house without any consultation. After the war it remained in use by the RAF but there was serious fire damage in 1979. One advantage of this was the rediscovery of Crace's scheme of decoration in the entrance hall, which has since been restored. The RAF is giving up Bentley Priory in 2008. Since it was from Bentley Priory that the Battle of Britain was master-minded there are plans under consideration now to make some sort of museum commemorating this, and the Bentley Priory Battle of Britain Trust has been set up, ready to take over the house.

CANONS

Of the three early 18th-century great houses which soon disappeared, Canons was the first to be built and the first to disappear. Like Wricklemarsh it was demolished as soon as its builder had died. It is also the best documented, with many drawings, inventories and sale documents.

Its name derives from the Augustinian canons of St Batholomew the Great in Smithfield, whose property it became c.1130. The land was in the parishes of both Great and Little Stanmore, and by the Reformation there was a moated manor house which was leased. It became Crown property and was sold to Hugh Losse, a City merchant who bought various pieces of ecclesiastical land as they came on the market. In 1604 his grandson sold the land to Sir Thomas Lake, Latin Secretary to James I. Lake rebuilt the house, possibly to a design by John Thorpe. His plan of the house shows a courtyard house with a loggia opening into the gardens on one side.[1] The manors and land were split between various members of the Lake family over the next generations, with the history of the great house beginning with the marriage of Mary Lake to James Brydges in 1696. They were cousins, and in 1709 Brydges bought the property from her uncle, although he was not able to use the house until he died in 1713.[2]

James Brydges (1674-1744) was the son and heir of Lord Chandos of Sudeley Castle in Gloucestershire, who died in 1714, and in 1719 Brydges was made 1st Duke of Chandos. In 1707 his patron, the Duke of Marlborough, made him Paymaster-General to the Queen's Forces Abroad, a post which gave its holder commission of three per cent on the sums which went through his hands. Since the war was long and expensive, this allowed Chandos to build up enormous wealth before his resignation in 1712. His first wife died that year, and the following year he remarried, again choosing a cousin. She was Cassandra Willoughby of Wollaton Hall in Nottinghamshire, step-daughter of Josiah Child of Wanstead; so Chandos was brother-in-law of the builder of Wanstead, Richard Child. First of all he rebuilt the parish church, St Lawrence, Whitchurch (or Little Stanmore). It is one of the grandest parish churches round London, designed by John James and with a family mausoleum added by James Gibbs. Top artists – Verrio, Laguerre, Bellucci, Sleter – were brought from London to decorate it, and all these architects and artists were to be involved in the new house.

This was begun in 1713 as the piecemeal rebuilding of the earlier courtyard house. Chandos was a difficult client, interfering with his architects and constantly changing his mind. As a result he had a succession of people submitting designs and building works going on for ten years, but all within the footprint of the early 17th-century courtyard house. From the 16th century these suburban houses experiment with compact plans, and were usually not excessively large; Canons was large (146 x 124 ft) and lavish, with a central courtyard and two service courts.[3] It was built of stone – no problem for a man as rich as Chandos, although part of the north front was of brick. After many changes of plan and of architect and considerable expenditure he had a Baroque house of great splendour, with its interiors richly finished by top London craftsmen; but in plan it was still an old-fashioned courtyard house.

Talman, never an easy man, was asked to prepare plans for the house in 1713, but his 12 plans were not executed and do not survive. He also designed some service buildings which were built before he was dismissed. He was replaced the next year by John James, who produced designs for the west, south and north fronts. Vanbrugh was asked to check James's work and to make designs, and from 1715-19 James Gibbs was working on the house. John Price was employed after Gibbs was dismissed, then Thomas Fort until 1723, followed by Edward Shepherd. With this bewildering number of architects involved it is remarkable that the house was ever finished.

John James was the architect in charge from 1713 until the end of 1715, and was also the contractor responsible for the building. He was replaced by James Gibbs and these two architects were mainly responsible for the building. The entrance was on the south front, as in the 17th-century house. The impressive south and east fronts were of rusticated stonework with columned centrepieces. They had two main storeys and attics, and the roofline was decorated with vases and statues. The north side had a five-bay projecting stone centrepiece flanked by grey brickwork. A service wing extended westwards from it, and an exceptionally large chapel designed by Gibbs extended north. On the west side were the two stable courtyards, linked to the house by colonnades which formed a deep service court. The courtyard of the old house was reduced to allow for a magnificent staircase and corridors behind the main rooms.[4]

The interiors were lavishly finished. The marble entrance had a ceiling painted by Sleter and was flanked by the family rooms, with the Duchess's bedroom and dressing room in the S-W corner. A dining room and parlour were on the north side, and in the angle was the marble bathroom – Canons was most unusual in having water piped to both floors, with a water closet on the first floor. A marble staircase with ironwork by Tijou and more Sleter paintings led to the saloon above the hall. This was decorated by Thornhill with Apollo and the Muses. An *enfilade* of state rooms on the east front led to the largest room in the house,

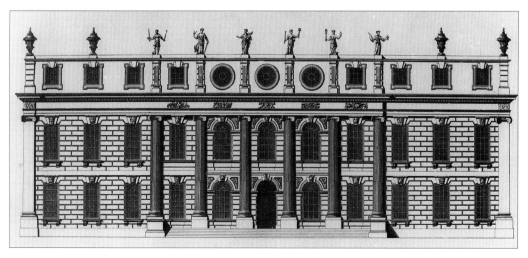

215 Stanmore, Canons. Elevation of south front, drawn by John Price and published in *Vitruvius Britannicus*, 4, 1739.

the 55 ft long library on the north front, which contained his collection of manuscripts and medals as well as his large collection of books.[5] Here Bellucci painted canvases for the ceiling with the liberal arts and sciences, and it was in this room that Chandos placed Grinling Gibbons relief panel of *The Stoning of Stephen*.[6] A detailed inventory made by John Gilbert, the steward, in 1725 describes the contents of each room.[7] The furnishings were as lavish as the house, there was a very large and valuable collection of silver and many of the paintings were of museum quality.

The household was as lavish as the house, with 83 servants on his payroll around 1720. From 1716-19 Handel was part of the household at Canons, and composed anthems and cantatas for the private orchestra. Dr John Pepusch was the Master of Music, and the Duke and Duchess listened to music during dinner from the adjoining music room. Defoe was more than ordinarily impressed by the house, writing that only Wanstead – built by Chandos's brother-in-law, Sir Richard Child – equalled its magnificence. He was impressed by the music in the chapel, writing that 'the duke maintains there a full choir, and has the worship performed there with the best music, after the manner of the chapel royal'.[8]

The large park was made by diverting the road further from the house. Lodges at the gates were manned by Chelsea Pensioners, and guards patrolled the grounds at night. Defoe approved of the drive, where the usual axial approach was dispensed with. 'The [Edgware] avenue is spacious and majestick [*sic*], and as it gives you the view of two fronts, joined as it were in one, the distance not admitting you to see the angle, which is in the centre; so you are agreeably drawn in, to think the front of the house almost twice as large as it really is.' There were 83 acres of gardens, and kitchen gardens where pineapples were grown – a sure sign of luxury. Visitors flocked to see this opulent house with its magnificent picture collection. They were admitted every day except Sundays, but were not allowed into the library.

Cassandra died in 1735 and Chandos remarried, his third wife being a widow who brought a considerable fortune. When he died in 1744 his widow went to live at the fairly modest Shaw Hall near Newbury, and Henry Brydges, 2nd Duke of Chandos inherited Canons. He was very extravagant and for two years struggled to maintain the house as in the past, then in 1747 decided to sell. There were sales of the pictures and other contents in 1747, and another sale over two weeks of the house itself.[9] It was then demolished, and the parts that had been sold were recycled. The painted glass and painted ceiling panels from the chapel went to the church at Great Witley in Worcestershire, the staircase to Chesterfield House in Mayfair, the gates to Hampstead parish church and some of the garden sculptures to the grounds at Stowe.

William Hallett's Canons

In 1753 the furniture maker William Hallett Senior (*c*.1707-1781) bought the site with 17 acres for £13,445 and built himself a smaller compact house on the site. Watts describes the house as 'a square of about 50 ft … nevertheless [it is] an elegant and commodious residence. The whole building is of stone, and the offices are underground, the cellars of the former house having been appropriated for that purpose.'[10] Hallett had attended the Canons sale in 1747, and it is possible that he was reusing some of the stone from the Chandos house; he is known to have bought some items there.[11] His portrait by Hayman shows him holding the plan of his new house. He remarried in 1756 and with his wife's fortune was able to retire and hand over his business to his son. He became interested in agriculture and turned most

216   Stanmore, Canons. The small house built on the site by William Hallett in the mid-18th century.

of the park over to farmland. His house changed hands in 1787, and again in 1812. The new owner, Sir Thomas Plumer, was Attorney-General and Master of the Rolls. He called in Humphry Repton to landscape the grounds, but no 'Red Book' has survived. After his grandson sold the house in 1860 the land was split into nine lots for sale. In 1896 the Canons Park Estate Company was set up to develop it, although Hallett's house and some of the land remained unbuilt on. This was bought in 1906 by Arthur du Cros of the Dunlop Rubber Company, who asked Charles Mallows to enlarge the house. The area was becoming a residential suburb of London, and when it was sold in 1920 some of the land was bought by Harrow Urban District Council to become a park. North London Collegiate bought the house and 10 acres and moved the school from Camden to this less restricted site. As usual the school has expanded and built large adjoining wings, but Hallett's house with its bows is still the core of the school, which remains a leading girl's school today.

TITSEY

Titsey Place

Two large estates lie only five miles apart and just inside the S-E stretch of the M25: Chevening in Kent and Titsey just inside the Surrey border, and of these Chevening is much better known. However Titsey also has a long and interesting history. It is a well-preserved house in a fine position just below the North Downs, with well-wooded hills behind it and a good water supply from a spring rising close to the house. In spite of its closeness to the M25 it has uninterrupted rural views over the park and farmland beyond. A remarkable example of continuity of ownership, the estate at Titsey has not changed hands since it was bought in 1534 by Sir John Gresham, a merchant in the City involved in the Baltic and the spice trades; he belonged to the Mercers' Company and was made Lord Mayor in 1547-8. His family came from north Norfolk and he founded Gresham's School in Holt. (His nephew was the hugely successful merchant Sir Thomas Gresham, founder of the Royal Exchange and owner of Osterley.) He bought up the nearby manors of Sanderstead, Westerham and Limpsfield in order to enlarge his estate, but did not rebuild the house before his death in 1556. His son William (1512-79) did that, but it was not recorded and the only part of it that survives is incorporated, much altered, into the back wing of Titsey. His portrait hangs in the hall, showing a large and determined looking man dressed in the severe dark clothes of a merchant. The family was Royalist and the house was confiscated in 1643 but was returned to Marmaduke Gresham in 1660, when he was given a baronetcy.

His grandson, the second Sir Marmaduke, was hopelessly extravagant and by his death in 1742 the estate had shrunk, the house had decayed and the family was indebted. The estate was rescued by Sir John Gresham, the last baronet, who inherited as a minor. He later married an heiress, demolished most of the old house and in 1775 built an unpretentious five-bay brick house which is encased today in Atkinson's entrance front. The remains of the old house became a stone-flagged servants' hall on the ground floor with a finely panelled bedchamber above in a slightly naïve Palladian style. The medieval parish church was removed from its site close to the house and rebuilt as a plain brick box beside the approach road to the village. His daughter and heiress Katherine married William Leveson-Gower (1779-1851) but she died only four years later and it was her husband who commissioned William Atkinson to enlarge the house in 1826. Atkinson did not have the free hand here which he had at Twyford Abbey in west London; the west-facing brick house remained as the core of the new house. He removed the trellis verandah which extended across the west-facing entrance front and encased it in 'Atkinson's cement'. The sash windows were replaced with mullion and transoms and were given hood moulds and a buttressed and castellated porch was added with the Gresham crest, a grasshopper, in the centre. His surviving interiors include the paved entrance hall and the staircase with its cast-iron balusters; he even designed the fine pair of Colza oil lamps at the foot of the stairs. The rather masculine decoration of the library with its black marble chimneypiece and simple oak bookcases is his, and the original drawing room (now the dining room) has Atkinson's restrained stone chimneypiece and frieze. It is an attractive room with its views south over the lake; the village and the mill on the little stream were moved away from this side of the house at the same time to improve the outlook.

In 1856 the house was given its present asymmetrical appearance by the addition of a three-storey castellated tower on the north side designed by Philip Hardwick. With its generous bay windows this provided a large dining room close to the service rooms behind. This was commissioned by William Leveson-Gower, but it was his son, Granville Leveson-Gower, who embellished the house slowly and carefully from 1860 when he inherited it till his death in 1895.[1] He was an antiquarian who wrote papers on local history and had the Roman site south of the park excavated. The small 18th-century parish church was rebuilt in 1861 to the designs of J.L. Pearson.[2] In the tiny village estate cottages were built in Surrey vernacular style by Whichard and Walker. A lodge was built to designs by George Devey, and the head gardener's attractive house beside the walled kitchen garden is probably also by Devey, who was particularly good at small buildings in vernacular styles. Leveson-Gower also carried his passion for history and genealogy into the house itself: the dining room was given heraldic decoration as a frieze, and the chimneypiece was given an overmantel with a 16th-century panel containing the Gresham arms. In these antiquarian interiors of this period old pieces are often artfully mixed with new, and this was flanked by new panels with the ciphers of Granville and his wife, the Hon. Sophia Leigh of Stoneleigh Abbey.

217 Titsey Place, entrance front. Atkinson refaced the 18th-century house in 1826. The large tower on the left was added in 1856.

The panelled sitting room was made to look more ancient by the introduction of old blue-and-white Dutch tiles into the fireplace and oak panelling onto the walls; this comes from various different sources, and frustratingly has no provenance.

During the Second World War the house was requisitioned for use by troops, after which it was lived in by two unmarried brothers, Richard and Thomas Leveson-Gower. They repaired the wartime damage to house and grounds and set up the Titsey Foundation to safeguard the future of the house and its estate of about 3,000 acres. Since the death of Thomas Leveson-Gower in 1992 the house has been carefully restored and its fine paintings and family portraits conserved and rehung. As intended by the two brothers who were the last private owners, both house and grounds are now open to the public.[3]

TOTTENHAM

BRUCE CASTLE

Bruce Castle is one of the most important early houses in the London area, but in spite of being a museum it is remarkably little known. It also has a complex history, as well as being linked with two noted antiquaries in the 17th and 18th centuries. Tottenham was a large village with several good-sized houses, on the main road north from the City through Hackney to Hertford (now the A10). This was a Roman road running parallel to the River Lea, with Tottenham on slightly higher ground west of the marshes. Bruce Castle was N-W of the village centre, close to the parish church and the house which is now the Vicarage; this is the only other important early house still standing in Tottenham. 'Lordship House' as Bruce Castle was then called was one of the manors of Tottenham and in 1254 became the property of a member of the Bruce family. In 1304 it went to Robert the Bruce but reverted to the English Crown when he became the Scottish king soon afterwards, although their name remained.[1] It seems to have been a manor house rather than a castle, and certainly shows no signs today of having been a fortified house. Nothing remains of the earlier house, but the irregularity of the plan does suggest that older fabric is incorporated into the house we see today: basically a 16th-century H-plan house with 17th-, 18th- and 19th-century additions. One of the puzzling features of the house is the large circular brick tower in front of the house, built in the 16th century but its purpose unclear. Might its corbels and battlements may have contributed to the name of the house?[2]

218 Tottenham, Bruce Castle. Entrance front drawn by Lord Coleraine in 1682, showing his alterations to the 16th-century house.

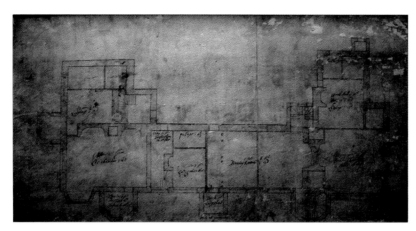

219 Tottenham, Bruce Castle. Plan of ground floor drawn by Lord Coleraine in 1682. The kitchen with its two big fireplaces is on the left.

Sir William Compton, the owner of Compton Wynyates and of large Midlands estates, bought it in 1513. He was a courtier and it would have made a convenient house for him to use when he was off duty, as his estates would have taken him several days to reach. In 1516 Henry VIII visited him here, meeting his sister Margaret who was travelling down from Scotland. For such a purpose its position close to a main road was advantageous. It is usually said that he rebuilt the house, but a recent report suggests that he built the brick tower but that the house was not rebuilt till the 1570s.[3] Recent dendrochronology suggests the timber was cut in the 1560s, so a building date shortly after that seems likely.[4] The rebuilding was probably carried out by the widowed Countess of Pembroke, formerly married to Peter Compton. She may have rebuilt it for her own use, or for her son Henry, later 1st Lord Compton (1538-89). The house was an irregular H-plan with the main front facing south into a walled forecourt. It was built of brick with stone dressings, and there are small surviving areas of the original diaper brickwork. It had a symmetrical two-storey front with gables (since removed) and a central porch which led into the screens passage. Above the single-storey hall was the great chamber. The front had two projecting staircase towers flanking the hall and the double-pile ranges beyond had service rooms in the west wing, with family rooms on the ground floor and state rooms on the first floor of the east wing. The 2nd Lord Coleraine's plan of 1682, when it was little altered, confirms that this was the arrangement of the house. It clearly shows the screens passage and a corridor leading to the kitchen with its two fireplaces and larders behind. The high end of the hall has two staircases, one in the tower and a second in the angle of the wing; but it was unusual for an Elizabethan house not to have a more imposing staircase leading up to the great chamber, and these were later rebuilt on a larger scale elsewhere.

In 1626 William, 2nd Lord Compton sold the Tottenham estate to Hugh Hare, who was later given an Irish peerage as Lord Coleraine. He also bought all the four Tottenham manors and later bought Longford Castle in Wiltshire, where he died in 1667; so Bruce Castle was his suburban house, not his main country estate.[5] His son Henry, 2nd Lord Coleraine (1636-1708), was to make important changes to Bruce Castle and to give it its name. He was a noted antiquary and wrote a history of Tottenham.[6] He was also a collector of books and coins, interested in architecture and added a family mausoleum to the church, possibly to his own designs.[7] With his antiquarian interests he appreciated the history of his house, and in 1682 he drew the plan of the house (already discussed) as a preliminary to carrying out work on the house. He carefully repaired the porch before adding a clock tower and cupola to its upper stage.[8] He then commissioned the view of the house by Wolridge which was painted in 1686, possibly fitted into an overmantel; it was recently rediscovered and restored.[9] This delightful scene shows a dog, a peacock and other birds outside the walled forecourt on the entrance front, a boy busily rolling the lawns, and a view through the house to the gardens at the back.

His grandson was the 3rd and last Lord Coleraine (1693-1749), who sold Longford Castle in 1717 and made Bruce Castle his main residence. He too made alterations there, increasing the size of the house by adding a north-facing range with a massive pediment behind the hall which bears the family arms. The room on the ground floor of the new north front became one of his libraries, for he, too, was a collector of books and prints. Above it was a splendidly furnished gallery, really a long formal drawing room. He also installed new staircases, one of which is probably by Nicolas Dubois, who also made the geometric staircase at Chevening.[10] He had separated from his wife and had had an illegitimate daughter, Henrietta, by his French mistress Rose Duplessis who lived with him at Bruce Castle as his wife. His young daughter was left the house, which caused many problems after his death. An inventory of the furnishings of Bruce Castle was drawn up in 1749, which provides fascinating evidence of the contents.[11] The legal issues were resolved when her husband-to-be James Townsend, a prosperous City merchant, bought the house in 1763. He was Lord Mayor in 1772-3 and around this time he modernised the house, in ways which surely would have upset the Coleraines. The windows on the entrance front were replaced with sashes, the gables removed and a brick parapet substituted. The east side of the house was given a tidy if slightly asymmetrical façade. Townsend's son sold the house in 1792 and it changed hands several times over the next few years before becoming a school in 1827. It was no ordinary school, but a progressive establishment set up by the Hill family, which banned corporal punishment and brought modern subjects and methods into this boys' school.[12] To accommodate class rooms and boarders a large N-W wing was added which still stands, and the old service rooms were replaced with more modern kitchens. The school closed in 1890 and the grounds were threatened with development. The site was preserved by Joseph Pedley who bought it in order to save it. In 1892 Tottenham Urban District Council bought it from him for £15,000, as usual because they wanted the 20-acre grounds rather than the historic house. Tottenham had expanded rapidly after the arrival of the railway to Enfield and 'in consequence of these cheap trains thousands of the working classes came to Tottenham to live'.[13] It was decided to turn the house into a local museum which opened in 1906, and it is still a museum today. It is also the most historic house in the LB of Haringey and houses the borough's archives and local history collection, with the restored Wolridge painting as one of its main exhibits.

220 Tottenham, Bruce Castle. Nineteenth-century photograph of east side, rebuilt by James Townsend c.1773.

TWICKENHAM

MARBLE HILL

Marble Hill, standing on the banks of the Thames in its own small park, is one of the most perfect Palladian houses in England. Like so many houses of the early 18th century it is not possible to point to one architect as the author of its design; it was the client – in this case, unusually, a woman – and a group of her friends and advisers who put together this remarkably successful design. With its compact plan and close integration with its garden, it is a house that can properly be described as a villa.

Henrietta Howard, Countess of Suffolk (1688-1767), was born at Blickling Hall in Norfolk, was orphaned early in life and brought up by relatives. At the age of 18 she married the dissolute and spendthrift Charles Howard, youngest son of the Earl of Suffolk and they lived a hand-to-mouth existence in London. It was only with the arrival of George I in 1714 that their fortunes improved, as they had already made contact with the Hanoverian court and were both appointed to minor posts in different royal households. Henrietta, now separated from her husband, became the mistress of the Prince of Wales. Before he became king in 1727 he had settled stock and some jewellery and furnishings on her, and with the help of her trustees she planned to build herself a house in the fashionable riverside village of Twickenham.[1] This would be her retreat from court life, as when on duty as Woman of the Bedchamber to the Princess of Wales she had lodgings in the various royal residences.

Her advisers on this building project were leaders of the Palladian movement: Henry Herbert, Lord Herbert and later 9th Earl of Pembroke and Archibald Campbell, Earl of Ilay and later 3rd Duke of Argyll; the latter was also one of her trustees, and built Whitton in another part of Twickenham. The earliest design of *c.*1723 is by Colen Campbell and shows a five-bay house of three storeys with a pediment and a pyramid roof, flanked by low pavilions which, curiously, are topped by obelisks.[2] Both plans and elevation are similar to what was actually built, but without the obelisks. Campbell does not seem to have been involved after this, and it is Roger Morris, who worked closely with Pembroke and Ilay and with Campbell, who supervised the building. So it is impossible to determine how much the design is due to the two professional architects, or to the client with her two knowledgeable advisers.

Since her position was a delicate one, land was bought in the names of her trustees, and in Campbell's illustration of the house in *Vitruvius Britannicus* it was named simply as 'a house in Twittenham [*sic*]'.[3] It was built quite economically, of stuccoed brick with minimal stone facings, and without the exterior stone staircase which Campbell shows in his plate. Instead, the entrance front was given Ionic pilasters to emphasise its importance, and the simple entrance was through a rusticated stone doorway into the ground-floor hall, opening into a tetrastyle hall which leads into the gardens. This type of hall, with its four columns supporting the floor of the grand reception room above, was a favourite device of the Palladians, as was the pyramid roof (seen in many of Palladio's *Quattro Libri* plates).

The breakfast parlour with its serving alcove was conveniently close to the kitchens, and the housekeeper's room next to it meant that Lady Suffolk (as she became in 1731) could keep a close eye on the running of the house.

The main rooms were on the *piano nobile* and were reached by a crisply carved mahogany staircase, probably made by James Richards, a master carver with a post in the Office of Works; it is particularly fine, and is comparable with Sir Robert Walpole's mahogany staircase being installed at Houghton Hall at about the same time. The Great Room with its three windows facing south towards the Thames is a splendid 24-ft cube, on which Lady Suffolk lavished more expense than on any other part of the house. Its white and gold colour scheme pays homage to Inigo Jones, and refers back to the Double Cube Room at Lord Herbert's Wilton House. The marble chimneypiece has gilded *putti* on the overmantel, the off-white panelling has gilded ornaments, and the plasterwork frieze is also picked out in gold. This makes a rich but unobtrusive background for the pier glasses and giltwood tables which furnished the room; one of the latter has recently been traced and bought back by English Heritage. The architectural qualities of the room meant that pictures could only be hung in certain positions, and a fine set of five paintings, signed and dated 1738, was commissioned from Panini in Rome and installed as overdoors and an overmantel painting. All these had been dispersed by the time English Heritage took over the house, but have been bought back.

The rest of the house made a comfortable and convenient home for Lady Suffolk and her second husband, the Hon. George Berkeley, whom she married in 1735 after retiring

221 Twickenham, Marble Hill. Plans and elevations from *Vitruvius Britannicus*, 3, 1725. The steps on the entrance front were never built.

from court. After his early death in 1749 she invited her great-niece, Henrietta Hotham, to live with her. The main bedroom with its bed alcove faced the gardens and had a dressing room behind it (Miss Hotham's room), with another bedroom and dressing room across the landing. The upper floor was approached only by the simpler second staircase, and had less accommodation due to the double height of the Great Room. It still provided three extra bedrooms and a gallery running along one side of the house, where Lady Suffolk hung portraits of the king and queen. It was probably used as her sitting room, as it had two fireplaces and a number of comfortable chairs and settees. In the pyramid roof were garret bedrooms for servants, lit only by small dormer windows. The two service wings were demolished in 1902, only the curving walls which hid them from the entrance front remain. One wing contained the kitchens, beyond which was Lady Suffolk's China Room, a curious and rather homely place to find it. Hidden in the trees was an ice-house, which survives.

222 Twickenham, Marble Hill, the river front. The original wings have been demolished.

Lady Suffolk was a keen gardener and a friend of Alexander Pope, who lived nearby and had made a famous garden behind his riverside house. So the setting of her house was carefully thought out, with Charles Bridgeman, the leading garden designer of the time, in charge with help and advice from Pope as well. An estate map of *c.*1735 gives a clear picture of the grounds, which were about 25 acres.[4] A drive led to the house past some simple farm buildings and orchards, and pleasure gardens were laid out between the house and the river. An oval lawn was surrounded by shrubberies, with newly fashionable winding walks leading on one side to a ninepin alley and on the other to a shell-encrusted grotto which she decorated herself. (Rather damaged, the grotto is still visible.) Towards the river a large lawn flanked with trees framed the view, and helped to distract the viewer from the public right of way which lay between the gardens and the river. There was also a walled kitchen garden of about an acre, and once she and George Berkeley had acquired a London house in Savile Row the head gardener was contracted to send produce there from Marble Hill.[5]

Horace Walpole was a Twickenham neighbour from 1747 and became a great friend, and Richard Bentley, a friend of Walpole's who had designed various parts of Strawberry Hill, designed the 'Priory of St Hubert' for Lady Suffolk in 1758. Walpole explained that the name referred to her maiden name of Hobart and that he, too, had a hand in the design.[6] It has since been demolished, but a drawing by Bentley shows a building in the fanciful Gothic style of Strawberry Hill, with blind arcading on the walls and a pinnacled tower. This 'imaginary church' was a farm, but did not last long, being demolished soon after Lady Suffolk's death in 1767.[7]

When she died, childless, the house and its contents were left in trust to her nephew, the 2nd Earl of Buckinghamshire; at his death in 1793 it passed to Miss Hotham for her lifetime. She did not live there, and the house was mainly let from 1767 until it was sold in 1824 to a neighbour, then was rapidly put on the market again and sold for £9,298 to Captain Peel, brother of the prime minister. Apart from rebuilding the stables, few changes were made by him or his widow, who lived there till her death in 1887. The contents were auctioned by Christie's that year and the house remained empty for some time, until in 1898 it was bought for redevelopment by William Cunard. Local residents were horrified at the prospect of this unspoilt stretch of the riverside being built on – which would also have destroyed the celebrated view from Richmond Hill – and a campaign to save it was mounted, which was ultimately successful. As so often, the park was opened to the public but the house was largely ignored, serving as a café for decades. It was only in 1965 that the house was restored by the GLC and opened to the public, and on the demise of that body was vested in English Heritage.[8]

Orleans House

The riverside village of Twickenham was always a favourite place for a suburban retreat, and in 1722 Macky noted that it was 'a village remarkable for abundance of curious seats … but I think that of Secretary Johnston, for the elegancy and largeness of his gardens, his terrace on the river, and the situation of his house, makes much the brightest figure here.'[1] While several houses of note have survived in Twickenham, Orleans House was demolished in 1927 and only the Octagon Room still stands.

'Secretary Johnston' was James Johnston (1655-1737), a Scottish politician who had spent some time in exile in the Netherlands, a time which must have influenced his architectural taste. He had been Secretary of State for Scotland from 1692-6, and in 1702 had bought the old house on the site which had fine riverside gardens. Johnston was a keen and knowledgeable gardener, and began laying out new gardens before he rebuilt the house.[2] John James was his architect, who may have been living in Twickenham at this time; he rebuilt Twickenham parish church 1714-15. In 1712 he dedicated his translation of Dézallier d'Argenville's *La Theorie et la Pratique du Jardinage* to Johnston. In 1710 the new house was completed, so it predates his house at Wricklemarsh by some 15 years and is in a much more restrained style. Campbell included the plans and elevation in his *Vitruvius Britannicus*.[3] It was a seven-bay house with a hipped roof, built of brick with Portland stone enrichments: a stone centrepiece with a Doric doorway and an arched window over, framed with drops – a touch which might have been inspired by Bruce's Kinross House or by Dutch examples. In plan it was a double-pile house with the service rooms in the semi-basement; there were attic rooms only on the sides of the house. The entrance hall opened into the main parlour, which with its

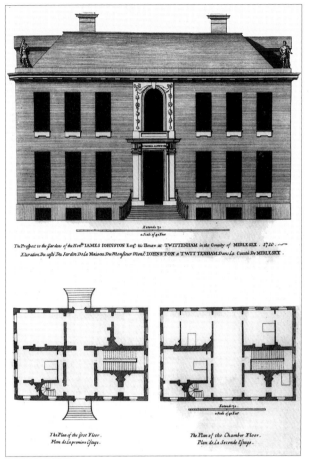

Twickenham, Orleans House. Plans and elevation of house by John James for Secretary Johnston. *Vitruvius Britannicus*, 1, 1715.

two flanking rooms could be opened up into an *enfilade*; these faced south towards the river. One of these rooms was an ante-chamber to the bedchamber and closet, which formed an apartment on the east side of the house. This was connected to a bedchamber and closet above by a small oval staircase, so these were probably the rooms for Johnston and his wife. The main staircase led up to the wide corridor or gallery running through the house with four suites of bedchambers with closets, most with corner fireplaces, opening off it. Macky describes the house as being built 'exactly after the model of the country seats in Lombardy, being of two galleries, with rooms going off on each side.'

Johnston was an expert gardener and laid out elaborate gardens. James was also very interested in gardening, but there is no evidence that he was concerned in the design of the parterres, wilderness or pleasure gardens here, all of which were much admired. Macky refers to 'the slopes for his vines, of which he makes some four hogsheads [of wine] a year' and noted that he had 'the best collection of fruit, of most gentlemen in England'. John Clerk of Penicuik, who prided himself on his skill at growing fruit, noted his 'dwarf apples on paradise stock and dwarf pears on quince stock' when he visited his fellow Scot in 1727 but also noted that the gardens were rather old-fashioned, having been laid out 20 years earlier.[4]

By this time Johnston had retired, and was able to spend more time at Twickenham. There seem to have been plans to enlarge the house, as a drawing by John Erskine, 11th Earl of Mar dated 1721 (when he was living in exile in Paris) shows the house with an attic storey as well as Doric pilasters and a segmental pediment over the entrance. The balustraded roof was to be given statues and a pineapple-topped loggia.[5] These changes were not carried out, but Mar may have been the link with James Gibbs, whose early patron he was. The major addition to the house was the Octagon, designed by Gibbs and completed in 1720; this is the only part of the house which we can see today. It was connected to the house by a terrace, later replaced by a corridor with various rooms off it. It is an octagonal brick banqueting house with rubbed red brick pilasters on the angles; the arched windows are given Gibbs surrounds in stone, and a brick parapet hides the dome. So the richly decorated interior comes as a wonderful surprise. Here the stuccadores who usually worked for Gibbs, Artari and Bagutti, provided a superb scheme of decoration. The niches in which the doors are set have cherubs playing on the pediments, the profile portraits of George II and Queen Caroline in roundels are surrounded by florid cartouches, the mirrored overmantel has reclining nymphs, and the ceiling has delicate patterning, almost Rococo in style.[6] The colour scheme is mainly white and gold with some light blue background, but current research suggests a different colour balance, which may be restored.[7] It is only 30 ft across but it is one of the grandest rooms surviving near London, and gives an idea of the sumptuous spaces for entertaining which were being created. In 1729 Mrs Johnstone entertained Queen Caroline and her children here for dinner, while her husband entertained the king in the main house.[8]

224 Twickenham, Orleans House. The Octagon, added by James Gibbs in 1720 as a riverside banqueting house and now the only remaining part of the house.

After Johnston's death in 1737 the house was sold to George Morton Pitt MP who died in 1756. It was bought a few years later by Admiral Sir George Pocock, also an MP, who had acquired a huge fortune through taking Havana in 1762.[9] He already had a house in Mayfair, but once he had pocketed his £122,000 share of the reward he married and bought Orleans House as his suburban retreat; when he died in 1792 he was buried in Twickenham. The house acquired its name from a tenant, Louis-Philippe, Duc d'Orléans, who rented the house while in exile 1815-17; his family was to return to this house after the 1848 uprising. A member of his entourage painted some charming views of Twickenham at this time, one of which shows the house from the river. The single-storey wing connecting the Octagon can be seen, as well as the canted bay which had been added to the garden front of the house by the late 18th century.[10]

From 1827-45 the house was owned by Alexander Murray MP, married to a daughter of the 2nd Earl of Lucan. He employed J.B. Papworth to make some alterations – the same architect as his father-in-law had used to design Laleham Park. The wing to the Octagon was raised to two storeys and he also designed the grate and fireback in the Octagon, which are still there. Lord Kilmorey, the next owner, sold the house in 1852 to the widow of Louis-Philippe, who had been living at Claremont since 1848. She gave the house to her son, the Duc d'Aumale, who added a library and ballroom. He lived there till 1871 and became a great friend of Countess Waldegrave of Strawberry Hill. But the future of these houses was already uncertain, as the growth of railways meant that people could reach their country houses with ease. From 1877-82 the house was a country club owned by John Astley, which did not make money. It was sold to Sir William Cunard, who also bought Marble Hill and was considering the development of these two properties. Public opinion was very much against this, and when he died in 1906 no development had taken place. But in 1926

225   Twickenham, Orleans House. King Louis Philippe visiting Orleans House in 1844. Lithograph after E. Pingret. The Duc d'Aumale lived there from 1854 until his death.

Orleans House was sold to the Crane River Sand & Ballast Company, who planned to extract sand and gravel from the riverside gardens. There was a sale of fixtures and fittings and the house was demolished the following year, leaving just the Octagon and some service buildings standing while 200,000 tons of sand and gravel were extracted. One woman played a vital part in saving the Octagon and this part of Twickenham from further unsympathetic development: Nellie Ionides. She was then the recently widowed Hon. Mrs Levy, and had begun collecting views of Twickenham and the Thames. She bought the Octagon to save it from demolition, and later helped the Council to buy the land which now forms Orleans Gardens. This was also a vital part of the famous view of Twickenham from Richmond Hill. After her marriage in 1930 to the architect Basil Ionides she bought Riverside House, so they lived next door to Orleans House. By the time she died in 1962 she had arranged to bequeath her house and art collection to the LB of Twickenham on condition that The Octagon became an art gallery where these could be displayed. Her remarkable collection has prints and drawings as well as some fine paintings, including some by Samuel Scott and Knyff. The gallery opened in 1972 in the adjoining buildings, and the Octagon also opened to the public. The buildings and six acres of gardens are now owned by the LB of Richmond upon Thames and is a refreshing example of council ownership preserving a building and caring for a collection of strong local interest.

POPE'S VILLA

The stretch of the Thames from Twickenham to Richmond still provides some of the most beautiful river views near London, and was considered as such in the 18th century, too. The house and garden which Pope created here became one of its major attractions. Long after the house was demolished in 1807 visitors continued to make their pilgrimage to the site, and print-makers continued to churn out views to satisfy the demand for pictures of it.

Alexander Pope (1688-1744) was a Roman Catholic, and as such barred from owning property within 10 miles of the capital. As a young man he rented a house in Chiswick and got to know Lord Burlington, then leased a modest house on the Thames at Twickenham in 1717. His father died that year and he needed a larger house to accommodate his widowed mother and family servants, and space for him to work on his various literary projects. Over the next quarter-century he was constantly developing his highly original garden and the house. The house was rebuilt using the Scottish architect James Gibbs, a fellow Roman Catholic. Gibbs submitted plans in 1719 for a five-bay house of brick with stone quoins.[1] The central block was of three storeys over a high basement, topped by a bold cornice and a hipped roof; the side wings were a storey lower.[2] The east front faced the river and his landing stage was across a small lawn. Just behind the house was a lane which separated the main garden from the house. Pope made a virtue from this inconvenience, linking the two gardens by a tunnel running diagonally through his basement; this is the only part of the house to survive. In the 1730s the river front was made more impressive by the addition of a balustraded terrace supporting a modest portico or porch, probably designed by Burlington. At first-floor level the roof of the unpedimented portico formed a balcony from the main room, possibly the drawing room; this looked across the river to the water meadows near Ham House on the Surrey side. The view of the improved house from the river, drawn by Heckell and others, became the standard illustration of the house.[3]

226 Twickenham, Pope's Villa, painted by Joseph Nickolls *c.*1765. There is a landing stage on the riverbank, and a tunnel beneath the house leading through the grotto to the garden across the road behind the house.

Descriptions are mainly of the garden and grotto, and no plan of the house is known. The main room on the *piano nobile* was approached up the steps from the river; it was furnished simply with busts and Windsor chairs, which presumably could be carried out into the garden. The Great Parlour had his main picture collection, and the little parlour in which he worked had his big damask-covered armchair. On the walls of the main stairs were *grisaille* panels painted for him by Kneller of three of the most celebrated antique sculptures, the Venus de' Medici, the Apollo Belvedere and the Farnese Hercules.[4] On the first floor was his library; his fame rested partly on his translations of Homer, whose bust presided here, along with English authors such as Shakespeare, Milton and Dryden.

The gardens displayed Pope's pioneering interest in the picturesque effects of a more natural looking garden, as Horace Walpole (who later came to live nearby) recognised. The garden at the back was wider than the plot where the house stood, but was still only 3½ acres, much smaller than the grounds of most suburban houses. On one side it was bounded by the road to Teddington and Lord Radnor's house was next door, so Pope's first aim was to plant out the boundaries to give as great a feeling of space as possible.[5] One side had a productive strip of kitchen garden and a little vineyard; the other had winding walks through the planting. Visitors approached through the tunnel, emerging with a view of the Shell Temple down the path. This small domed structure, encrusted with shells, was an early feature of the garden. But it fell down in 1735 and was rebuilt to William Kent's design. Beyond it lay a large mount, an old-fashioned feature which Pope employed to give height: it looked over the road and gave a glimpse of the Thames, while in the other direction were views of the more open central area of the garden which included that essential for entertaining one's friends, a bowling green. Two smaller mounts narrowed the entrance to the far part of the garden where Pope put up a stone obelisk set against evergreens; this was in memory of his aged mother, who died in 1733. Elsewhere urns and statues were strategically placed to enhance vistas.[6] The gardener in charge of all this was John Serle, handsomely rewarded in Pope's will, who published an invaluable plan of the garden soon after Pope's death.[7]

The grotto, 64 ft long, began as a fairly simple tunnel lined in tufa and minerals, but with the building of the portico the tunnel was extended and the river front had a wide light vestibule with a statue in a niche at each end. The tunnel was widened into an arched passage and opened into a vaulted oval space with a mirrored ceiling. Pope claimed that he could see reflections of the passing boats in this mirror, as if in a *camera obscura*. Kent's drawing of the author in his grotto shows him seated at a little table in this cool dark space, writing – though it could only have been an agreeable place in a heatwave.

In Pope's last years the embellishment of the grotto became almost an obsession, with urgent requests sent to his friends for shells, minerals, marbles and even semi-precious stones. The effect was rich, glittering and enlivened by the waters of a spring which he had found beneath his house when enlarging the grotto.

After Pope's death in 1744 the house and gardens were sold to Sir William Stanhope, who managed to buy another 1½ acres and also altered the house, removing the portico, adding canted bays to the wings and a pediment to the centre, and building a utilitarian service wing to the south. The house was so famous as a literary shrine, and the gardens so celebrated as precursors of the picturesque, that he produced a guide book for visitors. Less sympathetically, he cut down the dense plantings masking the boundaries of the garden behind the house, then found it so overlooked that he had to build a high wall. But the very popularity of the house proved its undoing. Baroness Howe, owner of the house from 1807, was so annoyed by the constant visitors that she solved the problem in a violent but effective way: the house was demolished and she built another one on the site. Turner's view of the house painted in 1808 is an implied criticism of her action, which drew much unfavourable comment: she was nick-named Queen of the Goths. Today only the tunnel survives, stripped of most of its ornament.

STRAWBERRY HILL

Strawberry Hill, a rambling Gothic house unlike any other, was the brainchild of Horace Walpole (1717-97) youngest son of the Prime Minister Sir Robert Walpole, who had rebuilt Houghton Hall in Norfolk as his country seat.[1] So Horace was brought up partly in London, and partly in one of the most magnificent of Palladian houses. Strawberry Hill was a complete contrast to Houghton: it was small, asymmetrical in plan, and highly individual, not to say eccentric, in style. Remarkably, the house itself and much of its decoration still exists, in spite of the often flimsy materials of which it was made.

Twickenham was among the most desirable of the villages near London with its cluster of riverside houses and proximity to the court at Kew. So by the mid-18th century land was short, and when Walpole decided to buy a house in the area he had difficulty in finding something suitable. In 1747 he leased and then bought an undistinguished little house which had been built in 1692-4 by the Earl of Bradford's coachman, and was therefore known as Chopped Straw Hall. It was west of the village and rather too close to the road to Hampton; but the four-acre site had views of the river, and he spent the next fifty years enlarging and improving both house and gardens, and filling the former with his eclectic collections. Since Walpole was also a brilliant letter writer and at the centre of social life in London, his little house became celebrated in his lifetime and was much visited, so there are many contemporary descriptions of it.[2]

227 Twickenham, Strawberry Hill. Horace Walpole's house is on the right, with Lady Waldegrave's 1856 addition on the left.

The original house had only three rooms on each floor, and they were small in scale. Walpole first dressed up the east front, disguising the earlier house by inserting gothic windows with quatrefoil openings above them, and adding a battlemented parapet with pinnacles. He had the professional advice of the minor architect, William Robinson, but the ideas were Walpole's. The whole was roughcast and whitewashed, a scheme which may be put back in the next few years.[3] He arranged the modest rooms to provide two parlours and a few bedchambers; one had a fireplace decorated with a Saracen's head, the Walpole family crest. Another was decorated with prints stuck on the wall – possibly the first print room to be made, and the first of three at Strawberry Hill. By 1753 his 'small capricious house' was becoming larger, and taking on an increasingly Gothic style. His 'Committee of Taste' was helping him with the design and decoration of new and larger rooms; the main figures of this committee were Richard Bentley, a talented designer, and John Chute of The Vyne in Hampshire. The trio searched through books of cathedrals and priories for evidence of medieval decoration, and visited medieval buildings in England and France. They were quite happy to adapt the design of a tomb for a chimneypiece, an attitude which would shock Gothic Revival architects of the 19th century. At the same time Walpole was beginning his collection of stained and painted glass, which he had inserted into the windows of the small original rooms as well as into the new additions. It came mainly from Flanders, some of it of fine quality, and was set into the upper parts of the windows with contemporary painted glass which Walpole commissioned from Price, Peckitt and others.[4]

In 1754 a large dining room, called the Great Parlour or Refectory, was added to the north-east with a library above it; and the entrance was rearranged, with a small entrance hall opening into a dramatically lit staircase hall. This had a wallpaper of Gothic design by Bentley, painted in dark greys; fragments of it were discovered in 1980, and it may be

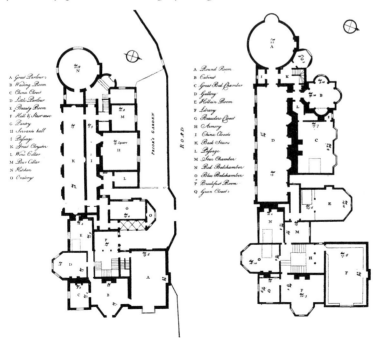

228 Plans of ground and first floors in 1784, after the addition of the Gallery and Round Room to the small original house.

reinstated. The staircase itself was by Bentley, with its flowing pierced design based on a staircase he had seen in Rouen Cathedral; he also designed a Gothic lantern which cast only the faintest light, adding to the Gothic 'gloomth'. On the newel posts were carved and gilded antelopes, supporters of the Walpole arms, and on the landing was the Armoury, an arcaded area crammed with armour from all over the world – again, Walpole being the first to arrange these obsolete objects as decorative features in a modern house. The library itself became the heart of the house for Walpole, whose rapidly growing book collection was eventually housed in seven rooms. Here Chute designed the crisply carved bookcases, based on a print by Hollar in Dugdale's history of Old St Paul's Cathedral, while the chimneypiece and overmantel were based on tombs in Canterbury Cathedral and Westminster Abbey. Walpole employed the decorative painter Andien de Clermont to paint various arms on the ceiling in homage to his Norfolk ancestors.

229 Twickenham, Strawberry Hill, interior of the library.

By now the house was much more comfortable and he could entertain in some style; but the house was to become larger still, and his next additions were the Treillage Passage leading to the Holbein Chamber. Because of the closeness of the road, the house could not extend far towards the north; but this did provide one good-sized bedroom, which was painted a deep purple. The bed was rather awkwardly squashed into its bed alcove just inside the door, and was hung with 'Lilac Broad Cloth, lined with white satin … adorned with a tufted fringe of black and white' and topped with had plumes of lilac and white ostrich feathers.[5] The ceiling was the first essay in Gothic tracery made in *papier-mâché* by the wallpaper manufacturer Thomas Bromwich. Vertue's copies of Holbein's drawings in the Royal Collection hung on the walls and gave the room its name, while the ebony furniture was Indo-Portuguese; it was 17th-century, but thought by Walpole to be Tudor. (This type of furniture became a favourite with antiquarians such as Sir Walter Scott.) The most spectacular addition followed in 1762–3, and opened up the house still more for entertaining. On the ground floor was the Cloister, an arcade (glazed in the mid-19th century) furnished with what must have been remarkably uncomfortable turned triangular chairs.[6] Above it was the new gallery (36 ft long) with its fan-vaulted ceiling based on the Henry VII Chapel in Westminster Abbey. Canopied recesses also had fanciful vaulting, and the dado was panelled in delicate tracery, all these details being made in *papier-mâché* by Bromwich. In contrast the walls were of red Norwich damask (or worsted) to make a conventional background for the densely hung collection of paintings. Off the far end of the gallery was the Tribune, a small room to hold the most precious of his possessions: miniatures, coins, medals and enamels. A tripartite screen separated the anteroom form the Tribune itself, and when unknown visitors came round they were only allowed to peer through it at the treasures within.

230 Twickenham, Strawberry Hill, interior of the gallery.

The house continued to grow, with the Great North Bedchamber built in 1770, then another extension in 1776. This three-storey tower had the kitchen on the ground floor – hardly convenient for the long journey to the Great Parlour. On the first floor was the Round Room, and here Robert Adam was called in, not to design the tower itself but only the chimneypiece and ceiling – not the happiest of commissions for Adam, who liked to have a freer hand. He produced a most elegant *scagliola* chimneypiece, based on the shrine of Edward the Confessor in Westminster Abbey, and for the ceiling design he drew on another of Hollar's plates of Old St Paul's; both of these surely the result of close collaboration with the client. Towards the very end of a long life, Walpole commissioned offices separate from and set at right angles to the house; the designer was James Essex, but the building was put up in 1790, after his death, by James Wyatt.

The gardens grew from the original four acres of 1747 to 47 at Walpole's death and were constantly undergoing changes. Like the house, he carefully avoided any sense of formality or regularity. The south side was planted with trees and had a serpentine walk, at the end of which was a shell bench from which he could watch the boats on the river. At the other end was the Chapel in the Woods, never intended to be consecrated, but in keeping with the gothic spirit of the house. In 1757 he set up the Strawberry Hill Press, printing fine volumes written by him and his friends; the simple building housing this was near to the house, but had to be moved later when the cloister and gallery were built. As the number of visitors increased he had admission tickets printed and wrote the *Description* of his house, which he revised and illustrated for a second edition in 1784.[7] He began to feel that his privacy was being invaded, and to escape the public built a thatched cottage with a flower garden on land across the road to the north, to which he could retreat for the day.

Walpole thought carefully about the future of his house after his death, and left it with its contents and an endowment to his niece and great friend, the sculptress Anne Seymour Damer. She found it expensive to maintain and in 1810 passed it on to Lady Waldegrave, who would anyway have inherited it after her death. It was the wife of her grandson, the 7th Earl Waldegrave, who rescued the house from dereliction and made it again a centre of social life.

Frances Braham (1821–79) was a beautiful and energetic woman, who had married Waldegrave as her second husband.[8] He had no interest in Strawberry Hill, and in 1842 arranged for the contents to be auctioned. It was a famous sale and the catalogue, available in Paris and Leipzig as well as London, allows us to piece together Walpole's extraordinarily rich and varied collection.[9] A temporary building was put up in the gardens for the auction, which lasted 24 days; the books and prints were sold in London later. The sale made £33,468. Lady Waldegrave bought back some of the finest family portraits, and also some of the stained glass, saving what we see today; she was already fascinated by the house which was to become hers at her husband's early death. By now a rich widow, she then married the much older George Granville Harcourt of Nuneham Courtenay. In 1856 she decided to restore and enlarge Strawberry Hill: she wanted to establish herself in a property of her own near London in case of Harcourt's death. She much admired Walpole's achievement, and decided to design the alterations herself rather than use a professional architect. She was also practical, and knew what standards of space and comfort she wanted her guests to enjoy.

Her most dramatic enlargement to the house was to fill the space between the Round Tower and the office range with

231 Twickenham, Strawberry Hill. The Chapel in the Woods, its stone façade based on a tomb in Salisbury Cathedral.

a large formal drawing room with a vast bay window facing over the gardens; the roof was given battlements and pinnacles to relate it to Walpole's work, and a new corridor connected this room to his gallery. She also had the Round Tower and Beauclerk Tower raised by one storey to make them more picturesque; the offices became guest rooms, and the Cloister was filled in to provide servants' rooms. Inside Walpole's house she was sensitive to his taste but made a few changes, such as adding mirrors to the alcoves and a Viennese marquetry floor to the gallery, tiling the entrance hall in Minton tiles and giving the staircase its ceiling decoration of gold stars on a blue ground. She also redecorated his Breakfast Parlour as the Turkish Boudoir, with a tented ceiling and velvet covered divans in the bay window. Possibly her friend the artist Edward Lear designed this, since he had travelled widely in the Eastern Mediterranean. If so, it would be only interior design by him. She also had the road moved back, allowing carriages to sweep up to the entrance. She splendidly entertained politicians and royalty, and became great friends with the exiled French Duc d'Aumale and the Comte de Paris, who were living at Orleans House nearby.

When Harcourt died in 1861 she married Chichester Fortescue, later Lord Carlingford, and spent her last years happily with him, entertaining in London and Twickenham on an extravagant scale. At her death in 1879 the house was sold and passed through various hands before being bought in 1923 by the Catholic Education Council for use as a teacher training college, a use which continues today. This meant massive enlargement with Sebastian Pugin Powell as architect; fortunately the new dormitories, refectory and teaching rooms were placed beyond Walpole's offices, thus preserving the views of his house. The Waldegrave Drawing Room became the library, and the priests lived in Walpole's part of the now extensive building. There was serious bomb damage in the Second World War and the College had to close down until the post-war restoration by Sir Albert Richardson, when attempts were made to recreate some of Walpole's interiors. He also designed a new chapel and library for the college, near the Chapel in the Woods; again, these did not interfere with Walpole's house.

Without the care of the College Strawberry Hill might have been lost; and although 20th-century development has blocked the view of the Thames, there is still a large area of green space to the south and east of the house. But the years have taken their toll of Walpole's house with its fascinating interiors, and it is clear that the house now needs major work to restore the structure and to preserve the often fragile decoration. It has recently been listed by the World Monument Fund as a site in urgent need of repair and conservation; the Strawberry Hill Trust has been set up and a programme of research established, and it is hoped that the current fund-raising will allow work to start soon on what will be a painstaking and long-term project.

WHITTON PLACE

'A villa is quasy a lodge, for the sake of a garden, to retire to injoy and to sleep, without pretence of enterteinement of many persons' wrote Roger North, and Archibald Campbell, Earl of Ilay (1682-1761, later 3rd Duke of Argyll) agreed with this in his garden and small house at Whitton.[1] Twickenham was probably the most fashionable village near London but he chose an unprepossessing spot on Hounslow Heath just beyond the hamlet of Whitton.

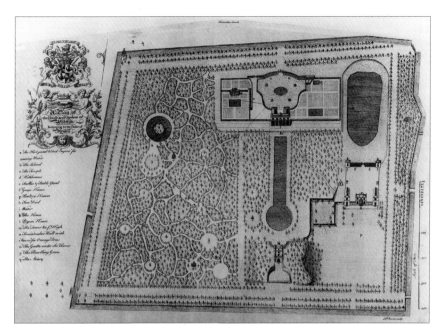

232 Twickenham, Whitton Place, plan of the grounds. The first house was above the canal, the second right of the canal. The nursery was outside the moat, on the right.

This was remote from the flourishing Thames-side social life of Twickenham: it was notorious for the criminals who waylaid travellers and for its desolate landscape. He liked a challenge and intended to grow exceptional trees in spite of the poor sandy soil and lack of water.[2] Sadly nothing remains of his gardens nor of the succession of buildings on the site.

In 1722 Ilay bought a farm and 12 acres which had been carved out of Hounslow Heath in the 17th century, and he soon acquired another 12 acres of heath.[3] By the time he died he had a total of 55 acres, but the main garden was a roughly square area of 29 acres which he surrounded with a 25 ft wide moat. This may have been partly for privacy – he cared little for social life, had a mistress but no wife, and spent most of his leisure time reading or conducting scientific experiments – and partly to have a ready supply of water for his grounds. This was raised by a 'wind-engine' from two small streams and also supplied water for the canal in the centre of the plot. Only at one corner was there a bridge over the moat, within which he planted a shelter belt of trees. The western side of the canal had a dense planting of trees with winding paths, the eastern side was more open. The canal was overlooked from the north by the orangery, built 1725-6. James Gibbs was his architect, a fellow-Scot who had already designed his brother's house at Sudbrook. The south front had a five-bay arcaded ground floor with some basic living accommodation over it and an entrance forecourt to the north. The forecourt had south-facing walls heated by stoves for the cultivation of oranges and was flanked by a hot house and small walled gardens where he could regularly inspect rows of plants. An early visitor was another Scot, Sir John Clerk of Penicuik, who reported in 1727 that 'he has a small spot of ground … but no house. His garden consists of wilderness works, on the north side is a large green house built of brick and finish'd with stucco without. Above this house is a dining room and 3 other chambers not yet finished. … My lord dined in the gardiner's house where he lies.'[4] Here was a man who put his garden first, and although Gibbs produced a series of designs for a house he did not build a proper house till 1732 and then used Roger Morris.[5]

233 Whitton Place. 1757 print by Woollett showing the Canal with well-dressed visitors fishing. The Gothic Tower in the distance has an arch allowing a view onto Hounslow Heath beyond.

From 1732 he employed James Lee as his head gardener, allowing him to use his own extensive botanical library and later encouraging him to set up a nursery at Hammersmith which became a major source for new and exotic plants.[6] Trees and shrubs were nurtured in the nursery, an enclosed area across the road from the moated garden, and transplanted. He had an impressive collection of trees, many of them from America such as maples, a scarlet oak and Virginian cedars. There were also many different species of conifers, some native and some American.[7] These can be seen flanking the 370 ft long canal which opened into a circular pond at the far end. Beyond this was a mount crowned with a round temple as any eye-catcher. By 1748 this had been replaced by the triangular tower seen in Woollett's print, designed by either Gibbs or Roger Morris.[8] This had an arch below, opening up a view to the heath through a break in the shelter belt – a perverse touch which would have appealed to Ilay. It was Gothic with battlemented towers and ogee windows, and relates to Ilay's rebuilding of Inveraray Castle in Gothic style.

Morris designed Ilay's house which was built in the eastern part of the grounds *c.*1732-3. It was a Palladian villa with a pyramid roof, a square block broken by two projecting bays each side, with a canted bay looking south over the lawns in front of the house. Henrietta Pye described it in 1760 as 'a regular handsome building'. She was shown his collection of porcelain 'consisting of the greatest curiosities. In the next room is a beautiful collection of butterflies and other insects; also drawings of birds, fishes and fruits.' On the ground floor was 'a long gallery … in which are all the instruments which the Duke uses in his mechanical and chymical experiments.' On the first floor was the drawing room 'in the Chinese taste … hung with India paper, the curtains and chairs of painted taffeta.'[9] His mistress, Mrs Anne Williams, had a small house nearby (and a London house in Argyll Street) and they had a

234 Twickenham, Whitton Place. 1757 print by Woollett of the 3rd Duke of Argyll's house, designed by Roger Morris in 1732.

son William. Ilay spent as much time as he could at Whitton, although his political interests meant that he had to be in London and Scotland too. When he died he left it to Mrs Williams and then to their son. He took the name of Campbell and allowed the Earl of Bute to arrange the transfer of several rare trees from Whitton to Kew Gardens before selling his father's estate. In 1766 it was bought by George Gostling, a lawyer, for £3,950; he enlarged Gibbs's greenhouse and turned the ground floor into rooms. He kept the western part of the grounds but sold the eastern part, which in 1781 was bought by William Chambers. He made various changes to Ilay's house, adding low wings each side with pedimented pavilions and filling the grounds with temples and sculptures. After his death it was bought back by Gostling's son (also George) and was leased to Sir Benjamin Hobhouse. Soon after the latter's death in 1847 it was demolished. George Gostling II made changes to his father's grounds, inviting Humphry Repton to loosen up the design, and the canal was turned into an irregular lake. Other than that it is not clear what Repton's proposals were nor if they were carried out. The Gostling family remained owners of Whitton through several generations and by 1900 the grounds were used by local families and as a sporting club. Demand for housing was growing since the arrival of the railway and in 1910 most of the land was sold for development, in spite of local protests. The Gostling house with its Gibbs core and the Gothic tower were demolished and the council bought 10½ acres to make Murray Park. This was land which had been Argyll's nursery, and of the gardens themselves only a few cedars survive among the streets of houses. The moat has completely disappeared and the lake was filled in but not built on, its position marked by the sports ground. The best memorial of Ilay and Whitton is his botanical knowledge and the transfer of many of his trees to Kew Gardens.

TWYFORD

TWYFORD ABBEY

Tucked in between the North Circular Road and the A40 is a surprising pocket of greenery surrounding and almost completely hiding a dilapidated house which has been empty for the last 16 years. It is Grade 2 listed, but may well not last much longer as it has been the subject of numerous unsympathetic planning applications. Ironically, its position so close to two major routes is at the moment what preserves it – the site would be seriously unhealthy for anyone living in housing on the outer fringes of the grounds, and development close to the house has been ruled out as it is designated as Metropolitan Open Land.

Twyford was a very small parish north of Ealing with the River Brent running through it from west to east. There were a few cottages and a very small brick church, near which was a moated site enclosing a medieval manor house. John Philpot, the grandson of a Lord Mayor of London, bought the house in 1432 and it remained in that family till 1540. By 1593 the manor house was the only house in the parish and the family used the church as their private chapel. Dr Stukeley wrote *c.*1755-62 that 'the fine old mansion house … about forty years ago was pulled down, being old and ruinous, of which some of the lower windows now appear in the great hall next the moat, and a building for a farm erected in its stead. It has a large moat round the house.'[1] The great hall (66 x 20 ft) remained, and a fairly modest house with four rooms to a floor was attached to it; this later became part of the service range behind the early 19th-century house. The nearby farm house was let to a succession of tenant farmers by the Herne family from 1735 and by the Cholmeley family from 1785. The property passed to John Cholmeley's two children, his spinster daughter Penelope and Sir Montague, but both houses continued to be let. By 1801 Thomas Willan was renting the house and five years later, after the death of Sir Montague, his sister and executors sold him the house and 29 acres for £2,100.

Thomas Willan (1755-1828) was a successful entrepreneur who had made his fortune through various enterprises: he owned a pub in the City, and stage coaches, and invested in a diary herd. He rented grazing in Regent's Park so his milk could easily be supplied to central London; and he bought a house called Marylebone Park.[2] Once he owned Twyford he immediately pulled down the old buildings, filled in the moat and commissioned a new house.[3] His architect was William Atkinson, a pupil of James Wyatt and already established as a successful architect working in a gothic style; he came from Co. Durham and had many commissions in the north of England and Scotland. In spite of having destroyed the old house and the moat, Willan wanted a romantic and ancient-looking house; the irregular building which resulted has similarities to Atkinson's Titsey Place in Kent. It was approached down a curving drive from the S-W, part of which is now Twyford Abbey Road. The roofline of the wide three-bay entrance front was broken by the two corner towers and the higher centrepiece, all battlemented. The brickwork was covered in 'Atkinson's cement' and the windows were given gothic tracery and hoodmoulds.[4] The drawing room faced south with its long windows giving easy access to the gardens, and this front too was castellated. A 43 x 18 ft conservatory with tall gothic windows extended eastwards and had a tall tower behind it. This informal grouping is very effective seen from a distance.[5] The kitchen and service rooms were on the north side with a brewhouse, dairy, bakehouse and stables beyond. The large kitchen gardens lay to the north and given high brick walls at this time, which can still be seen from the North Circular Road. The final touch was Atkinson's rebuilding of the little parish church west of the house, which became his chapel; it remains as the chancel of a larger church built in Brentmead Gardens in 1958. Having achieved a suitably picturesque appearance Willan renamed his house Twyford Abbey, although it had never been in monastic use.[6]

Willan's widow remained at Twyford after his death although it was inherited by their only daughter Isabella, married to John Kearsley Douglas; they took the name of Douglas-Willan. Her mother lived to be 90, by which time her husband had already died; so she subdivided the estate into three lots and let it, keeping just a lodge for herself. Her son inherited the house but never lived there himself, and let it to a succession of tenants. He sold it in 1890 to William Hull Allhusen for £11,000. Allhusen, who had a house in Kensington Gardens as well as a Scottish estate and a house in Italy, proceeded to spend almost £6,000 on the house, but did not keep it long.[7] The Ealing & South Harrow Railway Company applied for

235 Twyford Abbey. View of the house designed by William Atkinson in 1806.

a compulsory purchase order for two acres of his land close to the house in order to build a bridge over a new railway line. This would have meant putting his drive in a tunnel below the railway. He went to court but failed to stop it, and decided to give up the house. It has been in institutional use ever since. This is yet another instance of the railways ruining the surroundings of a house so that its appeal to a private owner is destroyed.

From 1902-88 the house belonged to the Congregation of the Alexian Brothers, a Roman Catholic order who used it as a care home and hospital. Over the years they made various additions, mostly fairly sympathetically. Only the entrance hall, main stairs, drawing room and morning room keep some of their original decoration. Their contributions included building a chapel in the stables and enlarging the service range in a style close to Atkinson's to provide more accommodation.[8] From 1940 the small farm was let to Guinness, who had a brewery nearby. They built a large cowshed north of the kitchen garden and kept their cows there until 1975, possibly the last dairy farm so close to central London; even after that, a herd of beef cattle remained on the farm. By 1988 the Brothers could no longer afford the upkeep of so many buildings and sold the house with its 15 acres. It was bought for its development potential by a property company and since then there have been several planning applications from different property companies. While standing empty the house must have deteriorated badly, but I have not been allowed to visit it to inspect its condition for myself.[9]

WALTHAMSTOW

HIGHAMS

Higham Hall was a substantial house belonging to the Rowe family in the 16th century. It stood on the high ground above Walthamstow and slightly to the south of Woodford Green, set back only a little from the road.[1] On the west side it overlooked falling ground towards Epping Forest, which became an important part of later landscaping.

In 1764 the old house was bought and rebuilt by Anthony Bacon, MP for Aylesbury. His architect was William Newton, a young and scholarly architect who visited Rome in 1766; building began in 1768.[2] Early designs show a central block with colonnades leading to kitchen and laundry wings down colonnades, but these were dropped in favour of a more compact villa plan. The five-bay entrance front faces east and was originally of brick, although now stuccoed. It was a two-storey house, without decoration apart from the Ionic pilasters and strong horizontal lines of the entablature, both of stone. On the west side the ground falls steeply, allowing the semi-basement with its arched windows to be fully lit. Low side wings contained more offices and each had a small service courtyard, hidden on the garden side by high walls. It was an austere but elegant design. Newton's drawings include designs for a 'stuco room [*sic*]' but this may never have been built.[3]

236 Walthamstow, Highams, entrance front. The top storey was added *c*.1790 and the wings were enlarged later.

In 1788 William Hornby, a former Governor of Bombay, bought the house and although he only owned it for two years it was probably he who added to it.[4] A second storey was added and the roofline was balustraded, not improving its proportions; the stucco was probably added at this time, to disguise the alterations. A cupola (since rebuilt) allowed access onto the leads to admire the view. The next owner, John Harman, was a City banker and in 1793 he called in Humphry Repton to improve both house and grounds. Repton was living nearby in Hare Street, just outside Romford, and this was clearly a project which captured his imagination. In his 'Red Book' we can see how he responded to the house and landscape.[5]

Epping Forest runs roughly N-S between the River Lea and the River Roding, and of course was much larger *c.*1800 than it is today. But even so London and the surrounding villages were expanding, and Epping's ancient oak trees and glades with herds of deer appealed to the romantic imagination. Repton wanted to emphasise the proximity of the Forest to Highams, and set out his plans to do so in his before-and-after watercolours. He also wanted to lessen the massy severity of the enlarged house. He suggested facing the basement level in heavily rusticated stonework with arches echoing the form of the basement windows. This would support a verandah right across the house and extending into the side wings, where colonnades would mask steps down to garden level. The windows of the main floor would be lowered to give access onto the new verandah from the main reception rooms. This was carried out, and the delicate ironwork of his railings is still there, although the verandah canopy (not shown in his designs) has gone. These were clever alterations, linking house and grounds and improving the view of the house from the grounds.

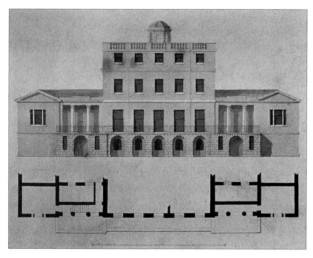

237 Walthamstow, Highams. Repton's 1793 proposals for the garden front, which were carried out. He added rusticated arches to the basement to support the long balcony.

The house stood close to the eastern boundary of the grounds with only Woodford Common separating it from the road. Its grounds extended east of the house down to the little River Ching, which formed the boundary to the west. Repton's ideas for the grounds were as effective as those for the house. The walled kitchen garden which partially blocked the view into the valley was to be moved to the side of the house, and the removal of some indifferent trees would do the same. The view down to the river and into Epping Forest beyond would thus be opened up, creating an extensive view of parkland belonging to the house, but also incorporating the Forest beyond. A 'sunk fence' would be built across the park to keep the deer away from the house. A circular walk was proposed, winding through belts of newly planted trees along the boundary which would block out the sight of other houses. In the bottom of the valley the Ching was to form a serpentine lake, with the drive passing on the far side between the water and the Forest. Repton's view shows the lake framed in clumps of trees and enlivened with a little sailing boat, with open ground rising to Epping Forest beyond. At one end of the lake he proposed a boat-house, which was also to contain a cottage and a tea room. It is one of his most engaging designs, seen from the grounds as a modest two-storey cottage with deep eaves; seen from the lake it is a more elegant building, with the arch of the boathouse below a tripartite window and a shallow pediment. This was the elegant room overlooking the lake where tea could be taken and sailing on the lake could be watched from the adjoining terraces. Sadly, although the rest of his plans were carried out, the boat-house was not.

238 Walthamstow, Highams. Repton's plan of the grounds. The house is on the left, with grassland sloping down to the lake and Epping Forest.

Harman died in 1816, and his son Jeremiah, a Governor of the Bank of England, inherited. In 1849 the estate was sold to the Warner family who had previously lived in Clock House, Walthamstow. They were largely responsible for the development of Walthamstow, so in buying Highams they were moving away from the increasingly built up village below. In the 1870s they sold some land for building, and in 1891 Sir Courtney Warner sold the lake and the adjoining strip of land to the Corporation of London to be added to their Epping Forest landholding; this land is open to the public today with the lake used for boating. The house was let, but these were its last days as a private house. During the First World War it was used as a hospital and afterwards became a school owned by Essex County Council. Large additions were made to the house in 1928 and 1938, providing wings to the forecourt in a style close to that of Newton's house. It is today Woodford County High School for Girls and what remains of Repton's grounds are now sports fields for the pupils, cut off from the lake by housing.

WALTON-ON-THAMES

PAINSHILL PARK

Painshill is probably the most celebrated recent restoration of a landscape garden, bringing back to life one of the most fascinating creations of the mid-18th century and allowing the visitor to wander through a carefully contrived but apparently natural sequence of views. Painshill House was never of more than minor importance, and has anyway been replaced so this is a description of a surviving landscape rather than of a house and garden.

The estate of Painshill began when the Marquis du Quesne bought three farms near Cobham in Surrey, although the land was in the parish of Walton-on-Thames. He built himself a small house, but lost money in the South Sea crash and had to sell. It was bought by William Bellamy, a lawyer and MP, who added another farm to the estate. The creator of the garden was the Hon. Charles Hamilton (1704-86), the ninth son of the Duke of Abercorn, who bought Painshill from Bellamy's executors in *c*.1737-8, financing the purchase by a loan from Henry Fox. Hamilton was a member of the household of Frederick, Prince of Wales, so was well connected if not well off, and was part of the circle in opposition to George II and Sir Robert Walpole. He was also thoroughly familiar with Carlton House and the William Kent gardens there. In 1740 he managed to buy another farm to the north, making Painshill into a 250-acre estate which he developed over the next thirty years. The land was a narrow strip about 1½ miles long, with the River Mole in the bottom of the valley forming the southern boundary and high ground running parallel to it, some of which had been open heath when Duquesne had bought it. Unlike much of the country round London it had natural variety in a small area combined with a good water supply. Hamilton and his wife used Duquesne's house which was not integrated into the garden but was close to the northern boundary of the estate and the Portsmouth road (now the A3). Painshill was not a *ferme ornée* like Philip Southcote's at nearby Woburn Farm, nor an Italianate garden like those which William Kent created at Chiswick and Claremont, although there were similarities to all these. It was a much more original creation made by Hamilton himself, a noted plantsman. He included flowering plants and shrubs as well as imported trees; many of these came from North America, which he bought via Collinson in London from John Bartram in Philadelphia.

The garden tour started from the amphitheatre, as it does today. This is a grassy area of high ground surrounded by trees and shrubs graded by height, with a lead cast of *The Rape of a Sabine* in the centre.[1] At one end of this is the Gothic Temple, an inviting airy wooden structure with ogee arches. From here a dramatic and carefully contrived view of the winding narrow lake unfolds; but the route to it is a circuitous one and only later is the south-facing vineyard revealed, planted on the steep hillside below the temple. Hamilton tried to finance his expensive passion for gardening by more commercial ventures, and claimed that his sparkling white wine was delicious and stood up well in blind tastings. The Ruined Abbey beside the lake housed his tile works, a less successful venture, although he could at least use home-made bricks and tiles in his garden works. It is very much an eye-catcher set against a backdrop of trees, the cream-painted brickwork pierced with Gothic windows and the upper storey looking partially collapsed; but it is simply a façade added in 1772 onto a utilitarian shed. The Chinese Bridge leads across to the mysterious wooded Grotto Island, which is scattered with chunks of rock and a tufa arch as a prelude to the grotto itself. This is one of the most elaborate of its kind, possibly designed by Joseph Lane of Tisbury, the leading grotto maker of the time. It has a rock and tufa tunnel through which one passes, stepping carefully close to the water and ducking one's head to avoid the stalactites. The cavern-like central room is encrusted with shells and minerals and echoes to the sound of trickling water.[2] A second bridge leads from the island to the winding walk between the lake and the River Mole, and takes visitors to the wilder and more atmospheric parts of the garden. In a bend of the river is a group of dense trees shading the Mausoleum, designed as ruined triumphal arch and decorated with some of the antique fragments brought back

239 Walton-on-Thames, Painshill Park. The lake seen from the restored Gothic Temple.

240   Walton-on-Thames, Painshill Park. The Abbey with the vineyard, recently replanted.

by Hamilton from his Grand Tour.[3] Today only a part of the original structure survives as stabilised ruin, the brick core clearly seen behind the stonework.

The River Mole was at a lower level than the lake but provided the water for it, so in a secluded corner was a mill-race to drive Hamilton's water wheel. In 1834 this was replaced by a dramatic Bramah Wheel installed in 1834 and still operating. The water is pumped up to the modest cascade and into the lake. Beyond here the ground rises to the most distant and wildest part of the garden, the sandy ground planted with deciduous trees and conifers. In this dank and dismal spot was the Hermitage, a thatched hut perched among the remnants of trees; but even the rural poor of the 18th century were not desperate enough to fulfil Hamilton's conditions of employment, and his hermit was sacked after three weeks for being found in a local pub. On the highest and most westerly point of the garden is the Gothic Tower, built of brick. The top room has large Gothic windows below the corbelled and battlemented upper stage. A round tower with a conical roof houses the stairs, and the roof platform gave magnificent views down the River Mole towards the great gardens at Esher and Claremont, or N–W to Windsor Castle. All this area is thickly planted with trees, about which Hamilton was very knowledgeable; many were native trees, others were species sent over from America. A route led back through glades in the woods to the Temple of

Bacchus, an imposing peripteral temple which housed one of Hamilton's most treasured purchases, a colossal statue of Bacchus which he had bought in Rome in 1732.[4] The last feature of the garden was the Turkish tent, with its canvas skirt which was draped in summer from a lead canopy.

The fame of this garden spread, and although it was not as close to London as the Thames-side gardens such as Pope's Villa it was much visited. Parties were brought over from Cobham and driven along grassy tracks through the grounds, and their tips helped supplement the wages of his head gardener, David Geneste. Not everyone was impressed: Thomas Jefferson compared it unfavourably to Esher Place and commented 'too much evergreen.'[5] Horace Walpole, always ready with a waspish comment, especially if the owner had not been a supporter of his father, dismissed the Gothic Temple as 'an unmeaning edifice … The Goths never built summer-houses or temples in a garden'. Nor was he impressed by the Mausoleum, writing 'You may as well suppose an Alderman's family buried *in* Temple Bar.'[6]

Creating a garden like this was expensive and Hamilton could no longer afford to live there, so in 1773 he sold Painshill. The buyer was Benjamin Bond Hopkins, who continued tree-planting and made a plunge bath in the park, the Roman Bath House. He also replaced Hamilton's house, employing the architect Richard Jepp Junior to build a new house further south, better placed in parkland and away from the main road. In 1925 the portico of the Temple of Bacchus was removed to form the centrepiece of this otherwise modest five-bay house. Hamilton, by now aged almost 70, moved to Bath and made a smaller garden there. The estate changed hands many times over the next two centuries and the garden became increasingly neglected. The vineyard went, the timbers of the Gothic Temple rotted, the roof of the grotto collapsed, the Hermitage and Turkish Tent disappeared and the portico of the Temple of Bacchus was removed, and after 1948 the estate was broken up into lots, although the main part of Hamilton's gardens survived as one unit. In 1980 Elmbridge Borough Council bought 160 acres and the Painshill Park Trust was set up to restore the gardens, with archaeological surveys and research underpinning the work. The result has been hugely successful with the landscape and its buildings restored, there are many visitors and in 1998 the gardens won a Europa Nostra award.

241 Walton-on-Thames, Painshill Park, the Gothic Tower. An electricity pylon was built unnecessarily close to it.

WANDSWORTH

WEST HILL

The Royal Hospital for Neuro-disability has a long and imposing façade on the highest part of West Hill. This masks a late 18th-century house of some distinction, which still exists behind the hospital and forms part of it. Indeed the design of the façade reflects the architecture of the earlier house. The house is between Wandsworth and Wimbledon and faces roughly east-west, making it 'a conspicuous object' on the road to Portsmouth, and giving it 'a beautiful prospect' with extensive views, especially east towards the City and the Thames, and beyond.[1] It was a desirable spot for a country retreat, and even if the first house on the site was modest it was set in 41 acres, bought in 1759. Lady Pitt, later Lady Rivers, built what was known as her 'casino'. She gave parties there, where she was admired for her 'superior beauty' and her house for its 'rural elegance'.[2] 'Capability' Brown worked on the landscape and made a lake at the bottom of the valley, where the West Hill estate bounded the Spencer's much larger one, where he was also employed. She also had a farm, and was said to invite her friends down to play at hay-making.[3] Later Lord Stormont rented it and made the small house somewhat larger; but there is little evidence for this house.

Johann Anton Rucker (1719-1804) bought the estate in 1789 and completely rebuilt the house, using the fairly undistinguished architect Jesse Gibson who had City connections.[4] Rucker came from Hamburg and had a successful career as a merchant in the City. He was unmarried and no longer young and his new house was stylistically old-fashioned, a competent essay in the neo-classical style of twenty years earlier. The house is set back from the road at right angles to it; its pedimented entrance front faces west, allowing the main rooms to take advantage of the views east to the Thames. It is a three-storey seven-bay house of yellow stock brick with stone enrichments, the roofline hidden by a stone balustrade. A Doric *porte-cochère* was added slightly later. The entrance hall has been little altered: a large square room with Ionic pilasters framing niches for sculpture and neo-classical plaster reliefs above the two fireplaces. A screen of Ionic columns leads to the corridor running N-S through the house. (The original main staircase was removed when it was converted into a hospital.) The elegant drawing room behind the hall is approached through pedimented doorcases and has a fine plaster ceiling in the style of Robert Adam; a more up-to-date feature is the use of tall arched windows leading directly to the gardens. The garden front is also pedimented, but with a recessed loggia on the first and second floors. Upstairs are the bedrooms, a billiard room and the library (38 x 22 ft), approached down a corridor the length of which is broken by arches and oval saucer domes. Although this room has lost its bookcases, the alcoves remain with elegant relief decoration above them; this and the carving on the marble chimneypieces relate to the arts and sciences. The long library windows open onto the loggia with its delicate ironwork, allowing one to step outside to admire the views. It was these, rather than the house itself, which most impressed writers. Rucker employed Humphry Repton to landscape his grounds, and Repton described staying with the 'venerable bachelor of nearly 80 years old, living happily surrounded by his nephews … charitable to his dependants, hospitable and kind to his equals'.[5] Angus praised the farm and dairy, and the boat-house on the lake and wrote rather condescendingly that 'The gardens, hot-houses, [and] pleasure-grounds … furnish a magnificent example of that degree of elegance and comfort enjoyed by English merchants, when they occasionally retreat from the industrious labours of the compting-house to share their well-earned wealth with their friends, in the hospitality of their country seats.'[6] The stables and service buildings were well away from the house, and had a tunnel leading directly into the deep basement, as at Claremont.

Rucker's nephew Daniel inherited the estate in 1804. He spent his honeymoon in Scotland, and was so inspired by visiting Sir Walter Scott at Abbotsford that he renamed the house Melrose Hall. But he could not afford its upkeep, and in 1824 sold it to George Granville Leveson-Gower, 2nd Marquis of Stafford and later 1st Duke of Sutherland. He managed to buy more land from Earl Spencer, making it an estate of almost 200 acres – a considerable extent for a place only six miles from London. His son, the 2nd Duke of Sutherland, inherited in 1833 and was even richer than his father, with his main estates at Trentham in Staffordshire and Dunrobin in Scotland. He and his wife came down often from their London house in St James's Square, which took them only an hour in their coach.[7] But they did not keep it long. Was this partly due to the growth of London, and the pollution brought by the prevailing west wind from industries in Wandsworth? Or did they simply

242   Wandsworth, West Hill. Repton's view of the garden front of the 1790 house.

243   Wandsworth, West Hill. The west front of the Royal Neurological Hospital, added 1864-81 and loosely based on the design of the house.

have too many houses, and with their lavish entertaining need to retrench? In 1842 it was sold for £43,000 to John Augustus Beaumont – a good example of the way in which City and aristocratic owners alternate as owners of these suburban houses. Beaumont's father was a leading figure in the establishment of the insurance industry, and his son ran the County Fire Office and the Provident Life Office, both founded by his father. But he was not simply going to enjoy it as a country estate, he planned to develop part of the grounds. In 1845 he also bought the Spencer's 600-acre estate next door, and when the Duke of Somerset, their tenant, left in 1862 he moved from Melrose Hall to Wimbledon Park.[8]

This was the beginning of the end for the West Hill estate. It was broken up into building lots, and in 1863 the Hospital Board bought 23½ acres from Beaumont for £18,000; this included the farm in the valley, which continued to provide produce for the big house. The hospital, founded in 1854 as the Hospital for Incurables, moved from smaller premises in Putney; this site with its large house and grounds was healthy and allowed for expansion, which followed rapidly. In 1864 a wing was added on each side of Rucker's house, with the design of the west front, facing the road, loosely based on Gibson's design. In 1868 a south wing was built to match it, and in 1881 the two were connected by a massive central block. Even this respects the height of Gibson's original house and is built in the same yellow stock brick. The effect is impressive, an example of Victorian philanthropy at its best. The hospital was not absorbed into the NHS in 1946; instead it has remained an independent charity, is proud of its history and maintains its buildings to a high standard.

WANSTEAD

WANSTEAD HOUSE

Wanstead was one of the great houses round London, rebuilt in the early 18th century by the immensely rich Child family on a massive scale and demolished only a century later. It was seven miles from the City, with the River Roding as the eastern boundary of the grounds and Wanstead Flats to the south. Epping Forest was very close, and Henry VII and VIII sometimes visited for hunting, possibly using the house as a hunting lodge. Sir Robert Rich was made keeper of the park and had use of the house. The 16th-century courtyard house then went to Robert Dudley, Earl of Leicester and favourite of Elizabeth I. These houses near London were conveniently close for royal visits, and she came to Wanstead in 1578. When his widow was unable to pay off his large debts the queen seized it from her, although she did then give it to her son by her first marriage, Robert Devereux, Earl of Essex.[1] From 1617-19 it belonged to George Villiers, later Duke of Buckingham, in the early years of his meteoric rise; he later settled on Beaufort House in Chelsea as his suburban house. The new owner was Sir Henry Mildmay, who paid the large sum of £7,300 for it, showing what a desirable property it was. However as a Parliamentarian it was forfeit at the Restoration and given by the king to his brother the Duke of York.[2] He sold it to Sir Robert Brooke, Mildmay's son-in-law; and it was Brooke's trustees who sold it in 1673 to Sir Josiah Child, Bt.

244   Wanstead House. The print of the house was published by Ackermann in 1824, the year of its demolition.

Child was an East India Company merchant and eventually Governor of the company, and made a fortune of about £200,000. He died in 1699 and his younger son, Richard, leased it and began laying out the gardens with George London as his designer. On the death of his elder brother Richard Child (1680-1750) became the 3rd baronet and owner of Wanstead. He was later made Viscount Castlemaine and in 1732, after his wife inherited the Tylney estates, Earl Tylney. He commissioned the new house from Colen Campbell in 1715, which established him as a major architect in the new Palladian style. Knowledge of the building was enhanced by the publication of a sequence of three of his designs for Wanstead in *Vitruvius Britannicus*. It was a magnificent stone house with a 260 ft frontage, the three-storey central block with seven bays balanced by two-storey wings of six bays. The entrance front had a pedimented portico and a balustraded roofline, with the *piano nobile* approached up stone steps, with the family entrance below. The external treatment was new in its careful massing and austere treatment, but the plan was hardly innovative. The long façade provided a main floor with a sequence of inter-connecting state rooms similar to Blenheim or to Castle Howard, one side ending in a chapel, the other with a gallery.[3] The ground floor had the family rooms and four apartments: for the owner and his wife and for guests. These were on a lavish scale. Macky described the remarkably large apartments of Lord Castlemaine, with a parlour, antechamber, bedchamber, dressing room and closet. His wife had the same, with Chinese wallpaper in her parlour and Chinese silk in her antechamber. The two other apartments on that floor were not yet finished on his visit, nor were the state rooms on

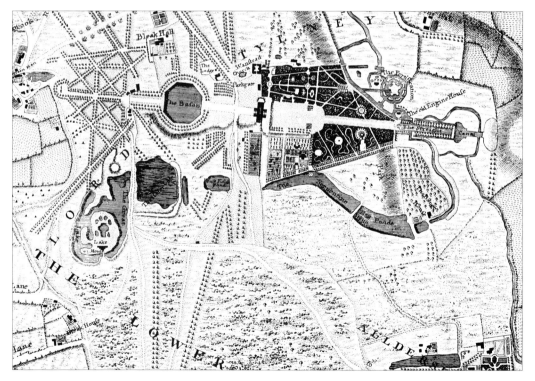

245   Wanstead House, from Rocque's map of 1745. The house overlooks the 'Bason' to the west and the 'streight canal' to the east. The 'Lower Forest' to the south is part of Epping Forest.

the *piano nobile*.[4] Sir John Clerk of Penicuik, down from Scotland in 1727, saw it in a more finished state. He described the house as 'one of the best in England' although he criticised the way the external stairs darkened the ground floor, and thought William Kent's decorative painting in the saloon 'a very indifferent piece of work'.[5]

Since Castlemaine had been laying out the grounds before he began rebuilding, these were more or less complete. Macky points out that the parkland appeared to merge into Epping Forest. 'The palace of Wanstead stands in a spacious forest … well planted with trees and full of deer.' He admired the great avenue which ended in a pond 'on which my lord [Castlemaine] keeps a gondola for his pleasure' and the green walk which ended with 'an unbounded view through forest'.[6] The formality of London's early designs were softened in the 1720s and 1730s, just as happened at Chiswick House at the same time; like Chiswick, these changes can be seen in Rocque's plans.[7] The canal was made into an irregular piece of water and lawns replaced the parterres close to the house, so by 1765 John Loveday could write that 'the garden just in view from the house is truly wild and rural … [with] a fine prospect of a woody country every way'.[8]

The reasons for the loss of the house were partly due to the expense required in keeping up the house and grounds, and partly to the lack of interest of later owners. After the death of Earl Tylney the house went to his son, who lived mainly in Italy and died childless in Naples in 1784. He left it to his sister's son, Sir James Long, who died ten years later leaving an infant son. So the house was let to the Prince de Condé from 1807 and was then inherited by Catherine Tylney-Long, who in 1812 married William Wellesley-Pole. They made some changes to the grounds, calling in Humphry Repton to advise them in 1813. He produced an illustrated report, rather than a 'Red Book' which survives, and shows his ideas for discarding outdated features such as the fortifications in the lake, and introducing flower beds close to the house. Soon afterwards Lewis Kennedy was called in to rethink the 18th-century American Gardens.[9] All these expensive changes were hardly carried out before financial problems hit the young couple. Under the terms of her marriage settlement they could not sell any land, so when their finances were in trouble they had to sell the house and its contents to raise some cash. In 1822 the contents were sold, and in 1823 the house was sold to a business in Norwich to be demolished and sold for scrap.[10]

The house and grounds were well known and much visited. Defoe reported that the gardens 'have been so much the just admiration of the world, that it has been the general diversion of the citizens to go out to see them, till the crowds grew too great, and his lordship was obliged to restrain his servants from shewing them, except on one or two days in a week only.'[11] Hassell a century later informed his readers 'the only day that the public are allowed to view the interior of Wanstead House is on a Saturday'.[12] There is not much left for us to see today. The grotto in the grounds was burnt in 1884 but the gatepiers in Blake Hall Road are still standing. In 1880 the Corporation of London bought 184 acres of the park, which again became part of Epping Forest. This was a result of the pressure, locally and nationally, which had led to the formation of the Commons Preservation Society and the 1878 Epping Forest Act. In 1920 the rest of the park was sold to Wanstead Sports Ground Ltd. It is now a golf club with the site of the house at the first hole. The Corporation of London administers Epping Forest and has recently set in hand a management plan for the grounds, not restoring the historic gardens but conserving surviving features, clearing views and replanting trees.

WATFORD

CASSIOBURY HOUSE

On the outskirts of Watford lies a country park called Cassiobury, on low-lying land beside the River Gade; but nothing remains of the great house which once stood there. The early house on the site belonged post-Reformation to Sir Richard Morison, and its rebuilding was completed by his son Sir Charles. His grand–daughter, heiress to the estate, married Arthur Capel in 1627, and it remained with their descendants till its demolition in 1927.

The house was rebuilt by Arthur Capel's son, who became 1st Earl of Essex in 1661. He turned to Hugh May for the design who produced a magnificent great house, unlike the more compact houses usually associated with his name such as Morton Hall or Eltham Lodge. May's entrance range with the main reception rooms was flanked by one wing of the earlier house, which was retained as lodgings. A new wing faced it but also extended into the gardens behind the house: so May designed T-shaped additions. This provided accommodation on a lavish scale, with a state apartment in the north range; the house

246   Watford, Cassiobury House. Early 19th-century print of east front, rebuilt by James Wyatt in 1799.

would certainly have been large enough for royal visits. Indeed Evelyn describes it as 'a very noble palace' and goes on to note the 'divers faire and good roomes, excellent carving by Gibbons … There is in the porch or entrance a painting by Verrio, of Apollo and the Liberal Arts. One roome parquetted with yew, which I lik'd well. The chimney mantles are some of them of a certain Irish marble (which his Lordship brought with him when he was Lieutenant of Ireland not long before).'[1] A *Country Life* article of 1910 shows the sumptuous overmantels and overdoors carved by Gibbons and the fine staircase with its richly carved acanthus panels. This staircase, now attributed to Edward Pearce, was sold to the Metropolitan Museum when the house was demolished.[2] But the house was never finished as Essex fell from favour with Charles II, was imprisoned in the Tower and killed himself. The 4th Earl of Essex was on the board of the Grand Union Canal Company, and the canal was cut through his park 1793-1805. Although it was landscaped by Repton in 1801 to make it an attractive feature of the view, it sowed the seeds of the eventual downfall of the estate. In 1799 the 5th Earl commissioned James Wyatt to update the house, and although several of May's interiors and his staircase remained some were altered. The whole house was encased in Tudor-style stonework, and was described by Prince Pückler-Muskau in 1826 as 'modern Gothic and splendidly furnished' with a 'long gallery hung with weapons'.[3] Massive extensions with service rooms were added to the N-W, making it a courtyard house. This was not one of Wyatt's most successful commissions. He died before it was completed, and Wyatville took over, although his plans may never have been implemented. The 5th Earl also agreed to allow the railway to run parallel to the canal, but these were not far from the house and its seclusion was gone. Queen Adelaide, living there as a widow in 1848, left after a few months because of the noise and lack of privacy. In 1909 the 8th Earl sold 184 acres to Watford Borough Council to make a public park. With the cost of running such a large house becoming onerous, the contents were auctioned in 1922.[4] The house was also auctioned but remained unsold, and it was demolished soon afterwards. The rest of the land was sold off for suburban housing, and only the stables and a lodge remain. The fate of this great house is therefore very different from that of The Grove nearby where the proposal for a railway was rejected, the views remained unspoilt and the house has been restored as a hotel.

THE GROVE

This large Hertfordshire house is on the outer fringes of the area covered in this book, just within the M25; its current postal address is Sarratt outside the motorway, ignoring its proximity to Watford, to which parish it originally belonged. It hardly qualifies as a suburban house, instead being an example of a country house and estate within 20 miles of London. The early house belonged to Francis Heydon in the late 16th century, and he probably rebuilt it; there are no traces of this house, nor any views of it. It passed through various hands in the 17th century, and was rebuilt piecemeal over the 18th and 19th centuries, producing the complex house we see today. Its plan is over-extended with its three fronts: the five-bay east front by Taylor, the 13-bay south front, and the earlier nine-bay west front; these do not relate well to each other.

The house stands on a hilltop, with extensive views over Green Belt land to the south and across the valley of the River Gade towards Cassiobury to the east. Charles Buck inherited the house from his father in 1717, and probably rebuilt part of it before selling it in 1728. The earliest part of the present house is the west front, still Baroque in style. It is built entirely of brick with rubbed red brick detailing and has slightly arched windows, giant pilasters framing the projecting three central bays, and quoins on the corner projections. Today this front is top-heavy, due to Blore's 1841-2 additions of a second floor with a panelled brick parapet. He also lowered the ground-floor windows to give access to the gardens through French windows and added a bow to the south. These later changes are due to the Villiers family: the Hon. Thomas Villiers (1709-86), created 1st Earl of Clarendon in 1776, bought The Grove in 1753, and his family kept the property till 1925. Thomas was a younger son of the Earl of Jersey, and in 1752 had married the Hon. Charlotte Capel, whose family lived on the adjoining estate, Cassiobury; so he was buying her the house next door.

The entrance was in the centre of the south front, flanked by two reception rooms. Clarendon (as he became) commissioned new chimneypieces for these from Robert Taylor, who had started his career as a sculptor. His library chimneypiece is particularly fine and is still *in situ* and another has been recreated from fragments. This led on to his architectural work at The Grove. From 1754-61 he was rebuilding Matthew Brettingham's east wing and turning the house round so this became a five-bay pedimented entrance front, with Venetian windows to two new reception rooms. One of these, the Doneraile Room in the south-east corner, keeps some of its original frieze and chimneypiece, although Taylor's refined style is overlaid with some florid later detailing. Taylor's façade was adjusted by Blore, who removed the pediment in order to add a substantial second floor here too and altered the Venetian windows. Apart from Taylor's exquisite marble chimneypieces there is very little original decoration – sadly, as the 1st Earl's records show that he also employed John Cheere and the French carver, Cuenot.[1] Even the main staircase, looking early 18th-century at first glance, turns out to be Blore working in early 18th-century style for the 4th Earl of Clarendon.[2] The stables to the west of the house appear to be by Brettingham. Like the Triumphal Arch at Holkham, they are built of brick and flint; the entrance in the south front is pedimented and there are corner towers with pyramid roofs. These have been restored as part of the conversion to hotel use. With the new entrance from the east these stables must have been less convenient, but were not replaced. Further changes came with the late 18th-century development of the canal system. As at nearby Cassiobury the 2nd Earl of Clarendon was asked if the Grand Union Canal could pass across his land. The route chosen was close to the River Gade, and the canal today is a picturesque embellishment to the park. However his successor wisely refused permission for the railway to run parallel, unlike the Earl of Essex at Cassionbury. Repton was consulted on the landscaping of the canal and the new approach, although no 'Red Book' was produced. A fine stone bridge carries the drive over the River Gade, with views of Taylor's east front on the hilltop.

Edward, 5th Earl of Clarendon inherited in 1875 and died in 1914; the estate at that time was 2,298 acres, and he added the four-acre walled kitchen garden north of the house, replacing the earlier one down by the River Gade. Clarendon was a courtier, and Lord Chamberlain from 1900-05. The house with its inter-connecting reception rooms, many bedrooms and generous staff accommodation was used for weekend entertaining, and many royal and political figures passed through.[3] This way of life was more than they could afford and could not continue after the First World War. The 6th Earl put the house on the market in 1922 and moved to Hampstead. It took three years to find a buyer: Watford

247 Watford, The Grove, from the S–W. The west front is the earliest part of the house.

was expanding, and country estates on the fringes of London were unattractive to private buyers.[4] After being a school for a few years it was bought in 1939 by the London, Midland & Scottish Railway as office space, safely away from central London with war looming. Bomb-proof shelters proliferated in the grounds. After the war it became the British Transport Commission Training Centre, and further low-quality additions were made, while the condition of the main building deteriorated. In 1996 it was bought for conversion into a hotel, the buyers attracted by the 312 acres of grounds, the fine site with extensive views, and the opportunity to replace the dilapidated mid-20th-century additions with good modern ranges. The architect Jeremy Blake of Fitzroy Robinson undertook the restoration, which elucidated much of the history of this otherwise under-researched house.

WEST WICKHAM

WICKHAM COURT

'Few rural villages, even in Yorkshire or Devonshire, are more sequestered than West Wickham' wrote Walford in 1884.[1] That is hardly true today, but even so the small parish church and Wickham Court are unusual in having a few fields around them; the Wickham and Keston area is a green lung between Croydon and Bromley. There are not many late medieval houses in this book, but Wickham is one of them, a late 15th-century manor house which was built as a suburban retreat by a Norfolk landowner. Sir Henry Heydon was the son of a Norfolk lawyer who had built Baconsthorpe Castle in north Norfolk. Henry married well, his wife being Ann Bullen (or Boleyn), the daughter of a prosperous mercer who was Lord Mayor of London. He had a post at court as steward to Cecily, Duchess of York and was

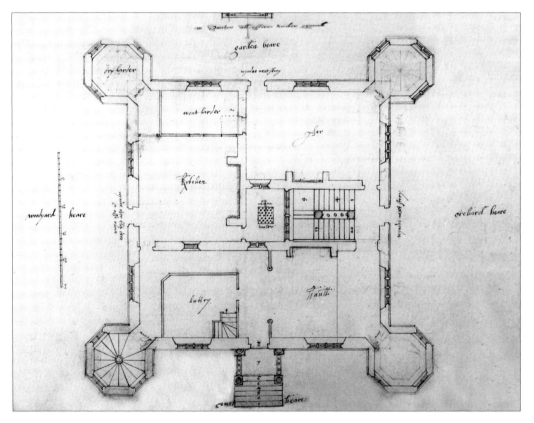

248   West Wickham, Wickham Court. Thorpe's *c.*1600 plan shows the screens passage with the hall lower right, the small courtyard in the centre and the parlour beyond.

running about 250 manors for her, so a house within easy reach of London was essential. It was also conveniently close to Eltham Palace and to his wife's family at Hever Castle. He bought the manor of West Wickham in 1469, soon after his wife had given birth to their first son, and probably rebuilt the house and the church soon afterwards, although there is no documentary evidence of the rebuilding.

His new house was almost a square with four corner towers, unusual in two ways. It was built of brick, an increasingly fashionable material at this time for élite houses, especially in East Anglia; and it was an early experiment with a more compact plan, the rooms outward-looking with only a small central light-well.[2] Fortunately John Thorpe recorded the plan, presumably because he was interested in this transition from the courtyard to the compact house, and this provides us with the best evidence for its original arrangement.[3] Today the west-facing house is entered through a later two-storey porch with the original oak front door, sturdy, studded and with massive bolts, moved forward into it. This led into the screens passage of the modest hall (about 20 ft long) with the buttery on the west and a corridor leading to the kitchen and larders; one of these was in the N-E tower. One side of the house was therefore service rooms, the other contained the hall, stairs and a parlour. It is most unusual to find the service rooms as tightly integrated into the plan as this, and suggests a strong desire on the part of the owner for a convenient house. Could it be a critique of the rambling courtyard house his father had built at Baconsthorpe?

The house was drastically altered in the 18th and 19th centuries and it is very hard to know how it appeared originally. The earliest depiction of it is a tiny drawing on a vellum estate map of 1659, showing the house with a walled forecourt and with conical roofs to the towers.[4] This is a stylised picture, but these conical roofs are also shown in the 18th-century print. The fenestration has been completely altered, as can be seen by comparing Thorpe's

249   West Wickham Court. Eighteenth-century print of the entrance front and a small service wing at the side.

plan, the 18th-century print and modern photographs. Thorpe shows an unusually large staircase, but this has gone and the small light-well was later filled with a staircase. Builders recorded finding 'curious ancient fragments … An old wood mullion of very good design … was found in the plastered wall of the principal staircase, supposed to have been an open court. There were several windows very perfect …'[5] These could have been fragments of the massive six-light windows onto the light-well shown by Thorpe, although the parlour and kitchen also opened into it. Internally not much remains, but one room has a stone chimneypiece with a four-centred arch, with love-knots and the initials of Henry and Ann carved in the spandrels on each side. This must have been imported from another part of the house as Thorpe shows all the fireplaces on inner walls, whereas today the flues are clumsily built out from the outer walls. Thorpe shows that two of the towers had spiral staircases; they have all been drastically altered, although two still have a vaulted ceiling on the upper storey, showing that they were rooms of some status.[6]

In 1480 Henry Heydon's father died and he inherited Baconsthorpe, after which he spent part of the year in Norfolk and part in Kent; when he died in 1504 he was buried in Norwich Cathedral. As so often with these suburban houses, his widow remained at Wickham, but after her death the house was let and increasingly the family was involved in Norfolk life. In 1580 William Heydon, great-grandson of the builder, sold the house and land for £2,700 to John Lennard, a London lawyer whose estate of Chevening was not far away. He bought it for his second son, Samuel, who moved there with his wife a few years later. Again his widow remained in the house after his death in 1618, and his son was only able to take it over after her death in 1630. The family remained there for several generations, sometimes letting it. At some point in the 18th century the fenestration was altered with sashes inserted; an eaves cornice was added, dormers put into the roof, a low wing was built on to the kitchen and a porch added to the front. Samuel Lennard died in 1755, leaving a five-year-old daughter Mary as the heiress. She later married John Farnaby and their son Sir Charles Farnaby Bt. was rector of West Wickham from 1815-48. When he died in 1859 the estate was surveyed for his widow, and consisted of 12 farms, with the house and outbuildings valued at £5,170.[7]

In 1866 his son, Colonel J. Farnaby Lennard, doubled the size of the house by building a two-storeyed gabled wing attached to the S-W tower of the house, designed by J.S. Anscomb. It is a peculiarly ugly and unsympathetic addition, which provided a vestibule leading to a large east-facing library with a new dining room beyond; these rooms were given Jacobean-style ceilings with ribs in geometric patterns. Above were bedrooms and dressing rooms, and behind these rooms was a glazed court, presumably for a winter garden. A new laundry block behind had service rooms with servants' bedrooms above.[8] The whole south side of the old house became a drawing room. A stone fireplace dated 1632 was brought in and given a heavily carved overmantel. The old kitchen was reconstructed to resemble a great hall with the 15th-century stone chimneypiece moved from elsewhere in the house and heraldic glass, most of it old, inserted into the windows. The sashes were replaced with rather unconvincing two- and three-light windows, so the brickwork of the exterior has been considerably disturbed. The house had probably been extensively altered before this intervention, but after this it had even less of its original fabric. It was probably at this time that the conical roofs were removed from the corner towers, which were raised and castellated. Between the towers the cornice was removed and a castellated parapet hid the dormer windows.[9]

250   West Wickham Court, garden front. The 19th-century wing is on the left.

It changed hands many times and the most unsympathetic changes were made when it was converted into a hotel, when the attics were converted into hotel bedrooms and the roof was raised with large windows inserted, which do nothing to enhance a Grade 1 listed house. It was bought in 1965 by the LB of Bromley, who built a secondary school in part of the service buildings. The remainder was let to the Diocese of Southwark as a teacher training college before becoming part of a university. In 2002 Wickham Court School took over the house and five acres, and it is now full of cheerful little children.

WIMBLEDON

EAGLE HOUSE

Eagle House is one of the most interesting of the group of merchants' houses built in the early 17th century. Robert Bell (1564-1640) who built the house had been born in Wimbledon, into a family of who farmed there but also had business interests in the City. Bell was a member of the Girdlers' Company and made enough money to become a founder-member of the East India Company when it was set up in 1599. He lived mainly in the City, but bought three acres in Wimbledon in 1613 and began building a house just on the edge of the village, set back from the road behind a high wall and facing south over Wimbledon Common. He had three acres of gardens, but although we know that he was well known as a plantsman and was involved with the gardens at Hatfield House we have no information about his Wimbledon gardens.[1]

It is a compact house with shaped gables front and back, three storeys high over a basement. The centre bay has an oriel window over the entrance, with canted bays on each side running through two storeys. The front has been stuccoed, with only the oriel and bays left as bare brickwork with stone dressings. Bell would have had no difficulty in acquiring stone: his

251 Wimbledon, Eagle House. The entrance front of this Jacobean house when it belonged to T.G. Jackson. 1899 lithograph by A.T. Way.

activity as a merchant included the import of stone from Caen, and he had provided stone for Robert Cecil's recently-built Hatfield House.[2] The garden front to the north reflects the front but more of the English bond brickwork is visible, showing the flat stone quoins characteristic of Jacobean building practice. The sides have been obscured by later additions. The plan is very interesting, with a cross hall running through the double-pile house from front to back, as at Charlton House, built just a few years earlier. The ceiling today is plain but the simple stone chimneypiece has a finely carved overmantel with strapwork panels, and the heraldic glass in the bay window to the north has Bell's coat of arms. The basement has the same plan, with the lower hall flanked by service rooms. The kitchen was ingeniously placed in the N-E corner and rises into the ground floor, with a mezzanine room above it.

The staircase leading from the high end of the hall was rebuilt when a wing was added to this corner of the house, but the discovery of painted balusters and a painted newel with its obelisk finial on the wall clearly reflected the design of the original stairs. (There are similar examples of painted balustrades at Kew Palace and Boston Manor.) A leaded window, covered over when the extension was built, was also discovered and both have been left visible. The secondary staircase, sturdy and less decorated, is still in place. On the first floor the great chamber occupies the same space as the hall below and is the same height, lit by bay windows at both ends. The chimneypiece is later and the panelled walls have been plastered, but the room still has its magnificent plasterwork ceiling, the ribs in geometric patterns with strapwork ornament within. In the centre are the arms of Robert Bell and his wife, Alice Colston. They were childless, and after the death of Bell's widow in 1647 the house was bought by Sir Richard Betenson, a Parliamentarian. It remained in his family till 1695 when it was bought by William Ivatt, a haberdasher and alderman in the City. The Ivatt family added an extension to the N-W corner of the house, which

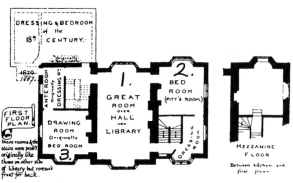

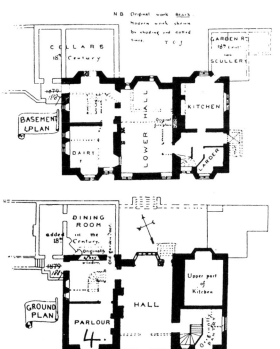

252 Wimbledon, Eagle House, plan of ground floor in 1891. The through hall has the great chamber above.

253 Wimbledon, Eagle House. The 1615 plasterwork ceiling of the great chamber with the arms of Robert Bell.

provided cellars in the basement, a panelled dining room with a corner fireplace on the ground floor and a bedroom and dressing room above. This may have been built soon after their purchase, although it is usually dated to *c*.1730. Externally this is marked by its brick parapet, narrow sash windows and the rubbed red brickwork of the string course and window surrounds.[3]

In 1789 the house was sold for £2,300 to Thomas Lancaster, who turned it into 'Wimbledon School for Young Noblemen & Gentlemen' which after a visit in 1805 by local resident Nelson was renamed 'Nelson House School'. It remained a successful school under various names, with Eagle House School moving there from Brook Green in 1860.[4] In 1886 the current owner, Dr Malan, decided to move his school out to Camberley and develop the land in Wimbledon, which was by this time growing rapidly with the railway providing easy access to central London. The house would probably have gone but for the enlightened actions of a distinguished architect, who bought it, restored it and lived in it for the next 30 years. Sir Thomas Graham Jackson (1835-1924) was living in Marylebone and running a quietly successful architectural practice when he visited his uncle in Wimbledon and heard about the probable demolition of Eagle House. As a great admirer of the English Renaissance style he was fascinated by a Jacobean house which still had many original features and decided to buy it, for £3,700. He carried out a sensitive restoration: the school additions were removed and he carefully repaired the four plasterwork ceilings and the panelled dining room, and used the great chamber as his library. He also bought old Dutch tiles and some by William de Morgan with which he lined some of the fireplaces. A panel of stone beside the door from the hall to the garden has a Latin inscription in which he recorded his work. In 1887 he, his wife and their two young sons moved in, and he remained there until 1924. He had just moved to a smaller house in Kensington when he died.

In 1947 Wimbledon Council bought it for £10,500 to use as a local museum and gallery. It was written up in *The Builder*, which shows it with a stucco finish and sash windows, both of which have since been removed.[5] The plans for a museum did not materialise; instead it remained in Council ownership and was divided into flats and offices, hardly a suitable use for a historic building. In 1985 it was sold to a development company, the flats were removed and the whole building carefully restored for office use. A new wing was added to the N-E designed by Quinlan Terry, as a three-storey wing with dormer windows in the attic. The house was bought by a trust and in 1991 the Al-Furqān Islamic Heritage Foundation was opened there. It is in excellent condition and is occasionally open to the public.

WIMBLEDON HOUSE

Demolished *c.*1717, this innovative house stood on a hillside overlooking what is now the All England Tennis Club. It was built *c.*1585-8 by Thomas Cecil (1542-1623), later 1st Earl of Exeter and owner of Burghley House. He had been brought up largely at Wimbledon Rectory but once married lived mainly at Burghley, supervising his father's rebuilding of that great house. Denied political office by his powerful father he decided to build an imposing house where he could spend time closer to the centre of power, and from 1575 he used the Rectory as a base while building up a large land-holding in the area. His new house was set in 266 acres, an exceptional estate so close to London; he was able to make a deer park, where he was later to entertain James I with a day's hunting.

The house, built of brick with stone dressings, was a half H-plan, innovative in its symmetry and room lay-out. Because of the steep terrain the usual axial approach was not possible, instead it was approached at right angles which would have given an element of surprise. Great terraces and stone steps led up to the forecourt and the balustraded terrace in front of the central entrance. This led conventionally enough into a screens passage, leading straight through the house into the gardens beyond. The hall windows were not differentiated on the façade, as the high end was lit only on the garden front. A pair of staircase towers with high slate roofs flanked the entrance, giving on to the leads with distant views northwards. The kitchens were in the west range, with further service rooms in the semi-basement; the state side of the house was to the east with lodgings and the long gallery on the first floor. The great chamber was directly above the one-storey hall (as at the much more modest Sutton House, Hackney) with an oriel window over the entrance. Possibly this was crowned by another storey: a marginal sketch in a survey of 1617 suggests this.[1] Another innovative feature was the chapel, tucked close to the main stairs and beside a door to the privy garden. Consecrated chapels had been in secluded corners of houses but by the later 16th century were placed at the heart of the house, where the household could participate in family prayers. The Wimbledon chapel was exceptionally well-lit with the east wall almost entirely glazed; and instead of solid walls there were just wooden screens separating the chapel from its peripheral spaces, so members of the household could hear and see services from outside the chapel itself, even from the staircase.[2] This can be clearly seen in Thorpe's plan, and is possibly one of the reasons he chose to record this house.

The gardens were recorded by Robert Smythson in 1609. The house is shown in outline and the kitchen range had doubled in size by this date; close to it was a herb garden. Outside the chapel in the east range a loggia or 'stone gallery' had been added at the lower level, opening into the privy gardens with its four plats; its roof provided a balustraded terrace overlooking the garden. The main gardens were on the hillside to the south; they were not aligned on the house, instead the large banqueting house was set in its own sunken enclosure. The gardens had bands of planting, one orchard planted with fruit trees 'with roses sett among them', the next edged by a walk with lime trees 'for shade and sweetness.' Higher up the hill was the vineyard, just planted when Smythson recorded it. It was edged with cherry trees and its walls 'sett with roses'. Cecil's gardens seem to have combined productivity and beauty, with views out over his park.[3]

According to the manorial custom of Wimbledon he left the property to his third son, General Sir Edward Cecil, in 1623.[4] He spent many years in the Netherlands as a soldier, and

254 Wimbledon House. 1793 print after Winstanley of the 1588 house, since demolished.

when in England divided his time between Wimbledon and his Chelsea house, now known as Lindsey House. When he was created a viscount in 1626 he chose Wimbledon as his title, and he added a family chapel to St Mary's church in Wimbledon. It was no doubt intended to contain generations of Cecils, but his restrained and elegant monument is the only one there. He had no sons and as soon as he was dead his three daughters and their husbands sold it for

330

£16,789 to trustees of Queen Henrietta Maria. This was in 1639, and she immediately began altering the house with the help of Inigo Jones, but hardly had time to enjoy it before she and Charles I left London for Oxford in 1642. However it was royal ownership which provides us with so much information about the house: both house and gardens were surveyed in 1649. Some interiors date from Cecil's time, such as the gallery 109 x 20 ft 'floored with cedar boards casting a pleasant smell' and the great chamber 'being a room intended for hangings'. Other rooms had been altered: the 'queene's new chamber' with its white marble chimneypiece, one of a suite of rooms which overlooked the gardens behind the house. There were also two rooms which together formed the 'bath roomes' one with a deal floor, the other tiled and with a piped water supply – a rare luxury at this date. A parlour in the S-E corner of the ground floor was converted into her private Roman Catholic chapel. There was also a grotto in the stone gallery with a fountain and shell decoration in 'the shapes of men, lyons, serpents, antick forms and rare devices'.[5] The grounds were redesigned by André Mollet, with an 'orange tree garden' outside the stone gallery and a wilderness and maze higher up the hill. It must have been a house of the greatest luxury and sophistication.

Wimbledon was confiscated and sold to various Parliamentarian supporters. General Lambert bought it in 1652; he later fell out with Cromwell and spent a few years of quiet retirement at Wimbledon, cultivating his gardens and growing tulips. The estate was restored to the queen in 1660 but she sold it at once, and in 1677 it was bought by Thomas Osborne, Earl of Danby and 1st Duke of Leeds. He had a London house and built Kiveton in Yorkshire, but spent only the autumn there; he lived mainly at Wimbledon for the rest of his life. He commissioned views of it from Henry Winstanley, which are precious sources for its late 17th-century appearance.[6] His trustees sold it in 1717 to Sir Theodore Janssen for the large sum of £27,000. He was a rich City merchant of Dutch origin, who planned to demolish it and build a new house higher up the hill. But he was a Director of the South Sea Company, and when that bubble burst his properties, including Wimbledon, were forfeit and his goods seized and sold, with the cash going to creditors. The house had gone, and another was to be put up nearby, by one of the most formidable women of her time.

The Duchess of Marlborough's Wimbledon House

In 1722 John Churchill, 1st Duke of Marlborough died. His widow, Sarah, Duchess of Marlborough (1660-1744) had always loathed Blenheim Palace, the country house given to her husband by Queen Anne and built for them by Vanbrugh. She much preferred to be in London at Marlborough House, or at the hunting lodge in Windsor Great Park which she held as ranger, a post given her by Queen Anne. She was immensely rich, a shrewd investor who had managed her own money for years, and she decided to build herself a house close to London for occasional use. In 1723 she bought lots 1 and 2 at the sale of Janssen's Wimbledon estate, which included the site of the Cecil house, its gardens and park. She reckoned that Wimbledon would be more convenient than Windsor, since it was only 'an hour's drive from London along a good road'.[7] She did not start building till 1730, partly perhaps because of her dislike of architects: 'I know of none that are not mad or ridiculous.'[8] Her final choice was Roger Morris, with the assistance of his patron Lord Pembroke. Morris was eventually dismissed and had to sue her to extract his £300 fee.

The duchess had strong ideas on what she wanted. She was no longer young and she did not want to go up steps to a *piano nobile*. So the basement was sunk, and a bridge over the area

255   Wimbledon House, designed by Roger Morris for the Duchess of Marlborough in 1732.

led to the front door. This was ridiculed by Horace Walpole, who went there not long before the duchess died. He wrote that 'the house stands in a hole, or as the whimsical old creature said, seems to be making a curtsy. She had directed my Lord Pembroke not to make her go up any steps … so he dug a saucer to put it in, and levelled the first floor with the ground.'[9] It was a compressed H-plan with a plain exterior; she had insisted that Wren make Marlborough House 'strong, plain and convenient' and she wanted the same again.[10] It was built of grey stock brick with the window surrounds, cornice and pediment in stone; the bricklayer was William Waterman and the stonemason John Devall, with William Kilpin as Clerk of the Works and Francis Smith of Warwick called in to check the building accounts in 1733.[11] Charles Bridgeman landscaped the grounds, and made a vista from the house across the valley. The cost of the house was the huge sum of £70,000.

The duchess lived on the main floor, with the service rooms below and an attic storey above. Her annotations on a plan show her requirements: the entrance hall was 'but for ornament and a passage' and led to a saloon facing south onto a portico with views over the park. The east side had a 21 ft square dining room, a drawing room 22 by 28 ft – larger but not too large 'for one who mortally hates all assembly's [sic]' and a state bedchamber. The west side had an apartment of three rooms and a closet, 'all this side entirely for my own use and not too much'.[12]

Copies of family portraits were commissioned for Wimbledon, and the duchess ordered leather wall hangings and marble chimneypieces. Some of these were based on ones she had seen at Southampton House in Bloomsbury, where her favourite grand-daughter Diana, Duchess of Bedford lived. She intended to leave Wimbledon House to her, so her early death in 1735 meant that it went instead to Diana's brother, John Spencer. He lived only two years longer than his grandmother, so it was his son John, later 1st Earl Spencer, who inherited as a minor. He and his wife Georgiana later used the house a lot, dividing their time between there, Althorp and Spencer House in London. James 'Athenian' Stuart was asked to update some of the interiors, and his designs survive for the dining room and a closet.[13] His trustees bought more land, doubling the size of the park to 1,200 acres, and he loved shooting there. The grounds were landscaped by 'Capability' Brown in 1760, with a new winding drive and an irregular lake. Later he added a large walled kitchen garden.

Wimbledon Park House

In 1785 the house was almost completely destroyed by fire. The 2nd Earl and his wife were away, and staff rescued many of the pictures, books and some furniture. It was not rebuilt; they simply converted a range of service buildings to a nursery wing for the use of their children. It was only in 1800 that a new house was commissioned by the 2nd Earl from Henry Holland, who had already worked for him at Althorp. The house was on a new site slightly to the N-W of the Duchess of Marlborough's house. Lysons described the position as 'singularly eligible, having a beautiful prospect of the park, with a fine piece of water towards the north, and an extensive view of … Surrey to the south'.[14] This house has now gone, but it was an interesting essay in the smaller house favoured by this date, two-storeyed, compact and austere. It was built of Portland stone, its severity broken by a bowed drawing room and library on each side. On the south front these two rooms and the central eating room opened onto a shady verandah supported by wooden Tuscan columns. The rooms inside were plain and well-proportioned, and there was plenty of space for their children.[15]

The Spencers gave up the house in 1826, after which it was let to the Duke of Somerset. In 1843 the 3rd Earl sold his Wimbledon property to John Augustus Beaumont, who had

256   Wimbledon Park House. 1813 print of the house designed by Holland for Earl Spencer.

recently bought West Hill in Wandsworth. Since both houses had large estates, these were adjoining properties. He planned to develop the land with large houses for the prosperous middle classes, who were able to commute to central London from this area by rail. The building he carried out established the Wimbledon area as one of spacious houses set in large gardens, a character they largely keep today. The house deteriorated during the Second World War and in 1949 it was demolished, and Wimbledon Park School was built on the site.

PART THREE

BATTERSEA

OLD BATTERSEA HOUSE

In the 19th century Battersea became heavily industrialised as small-scale river-related industries gave way to engineering and chemical works. Before that it was a small village on the edge of marshy ground with the parish church and a cluster of substantial houses. Old Battersea House is the only free-standing house to survive. Today a road divides it from the river, but when built in the late 17th century its grounds extended westwards to the Thames and it had large gardens to the south. The original entrance might have been from the river, and here the central door has rubbed red brick pilasters with consoles which support a pedimented porch. Between them is a delightful relief of ship-building instruments, probably placed there by Samuel Pett. He came from a prosperous family closely associated with the Navy and with ship-building, and was possibly the builder of the house. There is no architect associated with it, but it is very typical of London bricklayer's work: a substantial seven-bay house of double-pile plan, built of dark brick with red brick detailing. There is a deep coved cornice below the hipped roof, which has pedimented dormer windows. The door has two windows on each side, closely spaced, while narrow blind windows are set between them and the outer pair of windows, with the panelled chimneys aligned on them. It is altogether a competently designed and comfortable looking house. Inside the entrance hall is flanked by a pair of rooms and leads through to the staircase hall. The oak staircase with its twisted balusters dates from the 1660s and seems to have been re-used from another, unknown, house when Old Battersea House was built. Much of the house is panelled although some of the panelling has been brought in later. The most interesting fragment is in the little drawing room where the stiles are painted with *chinoiserie* decoration, similar to the painted room in Carshalton House, and suggesting that the room might once have had a complete scheme of decoration imitating lacquer. This was introduced into his wife's parlour when Sir Walter St John was living in the house. The house remained in private ownership till the mid-19th century; it then became a school, and ancillary buildings were added to the north, but without changing the house itself very much. In the 1930s the council bought it and drove a road between the house and the river to serve the housing estate which they were building behind the house. Plans were made to demolish the house to provide more space for housing, but local protests were taken up by SPAB and an Act of Parliament prevented demolition. Instead the council leased the house to private owners. Colonel and Mrs Stirling filled it with their fine collection, mainly of furniture, ceramics and Pre-Raphaelite paintings. Wilhelmina Stirling was the sister of Evelyn de Morgan, married to the ceramicist William de Morgan and her collection was particularly strong on her sister's paintings and his glazed pottery. Mrs Stirling died in 1965 aged 96, by which time the house was in need of attention. A happy solution was the acquisition of the lease by the American Malcolm Forbes, who took on the house in 1971 and carried out a meticulous restoration with the help of the architect Vernon Gibberd. The collection remained in the house, which was occasionally open to the public, with some objects on loan to suitable National Trust houses. The Forbes Foundation has now moved the collection to different premises in the LB of Wandsworth, and is building up a new art collection in Old Battersea House.

Cherry & Pevsner, *London 2*, pp.675-6; E. Croft-Murray, *Decorative Painting in England*, 1, p.230; J. Cornforth, *Early Georgian Interiors*, 2004, p.255.

BECKENHAM

BECKENHAM PLACE

Today this house looks forlorn and neglected, but also very odd: its entrance front is dominated by a vast portico which bears little relationship to the house behind, brought over from Wricklemarsh when it was demolished. The house is a plain seven-bay late 18th-century block, faced in stone and of two main storeys over a basement, and with attics in the hipped roof. On the S-W facing garden front the fall in the ground brings the basement above ground level and this side is enlivened by a bow running through all three storeys. The *piano nobile* was altered *c*.1800 when the sash windows in the bow were replaced by long windows opening onto an ironwork balcony supported on slim columns, with stairs down to the gardens. This is the only feature to relieve the utmost severity of this front. The house was built by John Cator (1727/8-1806) who bought the land in 1773 from the Earl of Bolingbroke; the St John family owned many manors in south London. Cator came from a Quaker family and had a timber business in London with wharfs on the site of Tate Modern, and he was also a developer. He chose a fine site for his house, looking down over parkland towards the River Ravensbourne; it is still parkland with some fine trees possibly dating from the late 18th century, and older trees in the woodland. Soon after he had built it Sir Gregory Page of Wricklemarsh died, and his heir decided to sell the John James house which Page had built 1724-7. This needed an Act of Parliament but once this was through Cator bought Wricklemarsh, not to live in but to demolish it and develop the estate. He paid £22,250 for the house, sold off the land in lots and in 1787 demolished the house. Four of the chimneypieces went to the Admiralty, but he brought the portico and other stonework to his new house at Beckenham. (This included some chimneypieces, which were later moved to Woodbastwick Hall in Norfolk, since demolished.) So the N-W facing entrance front was extended and the Ionic portico from Wricklemarsh added. However its scale dwarfed Cator's two-storey entrance front, so he added a steep pediment in which he placed his arms, resting on palm fronds and made of Coade stone so slightly browner than the surrounding stonework. This pediment with its steep angle and thin cornice sits most unhappily above the columns, looking more like theatre design than architecture. The front door with its Ionic half-columns and beautifully cut stonework is also from Wricklemarsh, and the side walls of the extension behind the portico have the Venetian windows from the sides of Wricklemarsh. Again these are very over-scaled for their position but of top-quality stonework. The main block of the house has large plain rooms, some with neo-classical plasterwork ceilings, set round a top-lit staircase. The house remained in the Cator family till 1928, although it was let after 1835 when they moved to Norfolk. In 1905 it became the Norwood Sanatorium, and local residents leased the park as a golf course. By that time the Mid-Kent Railway Company had built a railway across the park from S-E to N-W and as a

257 Beckenham Place. The *c.*1780 print shows the plain stone house before the addition of the portico from Wricklemarsh.

result the Bromley area was fast developing as a commuter suburb. The freehold of the house and park was sold by the Cator trustees to the LCC in 1928 and the grounds were opened as a 213-acre public park the following year, with the first municipal golf course in the London area. Part of the house is now used by the golf club, but it is very shabby and neglected, and a Friends group was set up in 1996 to try to improve both house and grounds. Beckenham Place Park has recently been renamed the Lewisham Country Park.

A. Crowe, *London Parks & Woodlands*, 1987, p. 67; Cherry & Pevsner, *London 2*, pp.428-9.

BROMLEY

Plaistow Lodge

This house was built by Peter Thellusson (1735-97), a distinguished Huguenot financier who came over from Paris in 1760 and was naturalised British the next year. He acted as agent for his brother's firm, Thellusson, Necker et Compagnie, before setting up his own bank in the City. He had great financial acumen and became extremely rich: at his death was said to be worth £800,000. In 1777 he bought up land to form a 126-acre estate between Bromley and Sundridge Park where he built himself a country house within easy reach of the City; it cost about £40,000 to build, making it a very expensive house. His architect was almost certainly Thomas Leverton, who exhibited drawings of a country house in Kent at the Royal Academy in 1780. He was Surveyor to the Bedford Estate in London and most of his commissions were in London, so it is a good example of his country house style: refined, elegant and well-planned. The house is approached diagonally across parkland, the entrance front making an attractive composition with its five-bay main block and pedimented wings. It is built of brick, although the ground floor of the entrance front is faced with rusticated stonework. The pediment is supported by stone pilasters with capitals of Leverton's own invention without an entablature below a stone cornice. The rustication is repeated in the central bay of the two-storey wing connecting the main house to the pavilions. These are very effective, with a wide pediment over a Venetian window and stone detailing: there are Coade

258 Bromley, Plaistow Lodge, anon. watercolour. The house with its pavilions was probably designed by Thomas Leverton *c.*1777.

stone relief panels at the upper level and brick niches with figures in them. The garden front is entirely of brick and has a deep bow running through all three storeys. The long windows in the ground floor bow room give access to the garden. Inside, the house has an arched corridor running through into the pavilions and dividing the front rooms from those facing the garden. It still retains its original staircase and spare neo-classical cornices. Thellusson died at Plaistow and his wife Anne continued to use the house till her death in 1805, when it passed to their eldest son Peter, 1st Baron Rendlesham. He preferred Brodsworth, the Yorkshire estate his father had bought in 1790, so Plaistow was let. In 1810 it was sold by the Thellusson trustees and in 1812 was bought by a group of men to be given to Walter Boyd in token of their gratitude to him. Boyd was a banker and friend of William Pitt and many other influential figures, and his wife was a great friend of Empress Josephine. They had remained in Paris throughout the Revolution, protecting the business interests of English merchants and those of the British government. This house was his reward, and he was a most hospitable owner. When he died in 1837 his son continued there but after his death it changed hands. From 1873 it belonged to Arthur, 10th Baron Kinnaird and then to his son, who decided in 1896 to sell it and break up the estate for building. The house with several acres of grounds was preserved by Gustav Loly, who took it over for his school. It remains Quernmore School today, and still keeps some of its original parkland and gardens.

E.L.S. Horsburgh, *Bromley, Kent*, 1929, pp.181-4; Cherry & Pevsner, *London 2*, p.170; J. Newman, *West Kent & the Weald*, 1969, p.182; G. Worsley, 'Jewels in a Rich Coronet', *Country Life*, 14 October 1993, p.68.

BROMLEY-BY-BOW

BROMLEY HALL

Blighted by its position right on the northern approach to the Blackwall Tunnel, the continuing existence of this house is remarkable. So is its current state, rescued from unsympathetic industrial use, carefully researched and meticulously restored. It is now owned by Leaside Regeneration, who with the help of English Heritage have pieced together its history. It does not appear particularly old at first glance: we see a four-bay house with a high hipped roof and dormer windows, the proportions, the sash windows and the deep eaves coving suggesting an early 18th-century date. But its origins are much earlier. There was a 12th-century manor house on the site belonging to Holy Trinity Priory in Aldgate, and during the recent restoration traces of Reigate stone walls were found below the present house; fragments can be seen through a viewing panel in the floor of the main room. This house was rebuilt *c*.1490 by the Priory as a hunting lodge, making it one of a small group of surviving early Tudor houses in the London area. It was leased by a courtier, John Blount, and post-Reformation became royal property. But the house was in marshy land close to the River Lea, and was hardly suitable for hunting; it may have been used by the king as a staging post between Greenwich Palace and Epping Forest. The west front is of brick as is the reconstructed east front; the north and south sides have been cemented over. The Tudor house was probably a storey higher than it is today, the leaded roof giving views over the marshes and mills of the nearby River Lea. Part of a stair turret still projects on the north side, and traces of the stairs remain internally. Externally the cement has disguised evidence in the brickwork; but polygonal corner projections survive. The plan is simple, with a corridor running from north to south, which on the ground floor still has original tiles below the later timber flooring. There were large rooms in the west front on both ground and first floors; these were subdivided later by stud partition walls, making four rooms per floor.

259 Bromley-by-Bow, Bromley Hall. Photograph *c*.1890 of the west front of this Tudor house in Brunswick Road, now Gillender Street.

There are traces of several layers of simple early decorative painting in both the hall and the ground floor front room. The latter has moulded beams, and in other parts of the house moulded beams have been turned around and re-used, possibly when the top floor was removed. Its position close to the increasingly industrialised River Lea meant that its later history was much less distinguished. During the Civil War gunpowder was manufactured in the grounds. The second floor was taken down in the late 17th or early 18th century, and the spiral stair replaced by a new wooden staircase with barley twist balusters; the upper part of this is still *in situ*. William Woolley, owner in 1704, moved the entrance from the east front to the west and gave the house its hipped roof. By 1760 there was a calico printing works in the grounds, by 1898 it was a nursing home, by the 1920s a hospital. After some bomb damage in the Second World War it was boarded up, but SPAB carried out an inspection in 1952 and recognised its importance; this did not prevent its conversion into a petrol station, handy for travellers heading for the Blackwall Tunnel. In its last phase it was home to a carpet trader, who had his warehouse in the adjoining buildings added by the hospital. The recent £1.1 million restoration has rescued the house as well as providing office space, and it can be visited by appointment.

SPAB Report 1952; Museum of London Archaeology Service; Cherry & Pevsner, *London 5*, pp.634-5; Heritage of London Trust report; *Survey* 'Parish of Bromley-by-Bow' 1, 1900, pp.17-18.

CHELSEA

ARGYLL HOUSE

This discreet private house on the King's Road in Chelsea was designed by a leading Palladian architect, Giacomo Leoni, a Venetian who was in England by 1714, and whose main claim to fame is his revised edition of Palladio's *Quattro Libri*, published in Italian, French and English from 1715-20. The five-bay house with a frontage of approximately 60 feet was built in 1723 for John Perrin (or Pierene), of whom practically nothing is known; but he did subscribe to Leoni's book. He paid rates on the house till 1740. His initials and the above date are on the rainwater heads, and his monogram is also on the fine wrought iron gate. The plan, with four rooms to the two main floors, was typical of many medium-sized houses round London, and it has none of the grandeur of Leoni's other works, such as Clandon Park, Surrey or Queensberry House, Mayfair. Only the central emphasis, with its Doric door surround and pedimented first-floor window and the neat parapet with a stone cornice mark it out from the run of houses of that date. Leoni comments on his use of grey brick with stone enrichments 'which in my opinion sorting extremely well with white stone, makes a beautiful harmony of colours' and illustrates the house in his translation of *The Architecture of L.B. Alberti*. The front door opens into a staircase hall which takes up almost one quarter of the floor area, and the two rooms at the back overlook the gardens. The rooms have standard panelling of the 1720s with no Palladian details, and the service rooms are in the basement. At the far end of the garden were the stables and coach-houses, with servants' accommodation above them. The house acquired its present name from John, 4th Duke of Argyll, who rented the house just before he died in 1770. The most famous later inhabitant was Lady Colefax, co-founder of the decorating business Colefax and Fowler, who lived here from 1922-38. After the Second World War it became the London house of

Lord Normanby, who added a wing in Georgian style on the east side of the garden. The house, comparatively modest in scale and preserving a small part of its original garden, is still a private house.

Survey, 4, ii, 1913, pp.82-5; Cherry & Pevsner, *London 3*, 1991, p.576; G. Leoni, *The Architecture of L.B. Alberti*, London, 1726, 3, plates 20-2.

DAGENHAM

VALENCE HOUSE

Dagenham, an industrial suburb of East London, boasts the largest pre-war housing estate in London, Becontree. Surprisingly there is a moated house tucked in beside it, one of the oldest in London. Valence is one of a small group of houses in the London area which have moats; here half of it remains. Today the building looks like a modest Essex farmhouse with its plastered walls and steep tiled roofs, although its origins go back to the 13th century. It takes its name from Agnes de Valence, owner in the early 14th century and sister of the Earl of Pembroke; in 1475 it became the property of the Dean and Chapter of Windsor who kept it till 1867. The timber-framed house was much larger. What remains is L-shaped and of indeterminate date, probably mainly 17th-century with some later additions. There is one ground-floor room with early 17th-century panelling, possibly rearranged. Its history explains why so little remains. The house was let to various families, the most important being the Fanshawe family in the late 16th century. A large wing was demolished in 1863, after which the house was let to a farmer. The photograph shows the 18th-century sash windows and a genteel early 19th-century verandah; it was by no means a semi-derelict farm like Eastbury Manor House nearby. In 1921 the house and land were bought by the LCC in order to build the Becontree Estate on the site. It only survived because Dagenham Urban District Council needed premises and bought the house from the LCC in 1928, thereby saving it from demolition. An extension was added on the east side to provide a

260 Dagenham, Valence House from the S-E, *c.*1918. The timber-framed house is mainly 17th-century beneath the later stucco. The verandah was removed when the house was enlarged as council offices in 1928.

suitable meeting room. When new council offices were built Valence became a museum and local studies centre, as it is today. In 1963 Aubrey Fanshawe, a descendant of the former owners, gave his remarkably fine collection of 17th-century family portraits to the house; these include a Lely, a Dobson and a Marcus Gheeraerts the Younger. Two arms of the moat survive in a modest garden; half the moat was filled in when the drawbridge was removed in 1863, with what remains providing a peaceful spot for fishing. The council most insensitively demolished the stables and farm buildings close to the house and replaced them with a factory and their depot; this blights both the approach to the house and the views from it. Recently it has tried to redress this by laying out an enclosed herb garden, designed in 1992 by Virginia Nightingale; and 18th-century wrought iron gates were brought from Dagenham church. So Valence and its small park do provide a green and comparatively attractive spot in the flat landscape of the Thames estuary.

VCH 'Essex', 5, 1966, pp.278-80; Cherry, O'Brien & Pevsner, *London 5*, pp.145-6; J. Howson, *The Fanshawe Family & Other Portraits*, 1983.

FULHAM

HURLINGHAM HOUSE

This late 18th-century riverside house with its large gardens is one of the few to survive close to central London; that it does so is due to its conversion into the Hurlingham Club in 1869, so its extensive grounds were used for polo, tennis and croquet rather than being built on. William Cadogan, a successful doctor with a London house, acquired a three-acre lease from the Bishop of London's Fulham estate, and managed to lease a further nine acres soon afterwards. In 1760 he built himself an unpretentious three-storey brick house which was left to his daughter and son-in-law at his death in 1797. They immediately sold it, and the new owner, John Ellis, built the present much larger house. Using George Byfield as his architect, he kept the north front of Cadogan's house as his entrance front. So there is a striking difference between the three-storey brick house seen from the north, and the stuccoed two-storey house which faces the river. In 1797-8 Byfield added a nine-bay south front

261   Fulham, Hurlingham House. Elevation from *New Vitruvius Britannicus*, 2, 1808.

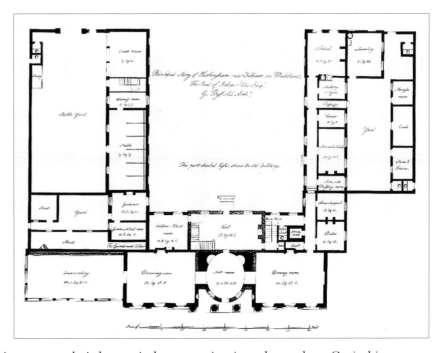

262 Fulham, Hurlingham House. Plan of house and service areas from *New Vitruvius Britannicus*, 2, 1808.

with two large reception rooms, their long windows opening into the gardens. Corinthian pilasters divided the bays, with the central three bays emphasised by columns and a recessed loggia below a shallow pediment. This masks the oval anteroom, actually part of the older house, which separates the drawing room from the dining room. This was on the east side, a practical position, for the new service quarters were placed to the north-east, and a corridor led directly from dining room to kitchen. Two new service areas were built flanking the north entrance, forming a deep courtyard. On the east side was extensive servant accommodation with a kitchen and laundry; on the other was the stable yard, with stabling for six and coach houses. Ellis bought the freehold in 1800, and also acquired 11 acres. To incorporate this new land he consulted Humphry Repton, although there are no surviving plans for this. A conservatory was built on the west end of the drawing room, unifying house and garden in a typically Regency manner; this has recently been rebuilt to the original design after destruction during the Second World War. In 1808 the house was sold to George Wyndham, 3rd Earl of Egremont of Petworth in Sussex. After changing hands between prosperous owners, it was leased from Richard Naylor in 1869 by the newly formed Hurlingham Club, which in 1874 acquired the freehold. With polo matches taking place there it became part of the London social season, and it expanded by buying up the properties to east and west. In 1906 Lutyens was called in to make improvements, designing the gate piers and iron gates across the forecourt, adding the two porches in the angles of the building and making a long gallery or hall to simplify access within the house. There was some bomb damage during the Second World War and the conservatory was destroyed, but a greater change came in 1946 with the compulsory purchase by the GLC of the land to the east, including the polo ground, to build housing and a school and provide some open space in what was then a poor part of London. Over the last fifty years the club has developed sporting facilities so it can remain open all year round: hard tennis courts, an indoor pool, squash courts and restaurants. So the 42 acres which surround the house are no longer wholly garden, and it is only the south front which retains a sense of being a suburban retreat. But there Byfield's elegant reception rooms still overlook lawns scattered with mature trees with the Thames beyond, and justify Richardson's description of it as 'one of the most beautiful villas on the banks of the Thames'.

C.J. Fèret, *Fulham Old & New*, 3, 1900, pp.242-5; D. Stroud, *Humphry Repton*, 1962, p.170; G. Richardson, *New Vitruvius Britannicus*, 2, 1808, p.4.

GREENWICH

VANBRUGH CASTLE

Vanbrugh, one of the most original English architects, built himself two houses which feature in this book: Chargate in Surrey, later renamed Claremont (demolished) and this house on Maze Hill in Greenwich, its modern name reflecting his passion for the castle style. Chargate was built *c*.1710 but he sold it in 1714, and in 1717 took a 99-year lease on 12 acres to the N-E of Greenwich Park, a convenient place to be as the previous year he had replaced Wren as Surveyor of the Royal Naval Hospital at Greenwich. The house, begun in 1718, was built by the bricklayer Richard Billingshurst, who was also working at the Hospital. It is a compact if eccentric house, three storeys high above a semi-basement; much of the wall surface is blank brickwork, with narrow arched windows and the semi-basement has circular windows punched through the thick walls. The square, battlemented corner towers and a circular staircase tower with a conical roof all rise above the roofline, giving it the dramatic skyline which Vanbrugh favoured. The house has the 'advance and recession' which Robert Adam so much admired, and from the tower roofs there are remarkable views to London and the Thames, as well as to the south. The house had only three main rooms per floor;

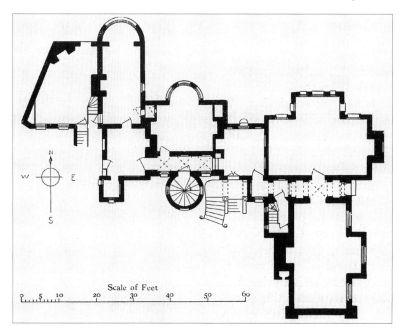

263 Greenwich, Vanbrugh Castle. Plan of the main floor, showing the irregular lay-out of Vanbrugh's house. The large room lower right was not part of the original house.

264   Greenwich, Vanbrugh Castle, showing Vanbrugh's 1718 entrance front with a later wing on the right.

by the time it was built was too small, as aged 54 Vanbrugh had just married and soon had children; it was enlarged to cope with family life. Sir John Clerk of Penicuik saw it in 1727 (just after Vanbrugh's death) and described it as 'great heaps of brick and thick walls but little accommodation within. There is scarce a room in them above 8 or 10 feet square ... The ornaments are such which the Goths and their successors put in place in castles and prisons viz: battlements, round towers, little windows and doors.' The house had a curtain wall around it, and low service buildings contrasted with the height of the house itself; these have gone, as has the gatehouse, another military touch.

Loosely grouped within the same plot of land Vanbrugh built houses for other members of his family, all in castle style. His brother Philip had a compact house of one main storey, its massive walls, narrow arched windows and arrow slits in the service wings recalling military architecture; his brother Charles had a two-storey house with heavily rusticated staircase towers at each side; while his two unmarried sisters each had a four-storey White Tower, the name recalling the Tower of London. All these have gone, leaving Vanbrugh Castle alone, without its gatehouse or service buildings, and with various later additions. Having been used as a school from 1921, it reverted to residential use and was converted into flats in 1979.

K. Downes, *Sir John Vanbrugh, a Biography* 1987, pp.374, 381-3; W.E.L. Fletcher, 'The Maze Hill Estate of Sir John Vanbrugh', *Transactions of the Greenwich & Lewisham Antiquarian Society*, 8, iv, 1976, pp.136-42; Cherry & Pevsner, *London 2*, p.273; H. Colvin & M. Craig eds., *Architectural Drawings in the Library of Elton Hall ...* 1964, pls.25-6; L. Whistler, *The Imagination of Vanbrugh* 1954, pp.200-7; A. Tipping, *English Homes*, Period 4, ii, pp.187-92; Sir John Clerk of Penicuik, NAS, GD18/2107, f.7v.-8r.

WOODLANDS HOUSE

Woodlands was built 1774-6 for John Julius Angerstein (1735-1823) a successful immigrant with a mysterious background: born in St Petersburg, son of a merchant from Hanover, he was rumoured to be the illegitimate son of the Empress Anna. He arrived in London in 1750 and became a hugely successful insurance broker and underwriter and a noted art collector. He and his wife had a house in Pall Mall, and wanted a house within easy reach of London where their two children could spend the summer. Sir Gregory Page of Wricklemarsh had a 41-acre plot available for development on the Westcombe estate. In 1774 Angerstein took a 99-year lease and began building a modest neo-classical house; they rented a house on Croom's Hill till it was ready. Angerstein lived to a great age and later enlarged the house, destroying its symmetry but making it more convenient. George Gibson was his architect, a local man with good City connections (his father had built Stone House, Lewisham). The result was 'a charming small villa [which] commands a pleasing but distant view of the Thames'. The five-bay two-storey house was of brick faced with Liardet's stucco, the cornice enriched with festoons below a mansard roof with attics. The porticoed entrance front faced east, windowless apart from a thermal window, and was 'enriched with two niches … containing elegant statues, representing the young Apollo and the dancing Faun' with bas-reliefs in roundels above them. About 1800 Angerstein, by now very rich, old and spending less time in London, added a west wing (mostly demolished). In 1808 and 1810 he bought about 6,000 acres of adjoining country estates on the Norfolk–Suffolk borders, and divided his time between there and Greenwich. By 1818 he needed a suite of ground-floor rooms at Woodlands, so added an east wing and filled in the portico to increase the warmth of the house. By this time the north front had become the entrance front and was faced in Portland stone; an elegant Ionic porch had been built. A pair of shallow bow windows had been added to the south front, and he also had a stable block, riding school

265   Greenwich, Woodlands, garden front in 2008. The house is empty and urgently in need of attention.

and conservatory. This held Angerstein's collection of exotic plants from China and South Africa, and produced the effect of 'walking in an evergreen flowery wood'. But his main interest was art collecting, and advised by Thomas Lawrence and Benjamin West he put together a superb collection which formed the basis of the National Gallery. Most of the exceptional works, such as Sebastiano del Piombo's *Raising of Lazarus* and Cuyp's *River Landscape* were in his London house, and were among the 38 paintings sold for £57,000 to the government in 1823. But the family portraits by Joshua Reynolds, Lawrence and others were in Greenwich and remained in the family. The house remained with Angerstein's descendants till 1876, when the property was sold to the Westcombe Estate Company for development. Mycenae Road was built right in front of the house, so the east wing had to be demolished. The whole house nearly went, but was saved by William Bristow of the development company who chose to live in it himself. It was sold to the shipbuilder Sir Alfred Yarrow in 1895; he stayed there till 1906. By that time much of its grounds had been developed, and it was no longer as desirable as a private house. It was bought in 1923 by the Little Sisters of the Assumption, and in 1967 by the LB of Greenwich, who restored it as a local history library and art gallery. With all these changes of use little has survived of the original interiors, but the north and south fronts still gives some idea of Angerstein's neat villa. However its present state gives cause for concern, as it is sitting empty, its south front boarded up, and the roof with gaping holes.

J. Young, *A Life of John Julius Angerstein*, 2006; *John Julius Angerstein & Woodlands 1774-1974*, LB of Greenwich exhibition catalogue, 1974; Lysons, *Environs*, 1, ii, 1811; Cherry & Pevsner, *London 2*, p.249; J. Young, *A Catalogue of the Celebrated Collection of Pictures of the late J.J. Angerstein*, 1823.

HADLEY

BEECH HILL PARK

Enfield Chace was sparsely wooded high ground belonging to the Crown and used from medieval times for hunting. The decline of deer hunting and changes in agriculture meant that by the 1770s there were plans to carve up the Chace into leasehold plots which could be farmed. Francis Russell was Crown Surveyor for Enfield Chace and financial adviser to William Pitt. Through Pitt's influence Russell was granted the freehold on 152 acres on the western side of the Chace and here he built his house, originally called Russell Mansion. Beech Hill Park is a good example of a medium-sized country house, comparatively little altered since it was built in 1781. Although no architect is known it has good proportions, elegant detailing and a well chosen site: it stands on high ground, looking south over what is still today an extensive, semi-rural landscape. The lodge (boarded up at present) and a short drive are to the north. The seven-bay brick house was originally an almost square block; four Doric pilasters frame the three central bays, and a simple cornice and parapet wrap round the house. The front door set in a depressed arch has a modest porch, added slightly later. The original entrance hall lay between the two south-facing reception rooms; the dining room was on the east side, and like the hall has neo-classical reliefs in plasterwork. Both the dining room and the bedroom above have their original chimneypieces, although most others have gone. The cantilevered stairs are restrained but elegant. North of the dining room were the service rooms, opening at the back of the house onto a small courtyard with the stables beyond; these survive, partly converted for residential use. Nearby were the barns and cottages required for the farm.

In the 19th century low wings were added each side, providing a conservatory and billiard room. The entrance was moved from the south front to the west side, and the service areas to the north were extended. In 1858 Charles Jack bought the property, and also more land in

266 Hadley, Beech Hill Park, south front. Built 1781, with two low wings added mid-19th century.

the area. After the agricultural depression of the 1870s he decided to develop part of his land as housing, but for this to be viable transport was required. He negotiated with the Great Northern Railway Company for a line to be built within easy reach, and partly paid for the new station at Hadley Wood. Gradually the area north of the house was developed as middle-class houses on leafy roads, but the farmland to the south remained. After Jack's death in 1896 the house was put on the market. The auction document describes it as 'A capital family mansion with choice gardens, stabling, farm buildings and several cottages in a beautifully timbered undulating park … [with] 261 acres.' But no buyer came forward and the house was empty for many years. In 1920 the house and grounds were sold to a property company for £31,500, and Hadley Wood Golf Club took out a lease, opening in 1922, and buying the freehold in 1976. Russell's house remains the club house, and has been carefully restored.

Cherry & Pevsner, *London 4*, 1998, pp.470-1; copy of auction document, Hadley Wood Golf Club.

HAMMERSMITH

BRADMORE HOUSE

The distinguished west front of this house is dwarfed by recent office buildings, has a constant flow of traffic past it and the elevated section of the A4 close by. But it is actually a reconstruction on a slightly different site of what was originally the east-facing garden front. Butterwick House was the old house here, owned 1500-48 by Sir William Essex, who had a London house as well as land in several counties. His grandson sold it in 1573, after which it changed hands many times. Henry Ferne (1660-1730), Receiver-General of the Customs, bought it in 1700 and according to Lysons 'built 3 handsome apartments in a spot of ground next The Old Hall and communicating with it'. This is the present Bradmore House, built to accommodate his mistress, the actress Mrs Oldfield. We see today a red brick Baroque façade of seven bays and two storeys with arched windows, the centre sweeping up and emphasised by tall stone Corinthian pilasters; Doric pilasters in brick frame the central window, and Doric pilasters in stone mark the outer corners. This suitably theatrical composition points to a builder or architect familiar with Thomas Archer's work. The house was sold by Ferne's

267 Hammersmith, Bradmore House. Drawing by R. Randoll of the front facing Queen Street, dated 1904. This side of the house and Queen Street have disappeared.

son-in-law in 1739 to Elijah Impey (father of the Chief Justice of India) and remained in that family until 1822. In the 19th century the old manor house had become a school, with Bradmore House in separate ownership. Mr Simpson owned it and lived in the main part, with the curate of nearby St Peter's church living in the back. In 1836 the adjoining Butterwick House was demolished. Faulkner describes the interiors as being 'wainscoted from floor to ceiling and handsomely ornamented … The mantelpieces are of Derbyshire marble … with fossil remains. The principal apartment is 30 ft long, 20 ft broad and 18 ft high, with three windows.' A contemporary drawing shows a fine Baroque interior with a richly carved cornice and Corinthian pilasters framing the arched windows. By the early 20th century Hammersmith Broadway was being built up as a shopping centre, the Metropolitan Railway had arrived, and it was no longer a desirable site for a private house. The Simpson family sold it in 1904 and in 1913 the London General Omnibus Company bought it, hoping to use the site as a bus depot. But after the demolition of the Old Palace in Bromley-by-Bow it was harder to demolish historic buildings in the London area, and the LCC stepped in. One panelled room was installed in the Geffrye Museum as a historic interior, and a garden niche of particularly fine brickwork was removed to the forecourt of the Geffrye Museum, where it now languishes behind a tree. The bus company built their garage on the gardens of Bradmore House, but was forced to reconstruct the east front of the house on a slightly different site, and to keep the main saloon intact with some public access. Access to the bus depot was provided by raising the whole front and cutting large openings on each side of the three centre bays. This unhappy compromise lasted for decades, the only change being the removal of the panelled room in the 1950s. (It is now in Trinity Almshouses, Mile End Road.) In the 1980s various schemes were put forward for redeveloping the centre of Hammersmith to provide office space and better transport links, all involving demolition of the bus garage. After a public enquiry and as a result of campaigns by local people a solution was eventually agreed with the developers and English Heritage. In 1993 the house was restored as a restaurant, the openings rebuilt with arched windows, the balustrade and ironwork on the roof taken out of store and reinstated. The house was completely reconstructed behind the façade, the sides and east front built in stock bricks with rubbed red brick details to match the west front. As people hurry to work in the morning they see this beautifully restored façade, which once stood where they wait for the tube trains.

Survey, 6, 'Hammersmith' 1915, pp.1–4; K. Whitehouse, R. White, I. McInnes, *Bradmore House, Hammersmith*, 1996; T. Faulkner, *History & Antiquities of the Parish of Hammersmith*, 1839; LB of Hammersmith & Fulham Archives.

HAMPSTEAD

FENTON HOUSE

Standing on the summit of Hampstead Hill is a brick house, built in the late 17th century and now owned by the National Trust. Historically Hampstead was not as desirable as village as Highgate across the Heath, and this house belonged mainly to a succession of merchants. It was built *c*.1686, possibly as a speculation by the bricklayer William Eades; there are odd touches, such as the asymmetry of the roofline, which point to its being designed by a builder rather than an architect. It was sold to Thomas Simpson, although he seems to have let it and never lived there. In 1706 it was sold to Joshua Gee, a Quaker silk merchant well known for his writings on trade. He lived in the City but had just remarried; his new wife had several children, and her money may have allowed him to buy this good-sized but compact house within easy reach of his work. The Gee family owned it until 1756, when the sale document described the house and its appurtenances: offices, brewhouse, orchard, kitchen garden and a brick building with two coach-houses and stabling for eight, which remarkably still survives in the service area to the west. The house was originally approached from the south. The brick gate piers with their contrasting plum and rubbed red brickwork are a foretaste of the house itself, which can be glimpsed through the fine early 18th-century

268   Hampstead, Fenton House, late 17th-century. Entrance front, moved to this side in 1807 and given a loggia.

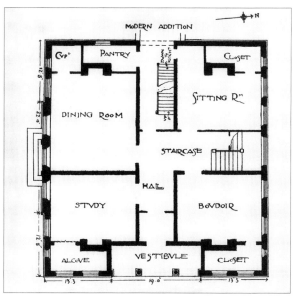

269   Hampstead, Fenton House, plan of ground floor. The house has four rooms to a floor, with the unusual position of the chimneybreasts allowing for corner closets.

wrought-iron gates. It is a good example of the compact plan with four rooms per floor which is so common in these suburban houses. The house has a through passage with four rooms off it, each with a closet ingeniously squeezed into the outer corners of the house and lit by tall narrow windows. These are next to the deep chimneybreasts, so the chimneys are close to the outer walls of the house. The first floor is approached by the main stairs with twisted balusters, lit by a long window overlooking the garden to the north. The plan of the first floor is similar, and again the closets are still there. A plainer secondary staircase, from basement to attics, is tucked off the corridor on the west side. The high hipped roof allows good-sized attic rooms, some of which still have their original fireplaces and panelling; these would have been used by the children and household, with servants using the service rooms in the basement or living over the stables. The house acquired its present name after it was bought in 1793 by Philip Fenton, a Riga merchant. His son James inherited it in 1807 and made various alterations, giving it its present appearance. He added the loggia on the east front, making that the main entrance; he also made two ground-floor rooms inter-connecting, fortunately keeping the corner closets. Although there were many owners in the 19th century, no further major changes were made. In 1936 the house was bought by Lady Binning, who used it as her London house when down from Scotland. She cherished it through the war and after, when so many houses were threatened, and bequeathed it to the National Trust at her death in 1952. She also left the Trust a fine collection of porcelain and some good pieces of late 18th-century satinwood furniture – both of a much later period than the house itself, but to be displayed there. The Trust added the Benton Fletcher collection of early keyboard instruments, again unrelated to the house itself. In 1973-4 John Fowler was appointed to redecorate the house, bearing in mind the display of these rather disparate objects. His decorative schemes respected the historic fabric while presenting it as a fashionably decorated and lived-in house and a backdrop for the collections. This would be controversial today, but the attractive result has its place in the history of taste and the presentation of historic interiors. The Trust also restored the gardens, keeping the terrace walk round the pleasure gardens but adding lawns and herbaceous borders rather than the original parterres, and restoring the kitchen garden. It is a fine example of the type of well-built medium-sized house which was once common in villages round London, but has almost entirely gone.

Information from Sheila Wilson; 1756 Sale particulars, 1920 Sale particulars, Camden Archives H728.3/Fenton House; Cherry & Pevsner, *London 4*, pp.215-6; *VCH* 'Middlesex' 9, pp.17,23,27; *Country Life* 24 March 1950, pp.802-6, & 30 January 2003, pp.50-3.`

HAVERING-ATTE-BOWER

The Round House

Round houses are uncommon, but this unique house is oval in plan in spite of its name. Built in 1793-4 by a London entrepreneur called William Sheldon, it was possibly designed by the architect John Plaw. His book *Rural Architecture* with many of his designs for compact houses and cottages came out in 1785 and Sheldon's name features as a subscriber. So he was an admirer of Plaw's work, although there is no documentary evidence that he commissioned the house from him. *Rural Architecture* included the circular Belle Isle, built 1774-5 and picturesquely sited on an island in Lake Windermere. The Round House stands on the summit of the hill at Havering-atte-Bower, now hemmed in by mature trees. But there are magnificent views south and east, which can still be admired from the roof. This has deep eaves supported on brackets, a rare feature as early as 1794. The three-storey house is of stuccoed brick with four pairs of astylar pilasters giving vertical emphasis, counterbalanced by the string courses between the storeys. There is also a basement ingeniously hidden under a grassy mound, which actually conceals an area which has occasional top-lighting through gratings; but the service rooms were poorly lit. The house is entered through a porch on one of its longer sides, with a small entrance hall opening into a top-lit staircase hall. The main room on each floor is semi-circular with a wider central window. On the ground floor the windows reach down to the ground, and the main room to the east has steps into the garden. This was probably the drawing room and used to have a rare example of a panoramic wallpaper made by Dufour in Paris in 1815, and known as *Le Petit Décor*. With its idealised scenes of people and buildings and its bold colouring, this covered the whole room above the dado, and the ceiling was painted with blue sky and clouds. The house was never lived in by Sheldon, who lost money on his Italian opera ventures at the Pantheon; he sold it in 1807 to William Jacobs, whose niece inherited it. She and her husband, William Whitehurst, may have put up the wallpaper *c*.1820, and possibly made some alterations to the arrangement of the rooms. The house was little altered by the Barnes family, who owned it from 1830 till the Second World War. After military use during the war it was in an appalling state, attacked by dry and wet rot and with guard dogs living in it. It was rescued by Michael Heap, whose father had bought it in 1952. He wanted to live in it and carried out a careful restoration with the help of the architect Julian Harrap in 1980-1. The wallpaper was by then in such a bad state that it was not possible to restore it *in situ*; it was carefully removed by English Heritage, and is now in store. In keeping with the modest scale of the house there was a small stable block, with space for just one pair of horses and a carriage; this survives. The short drive was flanked by a kitchen garden, and nearer the house was that fashionable accessory, a dairy, connected to the basement service rooms by a tunnel.

N. Burton, 'The Round House, Havering-atte-Bower', *Georgian Group Journal*, 1991, pp.57-9; N. Burton, 'The Round House' unpublished report for EH; Cherry, O'Brien & Pevsner, *London 5*, pp.171-3.

HENDON

HENDON HALL

This curious house stands on high ground about half a mile from the delightful little parish church of Hendon. David Garrick's name is associated with the house: he was lord of the manor 1765-78 but this was simply a property investment; he had his own country house in Hampton from 1755 and never lived in Hendon. However the link with Garrick is commemorated in a pair of stone obelisks, one with an inscription to Garrick, the other to Shakespeare, which are outside the house today. They have been moved from their original setting as the grounds have shrunk. Its most important owner was Samuel Ware (1781-1860) who owned it by 1828. With a busy practice as an architect and surveyor he lived in London and had a house in Portland Place; Hendon was for occasional use until his retirement in the 1840s. The house is said to have been rebuilt by Ware, but this seems unlikely: it is a three-storey triple-pile house with a six-bay entrance front, mid-18th-century in appearance.

270 Hendon Hall. The mid-18th-century entrance front is dwarfed by the portico with its banded brick columns, possibly brought from Wanstead House when it was demolished in 1824.

Apart from its off-centre entrance there is nothing unusual about the façade – except that it is dominated by an over-scaled portico with four columns of banded brick. The Corinthian capitals are of stone, as is the enriched entablature and the pediment. This portico could not possibly have been designed by Ware for his house, but might he have brought it from elsewhere? Keane suggests that it came from Wanstead House which was being demolished in 1823-4 and the materials sold. If so, it would be similar to the reuse of the portico from Wricklemarsh at Beckenham Place. The balustrade with its stone vases might also have been added to the more modest original house. The south or garden front is also of three storeys with a two-storey wing attached to the east side. This provides larger rooms than in the rest of the house and with its canted bay running through both storeys would have had good views of the gardens and beyond, although the site now is fairly restricted. One of these rooms has a good marble chimneypiece of c.1760, which would be a possible date for the addition of this wing. Unfortunately the house has been considerably altered internally so it is difficult to work out the dating of the various parts. Even the staircase, at first glance a good example of an early Georgian type, seems not to fit its space and may also have been brought in. On the west side of the house is a long service wing, the lower two storeys with mid-18th-century brickwork. The second storey was probably added by C.F. Hancock, a London jeweller who bought the house in 1869. He enlarged the service accommodation and in 1889 rebuilt the Home Farm using Wimperis & Arbour as his architects. Most of this has gone but the milking parlour is still there opposite the church, a most surprising survival in a village which has become part of London. The house became a hotel in 1911 and a conservatory was added to the south front, as well as a new garage and stable block with an arched entrance over the drive. During the Second World War the house was requisitioned as a convalescent home by the RAF, which had such a strong presence in Hendon. It has recently been restored as a hotel once again and is in good condition, although very much hemmed in by 20th-century residential developments.

Cherry & Pevsner, *London 4*, pp.164-5; Keane, *Beauties of Middlesex*, 1850, pp.237-8.

355

HESTON

SPRING GROVE

This large house of mainly early 20th-century appearance stands on the site of a small house built *c.*1645, which was demolished in 1754 by its new owner. He was Elisha Biscoe (1705-76), a local man who was developing parts of Brompton with new houses. He rebuilt Spring Grove as a neat five-bay, two-storey house with a central pediment, facing Smallberry Green. A drawing room with a canted bay window overlooked the gardens at the side; a service wing lay behind the house, with stables beyond. This house is still the core of the house we see today. In 1779 Biscoe's son let Spring Grove for £200 *p.a.* to Sir Joseph Banks, the noted botanist, who bought the freehold in 1808 for £6,000. A plan shows that it had pleasure gardens, kitchen gardens, a conservatory and hot houses as well as a small park and a dairy; with some fields in addition, he had about 49 acres. He kept Merino sheep here, and supplied George III with some for his farm at Windsor. Banks lived mainly here and Soho Square, with only occasional visits to Lincolnshire, till his death in 1820, and was buried in Heston church. In 1834 Henry Pownall inherited the house, and decided to update it. He enlarged the house by two bays to the east and moved the entrance from the south front to his new east wing. Some of the interiors were updated and Grecian chimneypieces installed, although the drawing room kept its delicate neo-classical plasterwork ceiling. The ground-floor windows were lowered and the exterior covered in Roman cement, presumably to disguise the new work. These changes lasted for about half a century, until an industrialist

271   Heston, Spring Grove, built in 1755 and later owned by Sir Joseph Banks. The south front overlooked Smallberry Green.

272 Heston, Spring Grove, west front. The bay window on the right was part of the mid-18th-century house, vastly enlarged after 1886 for Andrew Pears of Pears Soap.

bought the house and made major alterations, creating the house we see today. In 1886 Andrew Pears (1846-1909) of soap-manufacturing fame bought the house. This was not to be his suburban retreat; instead it was his main residence, conveniently close to the factory his father had established in Isleworth in 1862. The family had done very well out of the business, and in 1892-4 Pears spent around £120,000 on rebuilding Spring Grove, turning it into a much larger house where he could entertain. William Catherwood was his architect, a man who is only known to have designed one other building, and the result is not architecturally distinguished. Keeping the existing house as his south front, it was massively enlarged to the north. On the garden front new reception rooms opened from the drawing room and morning room: a large music room, with a minstrels' gallery dated 1894, opened into the Winter Garden. This top-lit space was decorated with Moorish tiles and had a fountain in the centre; beyond was a billiard room. The staircase was rebuilt in dark oak, and the window was filled with stained glass celebrating Manufacturing, Navigation and Commerce on one side, with Poetry, Music and Drama on the other. On the entrance front new service rooms backed onto a service courtyard, and the stables and coach-houses were rebuilt. More servants were needed for this enlarged house, and a mansard roof was added with nurseries and staff bedrooms. The whole house was refaced in warm red brick, replacing the Roman cement of Pownall's time. Perhaps Pears was not pleased with his rebuilt house, for in 1902 he moved to Mevagissey House nearby and put Spring Grove on the market. His reserve price was too high, and the house only sold in 1903. Mr Hossack, the new owner, sold off parts of the grounds for housing, and it became clear that the house was not likely to survive as a private house. It was used as a hospital during the First World War, and in 1922 was bought by Middlesex County Council in order to house Hounslow Polytechnic. By 1960 larger premises were needed and demolition of the whole site was proposed, so that a new building could go up on the site. A public enquiry rejected this, and instead some indifferent additions were made, especially to the north. In 1993 West Thames College took over the site, and a major restoration was carried out 1994-6, recognising the importance of Banks's ownership, as well as respecting the alterations made by Pears.

P. Rowlands, 'Spring Grove House: a History' 2001, unpublished booklet for West Thames College; J. Todd of Hounslow, 'Plan of an Estate at Smallbury Green' 1800.

HIGHGATE

BEECHWOOD AND THE ELMS

The hilltop village of Highgate had lost its aristocratic connections by the early 19th century but remained an appealing place to have a house, separated as it was from the expanding city below by farmland and market gardens. The most desirable sites were on the fringes of Hampstead Heath, with springs on the hillside providing a clean water supply. These two houses were built on adjoining plots, by the same architect, for two brothers. Fitzroy Farm, the *ferme ornée* developed by Lord Southampton, is mentioned elsewhere, and after it was demolished in 1826 some of its land was sold off which George and Nathaniel Basevi were able to buy. George Basevi (1794-1845) was a gifted architect who had joined Soane's office in 1810. He then travelled in Greece and Italy and set up an independent practice with offices in the Albany. He came from a well connected Anglo-Jewish family, being related to both Disraeli and Sir Robert Peel. In 1834 he designed Beechwood, close to Hampstead Lane and almost on the site of Fitzroy Farm, for his barrister brother. It is a five-bay house with widely spaced windows, the central one on the first floor being tripartite, matching the wide doorway below. The entrance front faces N-E, allowing the main reception rooms of this double-pile house to face over the Heath. Canted bays have been added to this front, otherwise the house is little altered. It is not one of Basevi's most striking designs, but he provided his brother with a comfortable family house which did not compete with the beauties of the landscape. There is a walled kitchen garden, and many fine trees still surround the house, some of them planted by Southampton and some of the oaks probably older still.

George Basevi had a large family and built his house *c.*1838 on slightly lower ground, off the lane now called Fitzroy Park. The entrance is marked by a stucco lodge. It is a stucco house of two main storeys, the entrance front also facing N-E and the main rooms therefore facing over the Heath. A spring feeds a little stream running through the picturesque grounds into Highgate Ponds. This house has been much more altered than Beechwood, and has additions of 1863 disguising his original design. Basevi died at the height of his career, falling from the tower of Ely Cathedral and his widow sold the house soon afterwards. Both houses have changed hands many times, but have remained as well-kept private houses with exceptionally large gardens.

Country Life, 'Beechwood, Highgate' 7 March 1952, pp.652-5; *The Builder,* 3, 1845, pp.510-11.

LAUDERDALE HOUSE

On the southern slopes of Highgate Hill stands a long low building, set back from the main road behind a fine early 18th-century gate. At first glance it looks Georgian but closer examination reveals that it is much more interesting: a late 16th-century timber-framed house, the oldest to survive in Highgate. It was built *c.*1580 by a City goldsmith, Richard Martin, son of a Lord Mayor, and was possibly a courtyard house on a modest scale. The hall was approached from the east; service rooms were to the north, but these went long ago, and there are now modern extensions on this side. It was one of the largest houses in Highgate, having 26 hearths in 1674. The original timber-framed structure can best be seen on the south and west fronts, where the jettied first floor is supported on slim wooden columns of 18th-century date; simple pediments and a thermal window were also added, and the early windows replaced with sashes. Much of the interior was badly damaged by fire in 1963, and the best of the early fabric is on the ground floor. The hall has simple panelling and a marble chimneypiece of the early 18th century; above it is a neo-classical plaster relief of moderate quality. The most interesting feature is the rectangular oak niche on the north wall, framed by fluted pilasters and finely carved coving. The interior also has Corinthian pilasters so cannot have had the fitted shelves of a typical buffet; possibly it was designed to take a side-table. The main staircase with turned balusters dates from the late 17th century; it is top-lit, with the opening framed with rich plasterwork, restored after the fire. The gallery on the first floor also suffered extensive fire damage, and has no original woodwork; it is hoped to complete its restoration with help from the HLF. The house belonged to City families in the early 17th century, and was let to Sir Henry Hobart of Blickling Hall. In 1641 the Dowager Countess of Home bought it, but was forced out during the Civil War by the Parliamentarian John Ireton; her daughter, Lady Lauderdale, reclaimed it after the Restoration. She and her powerful husband gave their name to the house, although he used it only until her death in 1671, when he rapidly remarried and moved to Ham House. The house changed hands many times, and like many of these houses became a school in the late 18th and early 19th centuries. Its history then becomes bound up with that of Fairseat, the nearby house rebuilt in 1867 by Sir Sydney Waterlow, a well-off printer and Lord Mayor. In 1865 he bought

273 Highgate, Lauderdale House, south front. The jettied first floor of the timber-framed 16th-century house is now covered in pebbledash and has a later pediment.

Lauderdale House and incorporated the grounds into his gardens; in 1889 he gave 29 acres to the LCC to make a public park, called after him. So Waterlow Park includes the original gardens of Lauderdale House, which had natural advantages: a good supply of water from the springs which feed the two lakes, and a magnificent view S-E over the City. This could be admired from an alcove seat which is set into a garden wall, or from the mount, which is a rare survival. Today the view is obscured by sycamores, but the gardens have otherwise been recently restored, with sculpture repaired and a simplified *parterre* below the house. Ownership of the house was, as usual, an unwelcome burden to the council and it was only in 1893 that its future was assured and some restoration was carried out. In 1971 the house was handed over to the LB of Camden, and is now run by a trust for community use.

Survey, 'The Village of Highgate' 17, 1936, pp.14-16; *VCH* 'Middlesex' 6, pp.124,136; J. Richardson, *Highgate*, 1983; NRO, Lothian Add.T.86a.

ISLEWORTH

GUMLEY HOUSE

In the centre of the Thames-side village of Isleworth is a group of brick buildings partially hidden behind high walls. Now a convent and school, this has at its core the house which

John Gumley (1670-1727) bought and rebuilt *c*.1700, hence its name. Gumley was a very successful furniture maker working in partnership with his mother, Mrs Elizabeth Gumley, then with James Moore, supplying some of the showiest and most expensive furniture in early 18th-century London. His showrooms were in Salisbury Exchange in the Strand, and he was also involved from 1705 in the manufacture of glass at a factory in Lambeth. He lived in Norfolk Street off the Strand and had a large family, presumably one of the reasons for acquiring a country house with good-sized gardens. It is a five-bay house with slightly arched windows and a deep wooden cornice; there was a single-storey extension each side, with a two-bay panelled room in each. It is not entirely clear where the service rooms and kitchens were, as the basement is low-ceilinged and includes cellars; possibly there was a service wing to one side, swept away in the post-1841 additions. A mid-18th-century drawing shows a pyramidal roof with tall brick chimneys, but both roofline and chimneys have been lowered. On both the entrance and garden fronts the

274 Isleworth, Gumley House. The garden front of the 1700 house with higher wings added for the Faithful Companions of Jesus in the mid-19th century.

roof is broken by a three-bay attic storey with a small brick pediment. The brickwork on these appears later than the original house, but the attic appears on the drawing and the attic bedrooms have their original chimneypieces and panelling; one room has a wall of Jacobean panelling, suggesting that it was reused from the early 17th-century house on the site. The windows of the two main storeys have brick aprons and rubbed red brick detailing, but there is no other ornament. The entrance hall extends right across the main front and still has its original fittings: painted panelling with fluted Corinthian pilasters, doorcases of exaggerated height and a black-and-white marble floor. As befits a furniture maker there is a shallow cantilevered staircase, with three twisted and fluted balusters per step; there is fine carving on the underside of the steps and a parquetry panel below the half-landing. On the garden front both ground and first floors now have a room the full width of the house, but there are two fireplaces in each room, one across a corner; these and irregularities in the panelling show that these were originally two rooms of unequal size. James Gibbs made poorly documented alterations to the house a few years later. These probably consisted of the brick gate piers and the colonnades with Tuscan columns which enclose the forecourt, as well as some chimneypieces. When Gumley died in 1727 he left a widow and seven children; the house in 'Thistleworth' was left to his widow unless she remarried (quite a common clause) and was entailed on his second son John. In 1841 the Faithful Companions of Jesus bought the house in order to establish a convent and girls' boarding school. It was enlarged by the three-storey wings each side which dominate it today and other buildings have since been added in the gardens, but Gumley's house has been little altered. With its elegant staircase, high-ceilinged panelled rooms and bolection moulded chimneypieces it remains a good example of the type of house that a prosperous entrepreneur could build for himself in the reign of William III.

VCH, 'Middlesex' 3, pp.91-2; G.J. Augier, *History of Syon … & the Parish of Isleworth*, 1840, p.228; *Dictionary of English Furniture Makers 1660-1840*, 1986, pp.379-80; *Country Life*, 27 February 1942, pp.406-7; information from Terry Friedman and members of the Faithful Companions of Jesus.

KENSINGTON

AUBREY HOUSE

Formerly known as Notting Hill House, this is a charming early 18th-century house on the summit of Campden Hill. Its comparatively modest size and its position in one of the smartest areas of London have preserved it as a private house when many others have gone into institutional use or disappeared. Chalybeate springs were discovered here in the late 17th century and were promoted by Dr Wright. He sold the land in 1720, and the house was probably built by Mr Reid who bought the site in 1721. He put up a simple five-bay three-storey house, astylar with a pediment, and with three-bay wings of two storeys. This is the house we see today, although there is a 19th-century extension to the N-W. It is a single-pile house; on the two main floors there is a wide corridor on the north (entrance) front, and south-facing rooms overlooking the gardens. These rooms are modest in scale, many of them with their original panelling and box cornices, some with original chimneypieces. The basement is deep and dark, and the original kitchen was probably in one of the wings. To the north are stables and service buildings. Lady Mary Coke rented it from Sir Edward Lloyd from 1767-86, and

275   Kensington, Aubrey House. 1825 print of garden front with lower wings each side.

her *Journals* give us a glimpse of it in the late 18th century. She was a daughter of John, 2nd Duke of Argyll, and was by this time the widow of Viscount Coke, from whom she had separated shortly after her marriage. In 1774 James Wyatt was commissioned to redesign the drawing room in the west wing. This interior has not survived, but a watercolour of 1817 shows his delicate decoration and the ceiling with low-relief plasterwork painted blue and white. She was an enthusiastic gardener, planting trees and opening up vistas; she had a flower garden, a kitchen garden, and kept cows, ducks and chickens. It was close enough to the West End for her to visit her friends, and every Sunday she could drive to Sudbrook to see her sister Caroline. But she complained about the state of the house, and about the danger of the roads (in 1776 a highwayman was shot in the road at the bottom of her gardens) and she removed first to Chelsea, then to Morton Hall in Chiswick. The house then became a School for Young Ladies, but with Lloyd's death in 1795 it was inherited by Sir Edward Price Lloyd, and was let to various families. From 1808-17 it was rented by the Huguenot de Visme family, and a charming group of watercolours, showing both interiors and exteriors, was painted by their married daughter Louisa Goldsmid; she records a comfortable if slightly old-fashioned family house. After another spell as a school the house was bought in 1873 by William Cleverly Alexander, a banker and leading art collector. He opened the two main ground-floor rooms into one and added the N-W extension and a loggia to the east. The house was filled with his eclectic collection, ranging from Dutch 17th-century masters through Hogarth to works by Whistler. The portrait of Cicely Alexander, his eight-year-old daughter, is one of Whistler's best known images. The house remained in the Alexander

276 Kensington, Aubrey House. Children playing in the simply furnished nursery, painted *c*.1810 by Louisa Goldsmid. Children spent as much of their time as possible in the healthy surroundings of suburban houses, rather than in London.

family until 1997, when it was sold for a record-breaking sum. The new owners have carried out a sensitive and thorough restoration, and it remains in its secluded corner of Kensington very much as it has always been.

The Letters & Journals of Lady Mary Coke, 1970; F.M. Gladstone, *Aubrey House, Kensington 1698-1920*, 1922; *Country Life* 2 May 1957, pp.872-5; 9 May 1957, pp.922-5; Louisa Goldsmid Album, RBKC Central Library.

LEWISHAM

STONE HOUSE

Architects can express themselves with greater freedom when designing for themselves, and one of the more eccentric houses round London is the villa which George Gibson the Younger built 1771-3. Gibson, son of an architect of the same name who may have designed this house, is said to have travelled in Italy. His output was small, and mainly for City families; he also designed Woodlands in Greenwich for Angerstein.

From 1766-8 he bought two parcels of land for his new house in 1766-8, a total of six acres on the high ground of Loam-Pit Hill. The house now sits uncomfortably close to the busy A20 between Lewisham and New Cross and has only one acre of grounds, but it had extensive views N-W towards the City, now obscured by the trees which have been planted to hide the surrounding buildings. The house is small, only 45 ft square with a bow on all four sides; and the exterior finish is most unusual. Stone is rarely used for these suburban houses because of the cost; the smooth finish of ashlar can be imitated in stucco. But Gibson chose Kentish ragstone – with its rough surface and small uneven blocks the very antithesis of ashlar. There is no other example of a sophisticated neo-classical house being built of this material. Only the quoins, string-courses and surrounds to the arched windows are in ashlar. Odder still are the massive ragstone buttresses which support the corners of the house at ground level. These, combined with the small proportion of window to wall, give it a slightly fortress air as one approaches. Above the low-pitched slate roof sits a stuccoed lantern with concave sides, lighting the central staircase and also containing the flues. The plan of the house is also striking, although sometimes ingenuity seems to overrule convenience. The house consists of a low ground floor with a *piano nobile* above; the entrance is on the east side, and the west has a deep portico with a wide flight of steps down into the gardens; it is unlikely that this was ever the entrance. There are some unobtrusive attic rooms on the east side only. The entrance hall has a bow at both ends, and still has its original floor of grey and white marble laid in lozenge patterns. This low and rather dark room contrasts with the extreme height and light of the very small toplit octagonal staircase hall. The stone stairs have simple upright banisters, but the walls are decorated with reliefs of William III and the first three Georges in profile. The visitor goes up the narrow stairs to the first floor, and is then dazzled by the high-ceilinged tripartite saloon, running the whole width of the west front and opening onto the portico. The central part is circular with a pair of columns screening the square end bays; the design is reminiscent of Roman baths, but on a miniature scale. In the 1830s the ceiling of the central part was painted with flowers on a dark background, and Rococo Revival overdoors were painted in the end bays. The other rooms on this floor

277 Lewisham, Stone House, seen from the N–W. It was built 1771–3 by George Gibson the Younger in 1771–3. Most unusually, this 1771–3 house was built of Kentish ragstone with dressed stone details. The portico leads from the saloon into the garden.

are small and simple, each with a bow and still with their original fireplaces. The dining room and service rooms were on the ground floor, and servants' bedrooms in the small attic rooms on the east front. The other surprise is the lantern on the roof: a small staircase winds up to the top, where a gallery gives a dizzying view down the stairwell. Four alcoves open out round the gallery with little slate benches from which to look at the distant views of City spires. Gibson lived in his creation for 25 years, before moving to Blackheath and then Hampstead. The radical MP Daniel White Harvey, founder of the *Sunday Times*, lived there 1822-6 and in 1842 Alderman David Williams Wire bought it. He added stars, a feature of his crest, to the groin-vaulted end bays of the saloon, and may have extended the dining room bow. He became Lord Mayor in 1858-9, and a print was made of the house to commemorate this. But he had a stroke while in office and died soon afterwards; his widow began to sell off land for development, and tall terrace houses now line the road beside the house. The late 19th-century coach house close to the house may have been built as a result of selling off the land with the earlier stables; and the ice-house is now in the gardens of a house nearby. Stone House was briefly a school in the 1880s, before reverting to private use and being the home of various surgeons and physicians. It was bought by the present owner in 1992, and has been meticulously restored.

Cherry & Pevsner, *London 2*, p.411; S. Ramsey & J. Harvey, *Small Georgian Houses & their Details*, 1972, pls.81-82; *Country Life*, 28 November 1991, p.77; information from the owner.

LOUGHTON

LOUGHTON HALL

Arts and Crafts country houses are rare in the London area as most were built slightly further from the capital, which makes the present forlorn and derelict state of Nesfield's interesting house all the sadder. Loughton and Twyford Abbey are probably the two houses in this book least likely to survive. The village of Loughton stands on high ground between Epping Forest and the River Roding, and the land was held pre-Reformation by Waltham Abbey. The house was probably early 16th-century, and from 1579-1745 the large estate was held by the Wroth family; in 1616 they owned 2,400 acres, although almost half of this was waste land. The old house had some major work done in the early 17th century, and was sold to William Whitaker, a City alderman, in 1745. His spinster daughter inherited it in 1770 and lived there till her death in 1825, when almshouses and allotments were set up under the terms of her will. The house was inherited by the Maitland family of nearby Woodford Hall, so it was not their main residence; when it was burnt down in 1836 it was not immediately rebuilt. Only the fine wrought iron gates remained, although they have disappeared since Ebbett illustrated them. In 1878 the Rev. J.W. Maitland commissioned a new house from William Eden Nesfield, who had made friends with Norman Shaw while they were both training with William Burn. Like Shaw he was experimenting with different styles, especially variations on vernacular architecture, and Loughton is a fine example of his picturesque old English style. The house stands next to the little flint church of St John the Baptist, which was once the parish church; but as the village developed on lower land to the west it was replaced in 1846 by a much larger church about a mile away, and St John's was rebuilt by Maitland in 1877, in effect becoming his private chapel. The high brick walls dividing

278 Loughton Hall in Essex, a listed house designed by Nesfield in 1878, is empty, boarded up and in poor condition. It is awaiting redevelopment.

the grounds from the churchyard are possibly 17th-century, although Nesfield cut a gate through to give Maitland direct access to the church. The house has a nearly symmetrical entrance front of two main storeys and a high hipped roof with attics, but two projecting bays rise through the attic storey giving it a strong vertical emphasis. Like many houses of this type the materials and windows are eclectic: the house is mainly of warm red brick with rubbed red brick detailing and a tiled roof, with sash windows on the ground floor and casements above; but the bays are plastered and have high four-light leaded windows on the upper floor. The entrance is asymmetrically placed in one bay, emphasised by a projecting porch topped with a wooden balustrade, and there is a low service wing to the east. The roof has a small bell tower topped by a weathervane, curiously placed to one side and almost hidden by the gables and tall brick chimneys. The effect of the whole is accomplished and welcoming. The wide hall leads straight through the house with the oak staircase opening from it to one side, with the main reception rooms facing south over the gardens. After the Second World War Loughton was zoned for development and the new estate of Debden was planned to the north. Commander Maitland sold 644 acres to the LCC and the house was left empty, although it was intended to preserve it as a community centre for the new residents. It was soon vandalised and the lead stripped from the roof, leading to serious dry rot. In 1951 an unsympathetic restoration began which removed much of the Nesfield detailing, after which it served as a school, community centre and college. Recently Essex County Council decided that the Grade 2 listed house was surplus to requirements and it has been sold to a private developer, who applied for planning permission to turn it into a residential care home. The house is in a very poor state, empty and boarded up, with dry rot in one of the gables and broken windows. Its future does not look hopeful.

D.J. Ebbetts, *Examples of Decorative Wrought Ironwork …* 1879, pl. 6; C. Aslet, 'The Country Houses of W.E. Nesfield', *Country Life*, 23 March 1978, pp.766-9; *The Builder*, 4 May 1951, pp.624-6; *The Guardian*, 22 October 2007; Essex County Council Planning Permission EPF/2131/06.

MILL HILL

BELMONT

Belmont and Holcombe House are the two most distinguished houses crowning Mill Hill, and both were built within the same decade. Peter Hamond, a brewer, began buying land in the parish of Hendon in 1768 and eventually built up a small estate. He was interested enough in architecture to subscribe to James Paine's *Plans, Elevations and Sections ... of Houses*, published in 1767. He employed Paine's son, also James, as his architect and the house was built 1771-3. This is the younger Paine's only major work before he switched his not very considerable energies to watercolours, but it is an interesting house and shows what he might have achieved had he continued in his father's profession. Belmont is much larger than Holcombe House, a five-bay three-storey house built of stock brick with minimal stone enrichments: a shallow parapet and string courses. The house has a plan of varied room shapes and some curious features, all designed to break its mass in unusual ways. The entrance was on the west side facing The Ridgeway, and had a two-storey elliptical bow which formed an entrance hall on the ground floor and a balcony on the first with a plain brick pediment above. (The ground floor bow has been rebuilt and the balcony glazed, but their form can still be seen.) The corners on the south side are chamfered and there is another plain brick pediment above a thermal window; below that is a deep recess framed in stone columns. The two windows set in the angles light the octagonal rooms within. On the first floor these open onto a balcony with delicate ironwork, on the ground floor they lead into the garden. On the east side a verandah was added in the 19th century, giving a homely look to this more irregular façade. An elevation of the entrance front shows that Paine had more ambitious ideas, perhaps cut back by his client in the interests of economy, but it is still an interesting design that breaks away from the ordinary run of late 18th-century villas. Hamond died in 1794 and the house changed hands several times before being bought in 1820 by Sir Charles Flower Bt., Lord Mayor of the City of London, who enlarged the estate considerably before his death in 1835. It was probably during his ownership that the lodge was added and a small castellated dairy with a Gothic window and a triple arcade, designed

279 Mill Hill, Belmont, from the S-W. The house was designed 1771 by James Paine the Younger. The recessed balcony overlooked the gardens.

by Robert Williams, was built nearby; these remain. His 441-acre estate was split up after his death, but because of its hilltop position and poor communications the little village of Mill Hill remained less touched by the expansion of London than surrounding areas. Its healthy atmosphere, well away from the smog of central London, meant that it was a favoured spot for schools, and in 1912 Belmont was bought by Mill Hill School for £6,700. At that time it was ivy-covered and had a large conservatory projecting from the south side. The ivy and the conservatory have both been removed, restoring this side of the house to its 18th-century appearance. New school buildings have been added to the north or service side of the house, but it remains in good condition with much of its interior intact and still has fine views over Green Belt land.

P. Leach, 'James Paine Junior: an unbuilt architect', *Architectural History*, 27, 1984, pp.392-405; BL Add. MS 31,323 AAA; *VCH* 'Middlesex' 5, 1976, pp.21-3; Cherry & Pevsner, *London 4*, pp.176-7; Mill Hill School archives; R. Braithwaite, *'Strikingly Alive', The History of the Mill Hill School Foundation 1807-2007*, Phillimore & Co. Ltd, 2007.

HOLCOMBE HOUSE

This very elegant small neo-classical house was built for a City merchant. In 1775 John Anderson, a Danzig glove merchant and Lord Mayor in 1797-8, bought the land. It was just to the west of The Ridgeway, then a more important road than it is today, and close to the hilltop settlement of Mill Hill. He chose John Johnson, Surveyor to the County of Essex, as his architect. The house was built 1775-8 and although now flanked by large late 19th-century buildings it is remarkably unaltered. Neat gate piers with urns announce the entrance into the forecourt; the three-bay house has a ground floor of rusticated stucco, left unpainted to resemble stonework: Johnson was promoting a type of stucco in competition with the Adam brothers at this time. The front has depressed arches and Coade stone keystones flanking the domed semi-circular porch. The first floor is smoothly stuccoed with the bays separated by paired pilasters, and the roof is hidden by a balustrade. The stables were on the south side of the forecourt (demolished) and a lower service wing was built on the south side. The old kitchen is still in use and retains its simple large stone fireplace. The steep fall in the ground behind the house not only means that it has a magnificent view west, but also

280   Mill Hill, Holcombe House by John Johnson, 1775. Entrance front with 1889 chapel on the right added by St Joseph's Missionary College.

that it has a well-lit basement. On this side attic windows pierce the balustrade, so the house is larger than appears at first glance, and it is neatly planned. The small circular entrance hall contains the elegant cantilevered staircase with its S-scroll wrought-iron balustrade. A small groin-vaulted lobby leads to the main reception rooms, both of which have lost their original chimneypieces but have retained their delicate neo-classical plasterwork. The two-bay drawing room has large circular panels on the walls with low-relief female figures in the centre and a figure of Eros over the chimneypiece. The three-bay dining room has plain walls but the ceiling has painted panels inset in the plasterwork. In both rooms the long windows reach down to the floor, drawing visitors to the extensive views westwards. Sir John Anderson died in 1813 and the house was then bought by John Shuter of Montreal, who became Deputy Lieutenant of Middlesex. The house remained the property of his widow till 1854, and of his brother till 1866. At that date the Roman Catholic church was setting up educational establishments and the house was bought by Father Herbert Vaughan, later Cardinal Vaughan, as a base while St Joseph's Missionary College was built next to it by the architects Goldie & Child; in 1889 they added the large red brick chapel to the north. The site remained in use as a college and school until 1977, when it was bought by the Missionary Institute London. This has carefully maintained the Grade 2 listed house but can no longer afford the upkeep of all these buildings, and the site is to be sold. Will it remain in as good condition as it is at present?

English Heritage files; Cherry & Pevsner, *London 4*, p.178; information from the Missionary Institute.

RAINHAM

RAINHAM HALL

This well-preserved house is a fine example of Early Georgian architecture in an area where little remains of the past. Rainham today has an old village centre surrounded by modern housing and industrial estates, with the Essex marshes extending to the Thames in the distance. Rainham Hall is itself part of that industrial scene, as it was built in 1729 by a sea-captain turned businessman called John Harle (1688-1742). He came from Northumberland and aged 30 married a well-off widow from Stepney; it may have been her money which allowed him to buy land where the River Inglebourne flows through the village and to build Rainham Wharf on its banks. Barges could reach the Thames from Rainham, and Captain Harle set up a successful business bringing corn and other agricultural produce from Essex to Rainham, then shipping it on to London. The city was undergoing one of its periodic building booms and he also shipped stone and other building materials, and brought coals and timber from his contacts in the Newcastle area. The house he built is a little old-fashioned in appearance, with hardly a trace of Palladianism. It stands next to the church, a tall five-bay house of three main storeys with a semi-basement and attics. Its quality is immediately apparent: it is built of stock brick with rubbed red brick window surrounds; the parapet has red and blue headers arranged in a chequerboard pattern; the quoins and keystones are of Portland stone, as is the string-course between the basement and ground floor. All these are materials which Harle was shipping. A quirky detail is the use of stone bollards shaped like skittles to protect the areas in front of the basement windows. The central bay projects slightly and the front porch is a *tour-de-force* of woodcarving, with its coffered segmental pediment

281   Rainham Hall, entrance front. The house was built by Captain John Harle in 1729 close to his business premises on Rainham Wharf.

and Corinthian columns. The east-facing garden front of the house is almost identical except that the tall staircase window is slightly off-centre, pointing to the house being the work of a competent local builder rather than an architect. The rainwater heads have the initials of John and Mary Harle and the date 1729. There is a fine wrought-iron gate separating the house from its forecourt also with their initials; at the back a pair of gate piers survives with a similar iron gate, although the formal gardens to which they must have led have gone. Beside the house is a two-storey brick range with a hipped roof and wooden eaves cornice; this pre-dates the house and was probably Harle's office. Nearby another range had stables and a coach house. In plan the house is simple, one of the many examples of the four rooms to a floor type. The front door opens into a marble-floored entrance hall, with the staircase at the back and a passage to the garden door. On one side two panelled parlours are divided by a deep chimneybreast, which allows a small closet off each room. The other corner was the kitchen, as it has a wide stone fireplace and a small service stair leading from basement to attics. A wide arch leads from the hall to the stairs which have finely turned balusters; the arched staircase window is flanked by Doric pilasters; the staircase walls are plastered and have panels painted with festoons of flowers. None of the rooms is large, most are panelled and have simple marble or stone chimneypieces. When Harle died in 1742 the house went to his son, then to his widow and it remained in her family until 1895, one of the reasons for its preservation. After the First World War it was bought by Colonel Mulliner, who carefully restored the rather dilapidated house and also researched Harle and his business interests. In 1949 the house went to the National Trust; a small part of the house is open to the public, while the upper floors are let as offices and a flat.

Cherry & Pevsner, *London 5*, pp.187-8; T. Small & C. Woodbridge, *Rainham Hall*, 1928; N. Lloyd *A History of English Brickwork*, 1925, pp.69, 232-3; A. Tipping, *English Homes*, 5, 1, 1921, pp.237-46; A. Richardson & H. Donaldson Eberlien, *The Smaller English House*, 1925, pls. 51-4.

ROEHAMPTON

DOWNSHIRE HOUSE

On the west side of Roehampton Lane and close to the road is an austere three-storey brick house, six bays wide with a lower canted bay added to the north. This is Downshire House, one of several country houses in this area which in the 18th and early 19th centuries belonged to well connected families for their occasional use. It is less architecturally distinguished than Roehampton House almost opposite. Its core is an earlier house, which in 1664 was assessed at eight hearths, and was then occupied by the retired agent to the Earl of Portland, who had lived at the much more imposing Grove House nearby. In 1769 the Hon. General James Cholmondeley bought it, and it is said that he rebuilt it. But an examination of the house shows this to be incorrect. The plain frontage must predate his ownership: its

contrasting brickwork and slightly arched windows point to an early 18th-century date, as does the front door with its robust Doric pilasters and segmental pediment. The entrance hall with its stone floor and simple marble chimneypiece could date from *c*.1710-20, as could the woodwork. But there are puzzles: the oak staircase is of early 18th-century type but appears much later, and there is some mid-18th-century work. The hall has an overmantel of rather coarse Rococo plasterwork, while the addition with the canted bay has a good chimneypiece of *c*.1740. All this work would predate Cholmondeley's ownership. However he did manage to buy more land on which to build stables and outbuildings, and there was a service wing, since demolished, to the south. It then went to George James, 4th Earl of Cholmondeley and to two other owners before being bought by Arthur Hill, 2nd Marquess of Downshire in 1798, whose

282 Roehampton, Downshire House. The early 18th-century Doric entrance.

name was given to the house. He immediately employed Robert Furze Brettingham, a minor architect (and grandson of Matthew Brettingham) to do some unspecified work there, and he also surveyed the grounds. Downshire, whose country house was Hillsborough in Co. Down, died in 1801, but his widow, who had become Baroness Sandys of Ombersley in her own right, remained in the house till her death in 1836. It changed hands many times after that, and in the early 20th century more work was carried out: the garden front was refaced and another canted bay added to it, while the drawing room inside was given florid Edwardian decorative details. Unlike the major Roehampton houses it was not requisitioned during the Second World War, and remained a private house till 1949. Since then it has, like the other houses, been in institutional use. It is now part of Roehampton University and is used as offices.

D. Gerhold, *Villas & Mansions of Roehampton & Putney Heath*, 1997, p.20; Cherry & Pevsner, *London 2*, p.692.

SOUTHGATE

BROOMFIELD HOUSE

One of the saddest sights in my research for this book was that of Broomfield, the shell of the house glimpsed behind scaffolding and hoardings while the LB of Enfield considers the options for restoration. It sits in the middle of a small park, overlooking a lake and not far from the much grander house on the hilltop, Arnos Grove. But the same artist decorated the staircase at both, so the interior of Broomfield belied its modest exterior. It was a timber-framed farm house bought by a City merchant, Geoffrey Walkenden, in 1566; the present entrance hall in the north range is one of the additions he made. In 1606 it was bought by Sir John Spencer (of Canonbury House) as an investment. Yet another City merchant, Joseph Jackson, owned it by 1624 and added a wing to the north. He probably also added the gateway to the east, built in English bond brickwork and a simplified version of the gateway at Forty Hall. The house remained in the Jackson family for the next 150 years and no major changes were made until the early 18th century when new gardens were laid out and the interior updated. The wooden alcove seat facing west over the garden must date from this time. With its pediment, Ionic columns and panelled back it is an elegant example of a once common type, but it too deserves better treatment. Inside the house panelling, fine chimneypieces and overmantels were installed in the main rooms on the ground and first floors and a new oak staircase was put in, with three fluted and twisted balusters to each step. In 1726 the artist Gerard Lanscroon was called in to paint the walls and ceiling. (These paintings were formerly attributed to both Thornhill and Laguerre.) He had come over from Flanders to work with Verrio, and established an independent practice working very much in Verrio's style; this commission follows shortly after his work at Arnos Grove. The walls, painted in oil on plaster, show mythological figures including Flora, Mercury and Vulcan, and there are figures representing the four seasons and the muses. The ceiling has a curious central female figure holding a carpenter's plane, flanked by a figure of Victory. In 1816 the house was inherited by Mr and Mrs Lybbe Powys who modernised it, removing the gables from the east and west fronts, adding a Tuscan portico to the entrance front and refacing the north wing in stock bricks. The stuccoed front showed no trace of its timber-framed origins, but curiously this was revived in 1928 when non-structural timber-framing was added to this west front; so the house has both an inner and an outer layer of timber-framing, with the Regency stucco surface in between. By this time the house had been sold: the last tenant left in 1901 and most of the land was sold for development. Southgate Urban District Council bought the house and 54 acres of the grounds for £25,000 and opened Broomfield Park in 1903. The house languished with no particular purpose until local opinion was mobilised by the discovery of mammoth bones in the area. It was decided to open the house as a local museum, with the startling combination of mammoth bones and Lanscroon paintings as the principal attractions. The guidebook states reassuringly that it 'does not wish to

283 Southgate, Broomfield, staircase hall with ceiling painted by Lanscroon in 1726. This has been in store since the house was badly burnt.

compete with the great National Museums'. Nor did it, but the end of the museum was due more to fire than to inertia: in 1984 a fire damaged the roof and upper floor, including the painted ceiling which was removed by the LB of Enfield to safe storage. Further arson attacks resulted in more fire damage in 1993 and 1994. The house is now an empty shell, supported by scaffolding and covered with a temporary roof. In 2008 no further progress had been made towards a solution, in spite of the foundation of Broomfield Historic Buildings Trust, set up by local residents specifically to prevent demolition of a Grade 2 listed building and to encourage the Council to start restoration work.

S. Brindle, *Broomfield: an Illustrated History of the House & Garden*, 1994; Richard Lea, *Broomfield House, Enfield: the Structural History of the House*, 1994; anon., *Brief History of the Museum*, 1955.

TOTTENHAM

THE PRIORY

Tottenham in the 17th century was a thriving village, almost a small town. The City was six miles away, easily accessible via Ermine Street, the old Roman road and still the main route to the north. It was dominated by Bruce Castle, but had many other substantial houses which were let to lawyers and City families. Of these only one survives, which since 1906 has been the Vicarage for All Hallows, the original parish church. It is set back from Church Lane and is approached by fine early 18th-century wrought iron gates, not original to the house but moved from the former vicarage at 776 High Road. Joseph Fenton bought the property in 1613 and in 1619 took out a 21-year lease on 179 acres of demesne land. He was a barber-surgeon in London and *c*.1620 rebuilt the existing timber-framed building, remains of which have been found within the brick walls of the present house. (Tottenham was noted for its brickfields at this time.) It is a five-bay house on two floors below a high-pitched tiled roof with attics, and has a projecting wing to the north. The garden front has a late 18th-century

284 Tottenham, The Priory, rebuilt by Joseph Fenton in 1620. His arms and rebus are on the ceiling of the dining room, and a finely carved chimney piece was added *c.*1740.

extension with a shallow bow. It is a modest exterior apart from the early 18th-century doorcase, but the interiors are interesting. The dining room has an exceptionally fine plasterwork ceiling with vines and foliage on the ribs and moulded decoration in the panels; it has Fenton's name and his rebus, a tun, in the centre of a strapwork cartouche. This room *c.*1740 was given a richly carved Palladian chimneypiece and overmantel, and the staircase was replaced at the same time. Another room has Jacobean panelling and a carved overmantel, one oval framing Fenton's name, the other the date 1621 – the later date showing that woodwork always went in after the plastering had been completed. By the late 19th century it was known as Carr's Farm, and was rather dilapidated. Tottenham had rapidly expanded due to the Great Eastern Railway, and it was bought by the LCC in the early 20th century for demolition. It was saved by the vicar, the Rev. Denton Jones, who bought it, restored it and made it into the vicarage, which it remains.

W. Bedwell, *A Briefe Description of Tottenham*, 1631, reprinted 1717; Cherry & Pevsner, *London 4*, p.585; F. Fisk, *History of Tottenham* 1913, p.138; *VCH* 'Middlesex' 5, pp.335, 350.

TWICKENHAM

KNELLER HALL

This house is not in the fashionable riverside part of Twickenham but in the hamlet of Whitton to the N-W, close to Hounslow Heath. The mid-19th-century Jacobethan house we see today masks the house built by the German artist Sir Godfrey Kneller in the early 18th century, then called Whitton Hall. Kneller (1646-1723) had arrived in England in 1676 and had immediately become a successful portrait painter, appointed Principal Painter to the king in 1688. His career was unaffected by the many changes of monarch, and he was rewarded with a knighthood and baronetcy. He was also well-educated, well-travelled and enormously successful. He lived splendidly and as well as his house in the Covent Garden area he wanted a country estate within easy reach of Hampton Court. He bought the estate at Whitton with about 100 acres of land and replaced the mid-17th-century house. A datestone recorded, 'The building of this house was begun by Sir Godfrey Kneller, Bart., A.D. 1709.' Our main evidence for it is the bird's-eye view *c.*1715 by Johannes Kip which shows an imposing two-storey house, the bays arranged as 1-2-3-2-1. It has a hipped roof

285 Twickenham, Kneller Hall, entrance front. George Mair's neo-Jacobean school buildings encased the old house in 1848.

with a central cupola and four corner gables or towers. In Kip's print these appear to be shaped gables, which would be an unlikely feature at this time; but a self-portrait by Kneller has a detail of the house in the background which shows that these were corner domes with concave sides. Two low wings on each side open directly into the gardens – these may have been orangeries. Wren or an architect in his circle, such as Robert Hooke, has been suggested as the architect; he and Kneller both worked for the Crown and in 1711 Kneller presented Wren with a portrait, possibly in gratitude. Here according to Vertue Kneller 'lives in summer courted by all people of honour and distinction'.

The south-facing brick house was set back slightly from the road (now Kneller Road) behind a walled forecourt with statues; grand iron gates allowed passers-by a glimpse of the façade. The gardens to the side and behind the house included a kitchen garden and orchard as well as pleasure gardens. There was a wide central *allée* leading to an avenue in open country beyond the garden enclosures. Some elements of the plan of the house can be guessed from a later record drawing in LMA, showing a large through hall in the centre. So on entering the house one would have a view through it and down the central axis of the gardens beyond. There were apartments with closets on each side of the hall, most with corner fireplaces. The main staircase was on the west side and was possibly painted by Kneller, although Vertue also records a 'small staircase' painted by Laguerre with an allegory of painting; this may be the secondary staircase in the N-E corner. The semi-basement had a groin-vaulted room below the hall, supported with four columns. Other service rooms were in separate buildings on the west side, including stables. The Kip print shows cows and poultry as well as horses in the enclosures beside the house.

The house was sold after Kneller's death and belonged to Sir Samuel Prime who landscaped the grounds. He probably added the irregular lake which can be seen in early OS maps. Charles Calvert, a brewer and MP, employed Philip Hardwick *c.*1830 to replace Kneller's low side wings with a drawing room and dining room, linked by a conservatory across the south front of Kneller's house. When his widow died in 1841 the house had 102 acres; but it soon ceased to be a private house. It was bought by the Privy Council on Education to become a teacher training college, and the architect George Mair was appointed to rebuild and enlarge it for its new purpose. Mair's building was described in *The Builder* as being based on Wollaton Hall, but this is very loosely interpreted. The new house was of brick with stone enrichments; the centre had a pair of lead ogival towers flanking large windows; the single-storey side wings were raised to three storeys and had balustrades with strapwork panels; and Calvert's conservatory was replaced by a screen with stone arches. Gas lighting was installed, furnaces for central heating were put in the basement, and steam power was used for the laundry. The work was carried out by Sir John Kelk, the building contractor who bought Bentley Priory in 1852. This, remarkably unchanged, is the building we see today. *The Builder* records that Kneller's house was dilapidated and 'was consequently taken down'. But is this true? The evidence of Mair's 1848 drawings suggests that much of the nine-bay main block of Kneller's house was simply encased in the new fabric; the through hall remained, and the vaulted central room in the basement. The college was not a success and the school closed in 1856. The building was taken over by the Army to become the Royal Military School of Music, which it remains.

LMA ACC/1155 1-9 drawings by Mair dated February 1848; LMA ACC/1155 10-20 drawings by Mair dated June 1848; *Walpole Society*, 18, Vertue 1, pp.27-8; 20, Vertue 2, pp.68, 121-5; 22, Vertue 3, p. 43; *The Builder*, 8, 9 February 1850, pp. 66-8; J. Harris, 'Kneller Hall, Middlesex', *The Country Seat*, 1970, pp.81-4; Roger de Piles, *The Art of Painting*, 1725, copy in BL with inserted 'Life of Sir Godfrey Kneller.'

YORK HOUSE

This imposing house, set back from a busy road in the centre of Twickenham, is now a sprawling complex of council offices with at its heart a 17th-century house. It was built on land belonging in the 15th and 16th centuries to the Yorke family, hence its name. By 1636 it was owned by a courtier, Andrew Pitcarne, as his suburban house, Twickenham being usefully placed within easy reach of London, Hampton Court and Windsor by road or river. He may have rebuilt the house, which in Moses Glover's 1635 map is covered in scaffolding. In 1656 his heirs sold 'Yorke Farm' as it was then called to Edward Montagu, 2nd Earl of Manchester, who resold it soon after the Restoration to Lord Cornbury for £3,500. Here the picture becomes confusing, for he was the eldest son of Edward Hyde, 1st Earl of Clarendon, who lived there and paid the local taxes. It seems that it was bought in the son's name, perhaps to protect his interests in case of Clarendon's fall from favour. When this did indeed happen it remained Cornbury's property, but when Clarendon died in exile it was left to his younger son Lawrence, later 1st Earl of Rochester. York House was clearly a very substantial house by Clarendon's time, as his house was assessed at 37 hearths in 1664, and 43 in 1666. He later sold it to Sir Charles Tufton, who may have transformed the early 17th-century house. What we see today is a three-storey brick house of seven bays, built of brick with stone dressings, the entrance front facing north. It is a truncated H-plan, the outer bays emphasised by separate hipped roofs. A deep cornice wraps round the house, its horizontality contrasting with the verticality of the design, which is emphasised by tall panelled brick chimneystacks on the side walls. There may have been a central cupola giving access to the main roof, although this is not shown in Ironside's view of 1786; this would have given glorious views over the gardens to the Thames. In plan the entrance hall led to

286 Twickenham, York House, late 17th-century. Garden front with extensions made for the exiled Comte de Paris and his son.

a room of equal size facing the gardens, flanked by three rooms each side. But today the hall has 19th-century Jacobean woodwork and plasterwork, and the main staircase is also 19th-century. Later owners made many alterations and additions, and few rooms have any original decoration. Many owners and tenants succeeded the Tuftons, including the Austrian ambassador who leased the house 1796-1818. It was then bought by the sculptress Mrs Damer, whose godfather was Horace Walpole. She had been made his executrix and had inherited nearby Strawberry Hill from him. She had given that up but knew York House well, having been a friend of Count von Starhemberg, the ambassador. She added a studio and lived there for the last ten years of her life and left it to her cousin, the distinguished lawyer and colonial administrator Sir Alexander Johnston. Since they spent many years in India and Sri Lanka the house was mainly let; it was inherited by their unmarried daughters, who in 1864 sold it to the Comte de Paris, one of several members of the French royal family living in exile in England. The house took on its superficially French appearance, with French windows and external louvred shutters. Their eldest son, the Duc d'Orléans, came back to the house after a period in English ownership, and enlarged it still further. But the most remarkable addition was made by his successor, the Indian merchant and philanthropist Sir Ratan Tata, who bought the house in 1906. The gardens of York House are divided by a lane running parallel to the river, a little pedestrian bridge connecting the two. He heard of some sculptures carved recently in Rome by Andreoni and delivered to a house in Sussex, the owner of which had committed suicide after being accused of fraud. In his riverside garden Tata built an amazing fountain for the sculptures, its luscious nymphs posing provocatively among shells, rocks and sea-horses. When Twickenham Urban District Council bought the house from his widow in 1924 the sculptures were startling white marble set against an evergreen niche. Now the LB of Richmond upon Thames seems embarrassed by their presence; the fountain is dry and the whole shut away behind rusty wire fences, as if to protect the public from such a riotous scene.

T. H. R. Cashmore, 'York House, Twickenham', *Local History Paper* No.4, 1990; LMA ACC/1789/006/02, Sale Particulars 1873; J. Payan, 'The Statues in York House Gardens in Twickenham' 1995, Twickenham Museum Archive; E. Ironside, 'A View of Twickenham' 1786.

TWYFORD

THE ELMS

A good Early Georgian brick house set back from the main road to Ealing, this house has similarities to Iver Grove in Buckinghamshire, attributed to John James. The Elms (also known as The Paddocks and Acton House) was built in 1735, probably by a London builder, at which time the owner was Henry Lloyd. Did he build it as a speculation, having inherited the land from his step-father? He did not keep the house, selling it in 1737 to Sir Joseph Ayscoffe Bt., a distinguished antiquarian who was Keeper of the State Paper Office; he also had a London house. The five-bay house has two main storeys over a semi-basement; it is built of brick, with rubbed red brick detailing. The south-facing entrance front has giant Doric pilasters supporting a steep pediment, while the garden front has angle pilasters of brick and had a central door into the garden, now a window. The windows are slightly arched with prominent keystones, and a bold cornice wraps round the whole house. In plan it is a double-pile house with four rooms to a floor. The fine cantilevered oak staircase has three twisted balusters to a tread, Corinthian newel posts and richly carved decoration on the tread-ends and along the landing; the secondary staircase is tucked behind it. The saloon, unusually, is at the front of the house, and had ceiling paintings by Sleter which have been removed to the V & A and Gunnersbury Museum. The rooms are mainly panelled, and the attic floor has four good-sized bedrooms with generously high ceilings and some original stone chimneypieces still *in situ*. In 1749 Samuel Wegg bought the house and added the two side wings. The two-storey east wing had a kitchen with a brick colonnade in front; the single-storey west wing contained one large room with a canted bay, but both these extensions have been much altered. The Wegg family lived there till 1842, when it was inherited by a cousin and leased to a succession of tenants. By the mid-20th century it was still lived in but the nearby farm buildings had become industrial premises, it was in poor condition and its future looked bleak. It was saved by Middlesex County Council, which bought it in 1954 for use as a school, replacing the industrial premises to the north and east with new school buildings; it is now flourishing as the Twyford Church of England High School, with the main house largely in office use.

T. & A. Harper-Smith, *The Elms*; Cherry & Pevsner, *London 3*, pp.158-9.

287   Twyford, The Elms, entrance front, *c*.1735. A large drawing room was added on the left in the mid-18th century.

WALTHAMSTOW

WATER HOUSE

Forest Road in Walthamstow is a main east–west route, built up and busy, and set back slightly on the north side is a bow-fronted brick house set in a small park. This was William Morris's family home, and is now the William Morris Gallery, a museum with a particularly impressive collection of Arts & Crafts paintings, furniture, textiles and stained glass. The early history of the site is unclear; behind the house is a moat, fed by a tributary of the River Lea. It may have had a house on it, but possibly had just an orchard and fishponds, with a house on slightly higher ground where the present house stands. The small estate belonged in the mid-17th century to the royalist Sir Thomas Merry, and then to William Piers, the Bishop of Bath and Wells. The present house was probably rebuilt as a speculation *c*.1745 (as a brick dated 1744 was recently identified in the east wall) by Thomas and Catherine Woolball; in their daughter's marriage settlement of 1756 it was described as 'lately rebuilt'. It was a three-storey house with four rooms to a floor, but later in the 18th century the south front was rebuilt in yellow stock brick laid in header bond, with deep bows enhancing all the front rooms. (This improvement is similar to the new south front at Valentines, not far away in Ilford.) This contrasts with the darker brick and slightly arched windows of the north or garden front, which is old-fashioned for its date. Most of the rooms retain their panelling, and several have good early 18th-century stone or marble chimneypieces. These, combined with some earlier panelling on the top floor, suggest that earlier material was re-used. The best feature of the house is the exceptionally wide hall running through the house on the two main floors, with an impressive cantilevered staircase of Spanish chestnut going to the first floor only. The landing has imposing Palladian doorcases opening off it, and the original secondary staircase is tucked in parallel to the main one. One-storey wings were built each side, the east one with kitchen and laundry (demolished *c*.1900) and the west wing with

288 Walthamstow, Water House, entrance front from the S-W. The *c*.1750 house was refaced with bows in the late 18th century. Until recently this was the William Morris Gallery.

additional reception rooms (now galleries). The poorly-lit basement was always cellars and storage space rather than servants' accommodation. The widowed Mrs Morris took the house from 1848-56, when William was at school and university; but he spent his holidays there, and swam, fished and boated on the moat with his brothers and sisters. After Mrs Morris left the house was bought by the local newspaper proprietor Edward Lloyd, who lived there for about 30 years with his large family. He added the rustic bridge which still crosses the moat, and the thatched boathouse which has gone. But the area changed once the Great Eastern Railway built a station in Walthamstow in 1870, and streets of low-cost housing rapidly followed. In 1885 Lloyd left, and his executors in 1898 offered 9½ acres and the house to the council to provide public open space; the remaining 86 acres were sold as 'ripe for immediate development'. Lloyd Park was opened in 1899, and the house was used as a school, a clinic and as offices. It was only after the Frank Brangwyn gift to Walthamstow and the increased interest post-War in William Morris and his circle that it was converted into the William Morris Gallery, fortunately leaving the fabric of the house intact; the gallery was opened by Clement Attlee in 1950. But the future of the house as a museum is unclear at present, with the LB of Waltham Forest making cuts in funding which threaten its survival.

Cherry, O'Brien & Pevsner, *London 5*, p.751; Kim Page, 'Lloyd Park: how a Medieval Moated Garden in Waltham Forest became a Public Park' Birkbeck College, Garden History MA, 2002; R. Cardew, 'The Water House', draft dissertation for North London Polytechnic 1977-9; 'Attested copy of Deed … 1756 …', *Walthamstow Antiquarian Society Monographs*, 11, 1923, p.30; Editorial, *Burlington Magazine*, June 2007, p.375; photographs in William Morris Gallery Archives (hereafter WMG) WMG 020/28, 31, 38 & 46; WMG V2/Z2525, 2526, 2379.

WIMBLEDON

WIMBLEDON RECTORY

The house nestles against the hillside below the parish church of Wimbledon, and at first glance looks like a rambling mainly 20th-century building. Then the steep tiled roof, small windows and brick tower point to its early Tudor origins. A small vaulted room probably dates back to the 13th century, so an earlier house must have stood on the same site. But it is best known as the first suburban house of William Cecil, later Lord Burghley and Secretary of State to Elizabeth I from 1558 until his death forty years later. Known as Wimbledon Parsonage in the early 16th century, it had probably been recently rebuilt. It was the home of well-paid rectors, and was a substantial brick house with barns, outbuildings and glebe land. At the Reformation it briefly became Crown property, before going to the Dean and Chapter of Worcester. They put the poorly paid vicar in rented accommodation in the village and let the house to a succession of courtiers. William Cecil took it over in 1550, when he was leading a retired life during the reign of Queen Mary; his rent was £49 *p.a.*, quite a substantial sum. The house and its 24 acres provided a home for his son Thomas by his first marriage, as well as the growing family he had with his second wife. But Cecil turned his attentions to his Hertfordshire estate of Theobalds after 1564, and the house was sub-let to friends from 1568. His son Thomas, later Earl of Exeter, had built up a substantial estate at Wimbledon before he built Wimbledon Manor House *c.*1585, down-grading the Rectory to an adjunct of the new house, and it was used over the next two centuries as a dower house, a laundry and a dairy. The Parliamentary Survey of 1649 gives the most

289 Wimbledon Rectory, entrance front. William Cecil lived here 1550-68. The remaining part of the
*c.*1500 house with its octagonal tower is in the centre, with 19th- and 20th-century additions each side.

detailed description of it, probably unchanged since the mid-16th century. It had a great
hall, withdrawing room, parlour and little chamber (this may be the ancient vaulted room)
and plentiful service rooms on the ground floor; there were ten chambers, five closets and
a gallery on the first floor, with attic rooms above. Outside were the usual brewhouse,
bakehouse, barns and stables, as well as two dovecots and a summerhouse. Its later history was
closely linked with Thomas Cecil's Wimbledon House which was sold by the Cecils in 1639.
When that was demolished *c.*1720, so was part of the Rectory, with the remaining wing
let to a farmer. Repairs were carried out in the 1770s when it was used by Earl Spencer's
agent, but it was in a state of picturesque decay when two watercolours were made of it in
the early 19th century, and it was empty for some time in the mid-19th century. In 1882
Samuel Wilson bought the house for £6,000, added the battlemented wing and brought
in early chimneypieces and doors from other houses; he also embellished the two acres of
gardens. By the 20th century its large and secluded gardens and its attractive position, close
to the centre of Wimbledon and within easy reach of central London, meant that it became
an increasingly valuable private house, and a succession of owners have enlarged and altered
it, leaving little of the original fabric visible.

C. Knight, 'The Cecils at Wimbledon', *Patronage, Culture & Power: the Early Cecils* 2002, pp.47-54; 'The Survy of the Rectory
of Wymblidon [*sic*]' NA Exchequer 317/71; R. Milward, *The Rectory, Wimbledon's Oldest House*, 1992.

NOTES

PART ONE

INTRODUCTION

1. D. Defoe, *A Tour through the Whole Island of Great Britain*, 1724, p.126.
2. P. Morant, *The History & Antiquities of the County of Essex*, 1, 1768, p.1.
3. *Walpole Society*, 'The Book of Architecture of John Thorpe' ed. J. Summerson, 40, 1966, T62, T225 & T226.
4. S. Switzer, *Ichnographia Rustica*, 1, 1718, p.xl.
5. C. Campbell, *Vitruvius Britannicus*, 1, 1715, pl. 28.
6. M-A. Garry, *An Uncommon Tenant, Fitzroy & Holkham 1808-32*, 1996, p.3.
7. J.B. Papworth, *Designs for Rural Residences*, 1818, p.89.
8. John Aubrey, notes for his 'Natural History of Wiltshire', Bodleian Library, MS Aubrey 2.
9. P. Leith-Ross, 'The Garden of John Evelyn at Deptford', *Garden History*, 25, no. 2, 1997, pp.138-52. A plan of the house and garden of Sayes Court *c*.1653-4 is in the British Library, Add. MS 78628.
10. R. Duthie, 'The Planting of some 17th century Flower Gardens', *Garden History*, 17-18, 1989-90, pp.77-102.
11. S. Morris, 'Legacy of a Bishop: the Trees, Shrubs & Plants introduced to the Gardens of Fulham Palace 1675-1713', *Garden History*, 19, 1991-2 pp.47-59; and 21, 1993-4, pp.14-23.
12. *Humphry Repton's 'Memoirs'*, ed. A. Gore & G. Carter, 2005.
13. The sale document for Hampton Court House is a good example of this.
14. *A Regency Visitor: the English Tour of Prince Pückler-Muskau, described in his Letters 1826-1828*, translated S. Austin, ed. E.M. Butler, 1957.
15. J. Strype ed., *Stow's Survey of London*, 2 vols., 1720.
16. D. Lysons, *The Environs of London*, 4 vols., 1792-6.
17. W. Watts, *Seats of the Nobility & Gentry*, 1787, illustrates no fewer than 14 suburban houses.

Chapter I MANNERS AND MONEY: THE SOCIAL CONTEXT

1. R. Garnier, 'Broom House, Fulham', *Georgian Group Journal*, 13, 2003, pp.168-80.
2. For instance the Pitts lived at Hayes Place, Bromley, close to their cousins the Stanhopes at Chevening; diaries and letters record many visits between the two families. In Twickenham Alexander Pope and Lady Suffolk were good friends and neighbours, as was Horace Walpole at Strawberry Hill.
3. Sassoon put on 'English Conversation Pieces' in 1930 and 'The Age of Walnut' in 1932. They took place in his London house and raised money for charity.
4. John, Viscount Perceval was created 1st Earl of Egmont in 1733. *Diary of Lord Egmont* 1, 1920, pp.149,166.
5. Farington's *Diary*, 1982, 8, p.3111, entry for Monday 24 August 1807.
6. Evelyn described the servants at Charlton making 'our coachmen so drunk that they both fell off their boxes upon the heath [Blackheath] where we were fain to leave them.' Entry for 18 March 1669, *Diary of John Evelyn* 3, p.525.
7. C. Williams ed., *Sophie in London*, 1933, pp.224-8.
8. J. Hassell, *Picturesque Rides*, 1817, 1, p.81.
9. H. Fincham, *An Historical Account of Canonbury House*, 1926, pp.13-14.

Chapter II THE DESTRUCTION OF SUBURBAN HOUSES

1. *Walpole Society*, 'The Book of Architecture of John Thorpe', 40, 1966, pp.62-3, pl.29.
2. C. Knight, 'The Environs of London: the Suburban Villa', *The Renaissance Villa in Britain 1500-1700*, M. Airs & G. Tyack eds., 2007, pp.136-8.
3. C. Knight, 'The Irish in London: post-Restoration Suburban Houses', *Irish Architectural & Decorative Studies*, 1998, pp. 63-7.
4. The only early evidence for this house is Thorpe's drawing in *Walpole Society, op. cit.*, T94.
5. P. Gaunt, *A History of Kensington Palace*, 1, 1988, pp.15-24 (unpublished).
6. Letter of 3rd Earl of Ailesbury dated 3 July 1745. S. Jenkins, *Portrait of a Patron*, 2007, p.176.
7. J. Salmon ed., *The Surrey Countryside*, 1975, p.156.
8. The Artists' Rifles was founded in 1860 as the 38th Middlesex (Artists') Rifle Volunteers.
9. It was a modest house, but on the site of a medieval moated house called Palingswick.
10. *Survey*, 28, 'Brooke House' 1960.

PART TWO MAJOR HOUSES

ADDINGTON

ADDINGTON PALACE

1. T. Allen, *History of Surrey & Sussex*, 2, p.308.
2. E. Walford, *Greater London*, 2, 1884, pp.132-3.
3. Walford, *op. cit.*, p.133.
4. G.F. Prosser, *Select Illustrations of the County of Surrey*, 1828, includes a print of the enlarged entrance front (no page number).
5. Sale brochure of 1911, p.5. Copy in Croydon Local Studies.
6. Sale brochure, p.15.

BARKING

EASTBURY MANOR HOUSE

1. P. Morant, *The History of Essex*, 1, 1768, p.5. The marshes are now industrial areas.
2. I am grateful to Nicholas Cooper for his information on the house.
3. T. H. Clarke, *Eastbury Illustrated*, 1834.
4. Will of Clement Sysley, NA, C142/185/71.
5. The complexities of ownership are given in *VCH*, 'Essex' 5, 1966, pp.201-2.
6. D. Defoe, *Tour*, 1, 1962, p.8.
7. A. B. Bamford, 'Eastbury House, Barking', *Transactions of Essex Archaeological Society*, 9, 1906, pp.29-30.
8. T. F. Hunt, *Exemplars of Tudor Architecture*, 1830, p.80.
9. *Survey*, 'Eastbury Manor House, Barking', 11th Monograph, 1917.

BARNET

WROTHAM PARK

1. D. Pope, *At 12 Mr Byng was Shot*, 1962, p.27.
2. Byng was the fifth surviving son of Sir George Byng, Lord Torrington, whose country house was Southill in Bedfordshire; but they came originally from Wrotham in Kent.
3. Tim Knox suggests that Ware may have designed the frame. *CL*, 21 February 2002, p.55.

BEXLEY

DANSON HOUSE

1. These are in V & A, Drawings Collection, 7078.2, 3861.19 & 20, E.4984-1910.
2. Vernet's painting is now in the Walters Art Gallery, Baltimore.

3. The temple was removed to St Paul's, Waldenbury in Hertfordshire.

4. Boyd bought this vase, made up of antique fragments by Piranesi, from Gavin Hamilton in Rome. It was sold to the British Museum by Hugh Johnston in 1868.

5. His art collecting is discussed by D. Hancock, *Citizens of the World*, 1997, pp.348-57, 369.

6. The architect of the stables is not known, but they have been attributed to George Dance the Younger.

7. The stonework had been rendered and painted after the war in an attempt to prevent water penetration. This was sand-blasted off in the 1980s, making the situation worse. Conservative repairs have been carried out using Bath limestone, and a limewash was applied to parts of the stonework to match the old with the new work.

8. C. Miele & R. Lea, *Danson, the Anatomy of a Georgian Villa*, 2007. I am grateful to EH for allowing me to see their unpublished research.

HALL PLACE

1. A. Ricketts, *The English Country House Chapel*, 2007, pp.257-8.

2. E. Hasted, *The History ... of Kent*, 2, 1972, pp.173-6. The rent was £280 *p.a.*

3. The 'Freehold Estate of about 540 acres comprising a fine old mansion known as Hall Place ...' was offered for sale by Messrs. Dann & Lucas of Dartford on 22 July 1912. Sale brochure in NAL.

4. R. Edwards, 'Hall Place, Kent', *Country Life*, 21 January 1922 has illustrations of the interiors with her fine collection of 17th- and 18th-century furniture.

5. There was also a working water mill on the River Cray not far from the house, which has been demolished.

6. The Trust is arranging a loan of some furnishings from the National Maritime Museum.

RED HOUSE

1. Sheila Kirk, *Philip Webb, Pioneer of Arts & Crafts Architecture*, 2005, pp.166-73.

2. Lawrence Weaver, *Small Country Houses of Today*, 1945, pp.180-5 discusses Red House and points out that the well was a source of water for the house at a time when no mains water was available in Upton.

3. Webb's contract drawings are in the V & A, Drawings Collection, E.59-64-1916.

4. Many pieces of furniture made for Red House went with Morris and were left to his daughter May. She left some to the late Emery Walker, which are now in his house in Hammersmith Terrace in London. Other pieces are in various museums, such as the Chaucer wardrobe in the Ashmolean Museum.

BLACKHEATH

THE RANGER'S HOUSE

1. NA, PROB 31/54/48.

2. Chesterfield did not get permission for this encroachment, and had to pay additional rent as a result.

3. Christie's sale, 28 April 1782.

4. Christie's sale, 21-22 March 1806. Copy of sale catalogue in NAL.

5. H. Colvin ed., *The History of the King's Works*, 6, 1973, pp.326-8.

6. Phillips Son & Neale sale, 31 July 1813. Copy of sale catalogue in NAL.

7. This can be seen in the painting by Anthony de Bree of Chesterfield House in 1884, in the Museum of London.

8. M. Hall, 'Furniture of Artistic Character', *Furniture History*, 32, 1996, pp.192-5.

9. J. Bryant, 'The Wernher Collection at Ranger's House', *Apollo*, May 2002, pp.3-9.

WRICKLEMARSH

1. I am grateful to Dr Sally Jeffery for information on John James.

2. S. Jeffery notes that the Ionic capital was based on a French design, published in London as recently as 1723.

3. E. Hasted, *History of Kent*, 1, 1778, p.427.

4. National Archives of Scotland, GD18/2107, f.7.

5. Woolfe & Gandon, *Vitruvius Britannicus*, 4, 1767, pls. 58-64.

6. John Brushe, 'Wricklemarsh & the Collections of Sir Gregory Page', *Apollo*, November 1985, pp.364-71.

7. C. Alister, 'Page of Greenwich', *Transactions of Greenwich & Lewisham Antiquarian Society*, 7, 1970, pp.255-63.

8. *Gentleman's Magazine*, 11 June 1787, p.634.

9. Woodbastwick Hall was demolished in 1971.

BRENTFORD

BOSTON MANOR

1. Claire Gapper suggests that the plasterwork and cornices of the hall are original, thus implying it was an early example of an entrance hall rather than a screens passage. RCHME, 'Middlesex' 1935, p.5 also suggests this.

2. There is evidence of an outer wall inside the attics, implying that the house might originally have been smaller. The roof timbers are not original, so the evidence is inconclusive.

3. A. Wells-Cole, *Art & Decoration in Elizabethan & Jacobean England*, 1997, pp. 90-3,102,164.

4. C.J. Richardson published drawings of the Great Chamber ceiling and chimneypiece in *The Builder*, 1844, pp.570-1.

5. A.J. Howard, 'Boston Manor & the Clitherow Family', unpublished thesis, 1969 (no university named; copy held LMA).

6. LMA, ACC/1360/292/2 shows the kitchen range to the north of the house.

7. LMA, ACC/1360/292/2-4 shows the garden.

8. This painting was in the Knight, Frank & Rutley sale of 1922, and has not been traced. It was sold for the very large sum of 450 guineas.

9. LMA, ACC/1360/245/1-2 are the accounts submitted to General Clitherow by George Hawksley in May 1847, detailing the work carried out at Boston Manor for the sum of £828 12s.6d. It includes painting the drawing room ceiling and adding gilding, as well as adding composition to the balusters and handrail of the staircase, and graining the wood.

BROMLEY

SUNDRIDGE PARK

1. There is some confusion over the earlier history, due to the village of Sundridge also in Kent. Sources are E. Hasted, *History of Kent*, 1797, 1, pp.559-60 and E.L.S. Horsburgh, *Bromley, Kent*, 1929, pp. 190-3.

2. H. Repton, *Memoirs*, *op. cit.*, 2005, pp.75-6.

3. Angus, *Seats*, *c*.1815, has a view of Sundridge supplied by Repton.

4. Samuel Scott died in Nice worth £1,400,000; J. Mordaunt Crook, *The Rise of the Nouveaux Riches*, 1999, p.291, n.91.

5. 'Sundridge Park Hotel' brochure, *c*.1935. Bromley Libraries.

6. A.C. Popham, 'Sundridge Park', 1982, pp. 1-4, unpublished paper in Bromley Libraries.

7. G. Worsley, 'Contemporary Classicism', *Country Life*, 10 September 1992, pp. 84-5.

BROMLEY-BY-BOW

THE OLD PALACE

1. *Survey* 1, 'Parish of Bromley-by-Bow', 1900; *Survey* 3rd Monograph, 'The Old Palace of Bromley-by-Bow', 1902.

2. SPAB Annual Report 1894, pp.21-3; C.R. Ashbee, *A Few Chapters on Workshop Reconstruction & Citizenship*, 1894, pp.18-19.

3. *Country Life*, 6 April 1907, pp.478-81.

4. Claire Gapper has pointed out that the V & A accepted many fragments of plasterwork from Godman for their collection, much of which is in store today.

CARSHALTON

CARSHALTON HOUSE

1. Defoe, *Tour*, 1962, pp.158-9.

2. A.E. Jones, *The Story of Carshalton House*, 1980, p.3. Jones attributed the rebuilding to Carleton, although it has recently been redated to *c*.1696. I am grateful to Andrew Skelton for his information.

3. The larger paintings were attributed to Robert Robinson, who died in 1706, by E. Croft-Murray, *Decorative Painting in England*, 1, 1962, p.224.

They are discussed by John Cornforth in 'Views from a Painted Room', *Country Life*, 7 September 2000, pp.174-7, and by Mireille Galinou in *City Merchants & the Arts, 1670-1720*, 2004, pp.38-40, 75, 111.

4. Jones, *op. cit.*, p.27.

5. D. Sherborn, 'Carshalton House, Surrey', *Country Life*, 4 March 1949, pp.480-3, perpetuates Aubrey's myth that Fellowes built the house.

6. Fellowes' inventory is in NRO, FEL 701.554.x.6.

7. Watts, *Seats*, 1779.

8. M. Girouard, 'Pure Ablutions: Country House Plumbing I', *Country Life*, 21 December 1978, pp.2131-2; and 'II', 28 December 1978, pp.2219-20.

9. This combination of orangery and bathroom may have been copied from Wanstead.

10. Auction 14 June 1887; BL, Maps, 137.c.4. (4).

CHARLTON

CHARLTON HOUSE

1. D. Lysons, *Environs*, 'Kent' 4, p.326.

2. Money for rebuilding the church was not mentioned specifically in his will, but the earlier church was replaced just after his death and traditionally was paid for by him. There is a fine monument by Nicholas Stone to Lady Newton, commissioned by her husband.

3. M. Girouard, *Smythson*, 1983, p.288.

4. Eagle House, Wimbledon is another example of this type. They may derive from Ashley House, Walton-on-Thames, built 1602-7 and demolished in 1925. This is discussed by John Gurney in *Architectural History* 43, pp.113-20.

5. These are 19th-century replacements of the original chimneys.

6. This was recorded by C.J. Richardson in a careful drawing. V & A, Drawings Collection, 93.H.15, plate 15.

7. Evelyn, *Diary*, 1955, 3, p.85.

8. This is discussed by John Newman in *Architectural History*, 27, pp.33-5.

9. *Diaries of the Earl of Egmont*, 1920, 1, p.33, entry for 7 February 1730.

10. LMA, E/MW/C, plans of the Maryon-Wilson estate, Charlton, 1903-39.

CHELSEA

BEAUFORT HOUSE

1. These are by William Spicer and John Symonds and are in the Hatfield Archives, CPM II. 6, 7, 9, 10, 15, and 16. They are reproduced in R.A. Skelton & J. Summerson, 'A Description of Maps and Architectural Drawings ...', *Roxburghe Club*, 1971.

2. Simon Jervis, 'Furniture for the 1st Duke of Buckingham', *Furniture History*, 1997, pp.50, 65-74.

3. This had been presented to Charles, Prince of Wales on his visit to Spain in 1625, and passed on by him to Buckingham.

4. Molly McCain, *Beaufort: the Duke & his Duchess 1657-1715*, 2001, p.103.

5. Ruth Duthie, 'The Planting Plans of some 17th century Flower Gardens', *Garden History*, 17-18, 1989-90, pp.88-94.

6. R. Davies, *The Greatest House at Chelsey*, 1914, pp.230-4.

LINDSEY HOUSE

1. C. Dalton, *The Life & Times of General Sir Edward Cecil*, 1885, i, p.376; and C. Knight, 'The Cecils at Wimbledon', *Patronage, Culture & Power: the Early Cecils*, 2002, pp.61-2.

2. Hugh Trevor-Roper, *Europe's Physician: the Various Life of Sir Theodore de Mayerne*, 2006, traces his career.

3. P. Kroyer, *The Story of Lindsey House*, 1956.

4. The Lutyens garden is discussed by Arabella Lennox-Boyd in *Private Gardens of London*, 1990, pp.55-9.

5. 'The Restoration of an Old London Palace', *The Graphic*, 23 July 1910 illustrates some of the interiors.

CHEVENING

CHEVENING HOUSE

1. A. Gomme, 'Chevening: the Big Issues', *Georgian Group Journal*, 14, 2004, pp.167-86; 'Chevening: the Resolutions' *op. cit.*, 15, 2005, pp.121-39.

2. The perspective view of Chevening is a small watercolour in an estate plan of 1679 by Richard Browne, in the house.

3. V & A, Drawings Collection, 3436.66 & 67.

4. R. North, *On Building*, ed. H. Colvin & J. Newman, 1981, p.71.

5. L. Wood, 'William Hallett's Lantern Stand for Chevening', *Furniture History*, 41, 2005, p.21.

6. Bradshaw worked at various addresses in Soho from 1728 and supplied tapestries as well as furniture.

CHISWICK

CHISWICK HOUSE

1. For the construction of the house see R.T. Spence, 'Chiswick House and its Gardens 1726-32', *Burlington Magazine*, August 1993, pp.525-31; for the interiors and furnishings see Treve Rosoman, 'The decoration and use of the principal apartments of Chiswick House 1720-70', *Burlington Magazine*, October 1985, pp.663-77.

2. Jane Clark, 'Lord Burlington is Here', *Lord Burlington, Architecture, Art & Life*, ed. T. Barnard & J. Clark, 195, pp.251-310.

3. These include a series of paintings by Pieter Andreas Rysbrack *c.*1728; a 1753 series of prints by John Donowell; and John Rocque's plan with vignettes of 1736.

4. Richard Hewlings has recently suggested Paine rather than James Wyatt as designer of this bridge; both architects were paid retainers by the duke.

5. I am grateful to Pamela Bater for information about the entertainments at Chiswick House at this period.

6. Osbert Sitwell, *Tales My Father Taught Me*, 1962, pp.154-5 describes seeing round the house at this time.

7. The Georgian Group Archives, Chiswick Box, have records of the discussions on the future of the house.

MORTON HALL

1. D. Defoe, *Tour*, 1, 1927, pp.12-13.

2. O. Millar, 'Artists & Craftsmen ...', *Burlington Magazine*, 137, 1995, p.521.

3. Description by Lord Gower in 1812, from 'Memoir of Lady Louisa Stuart' in *The Diary & Journal of Lady Mary Coke*, 1, 1970, p.cxxxv.

4. *Diary of John Evelyn*, ed. G. de la Bédoyère, 1994, p.290.

5. S. Jeffery, 'The Flower of all the Private Gentlemens Palaces ...', *Garden History* 32, Spring 2004, pp.1-19.

6. 'Particulars of a Valuable Freehold & Copyhold Estate ...', Report by Samuel Ware dated 12 June 1812, Chatsworth Archives, L/52/11.

CROYDON

CROYDON PALACE

1. The chapel is illustrated in 'The Old Palace, Croydon, Surrey – II', *Country Life*, 15 August 1965, pp.876-80.

2. E. Walford, *Greater London*, 1884, 2, p.164.

3. Andrew Coltée Ducarel, 'Some Account of the Town, Church & Archiepiscopal Palace of Croydon ...' in J. Nichols, *Bibliotheca Topographica Britannica*, 2, 1780.

4. Yvonne Walker, *The Story of Croydon Old Palace & the Archbishops of Canterbury 871-1780*, 1990, pp. 1-77.

5. William Varley painted it *c.*1800. Private collection.

6. He commissioned a new country house, Milton Ernest Hall, from his brother-in-law William Butterfield.

7. J. Thorne, *Handbook to the Environs of London*, 1983, p.130.

8. L. Thornhill, 'From Palace to Washhouse', *Proceedings of the Croydon Natural History & Scientific Society*, 17, ix, 1987, p.236.

DENHAM

DENHAM PLACE

1. It is possible that the entrance was always on the east front, and that the axial approach shown in the painting was a garden walk or for special occasions.

2. John Harris, *Records of Buckinghamshire*, 16, iii, 1957-8, pp.193-7.

3. A. Ricketts, *The English Country House Chapel*, 2007, p.247. Pevsner & Williamson, *Buckinghamshire*, 1994, p.272, suggest that the panelling

may have been installed by Lewis Way *c.*1816, and might have come from Stanstead Park in Sussex.

4. These are illustrated in G. Beard, *Decorative Plasterwork in Great Britain,* 1975, pls. 43-6.

5. *Country Life,* 18 April 1925, p.602.

6. It was illustrated in *Country Life,* 18 November 1905, pp.702-9, when lived in by Mrs Way.

7. C. Hussey, 'Denham Place …', *Country Life,* 18 April & 25 April 1925, pp.602-9 & 642-50. The house is also recorded in J. Cornforth & O. Hill, *English Country Houses: Caroline,* 1966, pp.203-10.

8. She was Sarita Enriqueta Ward, widow of Sir Colville Barclay, with an income of £40,000 p.a.

9. Sale particulars for auction 10 July 1968, by John D. Wood & Co.

10. RCHM, 'Buckinghamshire' 1, 1948, pp.119-21, and illustrated in *Country Life,* 1905, p.706.

11. Georgian Group Archives.

EALING

GUNNERSBURY PARK

1. *VCH,* 'Middlesex', 7, 1982, pp.125-6.

2. Plans and an elevation were illustrated by C. Campbell, *Vitruvius Britannicus,* 1715, 1, pls. 18-19, where it was attributed to Jones.

3. R. North, *op. cit.,* p.62.

4. *John Loveday of Caversham,* ed. S. Markham, 1984, p.363.

5. *Love*day, *op.cit.,* p.507.

6. R. White, 'As Finely Finished as Anything', *Country Life,* 11 November 1982, pp.1480-2.

7. 'The Particulars of the Capital Villa … 1787', Gunnersbury Museum Archives.

8. *Letters & Journals of Lady Mary Coke,* 1886-9, 2, p.341.

9. T. Faulkner, *History & Antiquities of Brentford, Ealing & Chiswick,* 1845, p.255.

10. This building was in a very poor state of repair, see Georgian Group Report, 1979. Recent investigations have confirmed that it has mid-18th-century foundations, so its name may have a basis in fact; and work will be carried out.

11. K. Bradley-Hole, 'Gunhilda's Graceful Grounds', *Country Life,* 22 July 2004, pp.56-9.

PITZHANGER MANOR

1. *VCH,* 'Middlesex', 7, 1982, pp. 126-7.

2. Ptolemy Dean, *Sir John Soane & the Country Estate,* 1991, p.91.

3. These were based on the antique lions at the Villa Medici in Rome.

4. *New Vitruvius Britannicus,* 2, 1808, p.9.

5. These have been restored since 1985.

6. *New Vitruvius Britannicus, op.cit.,* p.9.

7. Robins was also supplying furniture for Soane's Bank of England interiors. *Dictionary of English Furniture Makers 1660-1840,* 1986, pp.755-6.

8. The Council paid Walpole £40,000 for the house and grounds. P. Hounsell, *The Ealing Book,* 2005, p.81.

ELTHAM

ELTHAM LODGE

1. The three parks of Eltham were the Great, Old and New Parks, amounting to 12,000 acres before the Civil War.

2. Evelyn, *Diary, op. cit.,* 14 July 1664.

3. The tapestries, made by Jean le Clercq and Daniel Eggermans *c.*1675, are Crown property and were removed to the Queen's House, Greenwich.

4. The chimneypiece is illustrated by Tipping, *English Homes,* 1920, 4, part 1, p.104. The Chinese export wallpaper, dated 1725-50, is in the V & A and has a design of flowering plants and birds. Accession No. E.2083-1914.

5. *Country Life,* 'Eltham Lodge, Kent, Parts 1 & 2', 9 & 16 September 1919.

ELTHAM PALACE

1. A. Emery, *Greater Medieval Houses of England & Wales 1300-1500,* 3, 2006, pp.226-30.

2. Plan by John Thorpe, *c.*1603. NA MPF 228.

3. E. Hasted, *History of Kent,* 1, 1972, pp.465-8.

4. T.F. Hunt, *Designs for Parsonage Houses,* 1827.

5. H. Dunnage & C. Laver, *Plans, Elevations & Sections of the Great Hall of the Royal Palace of Eltham,* 1828.

6. A.C. Pugin, *Examples of Gothic Architecture,* 1831, p.37. Pls 43-49 are of Eltham.

7. Christopher Hussey wrote three articles about the old and new houses in *Country Life,* on 15, 22 and 29 May 1937.

8. Michael Turner researched the history of the Courtauld's house and wrote the 1999 guide book. The restoration cost £2.2 million.

ENFIELD

FORTY HALL

1. H. Colvin ed., *History of the King's Works,* 4, 1982, pp.86-9.

2. D. Lysons, 2, *Environs,* 'Middlesex', p.299.

3. Elain Harwood's research on Forty Hall, published in *The Renaissance Villa in Britain 1500-1700,* 2007, pp.206-16, is a valuable start for unravelling the history of this house.

4. LMA ACC/801/44 is the sale particulars, 1773.

5. E. Harwood, *op. cit.,* plate 9.

6. RCHM, 'Middlesex', 1937, pp.23-4.

ESHER

CLAREMONT HOUSE

1. Vanbrugh's drawings are in the V & A, D. 94-1891 & E.2124.177-1992. The latter are illustrated in H. Colvin & M. Craig, *Architectural Drawings in the Library of Elton Hall …,* 1964, pls. 37-8.

2. John Harris suggests an earlier date for the Belvedere in 'The beginnings of Claremont', *Apollo,* 1993, pp.223-6.

3. *Vitruvius Britannicus,* 3, 1725.

4. These are illustrated in J. Harris, *The Artist & the Country House,* 1995, pls.49-54.

5. H. Pye, *Account,* 1760, pp.33-34, 36.

6. The cost is sometimes quoted as £25,000, but Newcastle had a £15,000 mortgage from Clive.

7. RIBA has an album of designs by Brown, including interior details. One is signed by Brown and Clive, and dated 20 February 1771.

8. It took just over 1½ hours to get there from Kensington Palace. RA, QVJ, 16 May 1833.

9. Princess Charlotte's bedroom was still unchanged when Kilvert was shown in it 1871. *Kilvert's Diary,* 1977, p.112.

10. D. Millar, *Watercolours…* 2, pp.552-3, 640-2, 825.

11. Queen Victoria paid £74,100 for the estate. RA, VIC/Z208, f.49.

ESHER PLACE

1. Virginia Davis, *William Waynflete: Bishop & Educationalist,* 1993 discusses Wayneflete's various building projects at Tattershall, Wainfleet, Eton & Oxford. The 15th-century building accounts for Esher Place have not survived.

2. H. Colvin ed., *The History of the King's Works,* 3, London 1975, p.89.

3. Rev. J.K. Floyer, *Esher Place & its Association with Cardinal Wolsey & the Spanish Armada,* a privately printed pamphlet, 1920, p.4.

4. Michael Symes, 'The Landscaping of Esher Place', *Garden History* 8, iv, 1988 pp.63-96 covers the history and design of the garden in great detail.

5. Figure 1 in Symes 'Esher Place' 1988.

6. John Harris wrote up these discoveries in CL, 'A William Kent Discovery: Designs for Esher Place, Surrey', 14 May 1959, pp.1076-8 and 'Esher Place, Surrey', 2 April 1987, pp.94-7.

7. This and 37 other Kent drawings for Esher are in the V & A: E.356-1986 to E.394-1986.

8. Symes, 'Esher Place' 1988 shows designs for the various garden buildings.

9. BL Maps 137.b.5 (30); *Sale Catalogues of Landed Estates,* Surrey, 3, C-F, 1861-80.

10. *Daily Telegraph,* 23 June 1893.

FOOT'S CRAY

FOOT'S CRAY PLACE

1. E. Hasted, *History of Kent*, 2, 1972, p.138.
2. Woolfe & Gandon, *Vitruvius Britannicus*, 2, 1767, pls. 8-10.
3. R. Pococke, *Travels through Britain*, 1, 1899, p.69.

FULHAM

FULHAM PALACE

1. The history of Fulham Palace is covered by C.J. Fèret, *Fulham Old & New*, 3, 1900, pp. 94-154.
2. 1647 Parliamentary Survey of Fulham Palace copied from the original by William Dickes, Guildhall MS 10,464 f.45v – 46v.
3. R. Pulteney, *The Progress of Botany in England* 2, London 1790, p.105.
4. Jean O'Neill, 'Botanist to a Bishop', *Country Life*, 17 November 1977, pp. 1496-9.
5. Alice M. Coats, 'The Hon. & Rev. Henry Compton, Lord Bishop of London', *Garden History* 4, iii, 1976, pp.14-20.
6. Lysons, *Environs*, 'Middlesex', 2, ii, 1811, p.227.
7. The architect for this work has not been traced. Sherlock's tomb in Fulham churchyard was designed by John Vardy, so possibly he was also the architect.
8. Stiff Leadbetter's drawings are in Lambeth Palace Library, *Catalogue of Fulham Papers*, Terrick 19.
9. Letter from Horace Walpole to Hannah More, 20 July 1789.
10. Beilby Porteus, *A Brief Account of Three Favourite Country Residences in 1808* has a description of Fulham Palace, pp.27-46.
11. Seely & Paget requested this chimneypiece from the Ministry of Works, who had acquired Appuldurcombe House. It was installed in 1952.
12. LBHF commissioned three important reports on the history of the palace: Simon Thurley, 'Fulham Palace, an Architectural History', 1987; Warwick Rodwell, 'Fulham Palace, an Archaeological Appraisal', 1988; and Hal Moggeridge, 'Fulham Palace: Landscape', 1988. These are unpublished, but available in LBHF Archives.

HACKNEY

BALMS

1. *Survey*, 'Shoreditch', 7, 1922, p.79.
2. P. Metcalf, 'Balmes House', *Architectural Review*, June 1957, pp.445-6.
3. The watercolours are probably by Toussaint. Hackney Library, D 94-5.

BROOKE HOUSE

1. *Survey*, 28, 'Parish of Hackney Part 1, Brooke House', 1960.
2. *Survey*, 28, *op. cit.*, p.59.
3. S. Pepys, *Diary*, 7, p.181.

SUTTON HOUSE

1. The brick manor house at Standon has two stones dated 1546 and one with his initials. RCHM, 'Hertfordshire', 1910, p.208.
2. The indenture relating to the sale, referring to it as the 'bryk place', is in the Guildhall Library, MSS 1594.
3. Sutton lived at the Tanhouse on the adjoining plot. A plan showing the two houses is in LMA, D1/962.
4. One of the bargeboards was re-used inside the house in the 18th century. I am grateful to Mike Gray for his information about the house before and after the restoration.
5. An appeal was launched but did not cover the purchase price. The Robertson Fund, commemorating two brothers killed in the First World War, allowed the Trust to buy the house, while the appeal covered essential repairs.

HAMMERSMITH

BRANDENBURG HOUSE

1. T. Faulkner, *History & Antiquities … of Hammersmith*, 1839, p.279.
2. *Vitruvius Britannicus*, 4, Woolfe & Gandon, 1767, plates 26-29.
3. Melcombe's collecting is discussed by Clare Hornsby, 'Antiquarian Extravagance at Hammersmith', *Apollo*, December 1991, pp.410-14.
4. This was removed to Tottenham Park, Wiltshire by 1789.

5. *Gentleman's Magazine*, 1822, p.299.
6. The main sale was held at Brandenburg House in 1820 'By command of her Highness the Margravine of Anspach'. Sale catalogue in NAL.

HAMPSTEAD

KENWOOD HOUSE

1. *Survey*, 'Highgate', 17, 1936, p.128.
2. F. Russell, *John, 3rd Earl of Bute, Patron & Collector*, 2004, pp.23-6.
3. R. & J. Adam, *Works in Architecture*, 1, 1778, pls. 1-8.
4. G. Castle, 'The France family of Upholsterers & Cabinet-Makers', *Furniture History*, 2005, pp.28-9.
5. This David Martin portrait was moved to Scone Palace in 1922, but a copy has recently been installed at Kenwood.
6. Adam's interiors at Kenwood are discussed by Eileen Harris in *The Genius of Robert Adam*, 2001, pp.180-95.
7. Repton's proposals are discussed by S. Daniels, *Humphry Repton*, 1999, pp.219-26.
8. Repton's 'Red Book' is in a private collection, but a facsimile is held by the SRO, RH2 8/113.
9. Plans and elevations are illustrated in *Survey, op. cit.*, pls. 118-19.
10. *VCH*, 'Middlesex', 9, 1989, pp.75-81, traces the history of Hampstead Heath.
11. The sale took place over four days in November 1922. A copy of the sale catalogue is in NAL, 23.L. Some of the contents were removed to Scone Palace.

HAMPTON

BUSHY HOUSE

1. Unpublished leaflet by B. Garside, 'The Manor Lordship & Great Parks of Hampton Court during the 16th & 17th Centuries', 1951, pp.32-4.
2. E. Law, *The History of Hampton Court Palace*, 2, 1888, p.269, has the Parliamentary Survey of 1653.
3. A full history of the house is given by P. Foster & E. Pyatt in 'Bushy House', privately printed for the NPL in 1976.
4. The pavilions can be seen in Rocque's map of Middlesex, 1741-54.
5. The set of plans is in Sir John Soane's Museum.
6. Claire Tomalin, *Mrs Jordan's Profession*, 1994, tells her story.
7. NA, 'Miscellaneous Records of Bushy House 1802-68', Works 16/25/3.
8. In 1842 she commissioned a charming water colour of the house by H.B. Ziegler, which shows the verandahs opening out of the library, drawing room and morning room. Royal Collection SA I 3.
9. 'Bushy House & the National Physical Laboratory, Teddington', *Local History Notes*, 12, 1998, Richmond upon Thames.

GARRICK'S VILLA

1. C. Oman, *David Garrick*, 1958, p.184.
2. D. King, *The Complete Works of Robert & James Adam*, 1991, pp. 207-11.
3. C. Gilbert, *The Life & Work of Thomas Chippendale*, 1978, pp.236-47.
4. The architect of this is not known, although Roubiliac's name has been suggested.
5. *Local History Notes*, 46, 'Garrick's Villa & Temple to Shakespeare', LB of Richmond upon Thames, pp.1-6.
6. NAL, MS.L. 4631c-1970. Copy *c.*1823 of 'A descriptive Inventory of the Household Furniture & Pictures … and Fixtures belonging to the late Country Seat of David Garrick Esq. deceased … 1779.'

HAMPTON COURT HOUSE

1. J. Cornforth, 'The Menagerie, Horton', *Country Life*, 12 October 1995, pp.54-9.
2. Eileen Harris ed., *Thomas Wright's 'Arbours & Grottoes'*, 1979.
3. The grotto was restored in the 1980s. E. Harris, 'Villa for a Mortal Miss', *Country Life*, 5 August 1982, pp.92-4. The restoration was funded by English Heritage and the LB of Richmond.
4. G.D. Heath, 'Hampton Court House', 1985, a privately printed history of the house, has information on later owners.
5. The sale particulars suggest a guide price of £6,000. NMR, SC00723/PA.

HARROW WEALD

GRIM'S DYKE

1. *VCH*, 'Middlesex', 2, 1911, pp.12-13 & 4, 1971, p.186.
2. F. Goodall, *The Reminiscences of Frederick Goodall, R.A.,* 1902, pp.279-80.
3. W.R. Lethaby, *Philip Webb & his Work*, 1979, pp.76-7, contains Shaw's views on the unsuitability of the Gothic style for 'modern requirements'.
4. Messrs. Jackson & Shaw. *Building News*, 6 September 1872, p.182.
5. Goodall, *Reminiscences*, p.285. The statue was given back by his widow, and returned to Soho Square in 1938.

HAVERING-ATTE-BOWER

BOWER HOUSE

1. Harold Smith, *A History of the Parish of Havering-atte-Bower*, 1925.
2. A Latin inscription inset over the hall fireplace recorded this.
3. It is not clear how much land Baynes owned in Havering, although at his death he also had property in London, Buckinghamshire and Hertfordshire.
4. He was buried in Havering, and his monument was moved to the new church of St John the Evangelist when it was rebuilt in 1875.
5. A painting dated 1791 shows the north front without wings, while another anonymous painting of *c*.1800 shows the south front with the wings. In both the house appears to have been stuccoed.
6. Baynes died in London but was buried in Havering-atte-Bower.
7. An inventory was drawn up, dated 25 March 1776, probably at the end of Richard Neave's tenancy. Essex RO, D/DNeE2.
8. The stucco was removed in the late 19th century.
9. C. Hussey recorded the house and its collections in *Country Life*, 17 & 24 March 1944.

HESTON

OSTERLEY PARK

1. *Correspondence of Horace Walpole*, 1, 1965, p.125, letter to Lady Ossory dated 21 June 1773.
2. *VCH*, 'Middlesex', 3, 1962, p.109.
3. Quoted by J. Nichols, *The Progresses ... of Queen Elizabeth*, 2, 1823, p.107.
4. Elizabeth I is said to have complained during her visit in 1576 that the forecourt was too large. By the time she woke up in the morning a new brick wall had divided it in two.
5. 'An Inventory of ... the Goods and Chattels of Sir William Waller ...', NA, PROB 5/2019.
6. V & A, Jersey Papers, Box 5/1 has a list of all Adam's drawings at Osterley.
7. Eileen Harris, *The Genius of Robert Adam*, 2001, pp.156-79, discusses his work.
8. This had originally been in York House, Whitehall. It was moved to Jersey for safety during the war, but was destroyed by fire in 1949.
9. H. Hayward & P. Kirkham, *William & John Linnell*, 1980, pp.113-19, 164-8.
10. A transcript was published by M. Tomlin, 'The 1782 Inventory of Osterley Park', *Furniture History*, 1986, pp.107-34.
11. His will is in LMA Acc. 1128/11.
12. Moses Glover, *Map of Isleworth*, 1635, private collection; John Rocque, 'Middlesex', 1741.
13. H. Walpole, *op. cit.*, p.126-7.

HIGHGATE

CROMWELL HOUSE

1. *Survey*, 'Cromwell House' Monograph 12, 1926, has a full history of the house and line drawings of the interior details. The land extended N-E from the house, across what is now Archway Road.
2. They were illustrated in *The Art Journal*, 11, 1849, pp.85-7, and were drawn again for the *Architectural Review*, September 1910, pp.112-19. These drawings allowed the missing figures to be replaced recently.
3. His father had helped arrange the transfer of Catherine of Braganza's dowry to Charles II. His nephew was physician to Queen Catherine and the builder of Eagle House, Mitcham.

4. Defoe, *Tour*, 1974, 2, p.3.
5. It has been said that the ceiling was completely reconstructed, but Louisa Bain's diary describes visiting the house the day after the fire. 'The drawing room is damaged by water only, except that the beautiful ceiling has a large hole in it.' J.S. Bain, *A Bookseller Looks Back*, 1940, p.51.

ICKENHAM

SWAKELEYS

1. *Survey*, 'Swakeleys, Ickenham', 13th Monograph, 1933, and *VCH*, 'Middlesex', 4, 1971, p.104 cover the history of the house.
2. Evidence of this was found during the 1986 restoration.
3. It is possible that the screen and chimneypiece were installed by Harrington, which would suggest that the house was not completely finished in 1643.
4. E. Croft-Murray, *Decorative Painting in England*, 1, 1962, p.262, attributes it to Laguerre, but this has since been questioned.
5. The house may have been let or lent to Sir Robert Clayton, another Lord Mayor, at this time.
6. Pepys, *Diary*, 6, pp.214-16, entry for 7 September 1665.
7. It was recorded in photographs as a private house just before its sale. Avray Tipping, *English Homes*, 3, ii, pp.407-14.
8. The restoration is discussed by John Cornforth, *Country Life*, 11 December 1986, pp.1908-12.

ILFORD

VALENTINES

1. The west wall of the original entrance hall is exceptionally thick, suggesting it may have been the outer wall; the bow room on the S-W would therefore have been added in 1769.
2. J. Thorne, *Handbook to the Environs of London*, 1983, p.376, noted in 1876 that 'in the house is some good carving by Grinling Gibbons'. There is nothing today that resembles Gibbons' work.
3. This early example of a ha-ha with bastions was moved slightly to the east *c*.1870 in order to make a rose garden outside the walled garden.
4. Central Park, as it was called, was designed by Herbert Shaw.
5. I am grateful to James Hetherington, Conservation Officer for the LB of Redbridge, and Nigel Burch, project manager, who allowed me to visit the house and grounds during the £6 million restoration.

ISLEWORTH

SYON HOUSE

1. G. R. Batho, 'Syon House: the first 200 Years', *Transactions of the London & Middlesex Archaeological Society*, xiv, 1958, pp.1-17.
2. The excavations of 2003 and 2004 showed that the south wall of the church was on the same line as the south wall of the present house, and the north wall was on the south wall of the north range.
3. Somerset spent about £5,500 on building works at Syon. H. Colvin ed., *History of the King's Works*, 4, 1982, pp.272-3.
4. G. R. Batho, 'Henry, 9th Earl of Northumberland & Syon House', *Transactions of the Ancient Monument Society*, iv, 1956, pp. 102-4.
5. J. Wood, 'The Architectural Patronage of Algernon Percy, 10th Earl of Northumberland', *English Architecture Public & Private*, 1993, pp.74-7.
6. Eileen Harris points out that the floor differs from the design by Adam, and suggests it may be a 19th-century replacement. *The Genius of Robert Adam*, 2001, pp.68-9.
7. *The Life & Correspondence of Mrs Delany*, 1, 1862, pp.180-1.
8. Butter and other produce were regularly sent from Syon to Northumberland House.
9. J. Musson, 'Syon House, Middlesex', *Country Life*, 2 November 2000, pp.94-9.

ISLINGTON

CANONBURY HOUSE

1. In 1565 it was let to William Rickthorne for 31 years. *VCH*, 'Middlesex', 8, 1985, p.54.
2. Crosby Hall was re-erected in Chelsea in 1926, after the demolition of Crosby Place in 1908.
3. Print by John Hawksworth after F.W.L. Stockdale.

4. One of these is now part of 7 Alwyne Road, the other of 4 Alwyne Villas.

5. His fortune was said to be between £300-800,000. L. Stone, 'The Peer & the Alderman's Daughter', *History Today*, 11, 1961, pp.48-55.

6. James Boswell, *London Journal 1762-3*, 1985, p.256.

7. H. Fincham, *An Historical Account of Canonbury House*, 1926, p.19.

8. A. Tipping, *English Homes*, 3, ii, 1928, pls. 225 & 226 illustrate these.

9. 'Canonbury Tower Restored', *Country Life*, 28 April 1955, pp.1127-8.

KENSINGTON

HOLLAND HOUSE

1. Sir Walter Cope was made ranger of Hyde Park by James I.

2. 'The Book of Architecture of John Thorpe', *Walpole Society*, 40, 1964-66, p.71, T94.

3. C.J. Richardson recorded the decoration in *Architectural Remains …*, 1838.

4. Malcolm Airs, 'Inigo Jones, Isaac de Caux & the Stables at Holland House', *Georgian Group Journal*, 13, 2003, pp.141-59.

5. This was Kingsgate near Margate, which they used for two to three months a year.

6. SPAB Archives, report on bombed properties.

7. The house and grounds were sold for £250,000.

8. *The Builder*, 11 September 1959, pp.184-6; *Architectural Review*, November 1959, pp.237-41.

KESTON

HOLWOOD HOUSE

1. Soane's bound volume with drawings for Holwood is in the V & A, Drawings Collection, 3307/72.

2. Soane's plan is illustrated in G. Darley, *John Soane, an Accidental Romantic*, 1999, plates 66-7.

3. A. Gore & G. Carter, '*Memoirs*', *op. cit.*, p.56.

4. Drawing in V & A, Drawings Collection, D1894-1907.

5. J. P. Neale, *Views of Seats*, 1828.

6. Material from Georgian Group Archives, including Report by Dept. of the Environment dated 11 February 1988.

KEW

KEW PALACE

1. The exact site of Leicester's house is unknown. The brick vaults are hard to date, and could be of 16th- or 17th-century origin.

2. Fragments of red ochre limewash were found behind a rainwater hopper.

3. C. Knight, 'The Irish in London: post-Restoration Suburban Houses', *Irish Architectural & Decorative Studies*, 1, 1998, pp.72-8.

4. H. Colvin ed., *History of the King's Works*, 5, 1976, pp.227-9.

5. See S. Groom & L. Prosser, *Kew Palace*, 2006.

6. I am grateful to Lee Prosser of Historic Royal Palaces for his information on the house.

LALEHAM

LALEHAM ABBEY

1. RIBA Drawings & Archives Collection, PB1346/10.

2. NAL, Knight, Frank & Rutley Sale Catalogue, 27-29 November 1922.

3. RIBA Drawings & Archives Collection, PB1328/PAP[207]1-75.

4. The carpet was given to the V & A by the 6th Earl of Lucan in 1961. Accession No. T.178-1961.

MITCHAM

EAGLE HOUSE

1. A watercolour portrait of Mendes painted by his daughter is in the Spanish & Portuguese Synagogue, London.

2. The gates are illustrated in D.J. Ebbett, *Examples of Decorative Wrought Ironwork …*, 1879.

3. The plan and elevation are reproduced in M. Barley, *Houses & History*, 1986, p.211.

4. I am grateful to the staff at Eagle House School for allowing me unrestricted access to the house.

PETERSHAM

HAM HOUSE

1. The drawing by Robert Smythson is in the Drawings Collection, RIBA.

2. C. Rowell, 'A 17th century cabinet restored', *National Trust Studies*, 1996, pp.18-23.

3. For Ham and their other projects see J. Dunbar, 'The Building Activities of the Duke & Duchess of Lauderdale 1670-82', *Archaeological Journal*, 132, 1976, pp.203-30.

4. The inventories date from 1654, 1677, 1679, 1683 and 1728. See P. Thornton & M. Tomalin, *Furniture History*, 16, 1980.

5. R. North, *Of Building*, 1981, p.144.

6. John Slezer also worked for Lauderdale at Thirlestane, and used Jan Wyck to fill in the figures in his drawings.

7. N. Strachey, 'The Helmingham Plan', *The London Gardener*, 2, 1996-7, pp.36-41.

8. A 1649 miniature of the 1st Countess of Dysart, still at Ham, shows the towered house in the background.

9. William Bradshaw supplied a set of tapestries based on designs by Watteau in 1735, and giltwood pier glasses in 1743. *Dictionary of English Furniture Makers*, 1986, p.100.

10. Letter dated 11 June 1770, *Correspondence of Horace Walpole*, 10, pp.306-7.

11. M. Hall, *op. cit.*, *Furniture History*, 32, 1996, p.191.

12. A. Tipping, *English Homes*, 4, i, pp.111-44.

SUDBROOK PARK

1. T. Friedman, *James Gibbs*, 1984, p.323. I am grateful to Terry Friedman for his information on Sudbrook.

2. The source in Rossi's 1702 *Studio dell'Architettura Civile* was pointed out by John Cornforth in his *Early Georgian Interiors*, 2004, pp.28-9.

3. The drawing is in the Ashmolean Museum, Oxford: Gibbs III, 97.

4. James Gibbs, *Book of Architecture*, 1728, pl. 40.

5. Lady Louisa Stuart, 'Some Account of John, Duke of Argyll & his family' in *The Letters & Journals of Lady Mary Coke*, 1, 1970, p.xxxi.

6. H.M. Cundall, *Sudbrook & its Occupants*, London, 1912, p.63 lists the livestock as 4 oxen, 2 cows, 14 ewes with lambs, 35 sheep, 9 pigs and 3 old horses.

7. Coke, *Letters*, 1, p.40.

8. Cundall, *Sudbrook*, Appendix 1, pp.91-5. It makes clear that Caroline, Baroness Greenwich, had added about 27 acres to the estate when she had renewed the lease in 1784.

RICHMOND

ASGILL HOUSE

1. The house was completely refaced in Doulting stone in the 19th and 20th centuries.

2. *Gentleman's Magazine*, September 1788, 2, pp.841, 930.

3. He was Surveyor-General 1779-82, but this does not mean that he was a connoisseur of buildings. Howard Colvin describes him as 'a negative placeman, ignorant of architecture.' *History of the King's Works*, 5, p.77.

4. C. Hussey, 'Asgill House, Richmond', *Country Life*, 9 June 1944, illustration on p.992 shows this.

5. I am grateful to Mr Hauptfuhrer for showing me the house and discussing its history with me.

WHITE LODGE

1. C. Knight, 'The Irish in London: post-Restoration Suburban Houses', *Irish Architectural & Decorative Studies*, 1, 1998, pp.71-8.

2. Sir Robert Walpole used the old lodge, and his son Lord Walpole was Ranger.

3. These can be seen in Heckel's drawings, in J. Cloake, *Palaces & Parks of Richmond & Kew*, 2, 1996, p.106.

4. H. Colvin ed., *History of the King's Works*, 5, 1976, pp.230-3.

5. See Cloake, *op. cit.*, pp.110-13.

6. There is no 'Red Book' for this project, but three watercolours by Repton are in a private collection.

7. H. Colvin ed., *History of the King's Works*, 6, 1973, pp.354-6.

8. William Leitch, *The White Lodge, garden front*, 1861. Royal Collection, RL 19723.

9. Bedford Lemere's photographs are in the NMR, 11321-8.

10. NA, Work 32/590, has plans and elevations made in 1927.

RICKMANSWORTH

MOOR PARK

1. H. Colvin ed., *History of the King's Works*, 3, 1975, pp.16-17.

2. She and her husband had already made famous gardens at Twickenham Park, which they sold when given a lease of Moor Park by James I.

3. The 1687 plans of the ground and first floors were published by H. Colvin & A. Maguire in 'A Collection of 17th century architectural plans', *Architectural History*, 1992, fig. 36, catalogued on p.164.

4. J. Cornforth, *Country Life*, 10 March 1988, pp 138-41.

5. This is illustrated in G. Beard, *The Work of Grinling Gibbons*, pls. 57-9.

6. T.P. Hudson, 'Moor Park, Leoni & Sir James Thornhill', *Burlington Magazine*, November 1971, pp.657-61.

7. The decorative schemes are discussed by John Cornforth in *Early Georgian Interiors*, 2004, pp.31-5.

8. A set of four paintings of Moor Park still belongs to the Dundas family.

9. The tapestries were removed from Arlington Street to Aske Hall, North Yorkshire.

10. V & A house files, Moor Park, Hertfordshire.

11. D. King, *The Complete Works of Robert & James Adam*, 1991, pp.346-9.

12. Plans of the house with wings were published in *Vitruvius Britannicus*, 5, 1771, pls.54-5.

13. The auction was conducted by Knight, Frank & Rutley, and included in the sale was some of the furniture commissioned for Dundas, which had remained in the house.

ROEHAMPTON

GROVE HOUSE

1. D. Gerhold, *Villas & Mansions of Roehampton & Putney Heath*, 1997, p.14.

2. *Calendar State Papers Venetian*, 1632-6, p.367.

3. *VCH*, 'Surrey' 4, 1967, p.79.

4. In 1644 it was ordered to be sold 'towards the [2nd] Earl of Portland's assessment', but it was bought by the King's Brazier and survived until the Restoration. Portland's widow sold it to Charles II for £1,600 in 1675. *Calendar of State Papers Domestic*, 1627-8, p.86 & 1629-31, pp.165-7.

5. D. Howarth, *Art & Patronage in the Caroline Courts*, 1993, p.143.

6. Lysons, *Environs*, 1, Part 1, p.315. The Last Supper was one of the most popular subjects for private chapels. A. Ricketts, 'The Evolution of the Protestant Country House Chapel *c.*1500-*c.*1700', unpublished thesis, 2003, p.221.

MOUNT CLARE

1. It was cautiously attributed to Henry Holland in Christopher Hussey's articles on Mount Clare. *Country Life*, 26 January, pp.90-4 & 2 February 1935, pp.118-23.

2. D. Gerhold, *Villas & Mansions of Roehampton & Putney Heath*, 1997, p.31.

3. Anne Riches has cleared up the misattributions to Brown and Holland and has confirmed the attribution to Taylor. See 'Mount Clare, Roehampton', *Architectural History*, 1984, pp.255-62.

4. There were seven reliefs originally, possibly the Seven Liberal Arts. They are heavily overpainted and hard to distinguish. Two were replaced by the Shubin portraits, see n. 5.

5. Alison Kelly, 'The Shubin Plaques at Mount Clare', *Burlington Magazine*, April 1970, pp.224-8.

6. W. Watts, *Seats of the Nobility & Gentry*, 1779, no page number. Sir John Dick was a subscriber to this book.

PARKSTEAD

1. Letter dated 18 July 1823, *The Creevey Papers*, 1970, p.226.

2. D. Gerhold, *Villas & Mansions of Roehampton & Putney Heath*, 1997, p.29.

3. An early design by Chambers shows the house without its bedroom storey: visually more successful if much smaller. V & A, Drawings Collection, 3355.

4. *Vitruvius Britannicus*, 4, 1767, plates 11-13.

5. This room is labelled the hall in an undated sketch plan by William Newton. RIBA SE9/19.

6. Three ceiling designs are in the V & A, Drawings Collection, 2216.30, 41 & 42.

7. Giles Worsley suggests William Wilton, father of the sculptor Joseph Wilton, as the carver of this chimneypiece. Parkstead is discussed in *Sir William Chambers*, ed. J. Harris & M. Snodin, 1997, pp.80-2, 128-33.

8. A. Michaelis, *Ancient Marbles of Great Britain*, 1882, p.61.

9. His son put paintings and sculptures up for sale in February 1801. Christie's sale catalogue in NAL, annotated with prices.

10. Lysons, *Environs*, 1, Part 1, p.318 and sale catalogue. Bessborough had bought the valuable Salvator Rosa in the Canons sale of 1747.

11. *The Letters & Journals of Lady Mary Coke*, 1970, 2, p.264.

12. Bessborough's collecting is discussed by Rachel Finnegan, 'The Classical Taste of William Ponsonby …', *Irish Architectural & Decorative Studies*, 8, 2005, pp.13-43.

ROEHAMPTON HOUSE

1. *Vitruvius Britannicus*, 1, 1715, pls.80-81.

2. The quadrant walls are convex instead of the more usual concave, as at Hopetoun House.

3. It is possible that this pediment was never built.

4. Three designs dated *c.*1712 are in BM Prints & Drawings: 1865, 0610.1368-70.

5. It was described as over-varnished, giving it 'a glitter which makes photography of the walls impossible and of the ceiling most difficult.' *Country Life*, 14 August 1915, p.234.

6. Gerhold, *op. cit.*, pp.27.

7. The builders, who worked on several of Lutyens' buildings, were J. Parnell & Sons of Rugby. Warwick University Records Centre, MSS.14/4/1/1.

8. Lutyens' plan *c.*1911-12 of the proposed house and W. Walcot's 1913 perspective view are in RIBA Drawings & Archive Collection, PA1619/LUT [174] 1 and 10.

ROMFORD

HARE HALL

1. A. Searle & C. Brazier, *A History of Hare Hall*, [n.d. *c.*1960?], p.10.

2. James Paine, *Plans, Elevations & Sections*, 2, 1783, pp.18-19 & plates 60-3.

3. F. Cowell, 'Richard Woods (?1716-93): a Preliminary Account', *Garden History*, 14, No. 2 (1986) Part 1, pp.85-119 describes how he ended his days at Thorndon Hall, owned by Lord Petre, a friend of Southcote who had commissioned a large Paine house.

4. W. Angus, *Seats…*, 1787, pl. 28, has a view of the house.

5. F. Cowell, *op. cit.*, 15, Nos. 1 & 2, Part 2, fig. 44.

6. Wire's five photographs are at the Vestry House Museum, Walthamstow: 996.72.

7. Edward Castellan paid £12,000 for the house and 71 acres. Searle & Brazier, *op. cit.*, p.22.

SOUTHGATE

ARNOS GROVE

1. Richard Garnier's 'Arnos Grove, Southgate', *Georgian Group Journal*, 8, 1998, pp.122-34 covers the building history of the house, and suggests Talman as the architect.

2. The library was 25 x 20 ft, the eating room 35 x 24 ft, both 20 ft high, and the drawing room 36 x 27 ft. W. Watts, *Seats*, 1779.

3. Isaac Walker II bought the Minchenden estate in 1853, demolished the house and kept the land. His son bought Beaver Hall in 1870; he also demolished the house but kept the land.

4. I am grateful to Barbara Rees and her staff at Southgate Beaumont who allowed me access to much of the old house.

SOUTHGATE GROVE

1. *VCH*, 'Middlesex' 5, 1976, p.160.

2. T. Davis, *John Nash*, 1973, p.34.

3. G. Carter, *Humphry Repton*, 1982, p.158.

4. G. Richardson, *New Vitruvius Britannicus*, 1802, p.9. The house is illustrated in pls. 29-31.

5. Richardson, *op. cit.*, p.9.

6. J. Thorne, *Handbook to the Environs of London*, 1876, p.560.

7. The sale particulars are in the NMR, SC00707/PA.

TRENT PARK

1. Jebb's obituary in the *Gentleman's Magazine*, July 1787, pp. 642-3, states that he actually took on two additional 99-year leases in 1777, giving him a total acreage of 385 acres. The rent was £148 *p.a.*

2. 'The Ducal Estate & Contents of the Mansion' of Stowe was sold over 19 days from 4 July 1921 and included the garden buildings and statuary. Sale catalogue in NAL.

3. Lanning Roper, 'The One-Colour Garden' *Country Life*, 28 July 1955, p.186.

4. C. Hussey, *Country Life*, 10 & 17 January 1931.

5. The contents of the reception rooms were sold by Marler & Marler on 25 November 1924. They included French 18th-century furniture, Beauvais tapestry, Sèvres and Chinese porcelain. LMA, ACC/1358/001.

6. O. Sitwell, *The Scarlet Tree*, 1946, pp.133-4.

7. P. Stansky, *Sassoon, the Worlds of Philip & Sybil*, 2003, p. 241.

STANMORE

BENTLEY PRIORY

1. Soane's survey drawing is in Ptolemy Dean's *Sir John Soane & the Country Estate*, 1999, pl.3.2.

2. Dean estimates the cost of these changes at over £30,000, *op. cit.*, p.55.

3. Soane's designs are illustrated by Dean, *op. cit.*, pl.3.9.

4. He had already mortgaged both the Stanmore Park and Bentley Priory estates. LMA, ACC/0502/025.

5. RA, Letter to Prince Leopold dated 21 November 1848, VIC.Y.94 and QVJ, 15 November 1848, f.141.v.

6. D. Millar, *The Victorian Watercolours & Drawings in the Collection of H.M. the Queen*, 2, 1995, pp.560, 830-1.

7. BL Maps 137.a.11.(9), *Sale Catalogues of Landed Estates*, Middlesex, 2, K–Z. Sale brochure for auction on 20 July 1880.

8. Sale brochure for auction on 14 June 1909 with a guide price of £275,000. NMR, SC00720/PA.

CANONS

1. 'The Book of Architecture of John Thorpe', *Walpole Society*, 40, 1964-6, T 43 & T44.

2. He rented Sion Hill in Isleworth as his suburban house for a few years until 1712.

3. Ian Dunlop, 'Cannons, Middlesex, a Conjectural reconstruction', *Country Life*, 30 December 1949, pp.1950-4.

4. I am grateful to Sally Jeffery and Terry Friedman for their information on the design and building of this house.

5. Chandos bought Clarendon's library in 1709, and continued to buy books and manuscripts after that. S. Jenkins, *Portrait of a Patron*, 2007, pp.143-6.

6. This is now in the V & A.

7. This is now in the Huntington Library. Jenkins, *op. cit.*, p.66, n.29.

8. Defoe, *Tour, op. cit.*, 2, pp.5-8.

9. 'Pictures … by the most celebrated Italian, French and Flemish Masters …' were sold 6-8 May. 'Materials of the Dwelling House…' were sold 16-29 June; the auctioneer in both cases was Cock. Copies of the sale catalogues are in NAL.

10. Watts, *Seats …*, 1779, pl. 40.

11. *Dictionary of English Furniture Makers 1660-1840*, 1986, p.387. He certainly bought sash frames. G. Beard, 'The Quest for William Hallett', *Furniture History*, 21, 1985, p.224.

TITSEY

TITSEY PLACE

1. The family papers are in Surrey History Centre, Leveson-Gower of Titsey, Records 1308-1925: 2186.

2. The richly decorated church cost about £6,000 to build. It was about to be made redundant recently, so it too became part of the Titsey Foundation and is still in use.

3. I am grateful to the Chairman of the Trustees of the Titsey Foundation for information about the house and grounds.

TOTTENHAM

BRUCE CASTLE

1. *VCH*, 'Middlesex', 5, 1976, pp.325-8.

2. Nicholas Cooper suggests that it may have been a dovecot, a banqueting house, a prospect tower or a conduit house.

3. Nicholas Cooper carried out a structural survey of the house for the LB of Haringey, and I am grateful to him for his information on the house.

4. M.C. Bridge, 'Tree-ring Analysis of Timbers from Bruce Castle, Tottenham', *Ancient Monuments Laboratory Report*, English Heritage, 69/97.

5. Coleraine also owned a house in nearby Totteridge.

6. Published posthumously as R. Dyson & Henry, Lord Coleraine, *The History & Antiquities of Tottenham High-Cross*, 1792.

7. See H. Colvin, 'Lord Coleraine's Mausoleum', *Georgian Group Journal*, 2003, pp.78-83.

8. Coleraine notes that he found the Compton arms on the porch, which he retained.

9. I am grateful to Karen Hearn for her notes on the painting.

10. N. Cooper, 'The Work of Two Antiquaries at Bruce Castle', *Georgian Group Journal*, 2003, p.92. The original inventory is in NA, PROB 31/319.

11. Cooper, *op. cit.*, transcription of the 1749 inventory, pp.100-06.

12. Sir Rowland Hill (1795-1879) was headmaster for a while, and went on to reform the postal services.

13. F. Fisk, *The History of Tottenham*, 1913, p.13.

TWICKENHAM

MARBLE HILL

1. M. Draper, *Marble Hill House & its Owners*, 1970, pp.12-16.

2. WRO 2057/F6/14.

3. C. Campbell, *Vitruvius Britannicus*, 3, 1725, pl. 93.

4. NRO, MC/184/10/1. Plan of gardens *c.*1735.

5. NRO, NRS 8862 'Articles proposed to a man to keep Lady Suffolk's garden in the following manner …' dated 1751.

6. *Correspondence of Horace Walpole*, 35, 1973, p.644.

7. NRO NRS 8564 is a rough draft for 'An Inventory of Goods belonging to Marble Hill House taken 30th July 1767' and NRS 8546 is a tidy copy.

8. J. Bryant, *Marble Hill*, 2002, is a well-researched guide book.

ORLEANS HOUSE

1. J. Macky, *A Journey through England*, 1722, pp.62-4.

2. I am grateful to Sally Jeffery for information. Her Ph. D. on 'English Baroque Architecture: the Work of John James', Birkbeck, 1986 discusses this commission.

3. C. Campbell, *Vitruvius Britannicus*, 1, 1715, pl. 77.

4. John Clerk of Penicuik visited London with William Adam in 1727, partly to see the latest architectural developments. His record of this trip is in the NAS, GD18/2107.

5. This drawing is reproduced in *The History of Orleans House, Twickenham*, 1984, LB of Richmond upon Thames, fig. 16.

6. I am grateful to Terry Friedman for his information on this room. A plan, elevation and section were illustrated by Gibbs in his *Book of Architecture*, 1728, pl. 71.

7. John Cornforth in 'Orleans House, Middlesex', *Country Life*, 15 February 1996, pp.40-3, discusses the recent research into the original paint colours and gilding, and the possibilities of restoring these.

8. *The History of Orleans House*, pp.15-16.

9. He was a first cousin of John Byng, the builder of Wrotham, who also had a career in the Royal Navy.

10. L. Althalin, *Vue de la maison occupée par … le duc D'Orleans*. Ionides Collection, LB of Richmond upon Thames.

POPE'S VILLA

1. I am grateful to Terry Friedman for his information on Gibbs and Pope's Villa.
2. The only depiction of this phase of the house is *The Thames at Twickenham* by Peter Tillemans *c*.1730, possibly commissioned by Pope.
3. *Alexander Pope's Villa*, catalogue of a GLC exhibition at Marble Hill House in 1980, shows the many painted and printed views of Pope's Villa pre-1888.
4. These were bequeathed by Pope to 1st Lord Bathurst of Cirencester Park. The Hercules is now on loan to Chiswick House.
5. 'He gains all points, who pleasingly confounds, Surprises, varies, and conceals the bounds' as Pope wrote in his *Epistle to Burlington* in 1731.
6. William Kent designed two vases, which were published in J. Vardy, *Some Designs of Mr Inigo Jones …*, 1744, pl. 25.
7. Pope's will was published in *The Gentleman's Magazine*, June 1744, pp.313-14.

STRAWBERRY HILL

1. R. W. Ketton-Cremer's *Horace Walpole, a Biography*, London, 1940 is still one of the best books about him.
2. See W.S. Lewis, *The Correspondence of Horace Walpole*, 48 vols., London & New Haven, 1937-83.
3. A small area of the original external rendering has recently been discovered in a cupboard in the Great Bedchamber, proving that it was whitewashed.
4. A. Eavis & M. Peover, 'Horace Walpole's Painted Glass at Strawberry Hill', *The Journal of Stained Glass*, 19, iii, 1994-5, pp.280-314 includes a catalogue of his glass, and lists the pieces which have been traced elsewhere.
5. Henrietta Pye, *A Short Account of the Principal Seats & Gardens round Twickenham*, London, 1760.
6. These chairs were bought in 1775 from the Bateman collection at Windsor. Clive Wainwright, *The Romantic Interior*, 1989, p.106.
7. Horace Walpole, *Description of the Villa …at Strawberry Hill*, 2nd edition, 1784.
8. O.W. Hewett, *Strawberry Fair … Frances, Countess Waldegrave*, London, 1956 and K. Carroll, 'Lady Frances Waldegrave, Political Hostess at Strawberry Hill 1856-1879', *LB of Twickenham Local History Society*, Paper 27 (1998) are the best sources for her extraordinary life.
9. *A Catalogue of the Classic Contents of Strawberry Hill, collected by Horace Walpole*, London, 1842.

WHITTON PLACE

1. R. North, *Of Building*, 1981, p.62.
2. Ilay also bought some moorland near Peebles and planted trees at a place he called The Whim. I. Lindsey & M. Cosh, *Inveraray & the Dukes of Argyll*, 1973, p.17.
3. This can be seen on Moses Glover's map of 1635.
4. NAS, GD18/2107, f.9.r.
5. T. Friedman, *James Gibbs*, 1984, pp. 137-8. I am grateful to Terry Friedman for his information on Whitton.
6. For Ilay's library see D. Chambers, *The Planters of the English Landscape Garden*, 1993, p.89.
7. M. Symes, A. Hodges, J. Harvey, 'The Plantings at Whitton', *Garden History*, 14, ii, 1986, pp.138-72.
8. This was drawn by John Adam on his visit to London in 1748.
9. H. Pye, *A Short Account …*, 1760.

TWYFORD

TWYFORD ABBEY

1. Brother Cornelius Kearney of the Alexian Brothers researched the history of the house. This was privately printed in 1992 as *The History of the District & Manor House of West Twyford*. A copy is held by the LB of Ealing. For Stukeley, see p.38.
2. In 1811 he had to give up both his house and grazing when the Crown Estates began the development of Regent's Park.
3. The moat was close to the south and east fronts of Willan's house, and cut across the stable yard behind it.

4. Atkinson had developed a form of cement which could be used both externally and for moulding interior decoration such as friezes. The material for it was shipped from Lord Mulgrave's estates in East Yorkshire, where Atkinson had redesigned the house. H. Colvin, *Biographical Dictionary*, 1995, p.85.
5. Brian Rayment in his 'Appeal against Non-Determination of Town Planning Applications', 1983, p.14, for the LB of Ealing suggests that the various parts may have been inspired by the grouping of different buildings in medieval abbeys.
6. Kearney, *op.cit.*, p.60 notes that the land had belonged to St Paul's Cathedral in 925.
7. He sold the house for £9,000, so made a large loss. *Middlesex County Times*, 7 January 1899, p.6.
8. The 1916 altarpiece and reredos are described in Cherry & Pevsner, *London 3*, p.198.
9. LB of Ealing, Twyford Abbey Planning Application P2005/1167-LB. Permission for development was turned down.

WALTHAMSTOW

HIGHAMS

1. An anonymous 18th-century print shows the old house, and says that it had a frontage of 100 ft. Vestry House Museum.
2. Lesley Lewis, 'The Architects of the Chapel at Greenwich Hospital', *Art Bulletin*, 29, 1947, pp.260-7 discusses Newton's career.
3. A collection of drawings by Newton for Highams is in the RIBA, SC114/4(1-7). See also Jill Lever, *Catalogue of the Drawings Collection of the RIBA, L-N*, 1973, pp.137-8.
4. *European Magazine*, 1801 includes a print of the house by S. Rawle with its upper storey.
5. Repton's 'Red Book' of 1794 is on loan to Vestry House Museum, Walthamstow.

WALTON-ON-THAMES

PAINSHILL PARK

1. Michael Symes points out that this was a model made by John Nost, and was supplied to Hamilton by John Cheere. *Fairest Scenes: Five Surrey Gardens*, 'Painshill', 1988, p.41.
2. The grotto was restored by Diana Reynell.
3. *A Dictionary of British & Irish Travellers*, ed. J. Ingamells, 1997, pp.445-6.
4. Ingamells, *op.cit.*, p.446.
5. *Papers of Thomas Jefferson*, 9, 1950, p.370.
6. 'Horace Walpole's Journals of Visits to Country Seats', *Walpole Society*, 16, 19 27-8, pp.36 7.

WANDSWORTH

WEST HILL

1. Lysons, *Environs*, 1, part 1, p.390.
2. E. Rucker Davidson, *Rucker Kinsmen*, 1974, p.31. I am grateful to Cathal Moore for his help over researching this house.
3. D. Gerhold, *Wandsworth Past*, 1998, p.57.
4. Gibson was District Surveyor of the eastern part of the City from 1774. He may also have had Wimbledon connections, as he was buried there in 1828.
5. Gore & Carter, 'Memoirs', *op. cit.*, pp.130-1.
6. W. Angus, *Seats of the Nobility & Gentry …*, 1787 [1815?] no page numbers.
7. I am grateful to Pippa Thistlethwaite for information from family papers about this.
8. The Wimbledon Park estate cost him £92,000, which he financed through mortgages from the County Fire Office. D. Beaumont, *Barber Beaumont*, 1999, pp.195, 200.

WANSTEAD

WANSTEAD HOUSE

1. *VCH*, 'Essex' 6, 1973, pp.323-4.
2. *VCH*, *op. cit.*, p.325.
3. John Cornforth commented on the linear plan, in contrast to the circuit of rooms which became usual, as at Wricklemarsh. J. Cornforth, *Early Georgian Interiors*, 2004, p.13.

4. J. Macky, *A Journey through England*, 1, 1724, pp.20-1.

5. Sir John Clerk of Penicuik, visit of 5 April 1727. SRO, GD18/2107, f.7, r.

6. Macky, *op. cit.*, p.19.

7. John Rocque, *Plan of the house, gardens and plantations of Wanstead* …, 1735; and another 1745.

8. S. Markham ed., *John Loveday of Caversham*, 1994, pp.249-50, 534.

9. Sally Jeffery, 'How Repton saw Wanstead', *Country Life*, 14 April 2005, pp.98-101.

10. The contents were sold for £41,000, the house for £10,000. Parts of the house went to Wanstead House, Cambridge.

11. Defoe, *op. cit.*, p.90.

12. J. Hassell, *Picturesque Rides*, 2, 1817, p.81.

WATFORD

CASSIOBURY HOUSE

1. G. de la Bédoyère ed., *The Diary of John Evelyn*, 1994, p.265.

2. *Country Life*, 17 September 1910, pp.392-400.

3. *Puckler's Progress*, trans. F. Brennan, 1987, p.63.

4. Sales of the library and topographical works were sold by Messrs. Hodgson of Chancery Lane on 24 May, 22 & 30 November 1922. Copies in the NAL.

THE GROVE

1. J.T. Smith, *Hertfordshire Houses*, 1993, pp.166-7 and J.T. Smith, *English Houses 1200-1800: the Hertfordshire Evidence*, 1992, pp.123-4.

2. Jeremy Blake worked out that Blore raised the ceilings of the ground-floor rooms on the south front, so he had to recreate the staircase on its original site. The stone paving of the staircase hall is the original 18th-century floor. I am grateful to Jeremy Blake for his information on the house.

3. Sir Herbert Maxwell, *The Life & Letters of George, 4th Earl of Clarendon*, 2, 1913, pp.271-4.

4. There was also a sale of Old Master paintings on 4 July 1924; sale catalogue in NAL.

WEST WICKHAM

WICKHAM COURT

1. E. Walford, *Greater London*, 2, 1884, p.124.

2. In the 19th century it was thought to be an ancient fortified house, an idea demolished by N. Cooper, *Houses of the Gentry*, 1999, p.129.

3. 'The Book of Architecture of John Thorpe', *Walpole Society*, 40, 1966, p.91 & T175.

4. The estate then consisted of 303 acres. Kent RO, Lennard MSS, P2.

5. *The Builder*, 1847, p.279, showing profiles of the woodwork.

6. The house and its importance are discussed by A. Emery, *Greater Medieval Houses 1300-1500*, 3, 2006, pp.416-17.

7. The farms were not valued nor acreage given. The house itself was valued for £4,000. Kent RO, Lennard MSS, U.312/E.14.

8. About 50 plans and designs, mainly by Anscomb of Stratton Street, Mayfair, are in the Lennard MSS, P17.

9. Early photographs include *Country Life*, 24 May 1902, p.658 and NMR AA67/2756 dated 1914, both showing the house covered in ivy.

WIMBLEDON

EAGLE HOUSE

1. Treswell's 1617 'Survey of Wimbledon' shows that he bought cottages and small parcels of land, totalling 36 acres. Northamptonshire Record Office, Spencer Archives J 73.

2. L. Stone, 'The Building of Hatfield House', *Archaeological Journal*, 112, 1965, p.125.

3. English Heritage has a fragment of plain wallpaper with a block-printed border *c*.1745 from Eagle House. T. Rosoman, *London Wallpapers 1640-1840*, 1992, pl. 30.

4. It was called Eagle House from this time, although it is not certain when the eagle on the central gable was put up.

5. *The Builder*, 24 September 1948, pp.353-5.

WIMBLEDON HOUSE

1. The history of the house is discussed more fully by C. Knight in 'The Cecils at Wimbledon', *Patronage, Culture & Power: the Early Cecils 1558-1612*, 2002, pp.54-63.

2. Annabel Ricketts discusses this 'assembly chapel' in *The English Country House Chapel*, 2007, pp. 60-1, 72-3.

3. Paula Henderson, 'A Shared Passion: the Cecils & their Gardens', *Patronage, Culture & Power* …, *op. cit.*, pp.105-9 discusses the Wimbledon gardens; pl. 49 is the Smythson plan.

4. D. Lysons, *Environs*, 'Surrey' 1, 1792, p.523.

5. The 1649 Parliamentary Survey of Wimbledon is printed in W.H. Hart, *Surrey Archaeological Collections*, 5, 1871, pp.104-42.

6. In 1678 Winstanley produced two etchings, one of the entrance front, the other a view from the gardens. BM Prints & Drawings, 1881-6-11-353 & 354.

7. G. Scott Thomson, *Letters of a Grandmother*, 1942, p.142.

8. Scott Thomson, *op. cit.*, p.52.

9. *Correspondence of Horace Walpole*, 9, 1941, p. 61.

10. Frances Harris, *A Passion for Government: the Life of Sarah, Duchess of Marlborough*, 1991, p.151, n.81.

11. Scott Thomson, *op. cit.*, p.104.

12. WRO, 2057/F6/14.

13. RIBA Drawings Collection.

14. Lysons, *Environs*, 1, i, p.397.

15. D. Stroud, *Henry Holland*, 1950, p.44.

INDEX

Main references in **bold** and illustrations in *italic*.